ISLANDS AND CONTEMPORARY ART

ISLANDS AND CONTEMPORARY ART

GILL PERRY

REAKTION BOOKS

In memory of Rodney Graham, 1949–2022

Published by
Reaktion Books Ltd
Unit 32, Waterside
44–48 Wharf Road
London N1 7UX, UK
www.reaktionbooks.co.uk

First published 2024

Printed and bound in India by Replika Press Pvt. Ltd

A catalogue record for this book is available from the British Library

ISBN 978 1 78914 936 4

CONTENTS

PREFACE 7

INTRODUCTION
PARADISE OR PRISON? 9

1 **DESERT ISLANDS AND MYTHS OF PARADISE** 35

2 **ISLAND HOMES** 59

3 **DISAPPEARING AND ENDANGERED ISLANDS** 87

4 **ISLAND DETENTIONS** 125

5 **ISLANDS OF 'WHITE GOLD'** 145

6 **IRISH ISLANDS: OF MYTHS AND MAPS** 179

7 **FLOATING ISLANDS** 209

8 **GOING NORTH AND MELTING ICE** 229

CONCLUSION
ART ISLANDS, FUTURE ISLANDS AND END GAMES 251

REFERENCES 271

BIBLIOGRAPHY 291

ACKNOWLEDGEMENTS 297

PHOTO ACKNOWLEDGEMENTS 299

INDEX 301

PREFACE

This book has been a long time coming. Over the last two decades I became increasingly obsessed with the prevalence of the island theme in the visual arts and its relevance to my continuing research on installation art, the so-called 'global contemporary' and gender. I was surprised by the lack of a wide-ranging overview (to date) in art history. I soon realized why. For writers in the visual arts, the island theme is topical and seductive, but daunting and chaotic; it has huge interdisciplinary range and ecological implications and can test our definitions of what art is – or means. The use of the theme in literature, poetry and film is enmeshed with its imaginative visualizations in art. This is not just a book about contemporary art. Rather, it explores the myriad ways in which practices of the expanded field of modern art and visual culture have engaged with, and illuminated, our understanding of the island theme. I tentatively hope it will contribute to the cross-disciplinary richness of the evolving area of Island Studies.

CARGO

One day, long ago,
history arrived by boat
with its portable possessions –

its clothes and language,
weapons, redoubtable
genes, bulk seeds,

ancestral names,
and bloodshed.
                                        The islanders
sped headlong
through time and tides,
into the future

unwilling to forget,

or else with a need
to sink proximate horrors.

A conflict, close up
like a family at Christmas
which has got past
pre-drinks to the crackers.

'Don't grieve, islanders,'
A neutral voice pleads,
'move out of this fix

step by incredible step.'

Andrew Sant, from *The Lives and Times of the Islanders*

INTRODUCTION
PARADISE OR PRISON?

> An island can be both a paradise and a prison, both heaven and hell. Any island, any islander, is a contradiction between 'here' and 'there'.
> **Godfrey Baldacchino**[1]

'Sunday Showing for Tongan Castaways' ran the headline in the Australian newspaper *The Age* on 6 October 1966. It announced the rescue of six teenage boys who had been marooned for over a year on the uninhabited islet of 'Ata, at the southern end of the Tongan islands, an archipelago in Pacific Oceania (illus. 1).[2] Bored with the tedium of life at their boarding school in the Tongan capital Nuku'alofa, the boys hatched an ambitious plan to escape to Fiji or Aotearoa New Zealand. After setting out in a stolen fishing boat, they were caught in a storm and shipwrecked on 'Ata. Months after being given up for dead, they were finally rescued by an Australian fisherman and his crew in September 1966. Returning from a fishing trip off Tasmania, the fisherman Peter Warner saw fires on the green cliffs of the uninhabited island. He found six boys who had managed to survive for fifteen months living off coconuts, bananas, wild chickens and fish, eking out stored rainwater. Half a century later the Dutch historian Rutger Bregman researched the story for his book *Humankind: A Hopeful History*.[3] He tracked down Warner and used his unpublished memoirs to piece together one of the most remarkable island castaway stories of recent history.

Bregman compared this story with the fictional account of marooned boys in William Golding's dystopian novel *Lord of the Flies* of 1954. Golding's more pessimistic story also takes place on a deserted island in the Pacific Ocean: a group of schoolboys survive a plane crash and revel in their newly found freedom in an 'exotic' setting, and in the conspicuous absence of grownups. Their social cohesion and ability to govern themselves soon breaks down, revealing a dark sadistic bid for survival within the group. By the time they are rescued by the British navy, three of the boys are dead. In contrast, Bregman described the more harmonious organization of the Tongan children, who worked in teams and followed strict rosters. Warner reported that they had set up a small self-sufficient community, including a food garden with stored rainwater, a gymnasium, chicken pens and a permanent fire, 'all from an old knife blade'.[4] Both these desert island stories generated huge popular interest. Golding had a best-selling novel on his hands, and a film version of *Lord of the Flies*, directed by Peter Brook, was released in 1963 (illus. 2).[5] The surviving Tongan castaways have appeared in several TV documentaries and are (at the time of writing) negotiating a film contract.[6]

Island tales – both fictional and based on real life accounts – provide compelling dreams of 'exotic', often far-away places, adventure and 'otherness', and have been endlessly represented within anglophone and global cultures. Separated from other lands by water, islands lend themselves

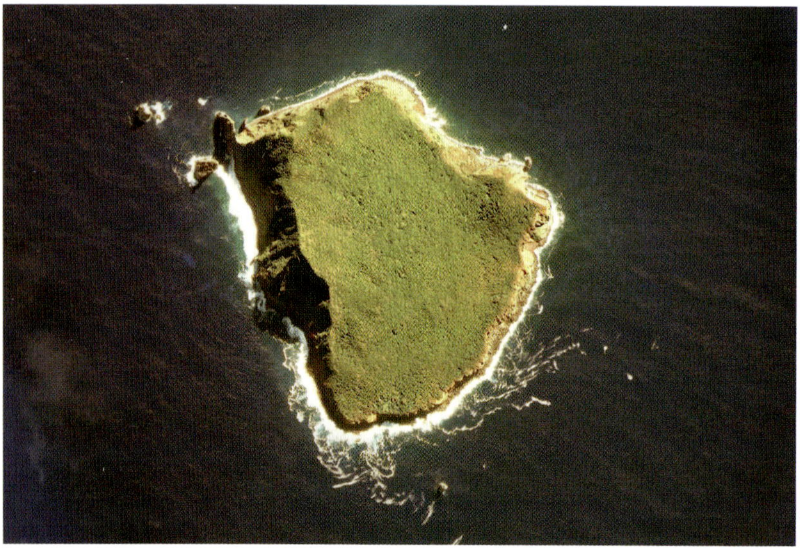

1 'Ata Island, Tonga Archipelago (or Tongatapu Group), South Pacific Ocean.

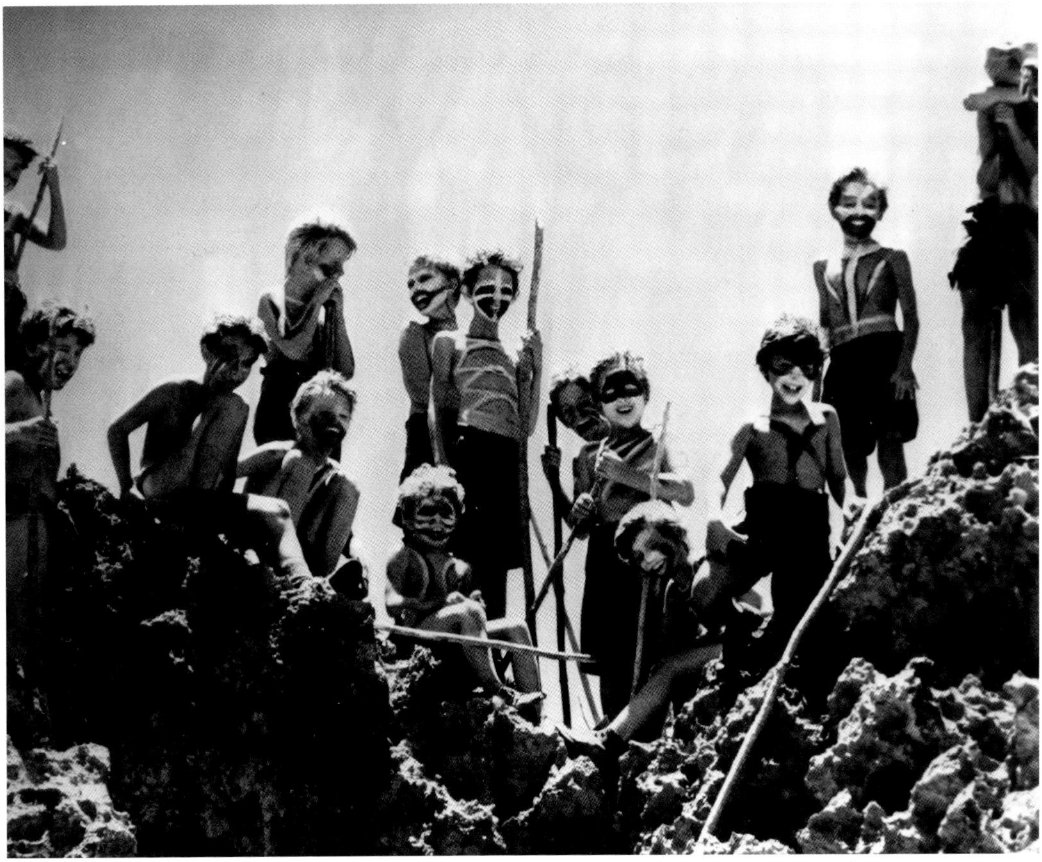

2 Still from the film *Lord of the Flies* (1963, dir. Peter Brook).

to extravagant mythmaking, and have inspired a host of artistic, literary, poetic, musical, philosophical and cinematic works over the centuries and across cultures. This book is primarily concerned with interpretations of the theme within the visual arts since the 1970s. I have found it impossible clearly to separate these from the visibility of island stories within the literary arts, popular culture and the media as we broadly understand it. Artists draw on, rework and challenge existing myths and tropes that circulate within both popular culture and so-called high art. I attempt to understand the popularity of the theme within some rich and overlapping forms of visual and written culture. Definitions are, of course, contested; in what follows, modern and contemporary art are seen as part of a complex web of interwoven values, visual currencies, fashions, beliefs and fantasies that connect across disciplines – and across different cultures. This is not just a book about visual art; it is an attempt to position some vivid examples of recent installation, sculpture, performance, video, film, painting and photography on the island theme within this 'complex web'.

I argue for a nuanced, interdisciplinary approach that is focused on art and visual culture but is also informed by models developing within the broadly labelled 'Island Studies' discipline. That said, I am all too aware that my project is hugely ambitious. Inevitably, it is also highly selective. It is not a survey; I could not hope to provide a comprehensive overview of the recurrence of the theme in art since the 1970s. The chapter headings reveal groupings that seem to me to raise some rich and topical issues addressed within visual art. In each chapter, I also include detailed studies of individual works that I believe address these issues in original and imaginative ways.

CASTAWAYS AND 'A SEA OF ISLANDS'

Many contradictory meanings have been attached to the idea of the island. When artistic or journalistic reinterpretations of popular island stories emerge, different narratives often compete for attention, as is exemplified in the Tongan tale. In 2020 the New Zealand online news journal *Newsroom* published a response to Bregman's book after an extract appeared in the British press. The sociologist Scott Hamilton describes a viral storm provoked by this tale of resourceful teenage castaways, when so many were 'depressed by a pandemic, a recession and a blundering and sinister American President'.[7] But he suggests that the only readers who had not been wildly enthusiastic about Bregman's account were the Tongans. He argues that the castaway story that Bregman tells is in many ways the product of Western, rather than Pacific, culture. He cites the Tongan writer Vika Mana, who wondered why Bregman relied on Warner rather than inviting the Tongan teenagers to tell their own stories. Other critics concurred, worrying that Bregman's emphasis on Warner's version might

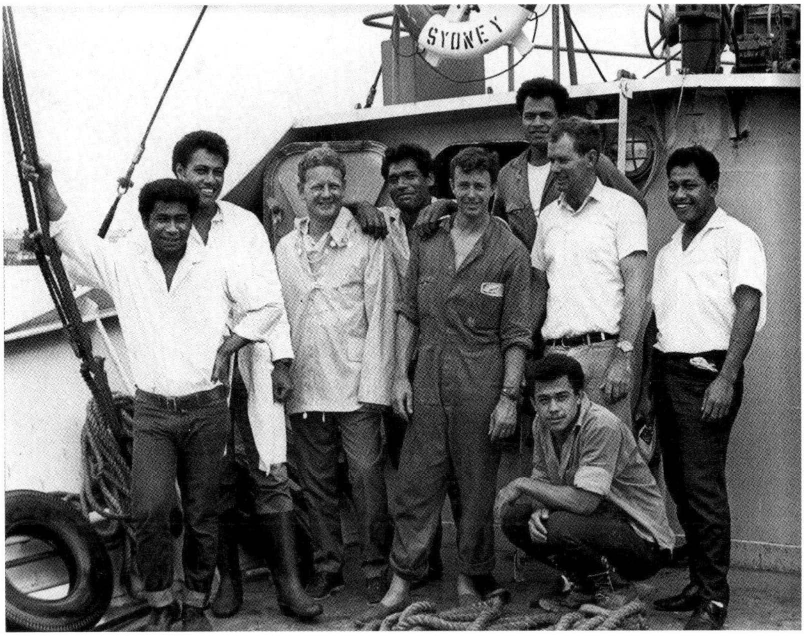

3 Tongan survivors from 'Ata with Peter Warner (third from left) and his crew, 6 January 1968.

be seen as inviting the construction of a 'white saviour story' in which a group of 'natives' are rescued by an enabling white sea captain. In contrast, Hamilton sees the story in the context of a sophisticated Tongan heritage that boasts an ancient literature and knowledge of the Pacific seas (illus. 3).[8] These boys drew on a close relationship with the oceans, including social and navigational skills, that is part of their cultural history. The influential writer and anthropologist Epeli Hau'ofa, born in Papua New Guinea in 1939, has written eloquently of the need for Western scholars to understand the different perspectives of those who live in Oceania. He replaces the term 'Pacific Islands' with that of 'Oceania', which denotes a connected 'sea of islands' with their inhabitants, rather than island states and territories that are defined by colonial boundaries. He describes a people who are at home with the sea, who 'played in it as soon as they could walk steadily, they worked in it, they fought on it. They developed great skills for navigating their waters – as well as the spirit to traverse even the few large gaps that that separated their island groups.'[9] The British writer Philip Hoare has also written eloquently of the Pacific as an ocean 'studded with twenty-five thousand islands, large and small, each with their own stories'. He describes these island narratives as criss-crossing the ocean 'in an embroidered web, drawn together in invisible lines of connection from shore to island sea, transversed in ancient feats of navigation and migration'.[10]

The island of 'Ata is one of many in the Tongan archipelago famously named the 'Friendly Islands' because of the reception offered to Captain Cook in the early 1770s. The irony of this naming has been widely acknowledged in view of the often unfriendly colonizing ambitions of Cook's voyages. Tonga is in the region of Oceania usually called Polynesia, an area that has long been subject to colonial fantasies of exotic 'isolation'.[11] As the geographer John Connell has argued, images of Polynesian islands, especially Tahiti, have emerged and evolved following encounters with (largely male) Westerners, and the 'pervasive image of utopia dominated the bulk of discourse in different phases'.[12] A key question for this book is how can visual art encourage us to think critically about such pervasive images, and what Hau'ofa describes as 'our sea of islands'? I consider some of the ways in which visual artists working in and around Pacific Oceania, the Caribbean and the Atlantic have conceived of their subjects as belonging to a fluid, connected sea of islands, rather than their isolated colonial boundaries. For example, Chapter One explores misconceived ideas of paradise in installations by Lisa Reihana, a Māori-born artist based in Aotearoa New Zealand and the Sāmoa-based artist Yuki Kihara.

In some ways, Bregman's account is closer to castaway stories that have dominated Western culture for centuries. From Shakespeare's *The Tempest* (1611) and Daniel Defoe's *Robinson Crusoe* (1719) to Johann David Wyss's *Swiss Family Robinson* (1812) and R. M. Ballantyne's *The Coral Island* (1858), or Robert Louis Stevenson's *Treasure Island* (1882), being shipwrecked or marooned on a desert island provided the geographical and social framework for a much-used literary trope. That is, the survival of a single – or group of – castaway/s, often male or largely male, who have come from a supposedly more sophisticated (that is, urban Western) culture full of elaborate codes and hierarchies. These islands are stages, or settings, in which protagonists usually discover personal qualities that they didn't even know they possessed. *Robinson Crusoe* is one of the most influential texts in this genre: a proto-modern account of how to control your environment to survive. The hugely popular story of Crusoe's 28 years on the island – his diligent labours, relationship with 'Friday', encounters with 'cannibals' and English mutineers and his perilous journey home – has helped to establish a template for Western castaway tales and films, as I show in Chapter One.

However, this template has been revised by a host of twentieth-century European writers and artists. Apart from Golding's gruelling story, the narrative has been challenged and modernized by H. G. Wells in *The Island of Doctor Moreau* (1896), or Jean Giraudoux's *Suzanne and the Pacific* (1921), among others. Michel Tournier's *Friday and the Other Island* (1967, titled *Friday and Robinson: Life on Speranza Island* in the United States) is a direct rewriting of Defoe's story that rejects Crusoe's status as a quasi-monarch on his island and explores the evolution of a more harmonious relationship with both the island and Friday, hence his title. More recently, in J. M. Coetzee's *Foe* (1986), the story is told by a shipwrecked woman, Susan Barton, breaking the model of intrepid masculine explorer. In Chapter One, I explore Defoe's castaway as an emblematic Englishman of the imperial era, a role model in dire need of revision, as is his version of a desert island. I also aim to show how the ubiquity of such castaway tropes in Western culture has prompted some imaginative interventions in the visual arts, epitomized in Rodney Graham's mischievous desert island film *Vexation Island* of 1997 (see illus. 15).

ART, ISLAND STUDIES AND 'ISLANDNESS'

In his essay 'Islands' (1978), which opens on the Scilly Isles, the novelist John Fowles provides a romanticized notion of the 'mysteries, symbolic and real, of all similarly situated small islands; about their silences, their otherness, their magic and their mazes, their eternal waiting for a foot to land'.[13] Using the metaphor of the body, Fowles emphasizes the inherent separateness of islands: 'It is the boundedness of the smaller island, encompassable in a single glance, walkable in one day, that relates it to the human body.' He describes the sea as 'an enabling evolutionary amniotic fluid', suggesting they possess a pseudo-human individuality and an 'obstinate separatedness of character, even when they lie in archipelagos'.[14] His writings would seem to counter John Donne's much-quoted line from his *Meditation XVII* of 1624: 'No Man is an Island entire of itself; every man is a piece of the continent, a part of the main.' Debates about the status of islands and their cultural boundedness, or 'isolation', versus connectedness have continued across decades and disciplines. It has also been argued that islands have appealed to modernist writers and artists because as separate or contained spaces they invite an imagining of potentially critical or fantastical alternatives to life on the mainland; they can inspire the production of radical or provocative work.[15] Throughout this book, I attempt to explore these questions in relation to recent artistic practices.

Academic studies of the cultural, geographical and ecological nature of islands feature regularly in scholarly anthologies, books and international journals. Since the 1990s 'Island Studies', or 'nissology', has won recognition as a separate discipline, encompassing anthropology, cultural and political geography, environmental studies and sociology (among other disciplines).[16] The influential cross-disciplinary *Island Studies Journal* was founded in 2006 in Canada, and *Shima: The International Journal of Island Studies* was founded in 2007 in Japan.[17] An island or isle is usually defined as any piece of sub-continental land surrounded by water that may occur in oceans, seas, lakes and rivers. But definitions are contested; the question 'what is an island?' continues to haunt Island Studies. Some scholars have claimed that small scale, isolation and boundedness are key characteristics, although there is little agreement on what constitutes 'small scale'.[18] Others have argued for a conception of islands as separate spaces that are qualitatively different to continents. The *Oxford English Dictionary*'s definition of an island as a 'piece of land completely surrounded by water' is, as the cultural theorist Barney Samson argues, 'practically meaningless: so is every land mass, if one zooms out far enough'.[19] And what if the 'island' is connected to the mainland by a causeway, or at low tide? Baldacchino explores this question of what constitutes the separate boundedness of islands when there are fixed links such as bridges, peninsulas, causeways or tunnels in his collection *Bridging Islands*.[20]

Most scholars would agree that Island Studies has evolved through different phases since the 1990s. A current interest in the study of archipelagos and groups of 'interlapping' islands connected by oceans, such as the Caribbean or Pacific Oceania, and Hau'ofa's influential notion of 'our sea of islands' is reflected in my selection and interpretation of artworks and projects. Most islands, however remote, are negotiating relationships and exchanges with other islands, mainlands, continents or colonial histories. Their spaces are often interconnected and dependent on fluid and evolving cultures. Within Island Studies there has been a move away from perceiving islands as static areas of land towards a more 'relational, archipelagic' approach.[21] The geographer Jonathan Pugh has made the important point that 'many places that are conceptualized as simply "mainland" or "island" are in reality archipelagos.'[22]

Taking a broad, fluid definition that includes some larger island nations (which are also archipelagos), such as Ireland and Iceland, not to mention islands with causeways and tidal flows, this book explores the remarkable range of artists' projects on the theme since the 1970s. I consider artworks in which the exploration of the physical, metaphorical, geographical, ecological, cultural or historical nature of an island is central to the artistic project; I explore how the idea of an island or its 'islandness' informs the work and contributes to its innovative potential. The references may sometimes be oblique, symbolic and/or allegorical, requiring the viewer to make imaginative leaps. Artworks that reference the island theme are not confined to representation of landscape or a clearly defined space, as is exemplified in my discussion of Cornelia Parker's *Island* (2022) in the Conclusion. I suggest that in the visual arts allegory has been revitalized as a device that can enrich our understanding of the idea of an island – both dystopian and utopian.

The island is a much-used metaphor in everyday speech. It has been adopted in several academic disciplines to indicate isolation or uniqueness, and a more complex notion of 'islandness'.[23] This term was first popularized by John Fowles in his novel *The Magus* (1965), the story of young British teacher on a small Greek island.[24] Fowles uses the term to denote a separate, contained culture that fears the threat of incorporation by other larger islands or nations. In contrast, Godfrey Baldacchino suggests that 'islandness' is a neutral term that should be used as an alternative for 'insularity', a word that has often been used pejoratively to suggest 'closed minded'.[25] Most researchers now argue for a more fluid conceptualization of islandness that takes account of the connected nature of archipelagos and modern communications and travel, and the different contexts and histories that characterize different islands. Peter Hay notes some of these complexities:

> Whatever islandness is, it seems likely to be quite different for islands that are unambiguously small as against those that are not; for tropical islands as against cold or temperate ones; for islands primarily inhabited by aboriginal people as against islands now dominated by immigrant peoples who have settled within the last two to three centuries.[26]

'Islandness' is a notion that has been contested across disciplines and cultures.[27] For Pugh, it is a productive, relational concept: he argues that islands have always been sites of 'relational entanglement'. They are interconnective spaces of culture, politics and metamorphosis.[28] Each chapter of this book explores these shifting meanings when applied to different aspects of artistic practice. Island sites are also often bound up with notions of identity, location and belonging. In Chapter Two I consider the relationship of islandness to the spatial imaginary of 'home', a concept that can denote anything from a private island emblematic of (global) wealth to a temporary lighthouse dwelling.

Many scholars have also explored islands to enable an understanding of the 'Anthropocene', a broad concept that is much debated across disciplines.[29] Islands have been identified as vivid indicators of an evolving epoch caused by human interventions, characterized by global warming, rising seas, intensifying storms and hurricanes, ocean acidification, species extinction, the loss of Indigenous Peoples and continued colonial exploitation. Pugh argues: 'In the Anthropocene, islands have become a topic of considerable interest, and not just because they are powerful symbols of global warming . . . islands have attracted interest lately because the West has become interested in developing relational ways of thinking about being and knowing.'[30] He claims that critical thinking about the Anthropocene involves recognition of the complex 'relational entanglement' between humans and non-humans. That 'entanglement' is also enmeshed with political and colonial histories and practices. I suggest that the study of visual art is slowly engaging with some of these evolving ideas of islandness and its capacity for metamorphosis and transformation. For example, in Chapter Three I explore some artistic responses to the effects of the Anthropocene in Pacific Oceania (including the work of Kathy Jetñil-Kijiner and Joy Lehuanani Enomoto on the Marshall Islands) and in the Galápagos Islands (including work done by artists on Gulbenkian fellowships).

In Chapter Five I show how the colonial myth of island isolation in the Caribbean has been challenged by both writers and visual artists who have explored complex patterns of migration, diaspora, detention and settlement, and the effects of living within a connected archipelago. In my discussion of the recent work of the Barbadian artist Annalee Davis and Trinidadian-born artist Karen McLean, I argue that both use their practice to mediate histories and memories of enslaved communities, especially women, on Caribbean islands. I also suggest that these art practices can contribute to a process of 'decolonization', as in the work of British artists of the Caribbean diaspora, including McLean, Sonia Boyce, Lubaina Himid and Steve McQueen. Reframed island histories can reveal traces of forced migration, slavery and resistance, and trans-island traditions of carnival and religious rituals. Moreover, the broader discipline of Island Studies has itself been seen as 'a decolonial project' in that it seeks to understand the ways in which 'the islandness of island colonies made itself felt'.[31]

Fowles's use of bodily metaphors and feelings of isolation surrounded by 'amniotic fluid' have an ironic echo in reactions to the recent global pandemic. The international crisis triggered by the COVID-19 pandemic of 2020–23 helped to reinforce theories of the virtues of the separateness of island communities, which can be more easily shielded from contamination by contagious viruses and unwanted invasion by foreign bodies. At the beginning of the pandemic, many so-called 'island nations', among them Taiwan, Iceland and Aotearoa New Zealand, managed to restrain the virus by closing and monitoring sea borders. As one medical expert pronounced: 'To be an island in 2020 or 2021 is probably the greatest geographical gift you could have.'[32] The particularly high infection and mortality rates in the UK early in the pandemic led to a cynical use of the label 'Plague Island'.[33] This controversial labelling reminds us that islands can also be deployed as sites on which secure boundaries can contain a community and incubate an infection, as in a leper colony. Likewise, they are seen as ideal spaces for prisons and penal colonies. In Chapter Four I consider some of the cultural associations of a 'plague island' in, for example, Martin Scorsese's harrowing film *Shutter Island* and Wes Anderson's animated film *Isle of Dogs*. I also explore the varied representations of islands as (similarly contained) detention camps, or 'migrant hotspots', in the work of Ai Weiwei, Alfredo Jaar and Isaac Julien, among others. On such sites, both place and space are seen (through the medium of visual art) to be intensely political constructions, vulnerable to abuses of power.

I was born and continue to live in England; my subject position as a white British woman has inevitably informed my choices of subject-matter and approach. As I was researching this book, the British people were immersed in a political and cultural crisis over Brexit, both before and after the controversial vote in 2016 to leave the European Union. In Chapter Seven I argue that this crisis has its roots in a much-used and ill-informed trope of the English imagination: a supposedly distinctive and separate 'island nation' – a notion that is implicitly challenged in the work of several British artists. I discuss Alex Hartley's floating *Nowhereisland*

(2012), a defiantly multinational, artificial island that was towed from the Norwegian Arctic to the south coast of England. The island trope can offer a seductive nationalist fantasy of separateness and self-determination. Islands can all too easily be seen to have immutable borders and uncontested geographies.

No wonder, then, that they have offered such rich material for writers, artists and filmmakers. The philosopher Gilles Deleuze has signalled the powerful imaginative pull of 'desert islands', where 'science makes mythology more concrete, and mythology makes science more vivid'.[34] Deleuze cites two kinds of islands identified by geographers: continental islands, which are separated from a major continent through fracture or erosion, and oceanic islands, which are formed from coral reefs or volcanic eruptions and can rise slowly and/or disappear. He argues that both types feed the imaginative idea of the deserted island, that dreaming of islands is always 'dreaming of pulling away, of being already separate, far from any continent, of being lost and alone – or it is dreaming from scratch, recreating, beginning anew'.[35] According to Deleuze, humans idealize this state of separateness, and an island doesn't stop being deserted if it is inhabited. As I suggest in Chapter One, the idea of the desert island is one of the most potent myths circulating across cultures. It often involves both a projection of the inherent value of being uniquely 'deserted' and a fantasy of the uncommon humans who can thrive in such circumstances. Hence the remarkable global appeal of the tale of the Tongan castaways.

Literary history is replete with islands as visionary or enchanted utopias and quarantined or dystopic sites. From the islands of Greek mythology, including tales of Atlantis (discussed in Chapter Three) or the islands visited in Homer's *Odyssey*, to Shakespeare's *The Tempest*, Francis Bacon's *New Atlantis* (1627), Thomas More's *Utopia* (1516) and Jonathan Swift's *Gulliver's Travels* (1723) to numerous castaway stories mentioned above, the theme has inspired literary, philosophical and epistemological musings on the nature of humanity. Moreover, many classic texts on the theme are increasingly subject to different interpretations, among them Shakespeare's *The Tempest*, in which Prospero, once Duke of Milan, has become a contentious symbol of islandness. He and his daughter Miranda are shipwrecked on a distant island once ruled by the witch Sycorax, but now inhabited only by her son Caliban and the spirit Ariel. Literary critic Stephen Orgel shows that Prospero has been seen 'as a noble ruler and mage, a tyrant and megalomaniac, a necromancer, a Neoplatonic scientist, a colonial imperialist, a civiliser'. Likewise, multiple interpretations of Caliban as 'an ineducable brute, a sensitive savage, a European wild man, a New-World native, ugly, attractive, tragic, pathetic, comic, frightening, the rightful owner of the island, a natural slave' remind us of the complex and evolving associations of islands and islanders as cultural signifiers.[36] The many identities of both Prospero and Caliban have provided rich source material for the visual arts.

Modern writers such as D. H. Lawrence (*The Man Who Loved Islands*, 1929), William Golding, Aldous Huxley (*Island*, 1962) and J. G. Ballard (*Concrete Island*, 1974) have also explored the dystopian possibilities of the theme, and its relevance to contemporary culture. Lawrence sought to expose some of the rose-tinted fantasies that propelled writer-islophiles such as Compton Mackenzie, who lived on the Scottish island of Barra in later life, and whose famous novel *Whisky Galore* of 1947 is an affectionate depiction of the camaraderie of a fictional Scottish island community who successfully defy local customs officers to salvage a shipwrecked convoy of whisky.[37] In contrast, Lawrence's hero builds his own kingdom, or 'Happy Isle': a utopian fantasy of isolation from the modern world. But Lawrence punctures this island dream; it ends in misery and madness.[38]

In the visual arts there is still considerable research to be done mapping artistic uses and reworkings of this popular subject and its wider imaginative and critical potential. The field is both enormous and daunting; I have encountered an extraordinary richness and variety of art projects for discussion across global landscapes and colonial histories. Moreover, the pairing of ideas of 'art' and 'island' has never been more topical, both literally and metaphorically. As I show in the Conclusion, many spectacular art museums have been positioned on islands, framing art, curatorial display and ideas of creative freedom within awe-inspiring contexts subject to the

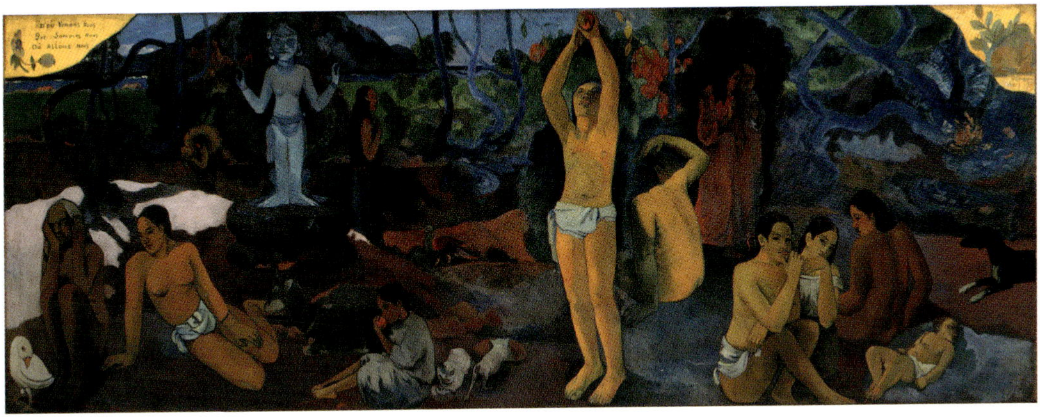

4 Paul Gauguin, *Where Do We Come From? What Are We? Where Are We Going?*, 1897–8, oil on canvas.

flows of oceans and rivers (illus. 127, for example, provides a dramatic arial view of the Arken Museum in Denmark). As one of the most potent motifs in contemporary art, film and literature, the island theme has been adopted to provoke audiences to think critically about many important issues in modern life. These include decolonization, the climate crisis, migration, detention, space and gender. The ecological and political potential of the theme and its relationship with so-called activist art is addressed in many chapters. Art that references the growing climate emergency has become increasingly visible over the last few decades.

Within art history, the popularity of the island theme has an important legacy in the work of nineteenth- and twentieth-century artists from Paul Gauguin's nineteenth-century Polynesian adventures (illus. 4; see also Chapter One) to the influential work of American artists Robert Smithson in the 1960s and '70s (featured below and in Chapter Three) and Christo and Jeanne-Claude in the 1980s (illus. 5). In 1983 Christo and Jeanne-Claude completed their spectacular installation *Surrounded Islands* in Biscayne Bay, Greater Miami, Florida. A group of eleven islands that had been used for dumping rubbish were surrounded by woven pink polypropylene for two weeks, tended by 120 monitors in inflatable boats, and extending 60 metres (200 ft) from each island into the bay. The project dramatically reconceived the island as a large-scale modernist installation, described by the artists as 'a work of art underlining the various elements

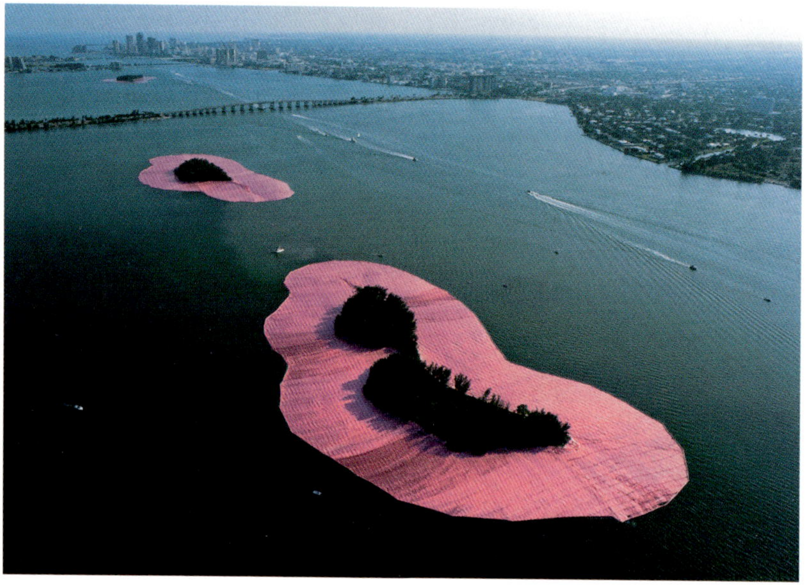

5 Christo and Jeanne-Claude, documentary photograph of *Surrounded Islands*, Biscayne Bay, Greater Miami, Florida, 1980–83, woven polypropylene fabric surrounding 11 islands, Styrofoam, steel cables and anchoring system, 603,870 square metres of fabric overall.

and ways in which the people of Miami live between land and water'. This book explores many projects within modern and contemporary art in which islandness is reconceived as part of the conceptual meaning of art.

Some of the most compelling works of the so-called expanded field of modern and contemporary art can engage a wide audience using analytical, playful, performative and parodic strategies of making, combined with an imaginative exploration of place and space. The power of the visual spectacle is not the only means to provoke lively debate on islandness. Aesthetic ambiguity, irony, pastiche, conceptual games, modern allegory and activism have informed some of the most interesting works on the island theme since the late twentieth century. This book explores the theme in a global context, with an emphasis on British and postcolonial British archipelagos and their imperial histories, especially in Pacific Oceania and the Caribbean. The complex colonial baggage of these islands and their vulnerability to climate change have inspired some compelling recent art projects.

GENDER, FEMINISM AND 'ISLAND QUEENS'

For centuries explorer and castaway stories usually featured men. Ship's companies were distinguished from terrestrial society by 'the almost complete absence of women, or at least their occasional – but almost always transgressive – presence aboard ship in the days before passenger ships and cruise liners. Ships are, very largely, "manned"'.[39] Nautical life and seafaring literature have been dominated by masculine codes. Until the nineteenth century women were largely excluded from life at sea – in the navy, as fishermen, explorers, traders or pirates; this applies to many global cultures. When relocated to the seas, gender relations could be reordered in complex (and often misogynistic) ways.[40] Fictional castaways were most often male, reinforcing patriarchal histories of discovery and empire/s. In *Robinson Crusoe* there is an absence of women – they are 'excluded as strictly as from a boys' boarding school. During Crusoe's time on his island they simply don't exist, not even in his memory.'[41] But modern literature has offered some challenges to this stereotype. For example, in Chapter One I consider Jean Giraudoux's *Suzanne and the Pacific* (1923), which mischievously instates a 'modest maid of Limousin' as an abandoned castaway who pursues a hedonistic life on her desert island – the opposite of Crusoe's resourceful 'monarch'. More recently, challenges to the Crusoe narrative have come from feminists who 'have wondered whether Robyn Crusoe might have done it better or more co-operatively than Robinson'.[42] Scholarship is also increasing on the women who cross-dressed as sailors or pirates in search of supposedly 'masculine' experiences of seafaring, exploring and naval conquests and battles.[43]

In Chapter One I also show how installation works by Reihana and Kihara have challenged gendered histories by deploying images and performances in which ambiguous gender roles are reimagined. Reihana introduces gender ambiguity into the traditional histories of Captain Cook's voyages in her panoramic video *in Pursuit of Venus [infected]*. As a Sāmoan/Japanese Fa'afafine artist, Kihara has deployed Sāmoan 'third gender' models to rework Gauguin's famous paintings of women on Tahiti

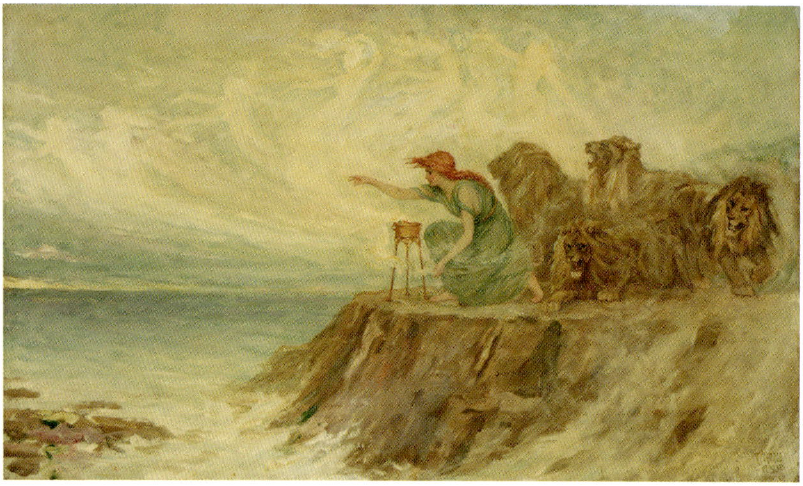

6 Frederick Stuart Church, *Circe*, 1910, oil on canvas.

and the Marquesas islands. Both artists challenge the traditional gender binaries of colonial histories.

Many modern women writers have also reworked the island theme to suggest some different narratives of 'island consciousness'. Jean Rhys's *Wide Sargasso Sea* (1966) explores the experiences of a Creole heiress, Antoinette Cosway, on the Caribbean island of Jamaica. As she negotiates an island of oppressive colonial legacies and patriarchs both absent and present, Antionette struggles to find her own identity, since it is enmeshed within the cultural and gendered prejudices of her family. Marina Warner's *Indigo; or, Mapping the Waters* (1992) is inspired by Shakespeare's *The Tempest* but is set on an imaginary Caribbean island where Ariel, Caliban and his wise mother, the healer and dyer of indigo, Sycorax, once lived. At the centre of the story is the fate of two English girls, Xanthe and Miranda Everard, whose family has settled on the island of Enfant-Béate. Prospero is side-lined as Warner evokes a sensuous Caribbean island and gives powerful voices to the characters of Sycorax, Miranda, Xanthe and Caliban.[44]

Women and aspects of their femininity have had long historical and cultural associations with islands. In Chapter Six I explore the ways in which women's bodies have been appropriated in gendered representations of both the geography and the national identity of the island/s of Ireland.

In Greek mythology many goddesses and sirens, among them Circe and Calypso, inhabited islands around the Greek archipelago, and their identities were enmeshed with these sites. Circe, a so-called sorceress and a minor goddess, claimed to be the daughter of the god Helios and the Oceanid nymph Perse, and was banished to the island of Aeaea when her gift of witchcraft was thought to threaten the gods. On Aeaea she honed her occult skills, gathering strange herbs and taming wild beasts. Homer's *Odyssey*, perhaps the best-known ancient tale of extraordinary island-hopping adventures, recounts the protagonist's visit to Aeaea on his way back from the Trojan wars. After changing most of his crew into swine, Circe is persuaded to change them back; she lives with Odysseus for a year on the island and bears him two sons. Over the centuries there have been numerous written and visual interpretations of her mythological roles and relationship with the island (illus. 6).

Circe has often been represented as an archetypal predatory female, a sexually free temptress and sorceress who used her intimate knowledge of nature's herbs and potions to entice or poison her (mostly male) victims on Aeana.[45] From Ovid's first-century poem *Metamorphosis* to Giovanni Boccaccio's *Famous Women* (1361–2), and many modern writers, including the British poet Carol Ann Duffy's *Circe* (1999), she holds remarkable staying power. As Judith Yarnall argues, different versions of the Circe myth 'can be seen as mirrors, sometimes clouded and sometimes clear, of the fantasies and assumptions of the cultures that produced them'.[46] Circe's intense relationship with her island and its magic herbs and animals are often at the heart of her various representations. Duffy's poem, written as a monologue, focuses on Circe's notorious tendency to transform men into pigs, describing her quasi-cannibalistic recipes for cleaning, dismembering and cooking these unfortunate beasts. Circe is presented as an earthy, sexual being, an island queen who avenges the abuse of 'sly', 'cowardly', 'cruel' men. Duffy reclaims her islandness for a resolute, self-sufficient womanhood.

In historical terms, the persistent, gendered association between women (fertility) and natural cycles has encouraged the essentialist fusion of ideas of Mother Earth and islands. Duffy appears to be mocking that association, reclaiming Circe for less passive, more vengeful culinary activities. Michel Tournier also offers a wry take on this association when his 'Cruso' develops a sexual relationship with the island, a territory he exploits, but sees as unquestionably feminine, and renames 'Speranza'.[47] He uses a moss-filled opening in a fallen tree to have sex with the Earth, feeling that 'a new man' was somehow coming to life within him, and was delighted to see mandrake-like plants growing around this spot, the offspring of his union with the island. As I show in Chapter Six, Ireland (as both nation and geographical island) has persistently been personified as female; Mother Ireland has 'always been a woman' – an earthy, corporeal, mythical presence.[48] The islandness of both Circe and Mother Ireland resides at least partly in their legendary fertile wombs and mythical powers. I show how the associations made between women, nature, islandness and witch-like powers are redefined or challenged in the work of several contemporary Irish women artists, including Alice Maher, Rachel Fallon and Jesse Jones. Circe and other female archetypes are resurrected in Maher and Fallon's embroidered sculpture *The Map* (2020; see illus. 97), which provides an epic archipelagic challenge to many of those historical associations. In Chapter Eight, which explores Roni Horn's work on Iceland, I also show how the Steilneset Memorial by French-born artist Louise Bourgeois and Swiss architect Peter Zumthor deploys the Arctic-Norwegian island setting of Vardo to celebrate and reclaim memories of persecuted 'witches'.

Following the traditions of classical myth, islands have provided spaces for unlikely tales of both mortal and immortal beings. The ancient history and folklore that surrounds the British archipelagos is replete with tales of island queens and women with magical powers. According to various legends, the Scottish Hebridean islands had a tradition of female rulers in medieval and pre-medieval times. A distinctive feature within this Hebridean folklore is the tradition of giant women.[49] Powerful women leaders based on islands are visible in many Celtic histories.[50] The remote nature of these northern land masses encouraged the dissemination of stories that could not easily be verified.[51] Throughout this book I reappropriate the term 'island queen' as a positive rewriting of a gendered history in which male leaders of island communities rarely warrant a comparable label ('island kings'?), suggesting an unusual or exotic association with the former. However, reappropriated through visual representation, my island queens are strong, visible and often transgressive. For example, in Chapter Five I explore the representation of another iconic female symbol of islandness: the Jamaican 'Nanny', a leader of slave resistance closely identified with the history of that island, and vividly represented in the work of Karen McLean.

Over the last few decades a category of 'Island Feminism' has emerged within Island Studies, drawing on research in geography, anthropology, cultural history and other disciplines. This developing area sees gender and sexuality as 'forces that contour the particular conditions of life – economic, geographical and ecological – and cultural and political manifestations on islands'.[52] Increasingly, scholars across disciplines are exploring gender relations in island locations as rich material for studying the links between gender and place.[53] So-called indigenous feminisms or postcolonial feminisms have also taken root since the 1990s, documenting the proactive cultures and responsibilities of native and Indigenous women. I suggest that *visual* culture reveals some related forms of re-presentation. For example, in Chapter Three I explore the ways in which Jetñil-Kijiner and Lehuanani Enomoto, who live and work in Pacific Oceania, have used their installations and performances to reveal an islandness that implicates gender, ecology and colonial history.

Around half of the contemporary artists featured in this book are women; I have been intrigued to find that an iconography that might traditionally be expected to attract the interests of male artists – around exploring, seafaring, mapping, castaways, dramas at sea, lighthouses and so on – has fired the creative imagination of many contemporary women. This book includes an exploration of women as co-creators of evolving, modern art practices in which gender, sexuality and colour are less likely (in comparison with historical conditions) to involve forms of social or institutional discrimination. My research suggests that over the last few decades there has been a flowering of original work by women on the island theme in varied media. Many have developed imaginative practices in which art is used to reframe or reinscribe gender and feminist concerns into island history. Such artworks are informed by evolving gender theories and actively interrogate the myths and histories of femininity that circulate around island themes. That said, I am also interested in the work of women who explore the theme for cultural, aesthetic, poetic or critical/environmental reasons, and whose practice makes more oblique or metaphorical reference to feminist or gender issues, if at all. 'Art' is seen as a dynamic set of material practices that intersects with culture and feminism in complex and diverse ways.

LANDSCAPING ISLANDS

Throughout this book, landscape is conceived not as a fixed object or topography to be faithfully represented but as a cultural practice rich in meaning. Art always presents carefully constructed re-presentations or imaginings of sites and locations; it mediates the visual characteristics and associations of a scene to an audience. In the process, the noun 'landscape' becomes more active; it implies a process of making and an act of depiction. In the Introduction to *Landscape and Power* (first published in 1994), W.J.T. Mitchell wrote: 'The aim of this book is to turn "landscape" from a noun to a verb,' an ambition that is shared in the following chapters.[54] Recent use of varied media in the expanded field, such as performance, film, photography and installation, has enabled some contemporary artists to make works that present landscape as active and shifting, as a process of image-making rather than revealing a fixed scene. In 1970 the influential American artist Robert Smithson (1938–1973) began constructing one of his best-known works, *Spiral Jetty* (illus. 7); the piece is made of local basalt rock and mud, and reaches 457 metres (1,500 ft) into the Great Salt Lake, near Rozel Point in Utah. Smithson had searched for a salt lake that had a red colouration caused by micro-bacteria, and he found his site a mile north of some abandoned oil seeps in Utah, in what he described as 'a world of modern prehistory'.[55] The spiral form was derived from a local

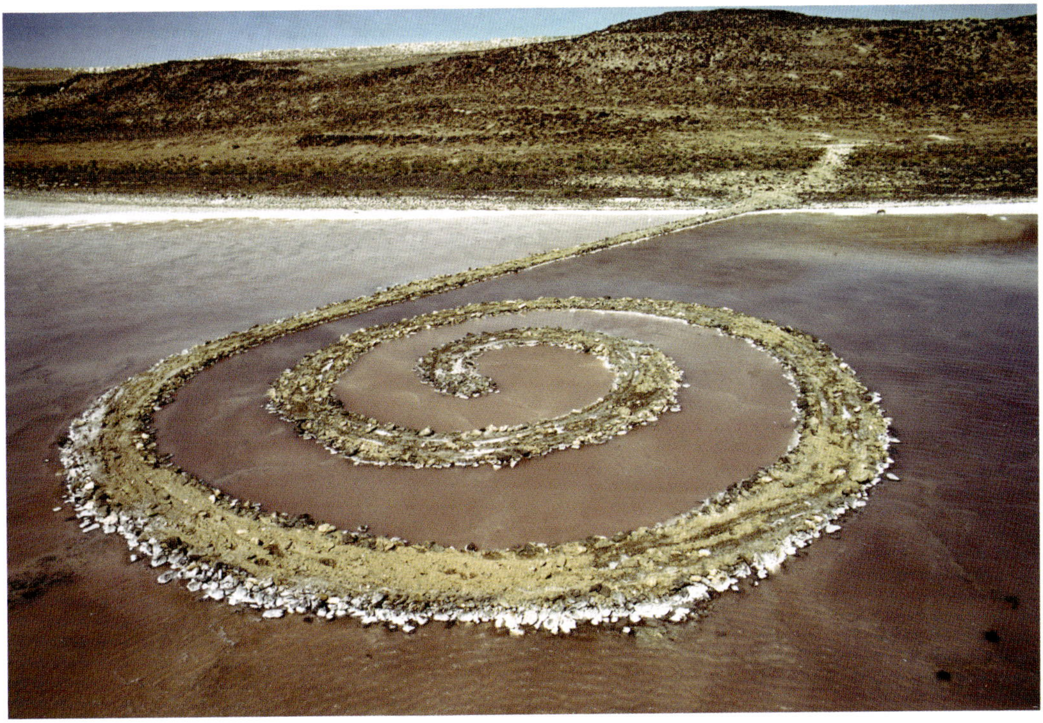

7 Robert Smithson, *Spiral Jetty*, 1970, Great Salt Lake, Utah, mud, precipitated salt crystals, rocks, water.

myth of a whirlpool at the bottom of the lake. A film and photographs were made to accompany the earthworks, but much of the jetty is now underwater, depending on fluctuating water levels; when they are low, a circular shadow of salt crystals is now visible. Smithson's strange spiral appears as an evolving and dissolving island that could be seen to exemplify a modern landscape practice that includes change through time, or what Smithson called 'entropy'.[56] As an impermanent site-specific work, it also encapsulates the transience of the expanded field of contemporary art that is frequently preserved only in photographs. As the art historian Craig Owens argues, this form of modern practice affirms the allegorical potential of photography. The photographic record fixes the transitory in a stabilizing image.[57] It creates a story that parallels the original ephemeral event. In Chapter Three I explore Smithson's notion of 'hypothetical' or disappearing islands that are not primary or 'authentic' art objects; they are rather earthworks that evolve through time, existing between sculpture, performance and photographic representation. I argue that modern and contemporary art have enabled some vivid and puzzling artistic representations of islandness, and such landscapes can be represented through the use of objects that stand as surrogates for an actual island. Allegory, metamorphosis, metaphor and metonym make regular appearances in my discussions. For example, I also show in Chapter Three that the Galápagos Islands can be evoked poetically through representation of their unique species, including iguanas in the drawings of Gemma Anderson, Alison Turnbull's butterflies or of the blue-footed booby in the playful disguises of Marcus Coates (see illus. 46). Such threatened species are metonymic signifiers of these islands.

Throughout his career Smithson was intrigued by the fact that islands, especially smaller ones, are largely defined by the areas of water that surround them, and the capacity of such waters to make them disappear. The sea is a fluid, unstable medium against which to frame a representation – whether literal or metaphorical – of an island. For many writers and artists (including Epeli Hau'ofa and the Martinican writer Édouard Glissant, cited in Chapter Five), the sea is also a vital connecting membrane that links and enriches the cultures of archipelagos. Oceans and water, in various geographical, ecological and metaphorical contexts, are of course inseparable from any study of islands, and have generated a rapidly expanding body of literature across disciplines. As a vehicle of colonization, migration, ecological disaster and melting ice caps, they have become an important and topical theme for curators and artists.[58]

Alongside his art projects, Smithson's lengthy writings and careful photographic records reveal cosmological, geological and ecological forms of exploration. Many years after his premature death in 1973, the evolving discipline of Island Studies has helped to bring together artists and scientists in observations of evolutionary biology, the climate emergency, geology and meteorology. Over the last few decades, expeditions, residences and field projects have brought together artists and scientists across different global archipelagos. The important Cape Farewell Arctic Expeditions (see chapters Seven and Eight) and the Gulbenkian

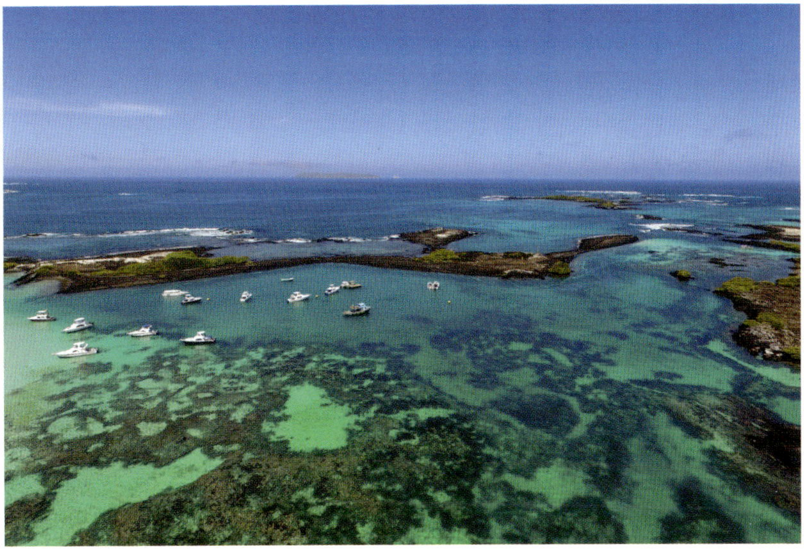

8 Aerial view of Isabela Island, Galápagos.

Galápagos Artists' Residency Programme (see Chapter Three) are among many cross-disciplinary projects that have nurtured some remarkable artworks on the island theme. The British palaeontologist Richard Fortey has written eloquently about the appeal of, and tensions involved in, multi-disciplinary studies of islands such as the Galápagos (illus. 8):

> Those isolated warts that poke up above the ocean floor in the Pacific and Atlantic Oceans will attract experiments from artists as much as documentation by scientists. Does an artist imagine themselves as a kind of Prospero, conjuring up an isolated world? It could be that the difficult questions of 'ownership' are best explored through art because it can refract the complex truth in more ways than political posturing or even scientific analysis.[59]

Artists have engaged with the island theme for a multitude of reasons, using a variety of media. Questions of ownership and refraction of 'the complex truth' are among many tricky issues that underscore the varied works that I discuss. Prospero will assume many different guises and genders.

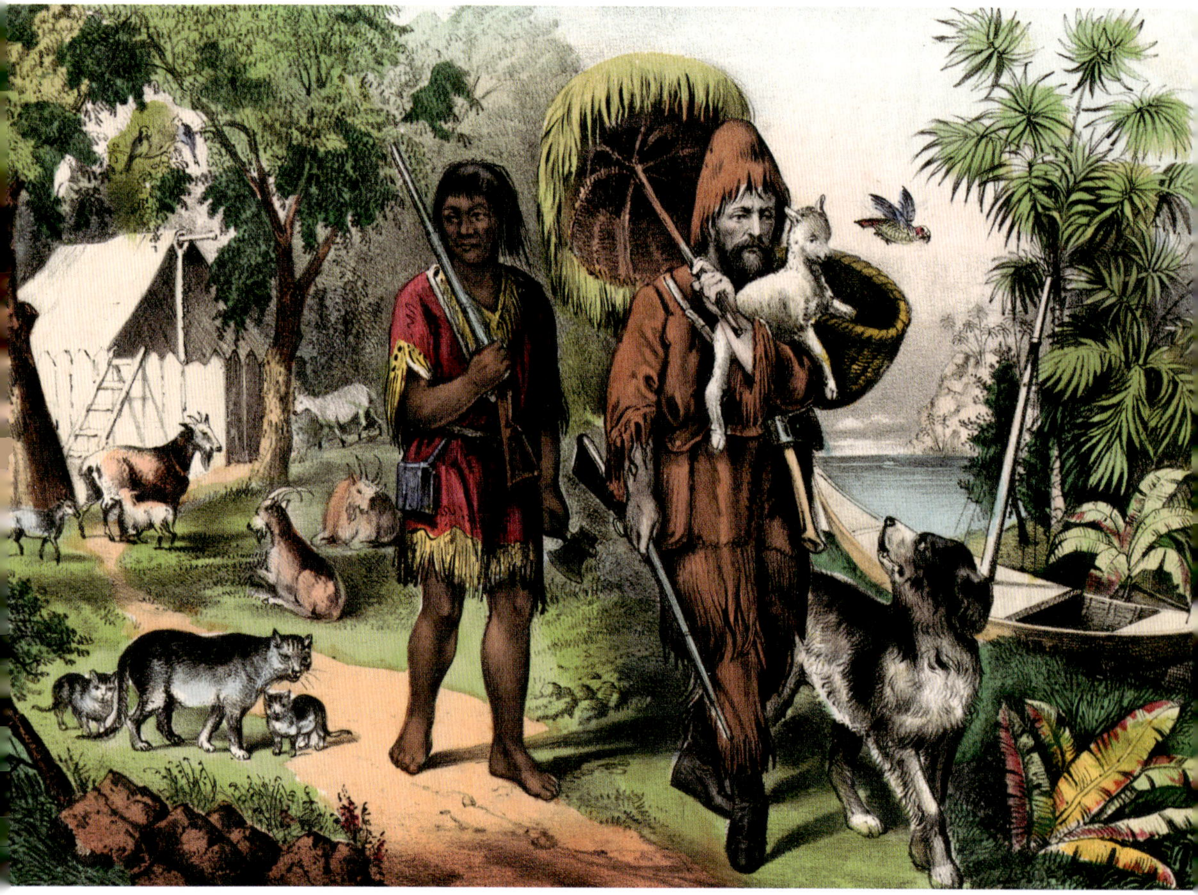

9 Robinson Crusoe
and his man Friday,
c. 1874, hand-coloured
lithograph.

1 DESERT ISLANDS AND MYTHS OF PARADISE

Defoe's *Robinson Crusoe* holds a special status in British, European and anglophone cultures. By the late summer of 1719 it had been reprinted three times, and a sequel, *The Further Adventures of Robinson Crusoe*, had been published (illus. 9). By the late twentieth century it had been reissued in several hundred editions, promoted in British schools for decades and adapted for the stage, film, television and even video games. This remarkable publishing history is paralleled by the number and variety of cover images – signifiers of changing approaches to the work, as I show below. For decades it was used as an educational text for teaching what Charles Boyle describes as 'the virtues of self-reliance, careful management of resources, and trust in the overall – if a little mysterious, but that's part of the appeal – wonderfulness of God'.[1] The book was widely deployed to promote the business of empire and 'discovery', and a public-school education promoting self-reliance and leadership. Washed up on his desert island for 28 years, Crusoe became the monarch of his domain: 'I thought myself very rich in subjects; and it was a merry reflection which I frequently made, how like a king I look'd.'[2] Boyle (among others) identifies a spirit of white male entitlement still visible in many aspects of modern life in the UK.[3] He cites the introduction to the 1900 Cambridge University edition, which hubristically invites readers to appreciate the values of resourcefulness, hard work and common sense 'that have made Great Britain the greatest colonising power in the world'.[4]

CRUSOE'S LEGACY

Crusoesque island myths lurk everywhere in the popular imaginary of modern post-enlightenment culture. In this chapter I map out some of the recurring tropes in literature, film and media that have fed into and overlapped with the visual arts. Through popular knowledge of Crusoe's exploits, islands have also become reference points in the evolution of social science. Robin Cohen has argued that

> Crusoe became the prototype of the gender-insensitive *homo oeconomicus* ('economic man'), an agent who makes rational calculations about scarcity and survival. Marxists used islands to expound their theories of primitive accumulation, exploitation and use-value. Anti-colonial and anti-racist discourses were grounded in the persona of Man Friday.[5]

When Crusoe teaches Friday to call him 'Master', the former assumes a symbolic status as an enduring political symbol of racism in a world of imperialist expansion. The changing visualizations that appear on the cover designs of different editions published since 1719 have helped to both represent and evade these shifting approaches. While the 2009 Arcturus edition reproduces the master/slave print from the 1754 publication, the HarperCollins 2013 edition avoids direct representation of both characters by using an aerial view of footprints – indexical traces in the sand of Friday's presence on the island (illus. 10, 11).

Many modern writers have also shifted the discourse. Michel Tournier replaced Defoe's first person with a third-person account in 1971. This allowed the author to imply a more wry and critical approach to a 'gender insensitive' Cruso, whose activities often appear to be ridiculous, especially when he fornicates with the island. Tournier's Friday is a part Indian, part Black teenager whom Cruso initially dominates as a 'slave'; he then realizes, however, that he can only have a harmonious relationship with both Friday and the island if he treats the former as an equal – an attempt to counter some of the original Crusoe's racism. Tournier explores what might constitute a utopia and seems to conclude that it does not come from dominating nature or Friday. Neither sex with Speranza (the island) nor controlling Friday offer Cruso a utopic space; that space could only

10, 11 Covers of editions of Daniel Defoe, *Robinson Crusoe*: Collins Classics (2013) and Arcturus Classics (2009).

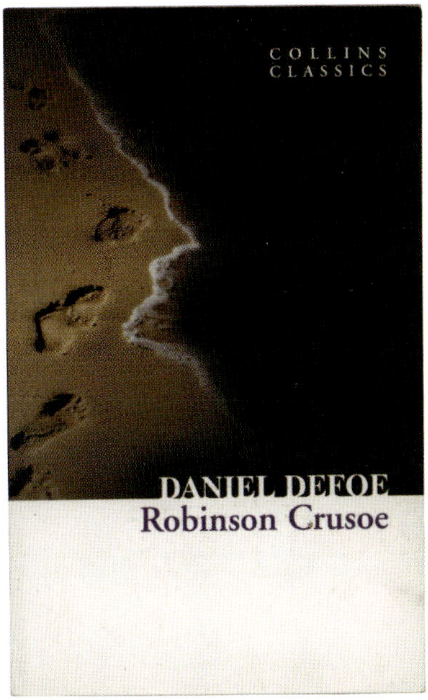

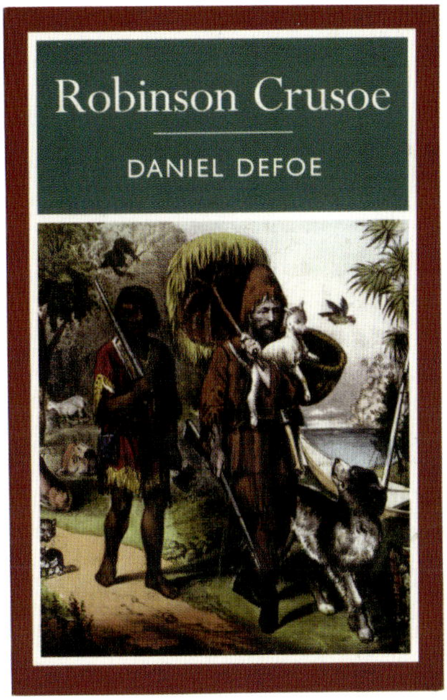

be found when he moved beyond ideas of domination. A childlike game of playacting, in which Friday dresses up as Robinson and vice versa, provides a symbolic resolution of that position. In J. M. Coetzee's *Foe* (1986), the story is told by Susan Barton, a woman castaway who lands on the same island as Cruso. She gives a voice to Friday, whose tongue has been cut off by former slavers (according to Cruso).[6]

Several decades before Tournier or Coetzee's playful rewrites, the French writer Jean Giraudoux changed the protagonist's gender in his desert island tale *Suzanne and the Pacific*, published in French in 1921 and translated into English in 1923.[7] A young French woman wins the Sydney Bulletin's competition for a trip around the world but is shipwrecked and marooned on a coral island in the Pacific for five years. During those years she explores her own and two neighbouring islands and is eventually saved by a group of astronomers studying an eclipse. Giraudoux's text describes Suzanne's irrational thoughts, fancies and fantasies; she is the opposite of Crusoe's stolid, resourceful colonial monarch. In a 1923 review titled 'The Lady of the Island', Ben Lucien Burman set out the contrast: 'Does she with palm-tree logs and conch-shell adzes attempt to erect a cabin, the hideous counterpart of civilisation's houses? Not Suzanne. True hedonist, she is content to live under a tree, to eat breadfruit in her right hand, to drink the juice of the wine tree on her left.'[8]

While Crusoe 'lacks imagination' as a 'stolid mechanician', Suzanne lies on a mossy bank. Another reviewer described Giraudoux as 'a new primitive', even a 'demi-dadaist'.[9] Suzanne emerges as a contradictory, proto-feminist modernist figure, both wedded to modern civilization yet also against all systems, continually affirming her spontaneity. As a modern reworking of the island myth, she is 'adorably' attached to the objects and symbols of modern life, hunting for rice powders, perfumes, tobacco and feather dresses and longing for railway stations, daily newspapers, moving pictures and crowds.[10] More recently, it is through the visual arts that some modern women and non-binary artists have repopulated desert islands myths of paradise.

Despite these literary interventions that break with the trope of the intrepid masculine explorer, Crusoe's legacy, and the fantasy of self-discovery in 'exotic', uninhabited settings, lingers in the Western popular imagination. Filmmakers have long been obsessed with the dramatic potential of

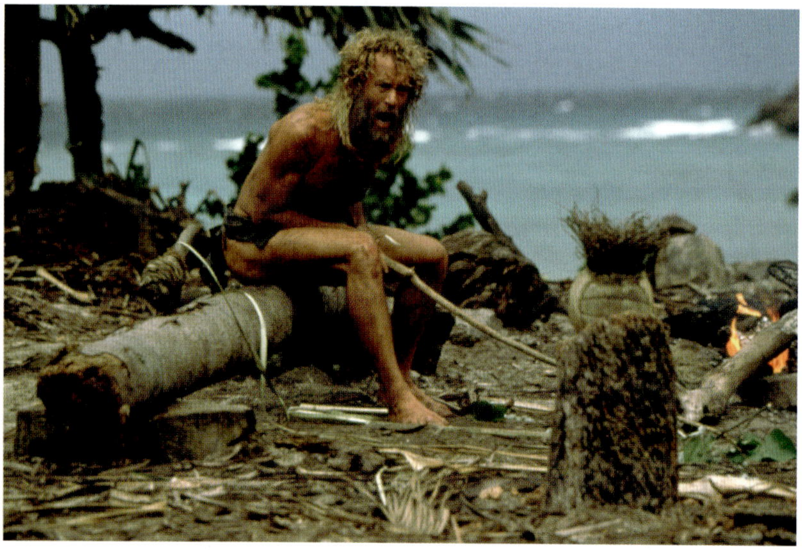

12 Still of Tom Hanks in the film *Cast Away* (2000, dir. Robert Zemeckis).

this genre, usually set in tropical archipelagos. Many of the desert island books listed in the Introduction to this book have been made into films, and Hollywood beckons the surviving Tongan schoolboys. One of the most successful modern survival films is *Cast Away* (2000, dir. Robert Zemeckis), in which Tom Hanks stars as Chuck, a time-obsessed FedEx trouble-shooter – a modern manager whose cargo plane crashes into the Pacific Ocean in a violent storm (illus. 12).

Chuck's fictional survival has inspired many modern myths; the Fijian island of Monuriki on which he was (supposedly) marooned for four years became a popular tourist attraction soon after the film was released. Festooned with awards, *Cast Away* achieved enormous global success – a testament to the ongoing appeal of the desert island story.[11] His character helps to both consolidate and evolve the trope of the resourceful white male castaway forced into a voyage of self-discovery. As the film progresses, his appearance – increasingly sunburnt skin, long hair, beard and loincloth – reinforces the Crusoesque look expected of every self-respecting castaway. Hanks himself claimed to have come up with the original storyline while reading an article about FedEx and their packages flying across the Pacific Ocean, adding a seductive 'authenticity' to the role.[12]

The stressed-out FedEx operator is called away for work while at a Christmas dinner with his girlfriend's family. After being washed up on a tropical island, he battles with isolation, acting out a search for the self. Chuck anthropomorphizes a volleyball retrieved from the crashed plane, naming it Wilson (after the brand), and chats with it throughout the film; Wilson becomes his obedient Friday. This narrative device enables Chuck to develop a one-sided speaking part that reveals his inner tribulations and triumphs. His character seems to critique aspects of modern, time-obsessed life while also applying Crusoesque survival strategies (unlike Suzanne's hedonistic spontaneity). Samson has argued that the opening scene seems to evoke 'a solid modern paradigm' of the mobile modern worker/manager who ensures free movement of consumer goods: it is shot from the viewpoint of a FedEx parcel speeding from a Texas ranch to its delivery. But Chuck's obsessive mobility also causes his temporary downfall; he is left adrift at sea.[13] At the same time, his search for companionship lies with a consumer product, an emblem of modern commodity fetishism.

Deleuze has argued that humans can create a fantasy of the potential unity of the island and its inhabitant: 'In certain conditions which attach them to the very movement of things, humans do not put an end to desertedness, they make it sacred.'[14] We might see the plot of *Cast Away* as contributing to this Western idealization of isolation. Chuck's ingenious survival through a diet of coconuts, fish and conversations with Wilson seems to affirm his natural resilience, his quasi-spiritual relationship with sacred 'desertedness'. But *Cast Away* is full of contradictions; Chuck is rescued and returns (with self-knowledge) to a modern, commodity-obsessed life; the film ends with him standing wistfully at a crossroads after making another FedEx delivery, before heading back north.

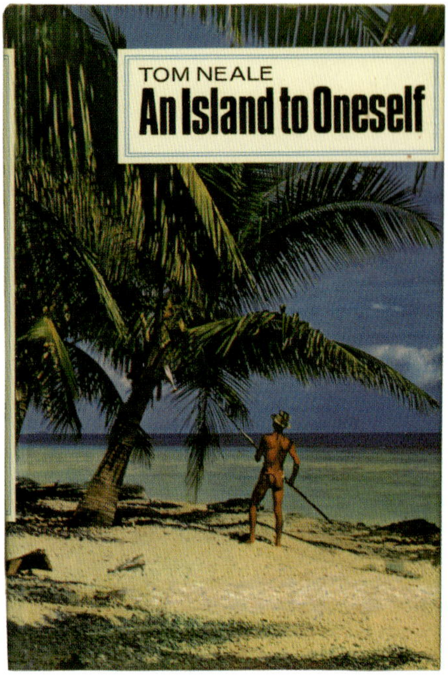

13 Cover of Tom Neale, *An Island to Oneself* (Ox Bow Press: Woodbridge, CT, 1966).

Accounts of real-life experiments in desert island isolation, and their visualizations, have proved equally popular with a modern public nurtured on post-Crusoe castaway myths. In 1966 Aotearoa New Zealand-born Tom Neale published a widely read autobiography, *An Island to Oneself*, an account of more than six years spent alone on the islet of Anchorage, close to Suvarov, an uninhabited coral atoll in the northern Cook Islands.[15] Neale spent three extended periods on Anchorage between 1952 and 1977. His autobiography, based on the second period on the atoll, documents his struggle to survive alone, described in one press review as 'an unforgettable tale of peril, beauty and solitude'.[16] Neale self-presents as a modern noble savage, contributing to the myth of the heroic white male castaway (illus. 13). The cover image depicts Neale with a deep tan standing under a coconut tree, naked apart from a loincloth and holding a spear, posed like a nineteenth-century Polynesian warrior in front of a clear blue ocean, a visual cliché waiting to be appropriated by a more cynical contemporary artist.

SLAPSTICK ROBINSON CRUSOE

Another male castaway (albeit fully clothed) posed against the white sand and clear blue sea of a tropical island with coconut palms is the subject of the Canadian artist Rodney Graham's film *Vexation Island*. Acted out by the artist and shown in the Canadian Pavilion of the Venice Biennale in 1997, the work was described by Graham (1949–2022) as 'a costume picture, that is to say, a travesty'.[17] He was a voracious consumer of literary and cultural sources, and this work mischievously references a host of themes that populate the desert island myth. Shot in brilliant colour in widescreen Cinemascope, the film opens with an aerial view of his island, surrounded by a glistening sapphire-blue ocean; coconut palm trees are blowing gently in the Pacific breeze, silhouetted in the white sand. After the camera has panned along the beach, Graham is first seen dressed as a shipwrecked eighteenth-century gentleman, sleeping (or unconscious) on a mariner's wooden chest with a parrot perched on a barrel beside him (illus. 14).

The scene loosely references the moment in Defoe's tale when Crusoe wakes up after trying to circumnavigate the island, as his parrot is talking to him.[18] The bird is also a reference to another icon of castaway stories, *Treasure Island*'s Long John Silver, an eccentric one-legged pirate who

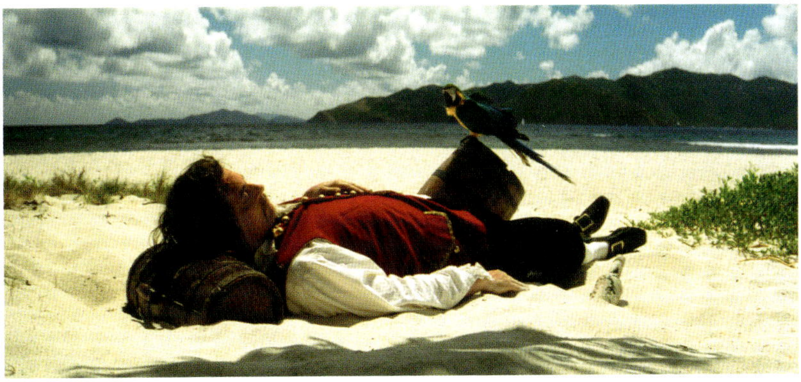

14 Rodney Graham, *Vexation Island*, 1997, still, 35 mm film, transferred to DVD, 9 minutes.

limps around with a parrot permanently on his shoulder. Graham chooses an early post-shipwreck moment before the meeting with Defoe's Friday; there is no reference here to the protagonist's negotiations with that tricky symbol of colonial domination. The sun-tanned castaway, who has a wound on his head, is disturbed by the squawking parrot, gets up and spots a coconut in a nearby palm tree. He proceeds to shake the tree to get the coconut – another desert island motif that has helped to sustain famous shipwrecked heroes from Crusoe to Hanks and Neale – but it falls out of the tree and hits him on the head. He is then knocked unconscious and falls down in the position and place in which the film started. This dramatic sequence is repeated on a nine-minute loop.[19]

When the film was first shown in Venice (another network of islands), Graham also sought to forge a relationship with the idiosyncratic architecture of the Canadian Pavilion. He specified that the partly open pavilion should be kept boarded up, as in winter.[20] The boards gave the space the appearance of a 'rustic hut', which reminded him of the stockade in Walt Disney's 1950 film version of *Treasure Island*.[21] The expensive production of *Vexation Island* mimicked that of a popular blockbuster supported by a full Hollywood crew. However, the viewer's expectations of struggle and final rescue in this popular film genre are thwarted on many levels; the glossy production values are undermined when the expected narrative is shortened, unresolved and endlessly repeated; temporality is rooted in paradox and playful humour. Graham's use of video looping defies the rules of Hollywood filmmaking that demand a beginning and an end, especially in desert island survival movies in which the protagonist's resourcefulness helps to propel the viewer to a happy(ish) ending in which the star manages to escape the island, as in *Cast Away*. In contrast, Robert Enright has described *Vexation Island* as 'slapstick Robinson Crusoe, all high-key Caribbean colour and low-grade coconut humour.'[22]

Repetition (aesthetic, metaphorical and as narrative) lies at the heart of *Vexation Island* and is evidence of Graham's interest in Freudian theories. Loretta Yarlow has suggested that Graham's protagonist is suspended between repeated states of 'prolonged unconsciousness and short-lived

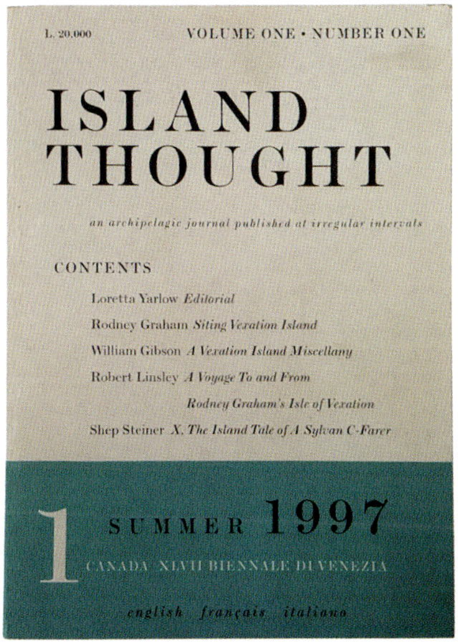

15 Cover of the journal *Island Thought*, I/1 (Summer 1997).

awakenings'.[23] In accordance with Freud's concept of neurosis, the artist creates neurotic heroes for whom repetition substitutes for past memories. *Vexation Island* echoes a frequent concern of Graham's film and video work: the cycles of waking and sleeping, and the 'repetition-compulsion' in everyday life.[24] He has acknowledged that it came out of an earlier piece called *Halcion Sleep* (1994), his first video using himself as performer. In *Halcion Sleep* the semi-conscious artist rides around Vancouver in the back of a van in a drug-induced sleep. The persistent positioning of himself as the performing artist and protagonist in most of his films reminds us that this is also a strategy of self-exploration, a self-conscious (even compulsive) repetition of the 'what's it all about?' cliché. Many of Graham's films and his 'neurotic heroes' leave us with a sense of the protagonist as feeling lost.[25] Art is presented as an unresolved pastiche of life and the myths that help to structure it.

Few commentators, however, have drawn attention to the central importance of the idea of a desert island, both literally and metaphorically, in *Vexation Island*. The protagonist's semi-conscious isolation in this glossy 'island paradise' colours every frame of the film. Graham's project, like so many of his works, is loaded with self-reflexive intentions, both mischievous and serious. To emphasize his exploration of the paradoxes of islandness, the artist led the production of a mock journal to accompany the exhibit in the Canadian Pavilion. Volume one, number one of *Island Thought – An Archipelagic Journal Published at Irregular Intervals* appeared in the summer of 1997 (illus. 15), nine years before the academic journal *Island Studies* appeared on the scene.[26] *Island Thought* includes an introductory essay by Graham titled 'Siting Vexation Island', in which he signals the appeal of aspects of Freudian theory. Drawing on his 'screen memories', he also describes his own performance as 'guided by a creative visualization of Brando's rendering of Fletcher Christian's death surrounded by his crew and the final shot: a pan away towards the sea and to the Bounty herself as the flaming ship and all hope of a return to England sinks at last beneath the waves'.[27] *Island Thought* is itself a key aspect of the performative, self-referential and multi-layered project that constitutes *Vexation Island*. The work comes with its own documentary 'evidence' and archival clues, albeit edited and performed by Graham and his collaborators. William Gibson's contribution, titled 'A Vexation Island Miscellany', cites the literary sources that help to explain the title, including Walter de la Mare's rambling anthology *Desert Islands* (1930). De la Mare cites tales of a tropical 'Vexation Island' that harboured 'the rotted relics of previous castaways'. He suggests that 'in the world of fiction there must somewhere be an island on the order of Vexation, but one wherein the sniffling swine-things are not wild pigs, and where the ghost that begins to chatter maniacally as each purple dusk descends is not a parrot.'[28] Are wild pigs and chattering parrots then disguises for a debased and self-absorbed humanity? Could Circe's – and Carol Ann Duffy's – pig-men find a home on Graham's Vexation Island? I like to think so.

IT'S MY ISLAND

Graham's gift for using playful, performative strategies to explore and critique cultural tropes has a mischievous echo in the diminutive desert island constructed by the Finnish artist Antti Laitinen (b. 1975), *It's My Island*. At the exhibition 'Earth' at the Royal Academy London in 2007 he showed a video triptych and photographs recording the process of building his island in the Baltic Sea, in a northern climate alien to that of a typical desert island fantasy. Using a spade and stacks, he spent three months filling bags with sand and dragging them into the sea, until a small outcrop of 'land' emerged above the water level. Positioning himself on this bleak island, he claimed it as a micro-nation paradise. As the single occupant, he also references the desert island cartoon trope famously repeated in the *New Yorker* magazine. The palm tree, another metonymic signifier of desert islandness, was deployed in his 2008 video *Voyage* (illus. 16). In 2009

16 Antti Laitinen, *Voyage*, 2008, C-print, Diasec.

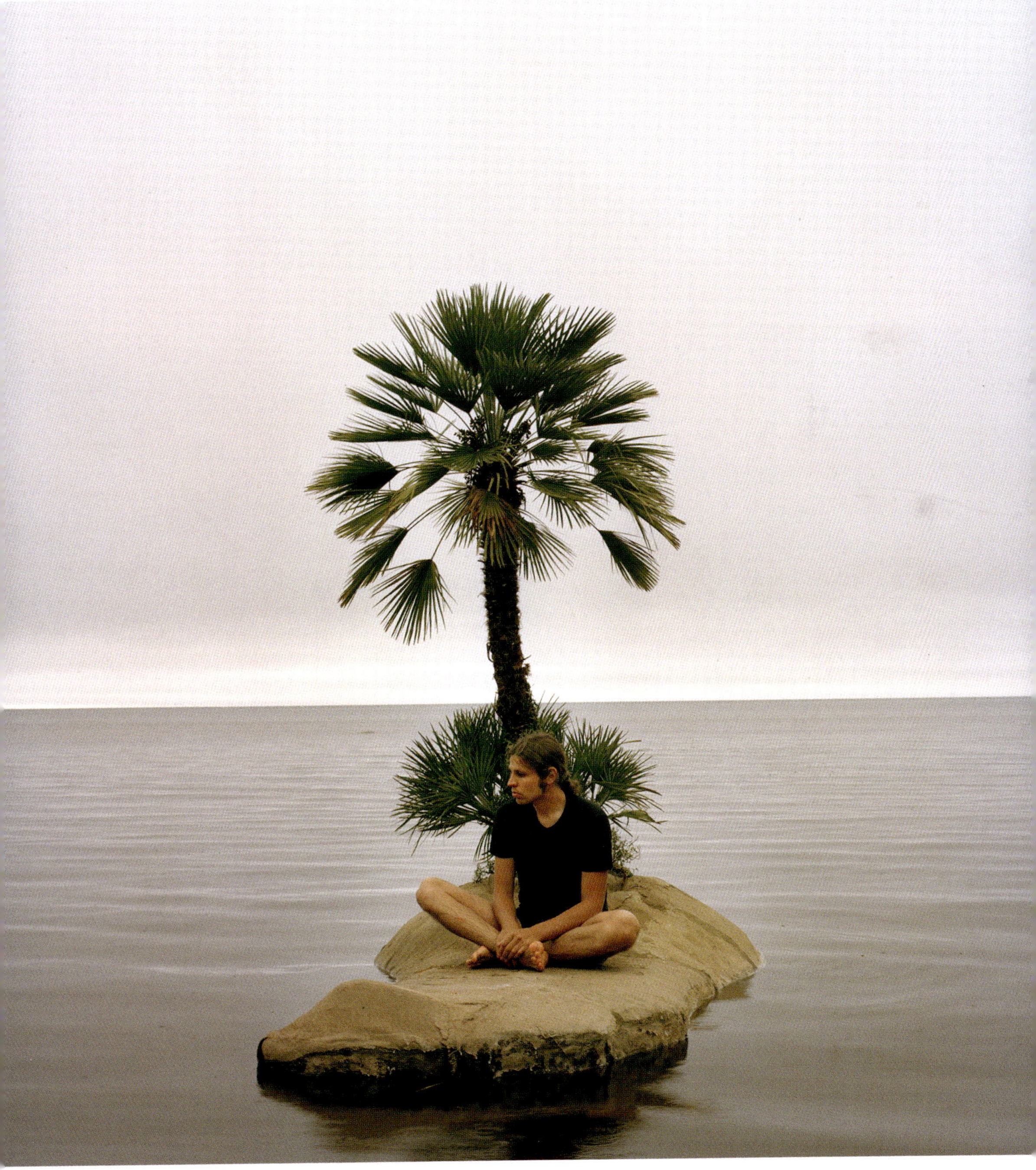

he rowed his homemade island (now floating) down the River Thames in London as part of a show entitled 'Hotel Meridian' (after the Greenwich Meridian) by the Vietnamese arts collective mahony.fm. The journey provided another mock-heroic narrative, since at one point he found himself stuck on a sandbank exposed by the tide. As he was rowing past the MI5 building (Head Quarters of the UK Secret Service) at Millbank, a police boat stopped his planned journey, towing him back up the river.

Another condition of Laitinen's work is its inevitable evolution and degradation. The sea quickly eroded the island and engulfed its tree in *Its My Island* of 2007, providing a Smithsonian form of entropy. But his comedic performances, influenced by his childhood love of *Monty Python's Flying Circus* in the late 1960s and '70s, are also a refusal to offer clear, authoritative meanings of his work.[29] While some have seen issues of climate change to be key concerns (changing and disappearing landmasses), others have identified contested ideas of nationhood and identity driving his playful performances. Both themes have been acknowledged by the artist as sources of inspiration, alongside his concerns with issues of Finnish identity and cultural imagery. He claims that the inspiration for *It's My Island* also came from thinking about what might actually constitute an island. Following his move to Berlin in 2007, he recalls sitting in a bathtub with his knees above the water line, wondering if such a visual image could be called 'islands': 'How small can an island be? What is the description of an island; everything which is coming from the bottom of the water and going above the waterline, is that an island? And then I thought, okay it is kind of a nice idea to try to build an island for myself.'[30]

The seeming naivety of his statement masks broader, epistemological concerns about how we use both language and visual representation to define an island, a conceptual problem discussed in the Introduction to this book. Laitinen's strategy, echoing that of Graham, is to foreground the marooned, performing self in the construction of his island/s. Both artists mischievously rework the trope of the resourceful (white male) protagonist, making choices alone; both artists appear to be going nowhere.

LOST AND FOUND

The incongruity of a floating palm tree in a northern Finnish context, or even in the middle of the Thames, reminds us of the ubiquity of sunny, tropical imagery in the desert island fantasy. Graham's cinematic use of the vividly coloured, castaway scene in a sun-drenched landscape has an ironic echo in the ongoing media fascination with the theme in film and television. Several popular TV series of the last few decades have also exploited and reworked its voyeuristic potential to attract and sustain a viewer's engagement as they witness the psychology of individual/s seeking to survive. Echoing the themes of *Lord of the Flies* and the Tongan schoolboys, producers have identified the lure of abandoned groups of people on remote tropical islands as a winning formula for reality TV. The high-budget and hugely successful American-made series *Lost*, originally broadcast on ABC between 2004 and 2010, features the survivors of Oceanic flight 815 from Sydney to Los Angeles, which crashed onto an apparently uninhabited island somewhere in the South Pacific when more than 1,600 kilometres (1,000 mi.) off course (illus. 17).[31] The castaways slowly discover that the island has a dark history, having been used as a centre for scientific research, and is home to a community called 'the Others', brought there by the islands' 2,000-year-old protector, Jacob, who guards the mysterious 'Heart of the island'. Filmed on Hawai'i, and using supernatural effects, temporal confusion and science fiction, *Lost* presents the island as both lush and mysterious, a dystopian fantasy backdrop for the unravelling of mysteries and personal secrets of each of the survivors. On one level the storyline of *Lost* conforms to desert island conventions. As Samson describes it: 'The island offers abjected characters the opportunity for renewal and self-fashioning, in the familiar paradigm of *Robinson Crusoe*.'[32] At the same time, *Lost* seems to deny viewers some common desert island tropes. The Smoke

17 Poster for the TV series *Lost* (2004).

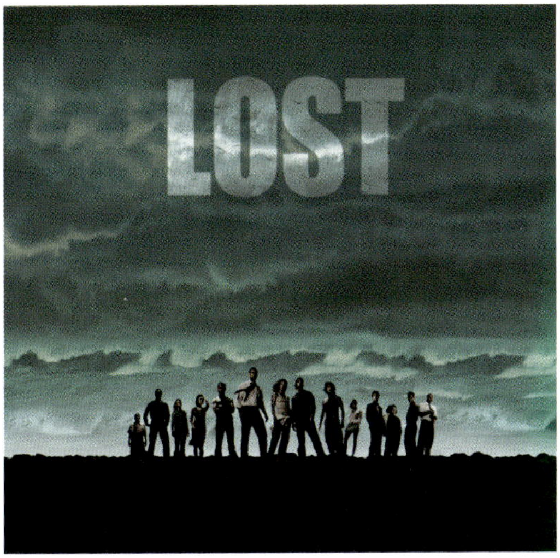

Monster, who attempts to start a global war between good and evil, is a far cry from suspicious or cannibalistic natives, and the giant frozen wheel in the underground research station that controls the island's position in space and time seems like an ontological conceit that catapults the series into science fiction.

Producers of reality TV have found the desert island theme irresistible. Over the last few decades many such shows in the United States and Europe have placed carefully selected volunteers of both sexes (usually with traditional binary representations of gender) in island settings, often wearing few clothes, in edited re-presentations of social and sexual 'survival' behaviour. By placing volunteers on a sealed-off island site, programme-makers can effectively manipulate and provoke conflict and distress. Remote and unfamiliar settings can also trigger a range of mental health issues among participants. As Nathalie Olah has written: 'The narrative arc of reality television involves the creation of villains, victims and oddballs, fictional constructions created by the editing process, of which contestants may only be partially aware.'[33] For example, the American TV series *Survivor* (launched in 1997, and now adapted in a British TV version) places a group of strangers on a remote tropical island with meagre supplies; they have to provide food, shelter and fire for themselves. Split between two teams, or 'tribes', and encouraged to compete for rewards such as food or luxuries, contestants are progressively voted out by fellow

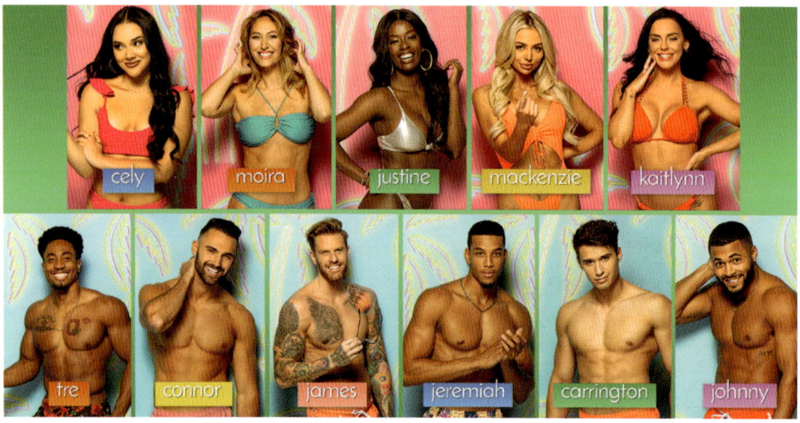

18 Cast of the reality series *Love Island* USA (2020).

participants, until only one remains who is awarded a large prize of $1 million (£100,000 in the British series). Sex, voyeurism, tribal conflict and financial gain are merged with the desert island myth. Deleuze's desert island fantasy is effectively contaminated (rather than contrasted) with the lure of modern global capitalism.

The successful British, Australian and American TV series *Love Island* (first launched in 2005 and revived in 2015 and launched in 2018 in the USA) develops some similar tropes, but in an affluent, hyper-sexualized context. It involves carefully selected single women and men, referred to as 'Islanders', who live in apparent isolation from the outside world in a holiday villa. Episodes are filmed to suggest an uninhabited landscape around the villa (Mallorca was in fact used for the British series). Under constant video surveillance, the protagonists mostly sport little more than skimpy swimwear. To survive, the Islanders must pair up and win a public vote for the 'favourite couple'. The island thus frames a voyeuristic fantasy of the inevitable sexual coupling – and recoupling – that happens when marooned in an 'exotic' place, separated by water from the familiarity of home or social community.[34] But this island setting is far from inhospitable; accommodation is luxurious. The warm climate, objectified bodies and the rules of the game produce intense jealousies, anxieties and exhibitionism; villains and victims inevitably emerge. Unlike some other desert island tales of community survival, the contestants are required to fight for their own individual status and desirability. They treat each other 'as a means to (unattainable) erotic or acquisitive satisfaction'.[35] A Paramount publicity page for the series displays three-quarter body shots of the female and male participants in skimpy swimwear, lined up as if on a dating site, in front of sketched palm tree leaves (illus. 18). Within this hugely popular sphere of modern visual culture, the ubiquitous leaves are all that remain of the original castaway signifiers. The contemporary version of the desert island myth has effectively morphed into a site for (mostly binary) sexual fantasy, narcissism and the manipulation of 'villains, victims and oddballs', forever competing with each other for self-preservation and visibility.

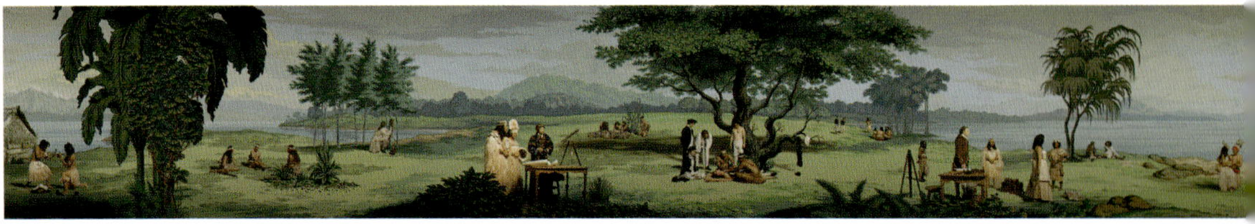

CAPTAIN COOK'S BREECHES

Pacific Oceania is often the ill-defined site of desert island tales. Images of a tropical Eden or paradise on these archipelagos have dominated Western island fantasies since the first colonial encounters by male 'explorers'. As John Connell has written:

> Linked processes of exploring, mapping, settling, administering and converting are implicated in a wider imperial politics of place, that in talking back to the homelands tended to glamourise the various enterprises that were linked to the colonial endeavour . . . Few islands can have excited imaginations more than those of the Pacific.[36]

James Cook's Pacific voyages made between 1768 and 1779 have attracted a vast amount of scholarly research, much of which has been written from the viewpoint of Western or European history-writing. Pacific historiography is evolving, however, and increasingly being written by scholars from the area itself, some of whom have deconstructed prevalent myths of Pacific settlement.[37] Several contemporary artists have also sought to reframe that history within a reconceived visual vocabulary of Pacific islandness.

Visitors to the 2017 Venice Art Biennale who managed to find the New Zealand Pavilion were transfixed by a video installation by Lisa Reihana (b. 1964), *in Pursuit of Venus [infected]*. Despite its location at the far end of the exhibition spaces in the Arsenale, it drew crowds and was claimed by some as 'the best artwork' in the show.[38] After Venice, it mesmerized audiences in Sydney, Perth and the Royal Academy exhibition

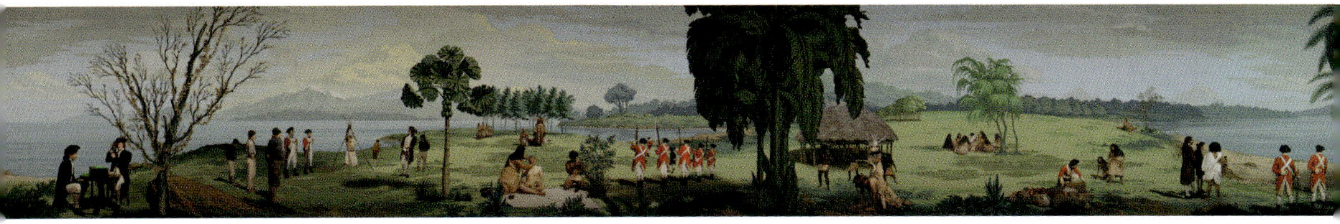

19 Lisa Reihana, Nga Puhi, Ngai Tu, Ngati Hine, *in Pursuit of Venus [infected]*, 2015–17, still, single-channel Ultra HD video: 64 minutes (looped), 7.1 surround sound, colour, AV 00:00:00. Transferred to DVD, 9 minutes.

'Oceania' in London in 2018, among other destinations. Reihana's spectacular reworking of stories of Captain Cook's voyages of exploration and conquest of the Polynesian islands, presented as a live-action, panoramic video, was hard to ignore. As the viewer sits at a fixed point in front of the 22.5-metre-long (74 ft) screen, which is in fact a wall, scenes set within local landscapes scroll past in an unusual combination of animation and film. Certain characters reappear in various juxtaposed scenes, with a backdrop of lush vegetation and sea vistas, evoking utopian versions of Tahiti.[39] Reihana's video-projection reanimates a controversial period of colonial history (illus. 19) that hinged on the idea that the intrepid British 'discovered' and claimed a cluster of 'exotic' islands, far from the imperial centre in London. Voyages of exploration were commissioned and funded with a view to open new markets and gain access to scarce resources, in order to extend the empire. The island coastlines featured in Reihana's work are presented as performative stages for social interactions and effects of exploration and colonization.

in Pursuit of Venus [infected] restages the sequences depicted in the celebrated nineteenth-century wallpaper *Les sauvages de la Mer Pacifique* (1804–5) illustrated by Jean-Gabriel Charvet. Charvet sourced his illustrations from accounts detailed in the journals of Pacific voyages by Captain Cook and others.[40] Designed to decorate the walls of wealthy European and American mansions, the wallpaper presents an idealized paradise in which Māori and Oceanic peoples are shown in inappropriate Hellenic poses and drapery and engaged in 'exotic' rituals, supposedly enjoyed by islanders.

Reihana is a leading Māori film and new-media artist based in Aotearoa New Zealand. After viewing Charvet's *Les Sauvages* at the National Gallery of Australia in 2005, she resolved to correct this 'fascinating concoction . . . that has nothing to do with her Polynesian roots'.[41] Years spent carefully researching histories of this 'concoction' compelled her to reconceive the wallpaper as a modern filmic project, and to invest it with a more nuanced understanding of Cook's voyages and their momentous effects on the lives and culture of the islanders of Pacific Oceania. In 1769 Cook had famously berthed the *Endeavour* in Tahiti, where he oversaw the building of an observatory to watch the astronomical transit of Venus across the sun – hence the title. On Tahiti Cook opened orders from the British Admiralty that charged him with exploring and claiming the so-called 'Terra Australis Incognita', a supposedly undiscovered southern continent, in the name of King George III. The rest is history. Or rather versions of that history.

Reihana's 'panoramic pantomime' lasts for eight minutes and consists of seventy vignettes that scroll across the landscape, combining historic and imagined scenes performed by indigenous actors, and including music and dialogue in several Pacific languages. Reimagined scenes include men wrestling, haka and hula dances, a kava-drinking ceremony, the trading of iron for sexual favours, floggings and Cook's violent death. Before staking Britain's claim in 1770 to what is now called Australia, Cook and his crew had spent eighteen months travelling around South Pacific Oceania and the west coast of Aotearoa New Zealand interacting with various First Nation Peoples, which marked the beginning of a colonial invasion that brought with it Western diseases and infections that devastated Indigenous communities, hence the final part of Reihana's title: *[infected]*. Cook's life and legacy has been researched and debated for generations, and lurid tales of his death and dismemberment at the hands of Hawai'ian warriors enthralled and horrified the British public. The nineteenth-century Hawai'ian historian Samuel Mānaiakalani Kamakau described the arrival of Cook in his 1866 *Mo'oleo*, or 'History' (unpublished in English until 1961). He emphasized the aggression and hostage-taking that preceded Cook's now mythical, ritualistic death, when his corpse was dismembered and body parts portioned out. The account concludes with an equally shocking list:

> The fruits and seeds that Cook's actions planted sprouted and grew, and became trees that spread to devastate the people of these islands:
> 1. Gonorrhea together with syphilis.
> 2. Prostitution.
> 3. The false idea that he was a God and worshipped.
> 4. Fleas and mosquitoes.
> 5. The spread of epidemic diseases.
> 6. Change in the air we breathe.
> 7. Weakening of our bodies.
> 8. Changes in plant life.[42]

Reihana presents a multi-layered critical engagement with these islands and their contested histories. She suggests that the colonial exchange involved has helped to define them ever since. Her moving tableau also reinforces the physical and geographical shape of the history that she explores; every scene is set against seascapes and lush island coastlines. Repeated images of the visiting *Endeavour* moored offshore also remind the viewer of the overarching narrative of exploration. Images are framed by the sea, from which invasions and encroachments arrive by ship or boat. In most sequences island coastlines are visible and landmasses appear to merge into each other as the video scrolls past its audience, emphasizing the connectedness between islands. Space is represented as archipelagic and fluid.

Moreover, as a woman artist, Reihana felt empowered to play with the gender roles embedded in this colonial history. In one scene a man pretends to give birth, and in another an islander pulls down Captain Cook's breeches. As she has explained: 'Because they couldn't see his genitals and he didn't sleep with the local women . . . they didn't know if he was a male or a female.'[43] For half the video he is played by a woman friend of the artist who was nicknamed Cook as a child because of a strong facial resemblance to surviving images of the captain. Reihana explains: 'Takatāpui is a Māori word meaning people of the same sex who are great friends . . . Fa'afafine is a word that relates to Sāmoa, where a man takes the manner of a woman and might look after the family and take on other duties. It's a kind of culturally known and accepted thing to do.'[44] *in Pursuit of Venus [infected]* thus engages with more ambiguous notions of gender and sexuality that are part of Polynesian island culture and integrates this ambiguity into the established historical narratives of conquest. Cook's breeches carry powerful metaphorical meanings. They represent both the invasion of alien Western dress (by the occupying male navy) into these islands, and the misrepresentations and social/sexual confusions that the uniform could carry, not to mention the infections that they hid. Removing Cook's breeches is an act of curious resistance; the events that subsequently resulted in his death and the notorious dismemberment of his body offer further evidence of the cultural conflict and confusions inherent in colonization.

in Pursuit of Venus [infected] explores and critiques the colonial representation of landscape and place, the 'contamination' of local cultures, alongside an ambiguous re-presentation of gender. Partly orchestrated through the participation of Māori and Pacific Islander performers, Reihana's fluid 'panoramic pantomime' offers a speculative reworking of visual tropes and established histories – a modern riposte to the 'soft primitivism' of Paul Gauguin's frieze-like nineteenth-century paintings of Polynesian women. Through such reimagining, contemporary visual art can play an important role in an ongoing process of decolonization and transformation by rewriting local island histories and their painted representations.

PARADISE CAMP

The TV series *Love Island* merges the idea of the island paradise with that of (the pursuit of) erotic satisfaction and voyeurism, albeit within a space of a largely traditional binary sexuality. Gauguin's paintings of a contradictory, romanticized Polynesian paradise dominated by his now-iconic images of women have contributed to the well-established visual conflation of ideas of (French) colonial island culture and seemingly 'exotic'

20 Yuki Kihara, *Fonofono o le nuanua: Patches of the Rainbow* (after Gauguin), 2020, installation view, Venice Biennale Arte 2022.

21 Yuki Kihara, *Paradise Camp*, curated by Natalie King, installation view, Venice Biennale Arte 2022.

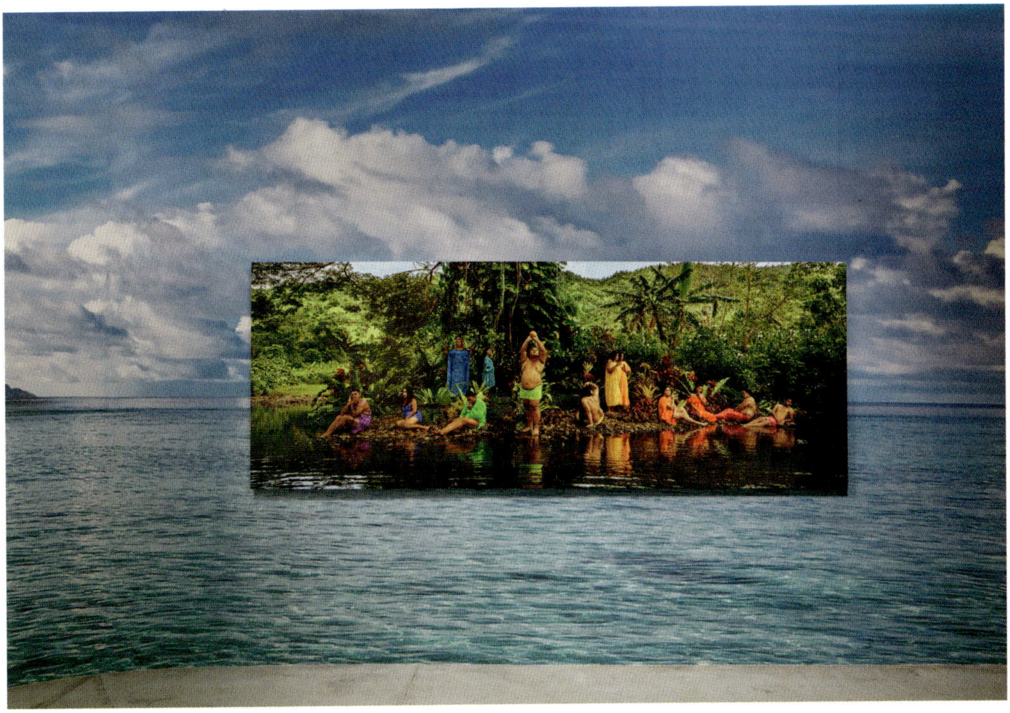

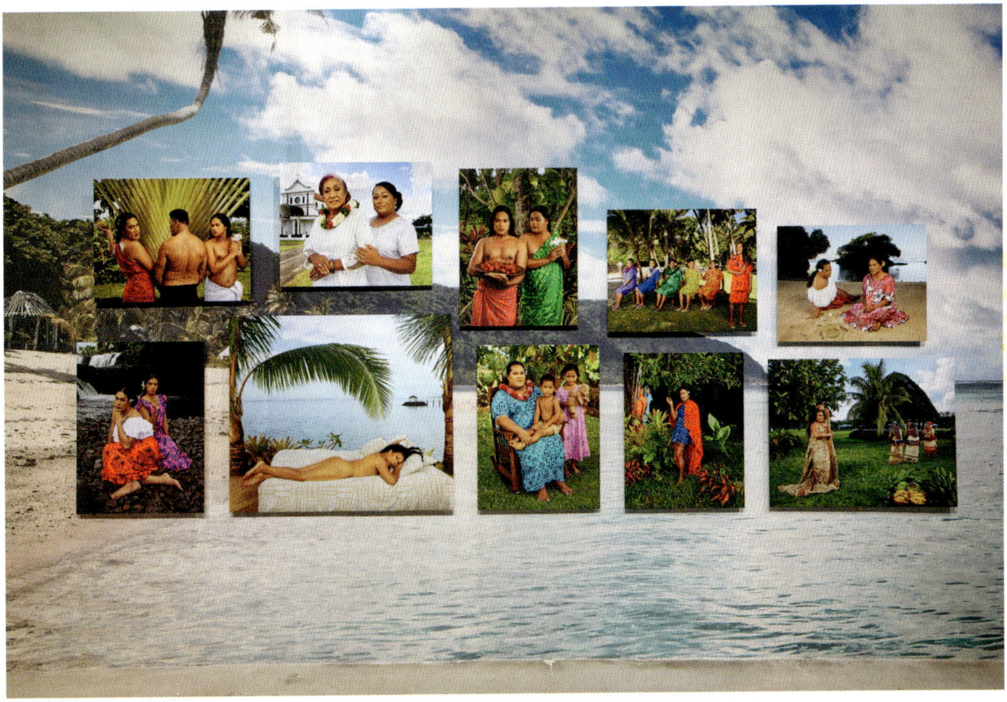

feminine sexuality.[45] Reihana is one of several Indigenous artists of Pacific Oceania who have challenged these Eurocentric tropes of Polynesian 'islandness'. A reframing of visual histories is also a key concern of the work of Sāmoan/Japanese artist Yuki Kihara (b. 1975).[46] She has spent many years researching the culture and worldviews of her Sāmoan ancestors, exploring genders and subjectivities in which land, belonging and identity are closely interconnected with oceans, island landscapes and seafaring. In her performative, photographic and film installation *Paradise Camp* for the New Zealand pavilion of the 59th Venice Biennale in 2022, Kihara revisits well-known works by Gauguin painted during his time on the islands of Tahiti and the Marquesas between 1891 and 1903. *Paradise Camp* consists of twelve photographs in bright, saturated colour (illus. 20, 21), in which Fa'afafine women (known as Sāmoa's 'third gender') re-enact well-known works by the French artist. In a five-part episodic series including film footage of Fa'afafine beauty pageants, a group of Fa'afafine offer their somewhat mischievous views on several Gauguin paintings, titled *First Impressions: Paul Gauguin*. Sāmoan sexual culture is thus playfully intertwined with the Polynesian colonial legacy visualized in his paintings, in what Natalie King describes as a decolonial strategy that 'reinstates Indigenous queer histories'.[47] Moreover, those histories are rooted in the islanders' closeness to, and observations of, land, kinship and oceanic life around them. The dominant male of the local pink skunk clownfish (*Tu'u'u-lumane*) changes its sex to female to ensure the survival of their species. Nicole M. Nepomuceno has explained that for Kihara, the Darwinian assumptions of heteronormativity are debunked by this kinship system: 'Samoans have long perceived and interacted with the world beyond heterosexual binaries, with four culturally recognized genders: *fafine* (woman), *tane* (man), *fa'afafine* (in the manner of a woman) and fa'afatoma (in the manner of a man), each with a specific familial and communal role.'[48] In each of Kihara's photographic reworkings, vibrant colours, exotic costumes and lush tropical sets evoke an exaggerated Gauguinesque palette and scenography. In their poses and facial expressions, the models carefully mimic those of the original works, creating an alternative, if no less seductive, invitation to 'gaze'.

The installation also includes what Kihara calls a 'Vārchive', derived from the Sāmoan concept of Vā, which describes the spatial and relational contexts that help to unite people and religions, enabling collective well-being. This Vārchive includes posters, colonial-type portraits, newspaper columns, local activist material and a three-dimensional geological sculpture of Sāmoa. The sculptural map, with sea levels defined by colour bands, reminds us of the precarious ecological status of the islands, an ever-present concern in any analysis of local culture. The film series includes a meeting in which Fa'afafine discuss the effects of climate change on their lives and community.[49] Issues of the climate emergency are thus intertwined with themes of sexuality and colonization, contributing to a highly coloured, provocative visual intervention, a bold reworking of a 'Polynesian paradise'.

Despite their different techniques of visual representation, both Reihana and Kihara deploy images and performances in which ambiguous gender roles are reimagined. Both also deploy layered historical sequences or art historical references, albeit presented through time in Reihana's carefully crafted, panoramic video. Kihara's multimedia photographic installation uses (perceptions of) gender and island queens to challenge dominant island histories, and to signify a present emergency. By presenting the Fa'afafine as a community actively addressing both visual history and the climate emergency, she invites a double-edged scrutiny of some potent myths of paradise.

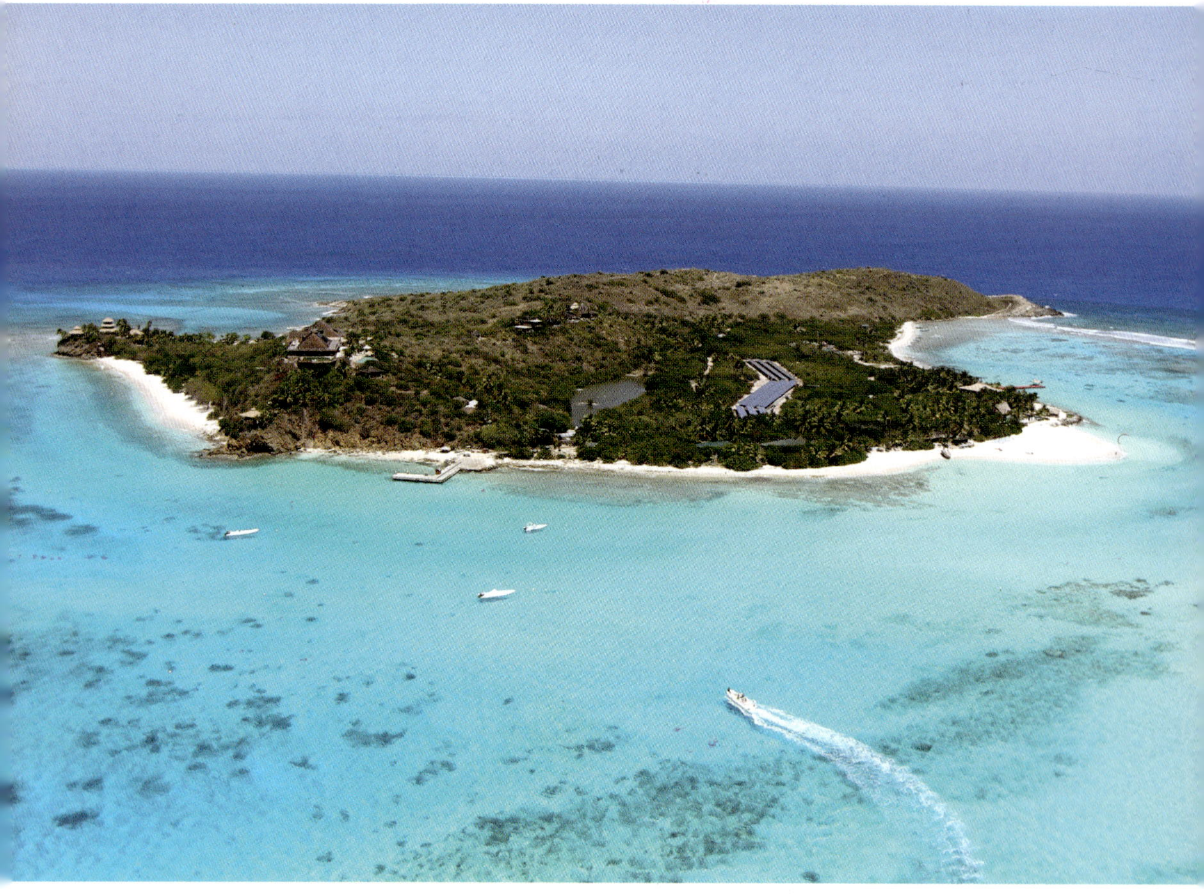

22 Aerial view of Richard Branson's Necker Island, British Virgin Islands, 2020.

2 ISLAND HOMES

'Incredible island homes for sale' ran the headline in the 'quintessential English' magazine *Country Life* in May 2020.[1] The dramatic social effects of the coronavirus pandemic of 2020–22 shone a light on the trials and health risks of urban living. Magazines and newspapers were full of articles on the appeal of island homes, and estate agents' portfolios featuring such properties were flourishing. In 2023 Sotheby's International Realty boasts a successful sub-division called 'Private Island Homes'. Catering for a super-wealthy global clientele, the website states: 'Infinite views, the serene sound of lapping tides and secluded elegance await on your private island paradise. Discover the true definition of escape and tranquillity.'[2] In the context of such hyperbolic claims, billionaire Richard Branson's privately owned 'paradise' of Necker Island in the British Virgin Islands, and the nomenclature of 'tax haven', come to mind (illus. 22). Not to mention the increased global movement of capital and exploitation involved in the culture of 'private island homes', which can place Indigenous cultures and ecologies at risk. Modern 'treasure islands' have been described by Nicholas Shaxson as 'the ultimate escape routes for our wealthiest citizens and corporations from a menagerie of laws, rules, financial regulations and democratic accountability'.[3]

Pandemic fears fed the fantasy of island escapes as potentially safe, secluded havens, away from metropolitan stress and bordered by 'lapping tides', although recent extreme weather effects have rendered some of these 'escapes' much less safe. The *Country Life* article featured some fabulous island homes, with prices ranging from £25 million (Isle of Man) down to £38,000 for a stone croft on the Isle of Bressay, just off the Shetland Islands in Scotland. Given the largely affluent, middle-class readership of

Country Life, the latter was added, one presumes, to provide a 'primitive' contrast, a fantasy of being alone in a supposedly wild, untamed nature. Some loose notion of the inherent romance of islandness infuses the desirability of these homes, from ludicrously expensive (with every imaginable and unimaginable modern convenience) to a semi-ruined ancient croft off Shetland. In each case, 'home' is inflected with an idealized notion of the island space, which helps to define the house.

'Home' is a multi-layered, fluid concept, much debated within the spheres of cultural geography, architectural and design history, anthropology, sociology and philosophy, among other disciplines. It is associated with concepts of belonging, identity and dwelling. As such it is often separated from its material correlate, the house. The architectural structure only becomes a 'home' when inhabited, when it is marked by the social, gendered, ethnic and cultural identities and traces that shelter within it. Home is a spatial imaginary where ideas, feelings and identities intersect. As a concept, it is both ubiquitous and complex, related to much-debated notions of domesticity, migration and homelessness.[4] Thus the idea of 'island homes' can carry a double dose of specialness. When imagined as a fluid and often 'exotic' space, a phantasmagoria of natural isolation, the island dweller attains a uniquely romanticized identity. What John Fowles described as the captivating 'otherness' of small islands, 'their magic and their mazes', can also infuse our perception of the homes that they host. But there are other, less desirable types of island homes that have also fired the popular imagination. Lighthouses situated on island outcrops or reefs can serve as one of the most extreme versions of this notion of 'home'; this spatial imaginary is often wild, isolated, dangerous, captivating – and usually temporary. Above all, the lighthouse is defined by the constantly changing force of the ocean by which it is positioned. It is both homely (as a protective haven) and unhomely (a vulnerable space of fear of natural forces).

The *Country Life* juxtaposition of the remote Bressay croft with fantasy homes for the super-rich sits nicely alongside some of the wry architectural and installation projects by the British artist Alex Hartley (b. 1963). Hartley has engaged with the island theme directly and indirectly in many works, including a series around the Scottish archipelagos.[5] Motifs of home, northern remoteness and the effects of surrounding water are recurring themes. While working on a series on the Outer Hebrides, he exploited the playful idea of scaling a crofter's cottage in a desolate area of the Isle of Skye (illus. 23).[6] He is renowned for his practice of so-called 'buildering', which involves a transgressive activity of scaling or climbing – of trespassing in and on (usually) modern buildings. The latter are often scaled for repair and cleaning in areas of modern, affluent high-rise structures, adding a note of absurdity to this performance on a tiny crofter's home, a prime example of abandoned Scottish vernacular architecture. Hartley's island projects often involve mischievously aggressive acts that de-romanticize the associations of specific places and landscapes. Now *un*-inhabited, such work punctures precisely the island home fantasy that the *Country Life* article seeks to perpetuate.

The representation of abandoned homes, replete with their uncanny associations, can de-romanticize the island home fantasy. The British artist

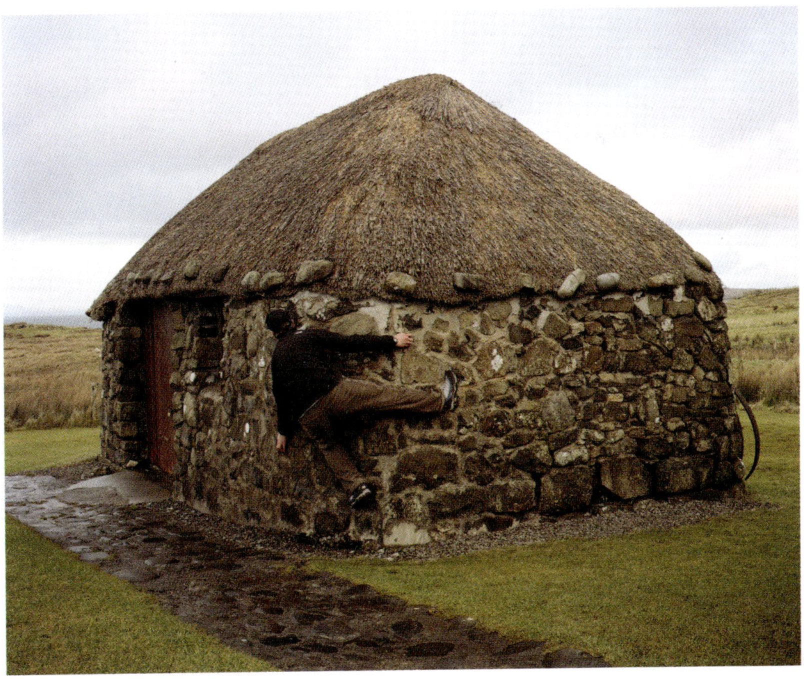

23 Alex Hartley, *Gnomic, Kilmuir*, 2007, west coast of north island of Skye, C-type photograph.

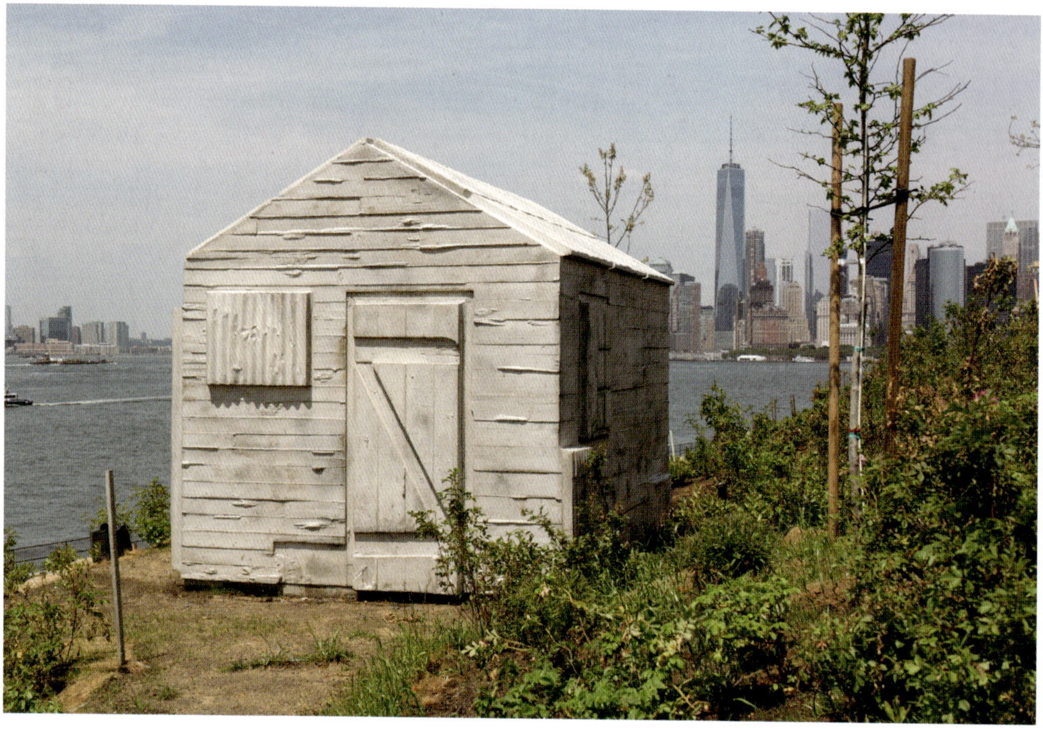

24 Rachel Whiteread, *Cabin*, 2015, concrete, installation Governors Island, New York.

Rachel Whiteread's *Cabin* (2015) atop (the significantly named) Discovery Hill on Governors' Island in New York's Upper Bay, looking out at the Statue of Liberty (illus. 24), references this idea of home, divided from – yet within range of – the seething metropolitan mainland (itself made up of connected islands, including Manhattan, Long Island and so on). *Cabin* is a negative concrete cast of the interior of an old shed or cabin. Inside Whiteread (b. 1963) has strewn bronze casts of discarded objects found on the island, such as bottles and cans – archival fragments that reference a lost history. The solitary nature of this installation, a simple space for introspection, is accentuated by its position. But this is an island site with a layered colonial history; 'Nutten Island' as it was named by the British, or 'Noten Eylandt' by the Dutch, was bought from the Lenape Native Americans by the Dutch in 1637, allegedly for two axe heads, a string of beads and a handful of nails. The British captured New Amsterdam from the Dutch in 1664, renaming it New York. As the site of the governor's home, fort and garrisons, the island held a vital military and political role for the British colonizers until the end of the wars of American Independence in 1783. Since then, it has been home to a U.S. government fort, army barracks and a Confederate prison. In 1911 it was expanded by 103 acres (to 172 acres) using rocks and construction waste to create more parkland and hills. By the 1960s the island was transferred to the U.S. Coast Guard and hosted a growing residential community. *Cabin* evokes memories of that coast guard community, with its unimpeded views across the water, as it sits on a bed of landfill. Centuries of military and post-military constructions and artificial shorelines have imposed a grid structure 'on a meandering landscape, reinforcing the isolationist logic of its islandness'.[7] As a strategic hub for colonial control, the island was perceived as isolated, impenetrable and in command.[8]

Cut off from lower Manhattan, Whiteread's *Cabin* invokes the local landscape as a series of visible and buried contradictions. A simple hut-like space situated on a (now) peaceful, partly constructed island mediates both the force of its own military history and the spectacle of the affluent New York City skyline, with its symbolic claims for global political dominance. Her permanent concrete cast stands as a monument to layers of colonial and neo-colonial activity on the island – a ghostly material memory that is far removed from the real-estate fantasy of an 'island home'.

HOMES FOR THE BIRDS

In June 2013 Hartley made St Kilda, the westernmost islands of the Scottish Outer Hebrides, his temporary home for three weeks as part of an artist's residency with Taigh Chearsabhagh Museum and Arts Centre. This evolved into a part-performative project as he spent five hours each day walking around the islands, watching and photographing the remarkable colonies of sea birds, including large numbers of Atlantic puffins and great skua, the only permanent residents of this remote archipelago. St Kilda is made up of three main islands and several 'stars'; the largest island, Hirta, boasts some of the highest cliffs in the United Kingdom. The last

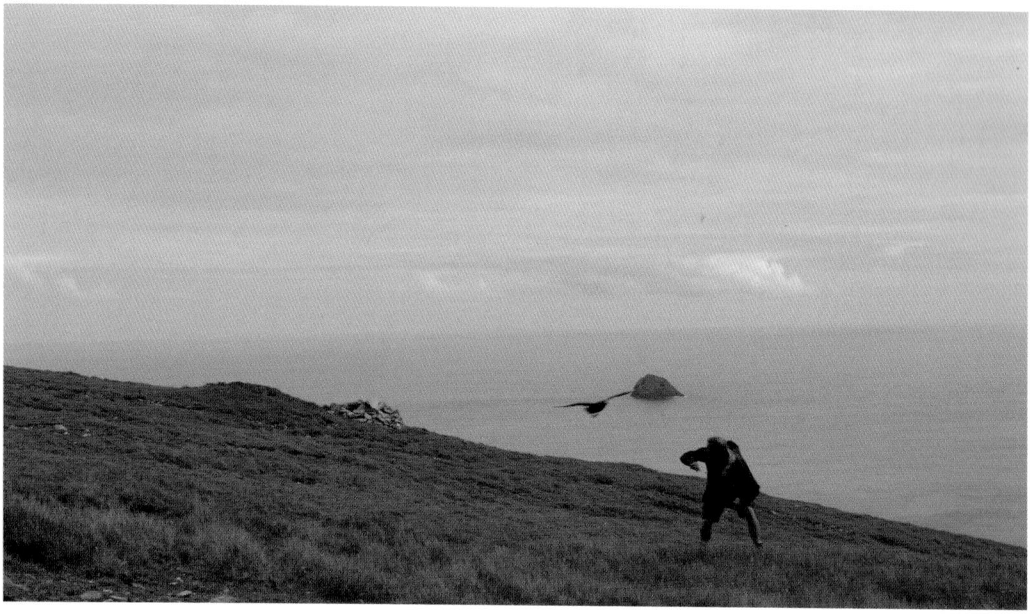

25 Alex Hartley, *Bird Attack*, 2013, still.

inhabitants (a population of only 36) were evacuated from Hirta in 1930 following a difficult period of social deprivation caused by illnesses brought onto the island by tourists, and the upheaval of the First World War. Now a ghost village of historic stone cottages known as *cleitaen* that are slowly falling into disrepair, Hirta is a temporary home in the summer months to a few military personnel, a bird warden and conservation workers.[9] The evacuation inspired the British film *The Edge of the World* (1937). Directed by Michael Powell, it charts the depopulation of this remote Hebridean island and the erosion of its traditional ways of living.[10] Hartley's arrival, and his closely studied interest in the character of this archipelago, reframes this nostalgic version of local history around the island's birds, and their defence of their territory.

In his short film *Bird Attack* (illus. 25) he walks along a misty coastline under prolonged attack by local birds, including great skua. His performance combines distanced footage (from a fixed camera) of the artist walking the cliffs on multiple trips, edited together with film from his hand-held GoPro camera, evoking dramatic Hitchcockian moments, including *The Birds* (1963), in which a seagull viciously attacks Melanie (Tippi Hedren) as she approaches Bodega Bay in California. Both films deploy the coastline as a frame for avian aggression in which the birds appear to defend their ocean homes. The effect in *Bird Attack* is both comic and daunting, an unexpected response to the mythically romantic 'edge of the world' that had become Hartley's temporary home, now only inhabited by hardy seabirds.

The Chincha Islands off the West coast of Peru have no scenery of note and are of no real strategic value. They have little to offer as romantic island retreats and are not on the main global trade routes. But in the mid-nineteenth century their inhospitable cliffs, stained with piles of bird excrement (guano) from huge colonies of sea birds, generated an international 'goldrush': according to Frank Uekötter,

> Guano's moment came in the 1840s when Western farmers were seeking new ways to improve their yields. English agriculturalists were the most prolific buyers; plantation owners in the United States were no less interested, as monocultures of tobacco and cotton were exhausting their soils. For farmers with an entrepreneurial soul, guano was the thing to buy.[11]

In the 1850s Peruvian guano was recognized as a most potent fertilizer, since it is enriched by the diet of the birds, mostly Peruvian booby, who feed off anchovies in local waters. Low rainfall on the Chincha Islands also prevents the nutrients from draining out of the guano. Given the mountains of fertilizer that had built up on these islands, they were soon contested by Peruvian, Spanish and American powers jockeying to control such valuable resources. At the height of the nineteenth-century 'Great Guano Rush', indentured Indigenous and Chinese labourers were forced to work under brutal conditions to harvest the guano. Although currently uninhabited, these islands are occasionally home to temporary labourers collecting new deposits.

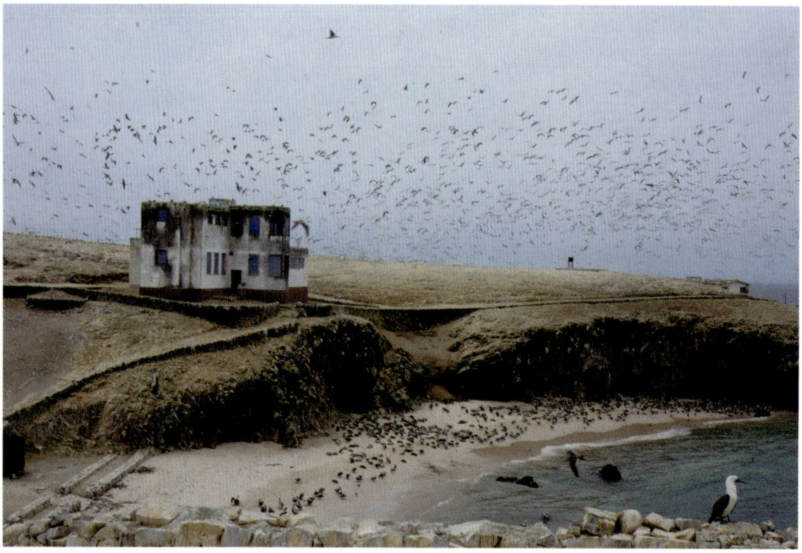

26 Dinh Q. Lê, *The Colony*, 2016, still from film installation.

In 2016 the Vietnamese artist Dinh Q. Lê (b. 1968) produced the video installation *The Colony* for the Ikon Gallery Birmingham and the arts charity Artangel, exploring episodes in the Chincha Islands' history. Fascinated by the global history of such a lowly material as bird manure, and its relevance for contemporary geopolitics, his three-screen film installation represents episodes of greed, suffering and exploitation in the island's history (illus. 26). He revisits the nineteenth-century wars between Spain and its former colonies Peru and Chile, the disturbing fate of the Chinese indentured labourers and the U.S. Guano Act of 1856. The latter was another imperial power-grab, passed by the U.S. Senate, which gave Americans the right to take peaceful possession of unoccupied islands with rich guano reserves, authorizing the president to declare them 'appertaining' to the United States.[12] As a Vietnamese-born artist concerned with the evolving geopolitics of his region, he sees parallels with China's power grab in the South China Sea: 'China is fighting for natural gas and oil (because the South China Sea is rich in these deposits) as well as fishing rights, but also critically wanting control of the shipping lanes.'[13]

The installation includes archive film and dramatic drone footage of a bleak, abandoned landscape of shit-stained cliffs and empty lodgings (illus. 26). Alongside the screens are nineteenth-century images of the island and a map of the territories claimed by the United States. A mournful soundtrack reinforces the inhospitable imagery and brutal narrative of exploitation and colonial greed. Dinh Q. Lê has expressed his desire to position and guide the spectator through a series of visual and physical experiences that evoke different aspects of this barren island. He looks to take the viewer back to the nineteenth century, to see that China's current behaviour has a precedent:

> So in the first chapter of *The Colony* you are like the eye of God looking down; then in the second chapter you slowly descend into the buildings; then in the final chapter you are given a human presence. These workers are covered in guano dust, their uniform appearance making it seem like an older time somehow.[14]

Later in the century the demand for guano collapsed as scientists were developing chemical fertilizers.[15] The footage of abandoned dormitories speaks to this history of commercial boom and subsequent neglect. The artist titled the installation *The Colony* because it reminded him of Kafka's *In the Penal Colony* (1914), a work that we will return to in Chapter Three. This short story focuses on a European dignitary who has just arrived on an island penal colony and encounters a brutal system of punishment dominated by executions. Kafka describes a stark landscape in which 'the Traveller' is numbed by the shockingly violent functioning of the local judicial system. Dinh Q. Lê's film evokes a parallel feeling of despair and disbelief at the intolerable conditions of hard labour and exploitation suffered on this bleak Peruvian island. The installation includes more recent footage of workers shovelling the guano into plastic bags with their bare hands, an antiquated procedure for a modern technological age. The only reference to technology is the occasional appearance of a drone, taking some of the spectacular footage of the barren, precipitous cliffs. As an artist's tool, it is an invaluable instrument of representation, but it also reminds us of the invasive role of a modern, potentially military, presence.

The artist has claimed a metaphorical function: 'I think the drone is an aggressor, a kind of alien of the future, but at the same time it is utterly a machine that we live with today . . . the drone to me has the visual power to suggest a form of knowledge that invades.'[16]

Invasion, imprisonment, exploitation, abandonment: these are all nouns that recur in the artist's account – and critical representations – of this work. Guano and its remote island home are elided in this exploration of colonial struggles for power and commercial dominance. Austerely beautiful island vistas, besmirched with guano dust and flocks of birds, evoke the penal colony as an inhospitable 'home' with resonant geopolitical implications.

TO THE LIGHTHOUSE AND OTHER TALES

> The Lighthouse was then a silvery, misty looking tower with a yellow eye that opened suddenly and softly in the evening . . .
> **Virginia Woolf,** ***To the Lighthouse***[17]

In mid-December 1900 the steamer *Archtor* was passing to the west of the Scottish Northern Hebrides on a journey from Philadelphia to Leith. The ship's log notes that the famous Flannan Isles lighthouse on the island of Eilean Mòr was not illuminated, despite the stormy seas (illus. 27). After the sighting was reported, the relief vessel *Hesperus* managed to reach the island by Boxing Day, after being delayed by bad weather. The crew were dismayed to find that all three keepers had vanished without trace.[18] The entrance gate to the compound was closed, beds were unmade and the oil lights refilled, suggesting an unexpected event. The *Hesperus* returned to Lewis, where the captain sent a telegram to the Lighthouse Board reporting the 'dreadful accident' and concluding: 'Poor fellows, they must have been blown over the cliffs or drowned trying to secure a crane.'[19]

It was concluded that the sheer force of the sea had probably swept them away.[20] As no bodies were found, this tragedy inspired feverish

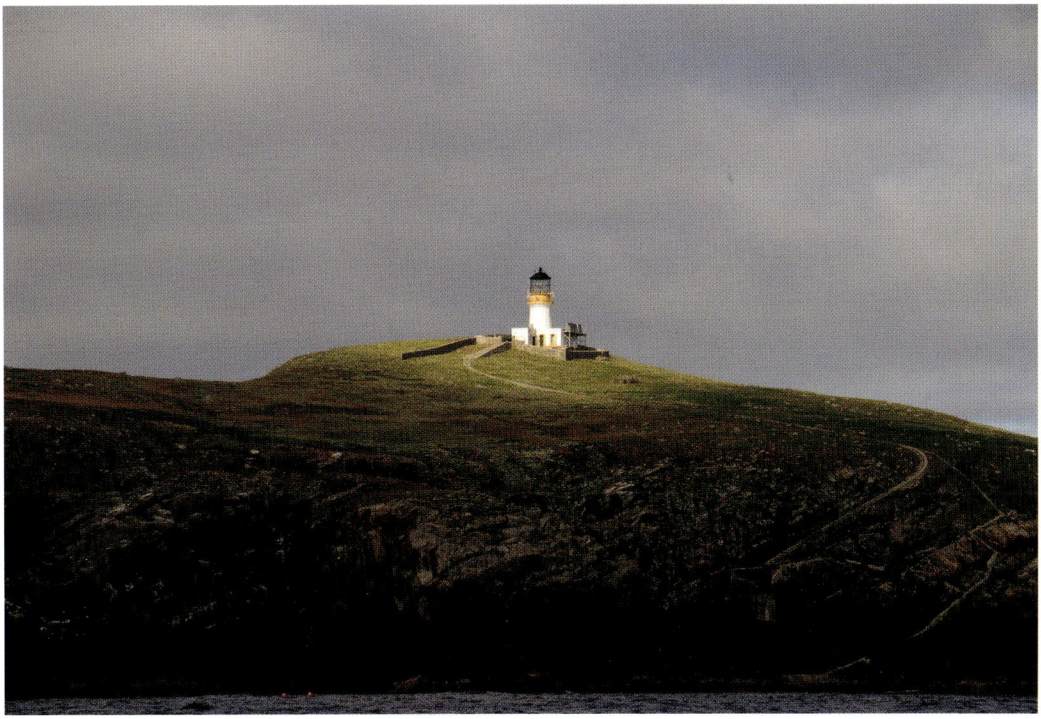

27 Flannan Isles Lighthouse, Eilean Mòr, Scotland.

speculation in contemporary newspapers and journals. The windswept lighthouse of Eilean Mòr became the focus of endless storytelling, generating a (pre-modern) media storm. Unlikely stories were spun about this cold, perilous site on the edge of the northern Atlantic, one of which included a serpent that had supposedly carried the Flannan keepers away; another, a ghost ship.[21] Fictional versions of the event abound in cinematic, literary and musical history, including the 2018 British psychological thriller film *The Vanishing* (originally called *The Keepers*), directed by Kristoffer Nyholm and set in the Flannan Isles, and a novel by Emma Stonex, *The Lamplighters* (2021).[22] The mystery also inspired a modern chamber opera by the composer Peter Maxwell Davies, *The Lighthouse* (1979), and a song recorded by the British rock group Genesis, 'The Mystery of Flannan Isle Lighthouse'.[23] The recurring theme of all these modern reinterpretations is the unexplained, ghoulish vanishing of the keepers, which continues to enthral audiences. The inhospitable, unhomely nature of this island lies at the heart of the popular narrative. According to the Genesis song, no one has ever come back from this bleak spot where the sea is always black.

Until the modern era of electrification and automation, lighthouses were temporary homes, sheltering their male keepers. They were monuments to both isolation and risk at sea – homely and unhomely. Tom Nancollas describes some of the most remote as 'seashaken houses', often constructed on desolate reefs or 'slippery rock formations in the middle of the sea, rising, mirage-like, straight out of the waves, with lights shining at their summit'.[24] Like the islands on which they are built, such edifices invite mythical constructs of masculine isolation, a subcategory of islandness that I have labelled 'lighthouseness'. While notions of home and domesticity have often been associated with femininity and the hidden lives of women, lighthouseness is implicitly gendered as masculine – a space of masculine interiority and even mental collapse, reinforced in many cinematic representations of the theme.

For nations that are characterized by extensive coastal archipelagos and miles of dangerous, craggy coastline, such as Britain, Ireland, Iceland or northern Canada, the lighthouse is a recurrent and reassuring marine landmark. Often painted white, or white and red (white and orange in Iceland), and usually with rounded wind-resistant walls, they carry immense symbolic power as beacons of light, guiding shipping in dangerous seas, not to mention the phallic potential of their thrusting vertical shapes. Their stable presence as navigational aids and temporary homes contrasts vividly with the intimidating, untamed nature around them. They can also mark the outposts of colonial cartography; on the edge of archipelagos like the Outer Hebrides they remind the seafarer of the British imperial oceanic sensibility, charting the waters and protecting its sailors.

When located on a remote island or rocky outcrop, the mythical potential of 'lighthouseness' has provided endless inspiration for writers and filmmakers. Lighthouse novels are a recognized British genre, from Edgar Allan Poe's *The Lighthouse* (1849) to Virginia Woolf's *To the Lighthouse* (1927) and P. D. James's *The Lighthouse* (2005), among others.[25] Woolf's widely acclaimed modern novel, set on the Hebridean Isle of Skye, is often read as a literal and psychic journey that merges synchronic time with the coastal landscapes of the Hebrides. Rich in metaphor, it has been interpreted by Nels Pearson as representing 'a turning point in England's imperial-oceanic sensibility' following Irish independence. The changing status of Britain's western archipelagos encouraged shifting perceptions of the Scottish islands: 'Wolf's novel relies upon a paradoxical construction of Scotland as both a primitive colonial hinterland and an utterly familiar, necessary component of British identity in the wake of Irish independence.'[26] Like Woolf, several British artists have worked with the themes of the lighthouse and the sea, drawing on their dramatic histories and the potential of both themes for the collapsing of time. Woolf's ability to evoke dense visual and emotional tableaux through written representation is paralleled and reconceived in the use of film and photography by the British artists Tacita Dean (b. 1965) and Catherine Yass (b. 1963).

Dean's two 16 mm films *Disappearance at Sea* (1996) and *Disappearance at Sea II* (*Voyage de Guerison*) (1997) were filmed in anamorphic format in two different lighthouses to the north and south of Berwick-upon-Tweed. Inspired by various stories of disappearance at sea, she used the light and lenses of each lighthouse and surrounding ocean to create evocative landscapes with multiple narrative possibilities. As she has written:

> The lighthouse is the last human outpost between land and ocean and built around human scale. Nonetheless, its presence hints at the other worldliness of the sea: a different sense of space that will never be domesticated by humankind, and which is more akin to Crowhurst's [whose disastrous voyage is described below] final and distorted sense of things.[27]

The lighthouse featured in the first *Disappearance* stands on St Abb's Head, a rocky promontory near the village of St Abb's in Berwickshire, first opened in 1862. Dean's fourteen-minute film charts the coming of dusk when the lights are switched on and the lighthouse comes to life. *Disappearance at Sea II* was filmed at Longstone Lighthouse in the Farne

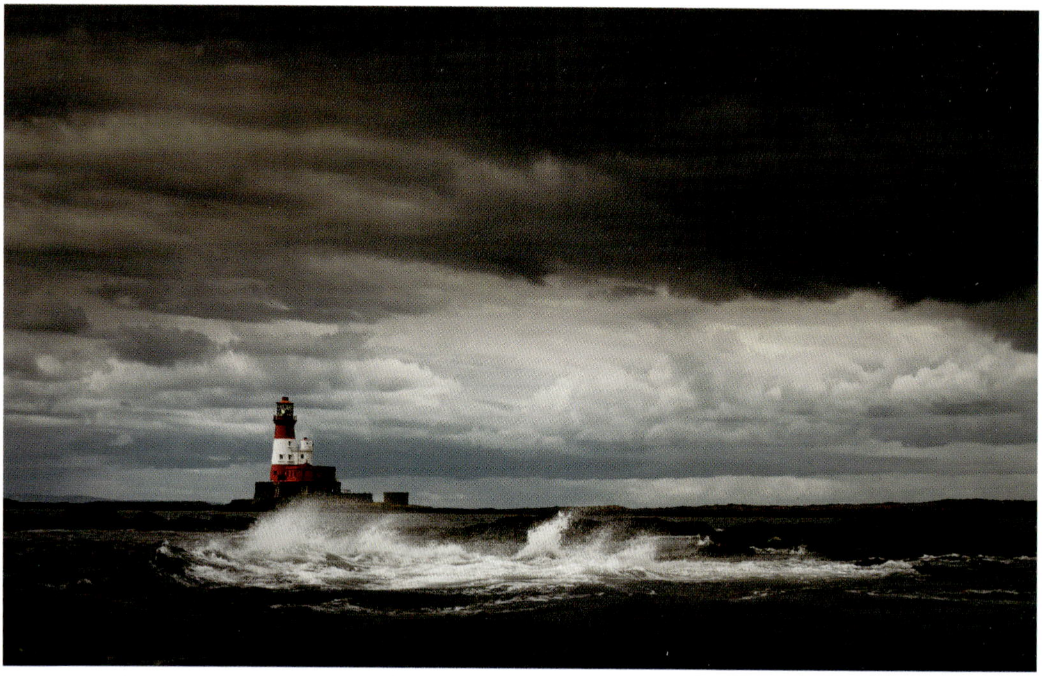

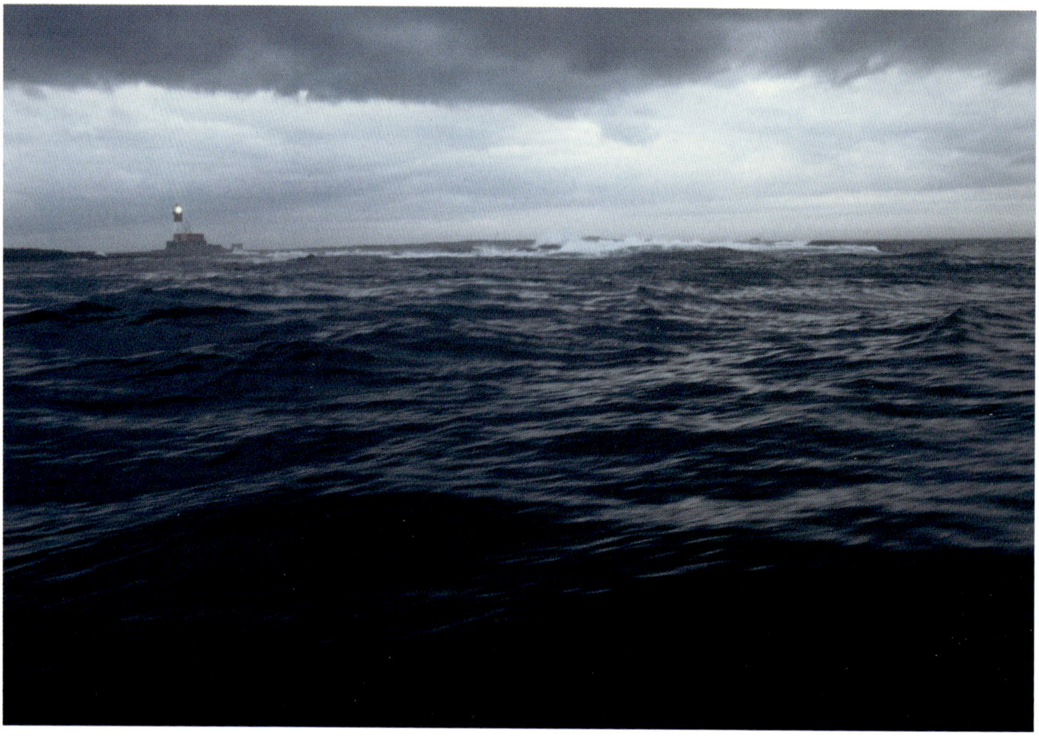

Islands in the North Sea off the Northumberland Coast (illus. 28, 29). Built in 1826, it was part of a network of navigational landmarks that saved many lives. Like St Abb's, its history is peppered with enthralling stories of wrecks and 'disappearances' that have inspired Dean's compelling films.

Longstone Lighthouse is best known for the tragic wreck of the *Forfarshir*, a paddle steamer travelling from Hull to Dundee that struck the rocks in a storm on the Outer Farne Islands in September 1838 while carrying 61 passengers. The boat ran aground on a rocky outcrop called Big Harcar. While eight escaped in a lifeboat, the remaining passengers were left to the mercy of the sea. The keeper's daughter, Grace Darling, spotted survivors on Big Harcar and persuaded her father to row out with her to the island in their unsuitable open rowing boat. Battling terrible conditions, they managed to save thirteen passengers and crew; 43 had perished. She and her father were subsequently awarded various medals for bravery, and the tale of Grace Darling has entered women's history as an exceptional story of a woman's courage and determination at sea. She is even commemorated in a civic institution: the RNLI Grace Darling Museum at Bamburgh.[28] Referenced obliquely in Dean's subtle, atmospheric work, she is an unlikely ghost, the island queen that haunts the film.

The other memorable ghost that haunts these two *Disappearances* is Donald Crowhurst, the English yachtsman who joined the first solo round-the-world *Sunday Times* Golden Globe Race in 1968 in his trimaran *Teignmouth Electron*, inspiring Dean's film of the same name (2000). A relatively inexperienced sailor and navigator, Crowhurst soon ran into difficulties; it seems that he never left the Atlantic Ocean. He secretly abandoned the race while reporting false coordinates and most likely suffered a psychological deterioration, possibly leading to suicide.[29] His boat was eventually found drifting and abandoned in the Atlantic, several hundred kilometres off the English coast. His disappearance sparked a media storm; it fed that voracious public appetite for yet another sensational story of the dangers of life at sea. For Dean, Crowhurst's tale was a mysterious, tragic story that inspired an obsessive interest as she sought out research documents and contacts, which involved trips to

28 Longstone Lighthouse, Farne Islands, off the Northumberland Coast, England.

29 Tacita Dean, location shot of Longstone Lighthouse, 1996, for *Disappearance at Sea II*, 1997, 16 mm colour film with sound.

relevant island sources.[30] J. G. Ballard, with whom she enjoyed an ongoing correspondence, describes her deceptively 'real' settings that stimulate the spectator's imagination: 'Tacita Dean's films are surveillance footage taken in some of the strangest spaces of the mind.'[31]

The subtitle of *Disappearance II* is *Voyage de Guérison*, referencing another sea-faring narrative, the medieval legend of the Cornish knight Tristan. According to legend, after defeating the Irish knight Morholt, Tristan sailed back to Cornwall to deliver the Irish princess Iseult for marriage to his uncle, King Mark of Cornwall. But Tristan and Iseult began a love affair, induced by a love potion. King Mark discovered her adultery, and after a series of perilous near-escapes the king agreed to let Tristan leave the country. After being seriously wounded, Tristan embarked on a 'journey of healing' and self-discovery, floating alone in a small boat without oars or sail. He believed the wind and the current would deliver him to an island where magical forces would heal his wounds.[32] After landing on the Irish coast he was taken by sailors to the palace of the Kingdom of Gormond and healed by the powers of the queen and her daughter Isolde. Dean links this tale of island hopping with that of Crowhurst. She cites the sixteenth-century story of a Portuguese governor sent to India who became ill and blind, and his ship drifted to an unpopulated island in the south Atlantic, which he named Tristan da Cunha, adding his own name to that of the legendary 'floating' figure of Tristan. Part of one of the most remote archipelagos in the world, midway between southern Africa and South America, it has often been the unintentional destination of those shipwrecked in the unpredictable seas of the southern Atlantic. As Dean reminds us, Crowhurst's boat was found adrift: 'Becalmed in the Sargasso Sea, a sludge of sea, thick with weed, where there is no wind or current, Crowhurst gave up his journey.'[33] Island mythologies rich in allegorical possibilities float in and out of Dean's multi-layered films.

Disappearance at Sea II was filmed by mounting the camera on the lighting apparatus of the Longstone Lighthouse. Dean used a continuous shot with an anamorphic lens, the camera's eye following the same trajectory as the lighthouse beam that comes alive at dusk. The visual narrative thus follows the seascape illuminated by the light of the beam and framed by the shape and mullions of the lighthouse's curved windows. The camera embodies the function of this emblematic building; filming follows the rotation of the lonely beam and looks out across a seemingly endless sea, evoking a sense of space akin perhaps to that experienced by those who have disappeared at sea. Real and cinematic space (mediated by the camera) seem to merge. A lack of human indicators of scale signals a remoteness or 'unworldliness' that characterizes lighthouses and the islands on which they stand. This slow, relentless seascape is thus loaded with possible floating signifiers and oblique references. Grace Darling, Donald Crowhurst, Tristan and Isolde and long-lost shipwreck victims inhabit the ceaseless movement of the greyish-blue waves. Moreover, Dean's fascination with the concept of navigation, both literally and metaphorically, shines through. Much like Woolf's journey to the lighthouse, ships' voyages have often been seen to mirror inner psychic journeys and revelations, hence the artist's interest in *Voyage de Guérison*. As Clarrie Wallis has written, Dean's 'work addresses the processes of plotting coordinates in space and time. Making connections between past and present, fact and fiction.'[34] The story of the *Teignmouth Electron* and its many voyages (with and after Crowhurst) encapsulates these unexpected coordinates and synchronic connections in time and space, and is illustrated in Dean's film of the same name.

Apart from Crowhurst's falsified positions and his ghostly disappearance, his trimaran completed several other voyages before being left to the elements on the southwest shore of a Caribbean island, Cayman Brac. After being found abandoned in 1969, it was sold at auction by his race funders, taken to Florida and then Jamaica, sold several times and repurposed as a small cruise boat in Montego Bay. Its final years were spent as a scuba diving boat in the Cayman Islands. During repairs, a sealed compartment was found containing Crowhurst's emergency rations, a poignant reminder of his fateful voyage. Despite plans to restore the boat, it was finally abandoned after being damaged by Hurricane Gilbert in 1988; the remaining hull now sits rotting on Cayman Brac. Intrigued by this multilayered story, Dean made a pilgrimage to the island of Cayman Brac in

1998, producing a film, photographs and writings documenting the boat's final retirement (illus. 30).[35] Dean describes her almost mystical experience when she finally found the boat:

> And we *found* it! Seeing it in the evening light was amazing because things become mythical in your own narrative, so to actually find its tangible form, to know it's not a spectre, was quite incredible. I was on the island for a week, the weather was terrible, and we were always ducking storms.[36]

Dean hoped the boat 'would remain what it is and not be duly transformed into what it is not'.[37] As an island relic, however, the rotting

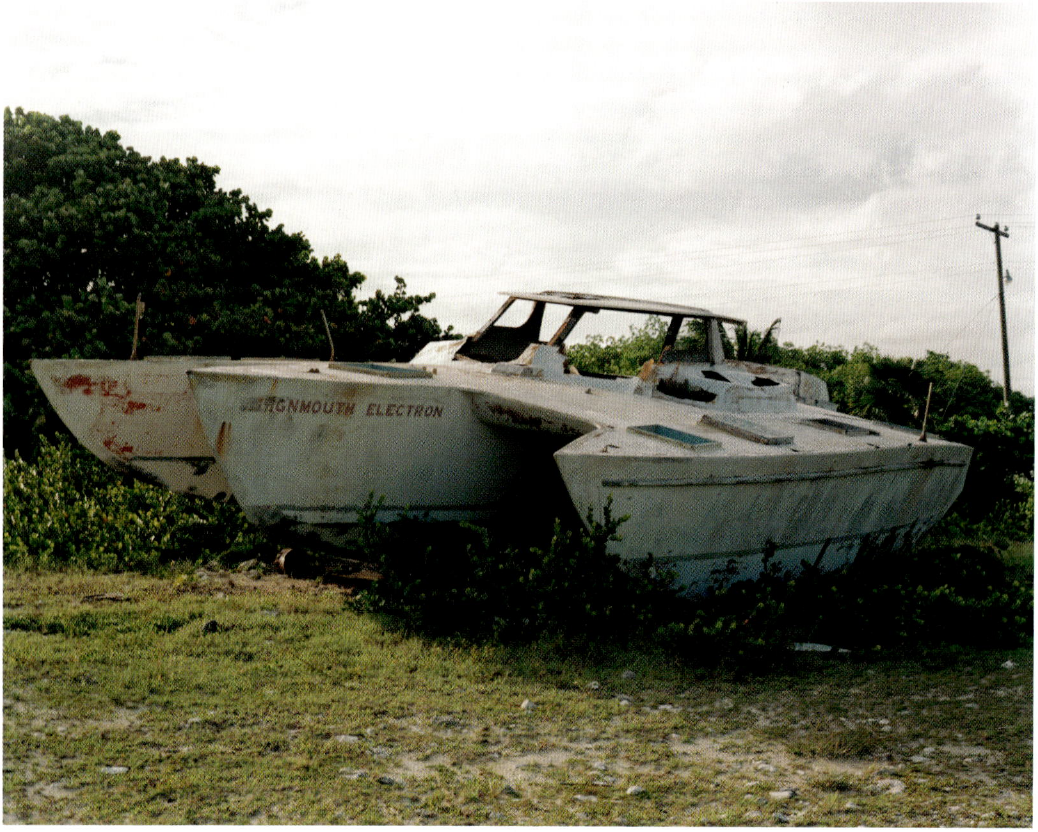

30 Tacita Dean, *Teignmouth Electron, Cayman Brac: General*, 1999, colour photograph.

structure has assumed other identities as a tourist attraction close to a remote beach, and a sad, diminishing trace, perhaps, of English hubris – an echo of the seafaring, exploring spirit of the British colonial past. Moreover, its final resting place is a British overseas territory, a vestige of empire that was first named 'Cayman' by Sir Francis Drake in 1586.[38] Scavenged by souvenir hunters, the boat is slowly deteriorating into island debris as it sinks into the sand. Yet the power of its dramatic history continues to inspire artistic projects. In 2017 the National Gallery of the Cayman Islands commissioned one of their first artists in residence, Blue Curry, and the Caymanian artist Simon Tatum to produce a series of photographs of the remaining wreck, *Teignmouth Electron (19 years after Tacita Dean)*.[39] These photographs reveal the progressive deterioration of a talismanic site, now in an advanced state of Smithsonian 'entropy'. The broken, scavenged hull, splintered and decaying boat parts, cracked and peeling paint traces and the shadowy trace of the word Teignmouth along the boat's side betray only a hint of its famous history, which lives on in the popular imagination. In 2015 a full-scale replica was constructed for a film of the Crowhurst story titled *The Mercy*, with Colin Firth in the lead role. This replica is currently stored on yet another island: Malta. Along with those storm-ravaged lighthouses, the myth and reality of the *Teignmouth Electron* belongs on, and has become part of, its successive island homes.

PLATFORMING IN BLUE

On a clear day an unoccupied lighthouse was visible from the roof of the De La Warr Pavilion, Bexhill, on the south coast of England, until its demolition in 2023. Eight kilometres (5 mi.) out to sea, the Royal Sovereign Lighthouse appeared to balance precariously on a corner of a massive square platform. While planning an exhibition at the pavilion, the British artist Catherine Yass became intrigued with this remarkable structure, the subject of her film *Lighthouse* and series of lightboxes of 2011 (illus. 31). Built in 1971, when it replaced a light ship, the platform is supported by a large concrete column rising out of the water. A monument to engineering ingenuity, its beam warned shipping of the dangerous shallow waters and currents around the eastern part of the English Channel. It was officially decommissioned in 2022. Yass has described her fascination with the difficult engineering project involved in boring down into the seabed: 'They concertinaed it up – one part was pushed up through the other. I'm very interested in modernist concrete structures. They represent a kind of aspiration, or Utopia, on a kind of community or social level.'[40]

Apart from holding the cylindrical lighthouse, the platform housed a cabin section and helicopter deck, and was originally staffed by three keepers – a 'utopian' surrogate island perched precariously on a single concrete pillar. Instead of being anchored firmly into a rocky outcrop (like the Flannan Lighthouse), it was lifted well above sea level by a seemingly riskier double structure of platform and pillar. This distinctive structure accentuates the way in which lighthouseness can embody a tension between being a life-saving navigational aid and a home, and yet a space positioned in a vulnerable, threatening environment. As Yass notes: 'it's supposed to represent a symbol for safety, and yet it looks so dangerous: the water is quite shallow and the lighthouse itself creates dangerous whirlpools of current.'[41]

A sense of danger and disorientation is created partly through her use of different perspectives and viewing positions; filming took place from a boat, helicopter and underwater. Twelve minutes long, the work begins at water level; the camera moves slowly over an uninviting expanse of grey sea, then circles the platform and rises and falls up and down each side of the lighthouse and the pillar. At regular intervals Yass inverts the film, turning the image upside down, contributing to an increased sense of strangeness and temporal confusion. The platform appears to hang from the column like a fragile model glued to its inverted base, with an equally fragile lighthouse suspended from one corner. The camera finally dives down into the sea, evoking a claustrophobic sense of drowning. The massive concrete pillar and its marine stains are viewed through a greenish underwater fog. The muted sound and slowed pace contribute to a sense of dislocation and fear. This lighthouse island is presented as both

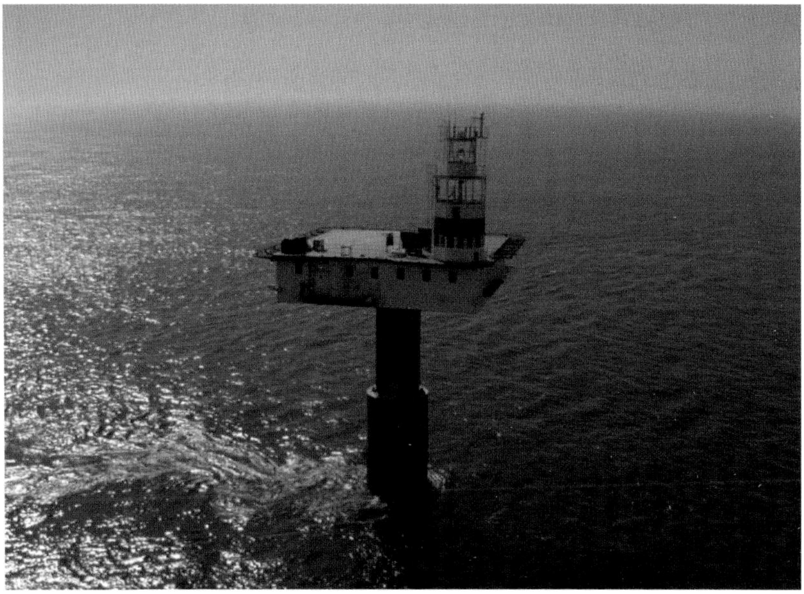

31 Catherine Yass, *Lighthouse*, 2011, still, 35 mm film and HD transferred to HD digital video, 12 minutes, 41 seconds.

majestic and ominous, 'like a siren attracting you in, but also signalling dangerous waters'.[42]

Alongside the film Yass produced a series of lightboxes that invite the viewer to observe semi-abstracted images of the lighthouse and platform. She laid a photographic colour transparency over a blue negative transparency, each taken a few seconds apart. Those areas that reflect light come out in a vivid blue, with the sun turned into a black ball, as in *Lighthouse (East)* or *Lighthouse (North north north west)* (2011; illus. 32), and there is 'a gap between the images . . . this little sliver of time is important for me, because it prevents the photograph from being one moment of truth'.[43] The effect is that the two images often don't quite register when laid on top of each other. The blue negative is always slightly smaller than the positive (due to temperature differences in the photographic process), creating a white halo around the image. These lightboxes invite the viewer to explore the physical and psychological effects of an iconic, yet also unfamiliar, architectural space.

The intense blue helps to create an image that is both compellingly beautiful and strangely uncanny and unsettling. Blue is a colour loaded

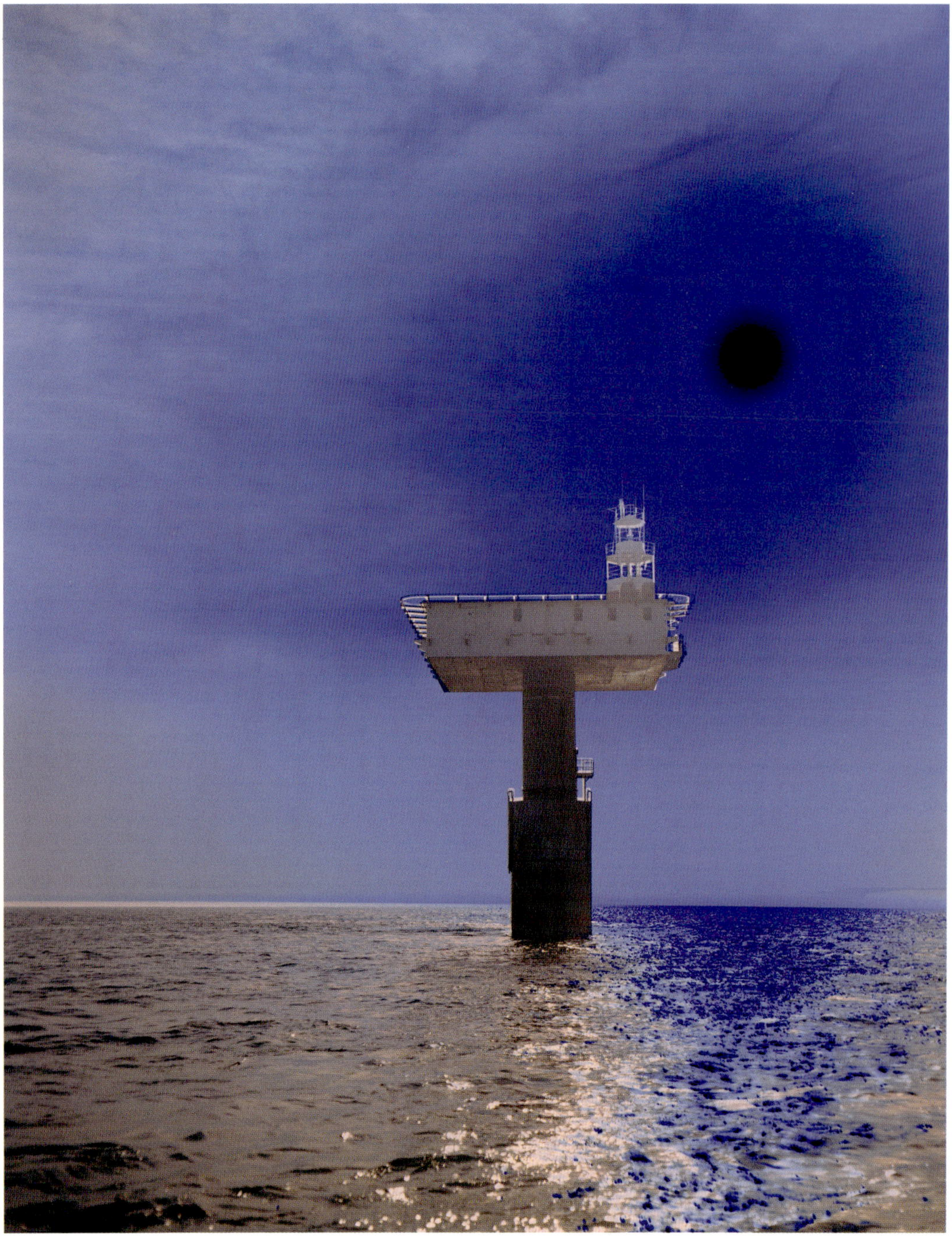

with cultural symbolism – political, religious, aesthetic and scientific. With the discovery of new pigments and dyeing techniques, not to mention the profitable trade in the mineral lapis lazuli from the Middle Ages onwards, blue became one of the most popular colours; it has been described as the favourite colour of Europeans.[44] Yass has used blue negatives in many of her photographic works, infusing them with other possible layers of meaning. An awe-inspiring lighthouse island and spectacular image of marine engineering is abstracted and aestheticized in a seductive shade of blue, albeit bordered by an eerie white halo. This is the blue of the legendary desert island paradise, rather than the ominous grey tones of the British Channel. Reconceived as a strange siren, Yass's lighthouse can confuse the expectations – and perceptions – of the viewer.

LIGHTHOUSE KEEPERS

> For how would you like to be shut up for a whole month at a time, and possibly more in stormy weather upon a rock the size of a tennis lawn? she would ask; and to have no letters or newspapers, and to see nobody . . . to see the same dreary waves breaking week after week, and then a dreadful storm coming, and the windows covered with spray, and birds dashed against the lamp.
> **Woolf, *To the Lighthouse***[45]

Along with long-distance solo sailors, lighthouse keepers, known as 'wickies', are often perceived as a race apart, masculine stereotypes from maritime histories of human resilience and solitary endurance before automation began in the 1950s and '60s.[46] In their 'seashaken' homes, they are also a popular subject for psychological thriller dramas. In 2019 the horror-thriller film *The Lighthouse*, directed by Robert Eggers, was released to wide critical acclaim, described by one reviewer as 'hallucinatory'.[47] Set in the late nineteenth century, it represents the devastating psychological effects on two keepers of being isolated on an island off the New England coast.

32 Catherine Yass, *Lighthouse (East)*, 2011, photographic transparency, lightbox.

Filmed entirely in black and white, it stars Willem Dafoe and Robert Pattinson as keepers Thomas Wake and Ephraim Winslow, who slowly descend into madness as violent weather cuts them off from the mainland, prevents a relief ferry from reaching them and spoils their rations of food for a four-week stint in their storm-ravaged lighthouse home (illus. 33). After they have consumed diminishing supplies of gin and a vile concoction of turpentine and honey, the storm floods their cottage, and they indulge in violent argument. Nature effectively destroys the island home and their psychological resilience. Winslow kills Wake, and is then seriously injured in the lantern room before falling down the lighthouse steps, as the violence of the weather parallels the protagonists' descent into madness. Hallucinations and horrific storm sequences seem to merge as the lighthouse appears to exercise mystic powers. The final scene includes gruesome footage of a barely alive Winslow lying naked on the lonely island rock, as seagulls feast on his exposed bowels. In a scene worthy of classical mythology, nature and the elements participate in an orgy of horror. The island home is reconceived here as a space of surreal physical and psychological torment, a hyperbolic expression of lighthouseness.

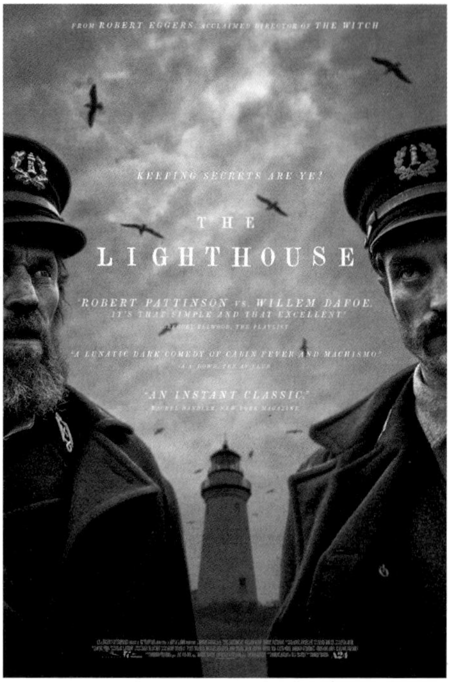

33 Poster for the film *The Lighthouse* (2019, dir. Robert Eggers).

Popular legends and multiple literary sources influenced this harrowing visualization of a lighthouse tragedy. The screenplay by Robert Eggers and his brother Max began as an attempt to adapt Edgar Allan Poe's short story 'The Light-House'. The work of Samuel Taylor Coleridge, Herman Melville and Robert Louis Stevenson has also been cited. The ghoulish story of the Smalls Lighthouse, another bleak station on a dangerous cluster of rocks 32 kilometres (20 mi.) off the Pembrokeshire coast in West Wales, was another influence on the screenplay. The Smalls (dating since 1776) is Wales's most remote and 'unhomely' lighthouse. In the late nineteenth century it was home to two keepers, who changed shifts every few weeks.

In 1801 one of the keepers became unwell and died, and the other kept his body in a makeshift coffin lashed to railings by the lantern, for fear of being accused of murder if he had thrown the body into the sea.[48] Fierce winds damaged the coffin and when blowing from a particular direction it appeared as if a decomposing arm was beckoning his fellow keeper. For four months bad weather prevented relief boats from reaching the island, and when eventually rescued, this wicky was described as unrecognizable both physically and mentally. As a result of this 'disturbing tale of death and insanity',[49] British lighthouse policy was changed to provide teams of three rather than two people. Even before Egger's grim psychological film, this macabre tale inspired scripts for several lighthouse horror films.[50]

Within film and literary culture, lighthouse island homes are generally characterized by the shocking mental and physical deprivations they imposed on their (male) wickies. It is their historical richness, isolated self-sufficiency and also their wry, even humorous, potential that inspired Rodney Graham's *Lighthouse Keeper with Lighthouse Model, 1955* (2010). Following his ongoing performative strategies, the artist plays the role of solitary, self-absorbed keeper in a photographic installation consisting of two aluminium lightboxes with trans-mounted chromogenic transparencies (illus. 34). The image is rich in visual clues and quotations offering up possible narrative meanings. The date of 1955 references the period when automation was increasingly reducing the work of lighthouse keepers; they had more time for hobbies such as model-making and reading. A 'seashaken' island home and a descent into madness are no longer framing features of Graham's lighthouseness. Rather, his wicky sits reading and warming his feet by the wood stove, with a model lighthouse on the table behind. Moreover, the protagonist is lit not by the lighthouse lantern but by the electric light of his kitchen.

In contrast with some traditional lighthouse narratives, the scene of an engrossed hobbyist appears mischievously quaint. But the carefully staged performance also functions as a comment on the effects of changing technology on their legendary keepers. Rather than struggling to maintain oil lanterns under stormy conditions, this wicky lounges comfortably with his

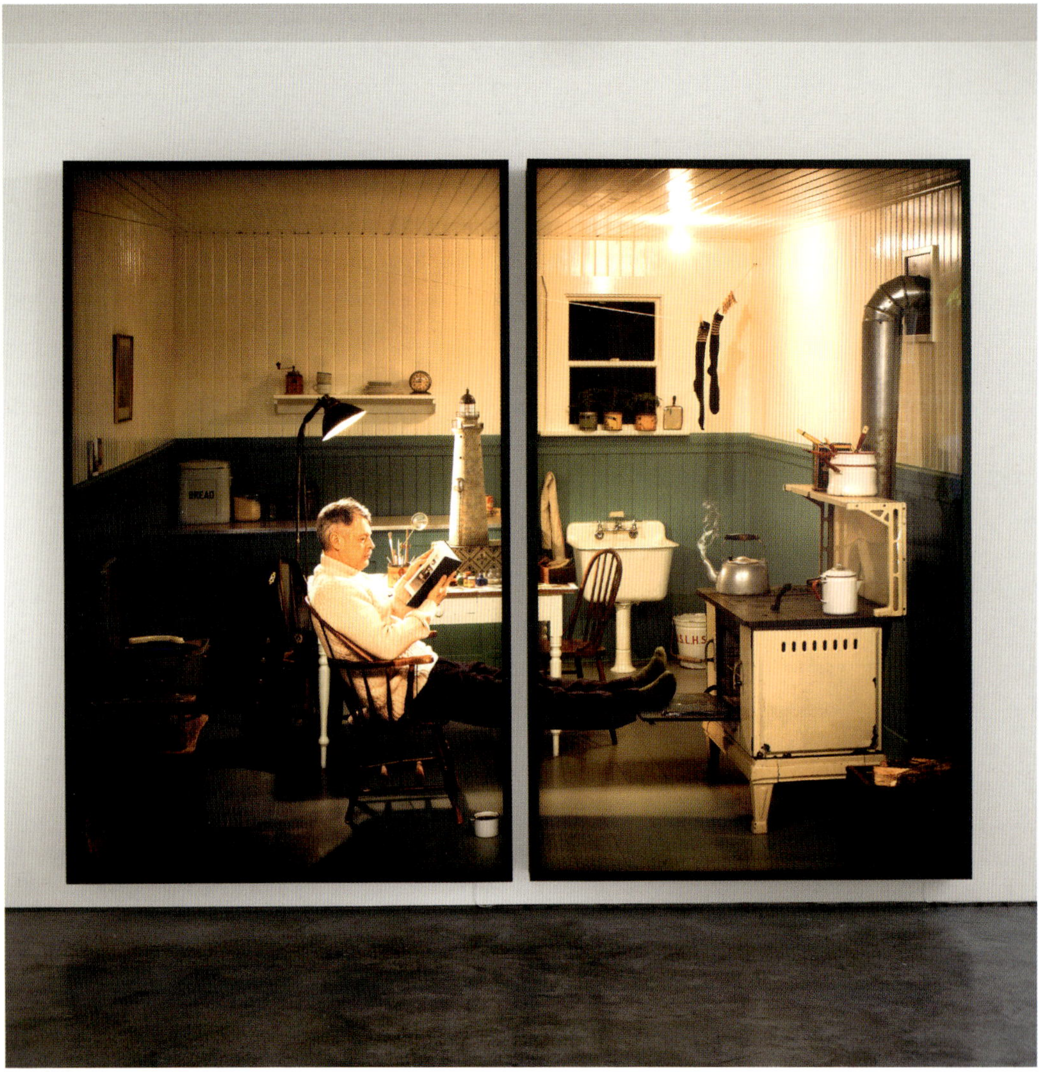

34 Rodney Graham, *Lighthouse Keeper with Lighthouse Model, 1955*, 2010, two painted aluminium lightboxes with transmounted chromogenic transparencies.

lighthouse paraphernalia, a hot beverage at hand and socks warming by the stove. The decor is carefully assembled to convey a sense of the style of the mid-1950s; Graham admits to drawing 'on childhood memories a bit. I was living on a logging camp for a time.'[51] He has also seeded some more dramatic referents associated with lighthouse history. The model is a replica of the famous Minot's Ledge lighthouse (also shown in picture postcards on the wall), which withstood fierce Atlantic storms on a rocky outcrop 4 kilometres (2.5 mi.) off Boston Harbor on the Massachusetts coast. These rocks plagued mariners for centuries; by the 1750s eighty ships and more than four hundred lives had been lost in the surrounding waters. After an eminent Boston merchant named George Minot lost a ship there in 1754, the ledge earned its name, and building work began on the lighthouse in 1849. Echoing other grim lighthouse tales, two keepers died in a terrible storm that destroyed the Minot's Ledge structure in 1851, and construction began on a new stone tower in 1855. But life continued to be testing for wickies, and 'the solitude and thunderous crashing of the waves drove more than one keeper insane'.[52] This iconic tower was used on the buttons and insignia of the U.S. lighthouse service, which can be found on Graham's uniform and hat. He has commented that he wanted to give the work 'a recursive lighthouses within a lighthouse feel'. This reflexivity playfully overstates the lighthouseness of this image in cryptic ways.[53] Even the book he is reading is titled *Keepers of the Light: A History of British Columbia's Lighthouses and Their Keepers by* Donald Graham (no relation) and is open on a page showing part of the illustration that inspired the work. Many of the lighthouses featured were built to guide gold prospectors on their way to the Klondike and are stationed on rocky islands and promontories along the North Pacific Coast, including the cover image. These lighthouse islands, much like the Peruvian guano islands featured in *The Colony*, are part of centuries-old histories of global capitalism and colonial power grabs. The relentless dangers of this tarnished history are ever present, despite the relatively relaxed, even contented, demeanour of Graham's wicky. One book review of *Keepers of the Light* includes a terrifying, yet familiar, summary: 'Can you imagine a wind strong enough to blow away a cow? It happened at the ill-fated light on exposed Triangle Island.' The book includes: 'stories of absurd and fatal government bungling; stories of suicide, murder, mysterious disappearance, heroism, starvation and occasionally happiness'.[54]

On closer inspection, the illustration on the open page of *Keepers of the Light* shows a keeper sitting in his lighthouse kitchen with his feet warming on the stove, a quotation that the artist openly deploys to show 'a figure on the verge of being redundant'.[55] The life-size scale of Graham's work (3 × 4 metres, or 9.5 × 12 ft) enables the viewer to carefully track the many visual clues and self-reflexive references. Its characteristic diptych form is partly determined by the large size, requiring two transparencies, and allowing Graham to use the break as a structural component. The division falls across his stretched-out legs, broken across the knee, and oddly separating the protagonist from the warmth of the stove. Graham's self-absorbed wicky forms part of this multi-layered palimpsest, packed with documentary cliches and humorous traces that mediate a well-established notion of lighthouseness.

3 DISAPPEARING AND ENDANGERED ISLANDS

PART 1: ENDANGERED ISLANDS

Island history is steeped in myth about landmasses that have supposedly disappeared. The story of Atlantis has inspired a host of speculative and pseudo-scientific writings – and some notable artworks. In his essay *Timaeus* (*c.* 430 BC) Plato introduced the fictional island of Atlantis, which fell out of favour with the gods only to be submerged into the ocean.[1] *Timaeus* included a theological account of the creation of the world, giving the island an allegorical and propagandist function as the home of a hubristic naval power that tried to besiege ancient Athens (the embodiment of Plato's ideal state). Plato located the island in the Atlantic Ocean:

> there was an island situated in front of the straits which you call the Columns of Heracles [the straits of Gibraltar, known as the Pillars of Hercules]: the island was larger than Libya and Asia (Turkey) put together and was the way to other islands . . . Now in this island of Atlantis there was a great and wonderful empire, which had rule over the whole island and several others, as well as over parts of the continent.[2]

Since Plato's time the myth has inspired countless writings, including Thomas More's *Utopia* (1516) and Francis Bacon's *New Atlantis* (1627). Fortunes have been lost searching for the island, and there are numerous publications, websites and film projects devoted to the subject. After analysing archaeological artefacts and geology, the navy veteran and historian Gavin Menzies claimed that Atlantis was part of an advanced Minoan civilization that extended worldwide from its Mediterranean base.[3] In a more fanciful vein, the American actor Patrick Duffy starred as *The Man from Atlantis* in a popular series on the American channel NBC in the 1970s. Duffy played an amnesiac (Mark Harris) believed to be the only survivor of the lost city and recruited by a California research foundation, where expert scientists were deployed to seek out Harris's origins and genealogy – in Atlantis.[4] The myth and its imaginative possibilities were given a twentieth-century reworking, while blithely ignoring the geological and biological effects of the passage of centuries.

Hypothetical Islands

The Atlantis legend, in all its cosmological and temporal glory, also informed the work of Robert Smithson. On a road trip to the Yucatan peninsula in 1969 he and the artist Nancy Holt stopped off at Sanibel Island in Florida, where he made a sculpture of shells, *Hypothetical Continent in Shells: Lemuria*, based on a similar prehistoric myth. A further work, *The Hypothetical Continent of Lemuria* (illus. 35), gives a pseudo-cartographical legitimacy to the myth and its artistic representation.

Lemuria was a hypothetical land bridge from the Eocene period believed to have sunk beneath the Indian Ocean. Appropriated by occultists, this account was disputed by the scientific community in the 1960s. Smithson's collage includes maps of the fictional island and a drawing of his sculpture of shells interweaving myth and artistic project to connect and emphasize differences between the material form of the beach and the fluid stories that circulate around islands and sea borders. For Smithson, islands were speculative sites that raised interesting questions about geology and the role of artistic intervention; hence his prescient fascination with the effects of natural erosion, tidal flows, volcanic eruption and sea-level rises.

The Hypothetical Continent of Lemuria was one of a several projects based on mythical islands that Smithson proposed in the late 1960s and early 1970s. In 1969 he published an essay describing a series of 'mirror displacement' works designed for island sites along Florida's Gulf coast.[5]

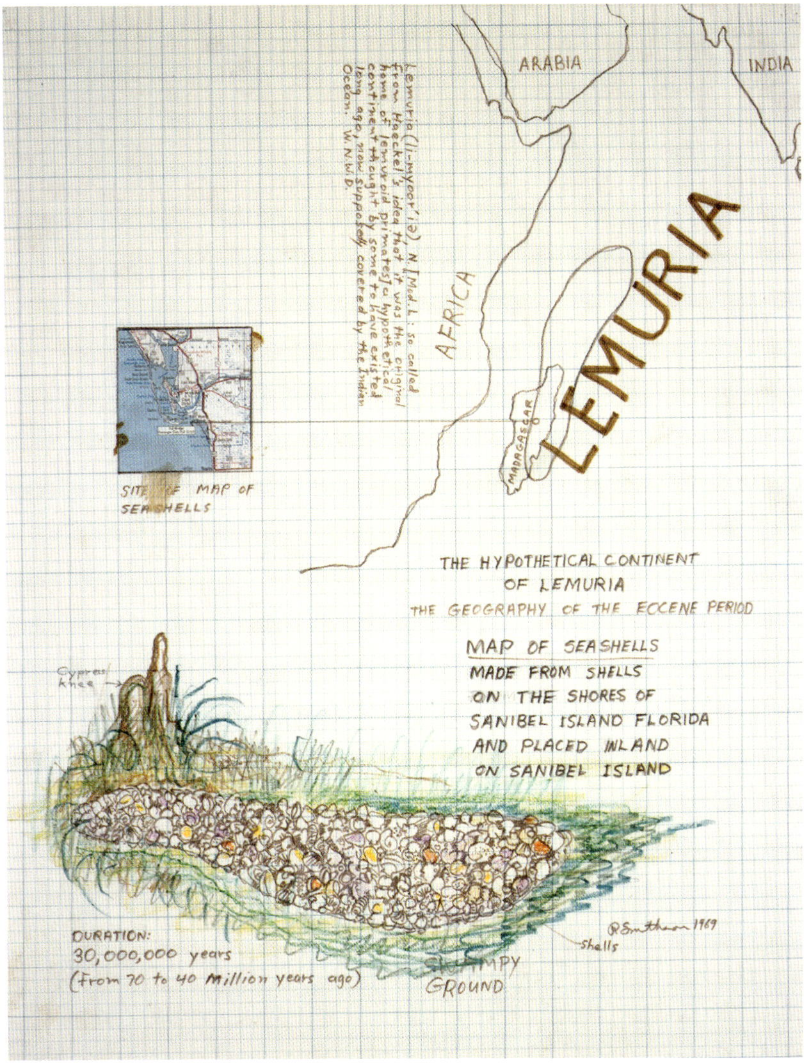

35 Robert Smithson, *The Hypothetical Continent of Lemuria*, 1969, brown ink, crayon, graphite and collage on paper.

He cites other contested islands including the 'Land of Mu', the existence of which was based on an 'imaginative translation' of a Mayan codex.[6] In a footnote he goes further:

> Conjectural maps that point to this non-existent site [of Atlantis] fill many unread atlases. It very well could be that the Maya

> writings that alluded to 'the Old Serpent covered with green feathers, who lies in the Ocean' was Quetzalcoatl or the Sargasso Sea [*sic*]. Every wayward geographer of Atlantis has his own curious theory, they never seem to be alike. From Plato's *Timaeus* to *Codex Vaticanus A* the documents of the lost island proliferate.[7]

Smithson's first 'hypothetical island' was made on the beach at Loveladies, New Jersey (illus. 36), following an ambitious but unrealized plan to cover a small island in the Georgia Strait, British Columbia, with broken glass.[8] Assembled in a sandy carpark next to a sprawling urban area of Loveladies, this was an intensely ironic island made of different sized pieces of glass, sited on a real island – Long Beach. Broken glass offered 'an allegory of shoreline', positioned close to a real shoreline.[9] Smithson again used cartography to sustain the island fantasy in his *Map of Broken Clear Glass (Atlantis)* (illus. 37). Atlantis has become a continent, with

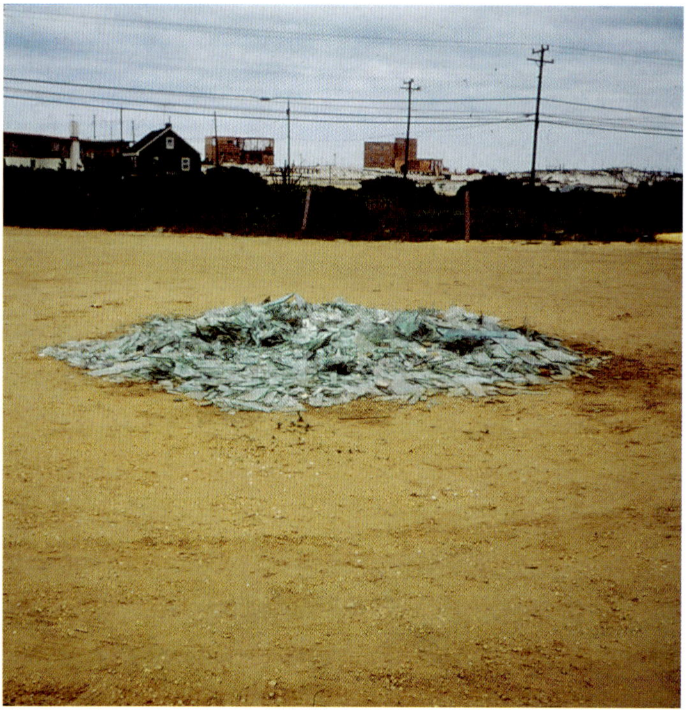

36 Robert Smithson, *Map of Broken Glass (Atlantis)*, 1969, Loveladies, New Jersey, glass.

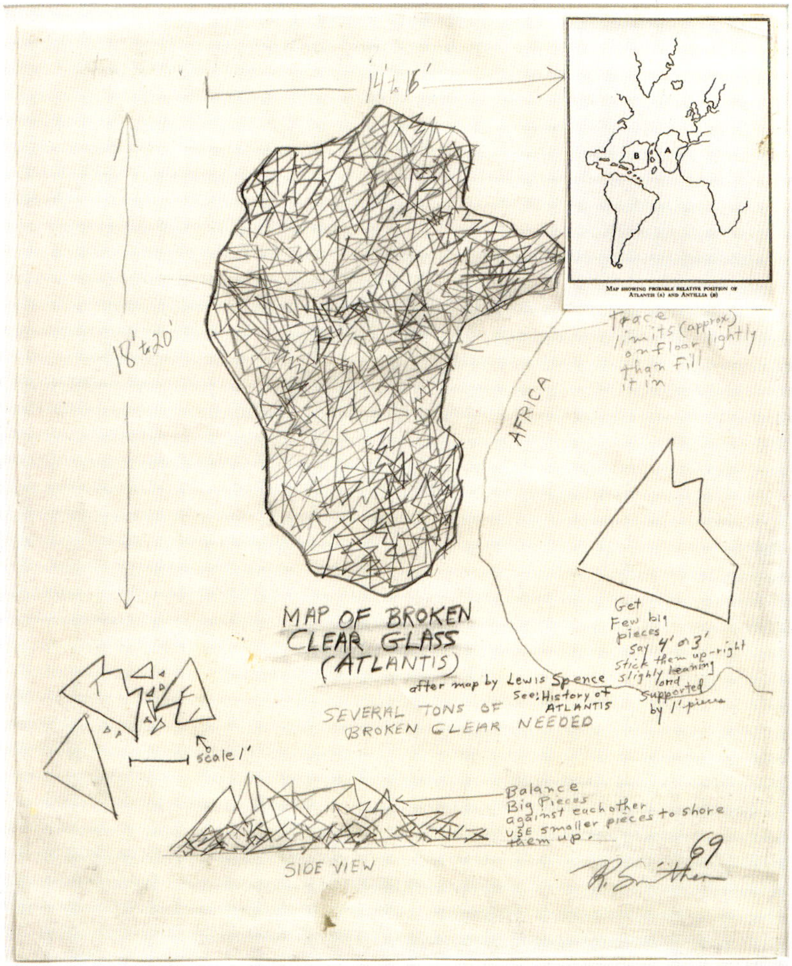

37 Robert Smithson, *Map of Broken Clear Glass (Atlantis)*, 1969, collage, photostat, map and graphite on paper.

neighbouring landmasses of Africa and America clearly delineated in the smaller map in the corner.

Smithson's islands are un-picturesque 'Nonsites' that draw on speculative histories to complicate meaning. They often involve some form of physical and material displacement. Many of his hypothetical islands on the Yucatan Peninsula in 1969 involved 'Mirror Displacements', sculptures made up of angled mirrors positioned in, and reflecting, the changing nature around them. 'Displaced' onto the mirror, expectations of nature, geology and place are confused. Most of these transitory works are now only accessible through his photographic records.[10] His *Eighth Mirror Displacement* was sited on the Island of Blue Waters on the Usumacinta River. This area of sand and sediment changed character with the movement of the river water, producing a 'non-island' that echoes Smithson's notion of entropy. He describes an island 'that annihilates itself' as bits of sediment dropped

38 Robert Smithson, *Mirror Displacement*, 1969, Chesil Beach, Dorset, 126 format transparency.

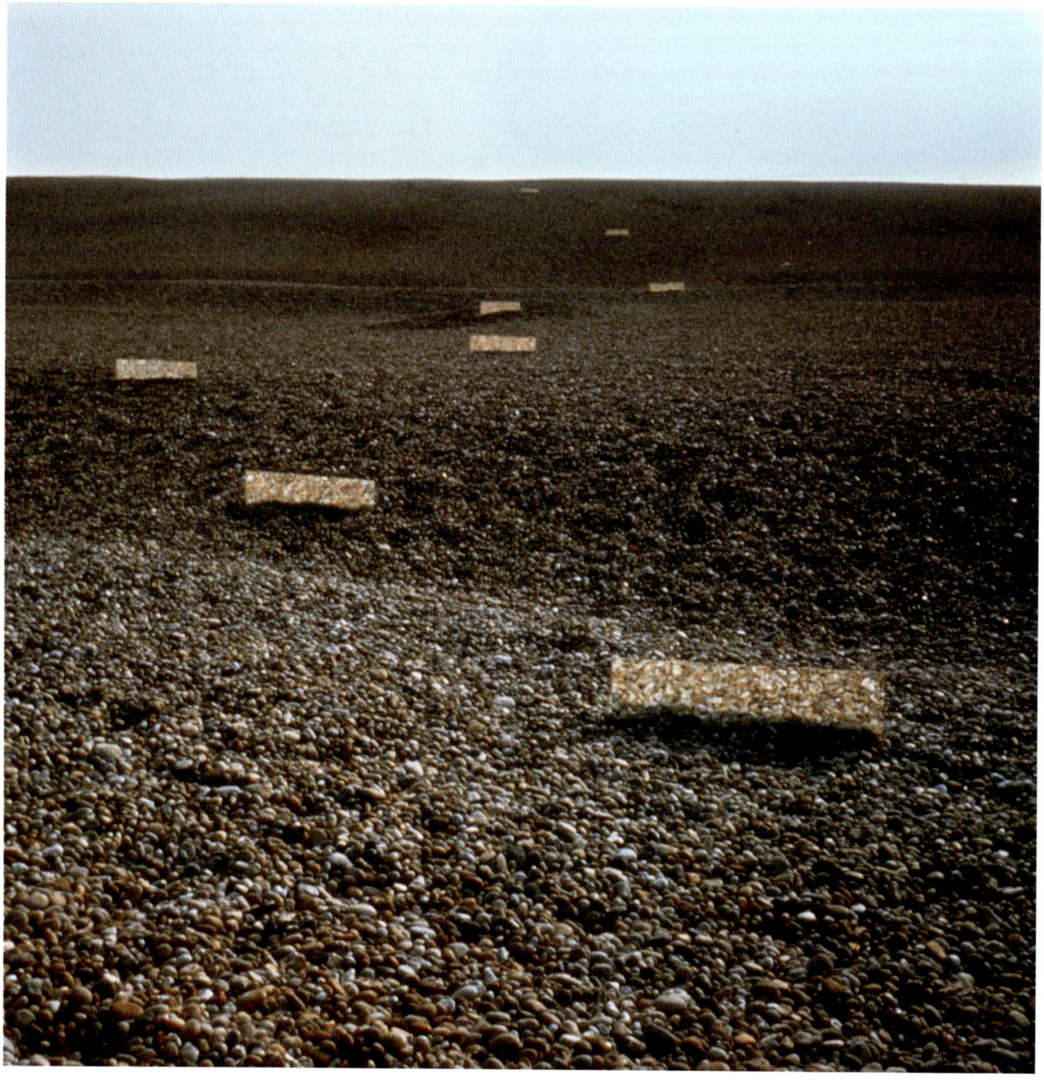

away from the sandflats: 'Small bits of perception dropped away from the edges of eyesight. Where is the island? The unknowable zero island. Were the mirrors mounted on something that was dropping, draining, eroding, trickling, spilling away?'[11] Recorded for his archive on an Instamatic camera using Kodachrome film, most of these transitory works now exist only through the artist's photographic documentation.

Smithson continued to construct 'Mirror Displacements' in 1969 on a trip around England and Wales with Holt, when they visited archaeological sites, quarries and ancient ruins.[12] Chesil Beach, the immense stretch of pale shingle that runs for 29 kilometres (18 mi.) from the Isle of Portland along the Jurassic Coast in Dorset, England, provided Smithson with an ideal site for another *Mirror Displacement* (illus. 38). Eight mirrors reflecting the rippling mounds of shingle that cover the southern end of Chesil Beach created the effect of a mottled pathway composed of the image of pebbles, reflecting back onto a sea of pebbles. Chesil Beach led to another island, the Isle of Portland, where dramatic white cliffs sit resolutely at the southernmost tip of Dorset, a site to which I will return later in this chapter.

Small Islands, Oceans and Inundation

> Fluctuations in solar radiation have melted the ice caps, sending the planet into a new Triassic Age of unendurable heat. London is a swamp; lush tropical vegetation grows up the walls of the Ritz and primeval reptiles are sighted swimming through the newly formed lagoons.
>
> **J. G. Ballard, *The Drowned World***[13]

J. G. Ballard's *The Drowned World* opens with the sentence: 'Soon it would be too hot.' His 1962 science-fiction novel describes an inundated, over-heating planet. An underlying question runs throughout the book: as oceans and temperatures rise, why don't people do anything significant to stop it? Ballard's dystopian world posits what the geographer Alastair

Bonnett describes as a curious speculative theory that people are following 'a primal urge to go back to the place where we first evolved and to slip, slither and fall away into the amniotic ocean'.[14] Bonnett suggests that 'aquaphilia' could help explain some aspects of our current crisis, especially our tendency to simultaneously run away from and towards the retreating shoreline.[15] But the evidence is clear: 'Disappearing islands are the star exhibit of sea-level rise.'[16]

As the 'star exhibit' of the contemporary climate emergency, small low-lying islands in Pacific Oceania, the Indian and Atlantic Oceans, as well as the Caribbean and Mediterranean Seas, are especially vulnerable to the effects of rapidly rising sea levels. Many have already disappeared. Others are experiencing severe coastal erosion, diminishing freshwater resources, more frequent and extreme hurricanes and cyclones and variations in local patterns of wave action. What is happening to them is an early warning to the rest of the world. Nearly half a century after Smithson's preoccupation with eroding landmasses, the plight of small islands has taken on a much wider ecological and geopolitical relevance. So-called Small Island Developing States (SIDS) have become the focus of urgent political concern. Their representatives have become increasingly vocal in arguments for global initiatives to counter the effects of the climate crisis, especially since these island nations are responsible for far lower emissions per capita than the rest of the developed world.[17] Impassioned lobbying on behalf of those threatened communities has informed a host of artistic initiatives across different media. T. J. Demos notes that as a system of global governance to address the crisis appears to be failing, we have seen 'a flourishing of contemporary artistic and activist practices that address and negotiate environmental conflict in other ways'.[18]

In 2009 Mohamed Nasheed, president of the State of the Maldives, convened an underwater cabinet meeting to draw global media attention to the disastrous effects of climate change on SIDS, notably his own low-lying archipelago. Dramatically staged with Nasheed's cabinet in full scuba gear 6 metres (20 ft) underwater, a resolution was passed calling for global cuts in carbon emissions (illus. 39). This underwater meeting passed

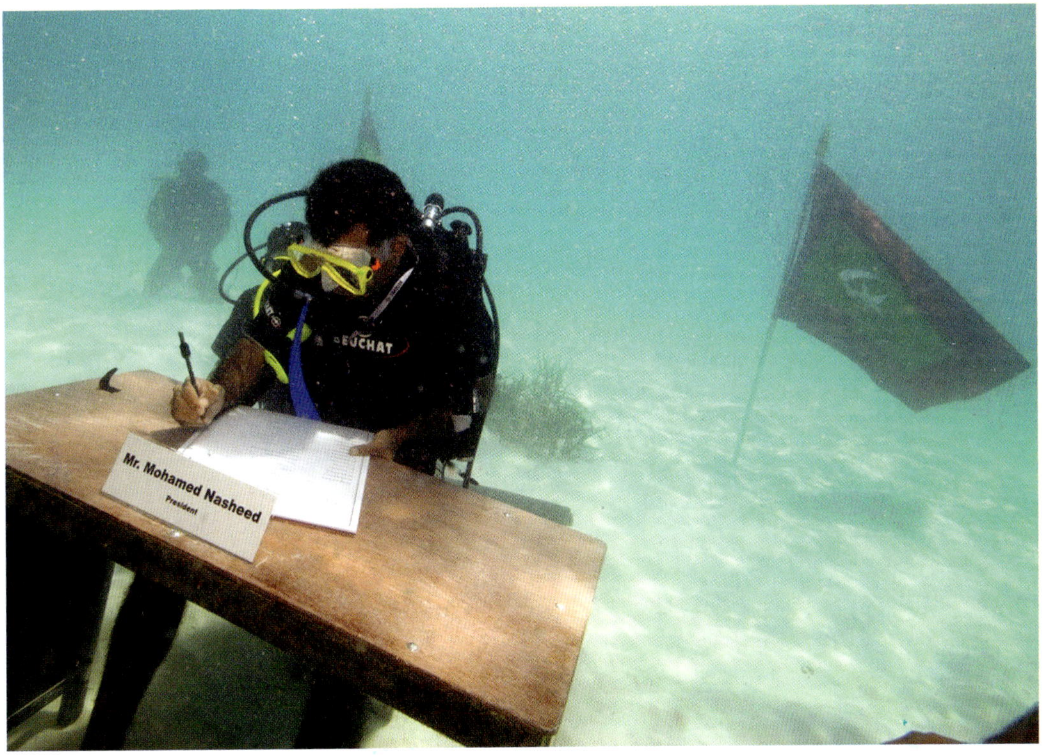

39 Mohamed Nasheed, president of the Republic of Maldives, chairing an underwater cabinet meeting, 2009.

a resolution calling for global cuts in carbon emissions, and Nasheed wrote on a plastic slate: 'We must unite in a world war effort to halt further temperature rises.' Staged shortly before the Copenhagen Climate Change Conference of 2009 (COP15), it provided a persuasive example of theatrical performance mimicking some of the characteristics of performance art, deployed for political ends. It attracted worldwide media interest. Since then, both politicians and artists have deployed strategies of self-representation partly submerged in seawater. For example, in 2021 a Tuvalu government minister, Simon Kofe, appeared by video at COP26, standing knee-deep in seawater behind his lecture stand.

Oceans and water have also become important sources of imagery for feminist artists concerned with global ecologies. A widely viewed video-poem, *Rise: From One Island to Another* (2018), a collaboration by the Marshallese poet, artist and activist Kathy Jetñil-Kijiner (b. 1989) and

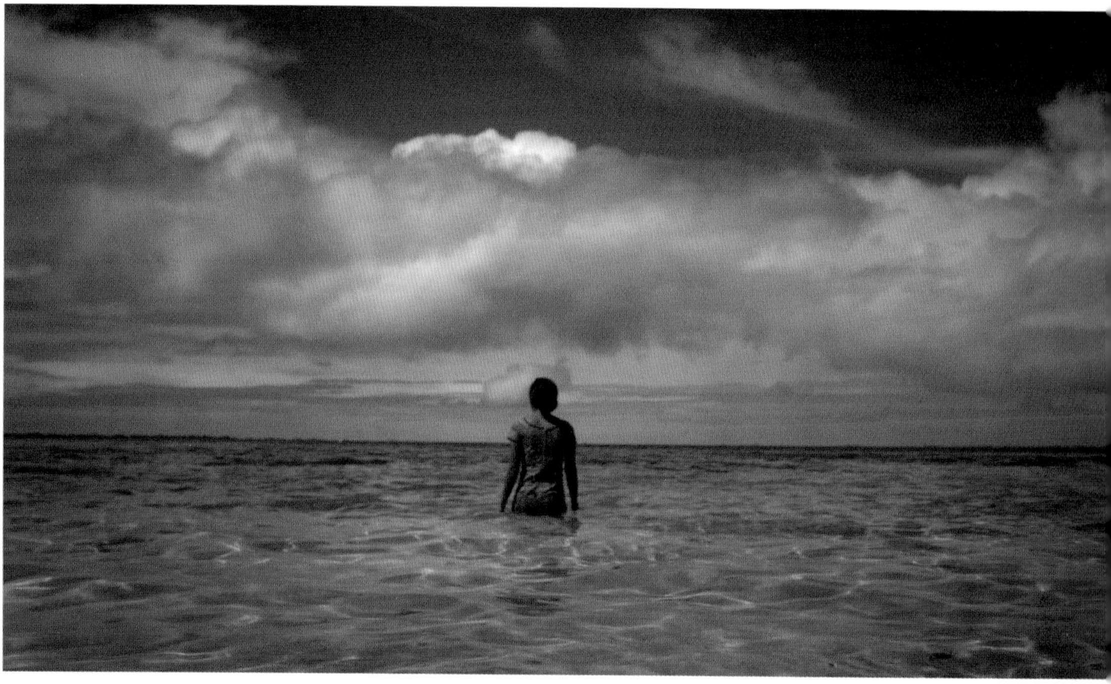

40 Kathy Jetñil-Kijiner and Aka Niviâna, *Rise: From One Island to Another*, 2018, video still.

the Inuk poet and activist Aka Niviâna from Greenland, is replete with images of the former partly submerged in seawater (illus. 40). While Jetñil-Kijiner stands in rising seawater off the shores of Majuro island, Niviâna walks on melting icecaps of Greenland. As the largest non-continental island in the world Greenland has a similar population to that of the Marshall Islands, about 56,000 inhabitants. The artists' subject positions as Indigenous islanders are used strategically to signal the shared problem of rising sea levels and ice-melts, invoking what Jaimey Hamilton Faris has described as 'an Indigenous transoceanic solidarity'.[19]

The Marshall Islands are described early in the video by Jetñil-Kijiner as 'a country more sea than land'. While the imagery of the video might lend itself to exoticized tropes of islands and islanders as disappearing, the voices of the two poets counter this objectification, asserting a 'sisterhood of ocean and ice'.[20] Hamilton Faris has argued that this strategy can be seen as 'aquapelagic', a form of representation (in relation to sea or water) that responds to the global climate emergency and climate representation.

She uses the label 'hydro-feminism' to represent the ecological and gendered ambitions of this video-poem in which both artists use voice and visual performance to address and critique the politics and popular imagery of the climate emergency. Water and its relationship to human bodies is important to evolving theories of feminist ecology.[21]

It remains to be seen if global responses (including successive COPs) to the climate crisis will produce results that might secure the future of these SIDS. As of 2023, the Marshall Islands, along with other low-lying coral atolls in Pacific Oceania north of Australia, are predicted to be partly submerged by 2035.[22] Several uninhabited islands in this archipelago (including Majuro Atoll) are already beneath the water line. Rising sea levels also cause salt-water contamination of aquifers, forcing islanders to migrate away from their homes. Like many SIDS, the colonial history of the Marshall Islands has inhibited independent action, since they are dependent on foreign aid largely from the United States, who continue to occupy military bases there and retain responsibility for 'defense matters'.[23]

Inhabiting these island communities and witnessing their progressive disappearances has encouraged many artists to adopt strategies that inflect contemporary art and visual culture with pressing ecological and geopolitical issues. They have used film, installation and performance as strategic devices to engage both local and global audiences. In 2020 an exhibition and associated community events, 'On Inundation Art and Climate Change in the Pacific', was staged at the University of Hawai'i Manoa. It included multimedia work by nine Pacific artists that addressed the vulnerability of Asia Pacific Island communities in Hawai'i, the Kingdom of Tonga, the Philippines, Okinawa, the Marshall Islands, Tuvalu and Singapore. Curator Hamilton Faris wrote that the exhibition 'create[s] a space to process raw emotions, inspire collective imagination, and generate capacity for creative, actionable, and communal responses to our watery climate'. An engagement with the effects of floods and ensuing disasters was imaginatively woven through each exhibit. In the installation *Sounding*, crowded with Marshallese hanging baskets, Kathy Jetñil-Kijiner and the artist Joy Lehuanani Enomoto (of Kanaka Maoli, African American,

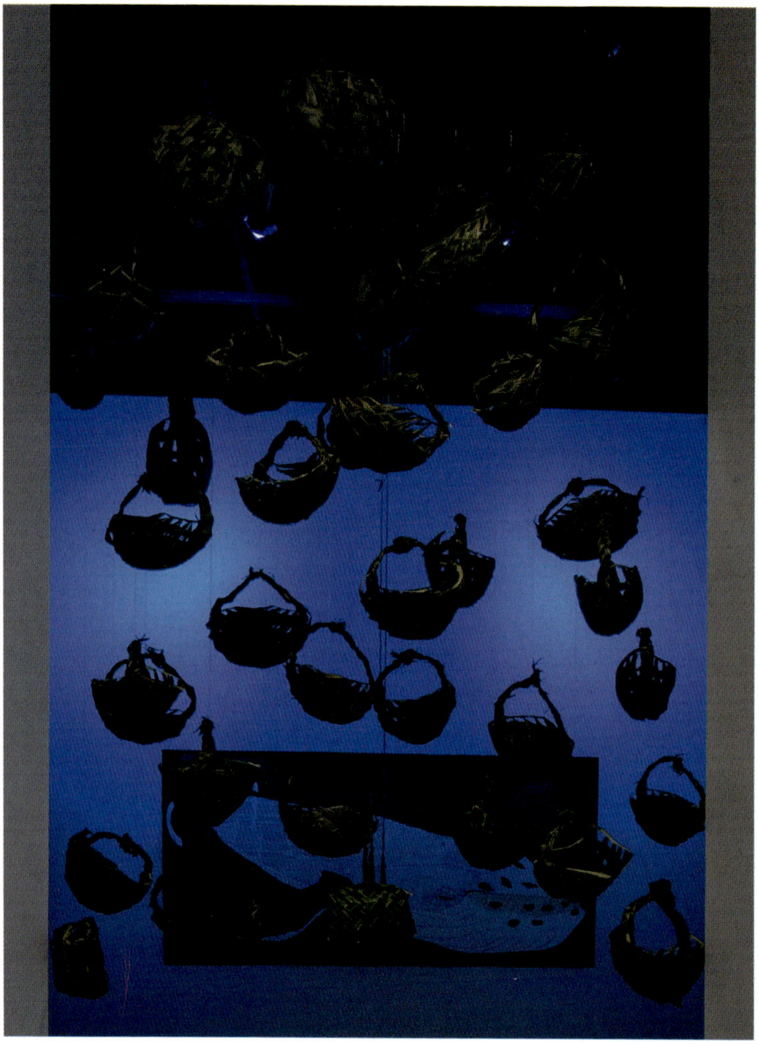

41, 42 Kathy Jetñil-Kijiner and Joy Lehuanani Enomoto, *Sounding*, 2020, installation with baskets, sounding line, drawing and sound recording, University of Hawai'i.

Japanese, Caddo Indian, Punjabi and Scottish descent) combined the patterned strands of basket-weaving with sounds of sonic vibration and water, a large drawing of a whale and wall text to suggest that all Indigenous Pacific island voices and ancestral sounds, including those of women, should be acknowledged in the solutions to the climate crisis (illus. 41, 42).

Woven baskets carry important cultural and gendered meanings in Pacific Oceania. Usually made by women, and often characterized by local

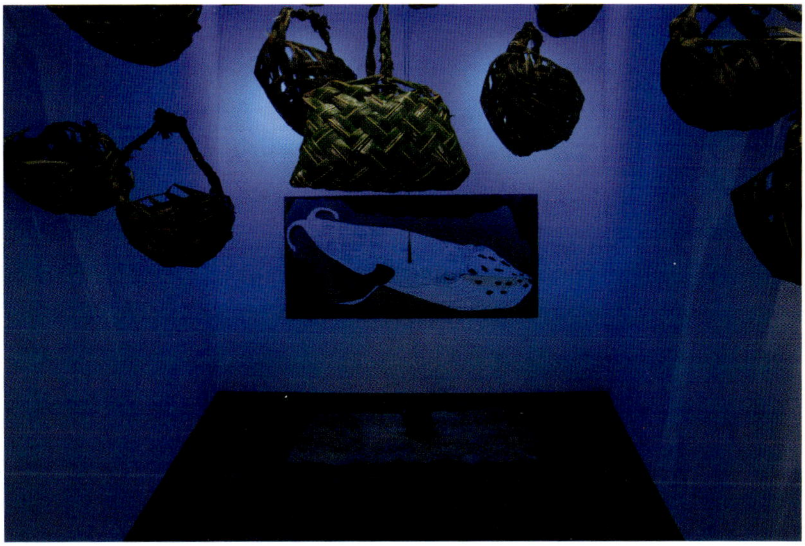

island styles and patterning, in recent history they were the main form of container used for food and possessions. A popular motivational Māori proverb translates as: 'With your food basket and my food basket, everyone has enough to eat.'[24] Jetñil-Kijiner's accompanying poem to this work explains what happens when 'strands' (literal and metaphorical) are left out of the conversation, signalling the effects of 'islands dying':

> There are islands dying. There are voices telling us to destroy
> thousand-year-old limbs like it's nothing.
> Like it's not another strand unravelling. Like it's not another
> woman sinking to the bottom. Sinking boulders tied to feet,
> body caged in a woven tomb.
> We missed a strand and we named her monster.[25]

Sounding references multiple aspects of this gendered and colonial island history, including a single hanging 'sounding line' traditionally used to measure shallow bays or sounds for navigation and exploration. Hanging amidst the baskets, it relates the development of the science of hydrography to the associated 'colonization, militarization, and industrialization of the Pacific'.[26] In the early twentieth century the sounding line was replaced by sonar. During the atomic tests on the Marshall Islands in the late 1940s and '50s, sonar was used to measure damage to the land, sea and reef systems. Researchers are increasingly identifying both local and global damage inflicted by nuclear fallout and its likely contribution to ecological change. Hence the relevance of the drawing of a humpback whale, juxtaposed with reports and lawsuits on the effects of naval sonar devices on marine creatures, and the article headline 'Stranded Whales Die Again on Hawaiian Shore' shown in enlarged text. In Hawaiian history the whale carries an important status as a valued ancestor, or 'aumakua, to which the living community owes a responsibility.

Elizabeth DeLoughrey has explored a body of writing from Oceania that critiques the militarization and radioactive contamination of military ecologies. Drawing on the French philosopher Paul Virilio's notion of the 'wars of light', DeLoughrey identifies a group of Pacific writers who explore 'the desacralisation of light and land'.[27] For example, in *The Whale Rider* (2005), a novel by the New Zealand writer Witi Ihimaera, a pod of ancestor whales are disorientated and eventually beached following French nuclear tests on Tahiti. Likewise, *Soundings*, through its imaginative use of drawing (of the whale), objects and text juxtaposed with emblems of scientific measurement, provides a visual equivalent that signals this 'desacralization' of light, land and the multiple functions of sound.

The 'Inundation' exhibition also included a community event, *HighWaterLine Honolulu*, which invited people to visualize and mark the levels at which rising tides will impact the Kaka'ako area of Honolulu. Organized by Christina Gerhardt, this was a recreation of artist Eve Mosher's original project, *HighWaterLine* staged in New York in 2007, in which local volunteers were invited to use a chalk liner to mark more than 113 kilometres (70 mi.) of New York boroughs at risk of tidal flooding; the line represented the point to which scientists and government assessments believed water would rise after a major storm. Mosher handed out leaflets on climate change and its impacts and encouraged other coastal communities to create their own HighWaterLine walks. In Honolulu walks and talks were organized around Kaka'ako, previously an area of wetlands with fresh water springs. The HighWaterLine walks were designed to engage the local community and beyond, raising difficult questions about how artistic practice can effectively mediate important political and social issues while also retaining some artistic value.

The complex relationship between contemporary art and 'political ecology' has informed many recent debates and related publications and is an inevitable concern of any study exploring the island theme in recent art.[28] That said, art practices engage with pressing ecological issues in different ways and are not necessarily self-defined as political 'activism'. Within the gallery or in public sites, art can provide channels through which people encounter ecological issues. The imaginative and novel strategies deployed can inform and inspire communities to address such issues, as in the community engagement of the 'Inundation' exhibition, or through multimedia forms and channels (publications, writings, independent video- and podcasts and so on). The loose label 'Eco art', which I have largely avoided, has become something of a modern buzzword, although it can signify different levels of engagement with environmental issues. Unlike the scientist following established research methods, the artist has the freedom to use metaphor, imagination and varied media to question and critique aspects of island life and its global implications.[29] The all-too-visible effects of the climate emergency on so many small island states have encouraged a flourishing of innovative, interdisciplinary art practices that address such issues.

Las Islas Encantadus: Galápagos

Known in Spanish as Las Islas Encantadus (the Enchanted Isles), the Galápagos Islands are often described as magical and strange (illus. 43). Close to the Equator off the Pacific coast of Ecuador, they are famously inhabited by animal species not found anywhere else on earth, including giant tortoises, marine iguanas and Darwin's finches (small land birds indigenous to Galápagos). With their origins in volcanic eruptions and ancient tectonic movements, some of the newest of the 120 islands are about half a million years old. Largely uninhabited and best known for its

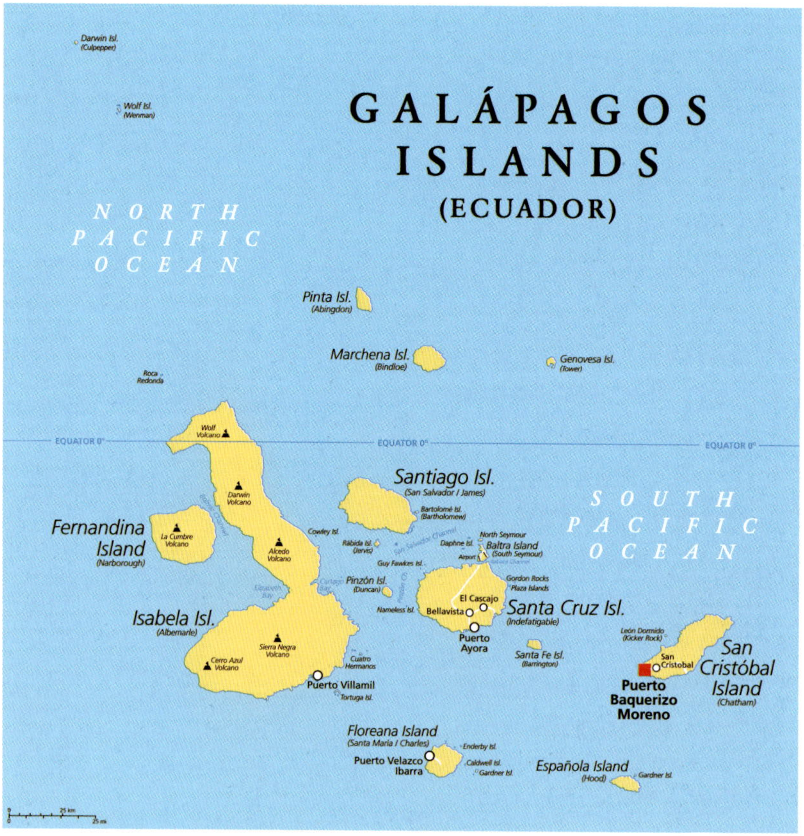

43 Map of the Galápagos Islands, Ecuador.

unique ecosystem first described in Charles Darwin's *On the Origin of the Species* (1859), this extraordinary archipelago is now threatened by climate change, tourism and the migration of Ecuadorians to four of the islands. Their unusual conditions have helped to create a vivid island imaginary, inspiring a host of strange, phantasmagoric visualizations. As the curator Greg Hilty writes: 'the Galápagos are . . . a mental construct. People bring their partial knowledge and more or less intense imaginings to the Islands, physically or virtually.'[30] In 2010 the British artist Gemma Anderson (b. 1981) spent a month there retracing the route of Darwin's voyage and produced a series of mysterious, dream-like etchings (illus. 44). She recalls lying beside iguanas on Isabela Island and drawing them directly onto copper plates: 'As I was drawing, I let a strange landscape develop from what I observed . . . iguanas, lava, a blue-footed booby foot and a bird's skull . . . which I added as a flying chimera to the scene.'[31]

However, humans now constitute one of the most significant invasive species. Both terrestrial (including feral goats, pigs, rats, ants, as well as humans) and marine species (including invasive organisms), not to mention industrialized fishing and widespread pollution, threaten the survival of many of the famous Galápagos creatures. Marine debris – notably plastic – transports invasive species and deposits its own contaminating particles or microplastics. A research project in 2019 found that 25 per cent of all plastic debris found on Galápagos beaches was colonized by at least one animal or plant.[32] At the time of writing, six famous Galápagos species are

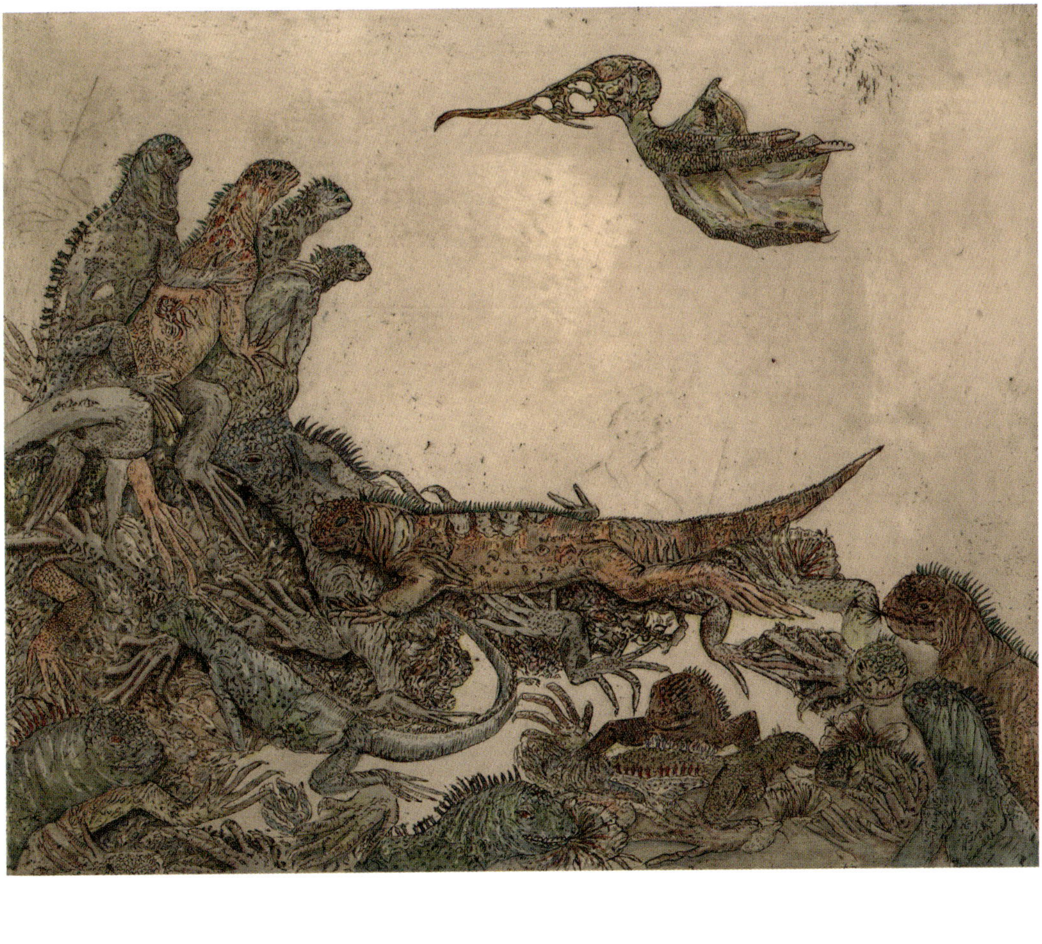

44 Gemma Anderson, *Amblyrhynchus cristatus, Pahoehoe Lava, Blue Footed Booby Chimera*, 2010, copper etching, hand-coloured with colour pencil and Japanese inks.

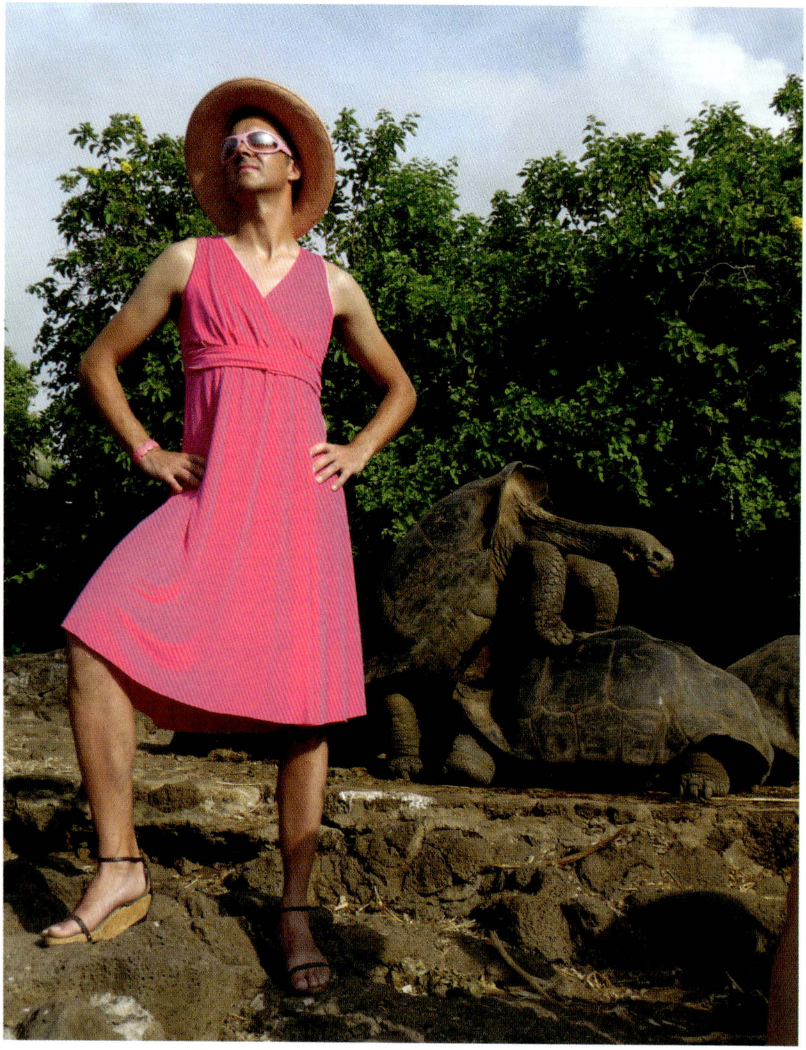

45 Marcus Coates, *Galápagos Fashions*, 2008, photograph by Elke Hartmann.

listed as endangered: the giant land tortoise, marine iguanas, blue-footed boobies, Galápagos penguins, green sea turtles and sea lions.

Tourism now defines the appeal of these islands in relation to some of these rare and endangered species, a tension that preoccupies scientific communities, including those based at the Charles Darwin Foundation on the islands. 'Visitor maps' often represent the islands of the archipelago according to the species found in and around them, visualizing the expectations of the tourist gaze. Undeterred by tensions caused by tourism, the Gulbenkian Galápagos Artists' Residency Programme was established to encourage encounters between art and science over a period of five years up to 2011. As more artists became involved in the politics of environmentalism, residences were offered to those whose practice engaged with global ecological issues raised. Organized by Siân Ede of the UK branch of the Calouste Gulbenkian Foundation, and curated by Greg Hilty and Bergit Arends, eleven artists were invited to take up residencies between 2007 and 2011.[33] Each commissioned project was informed by the perceived 'islandness' of the Galápagos and its threatened species, albeit using different aesthetic strategies. The dominant view held by scientists and biogeographers of the Galápagos as essentially a 'laboratory' for ecological research was imaginatively reconceived and reframed.

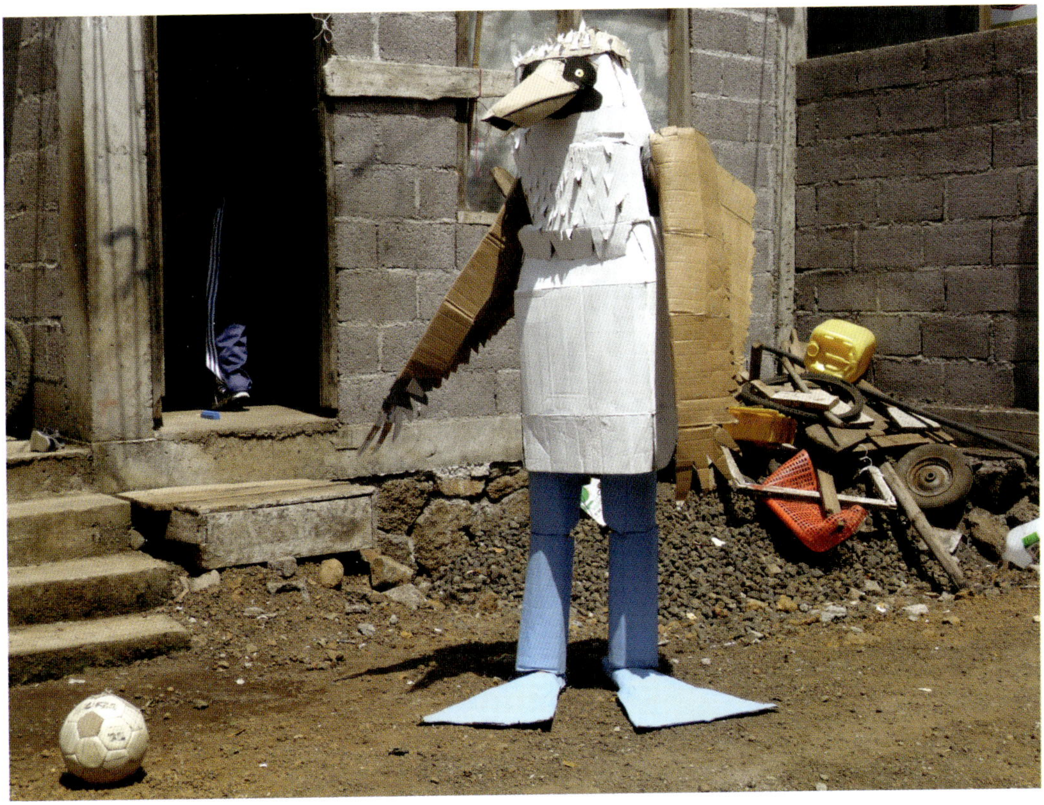

46 Marcus Coates, *Human Report (Blue Footed Booby)*, 2008, production still from broadcast on Channel 9 TV Galápagos.

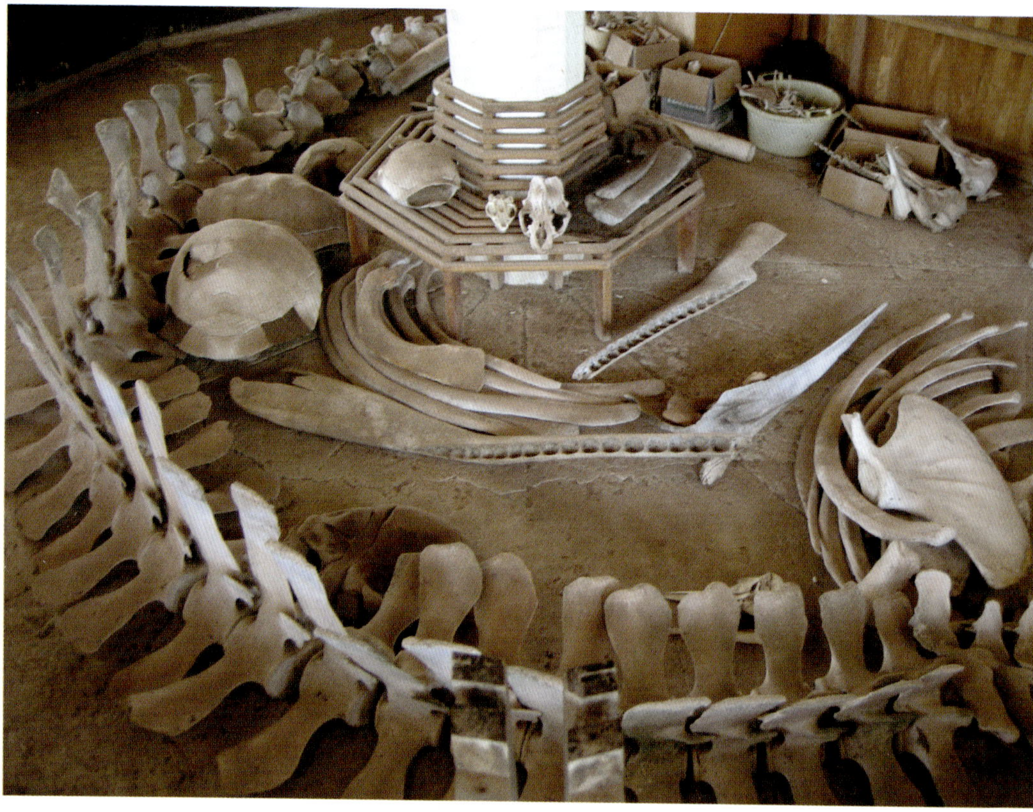

47 Dorothy Cross, *Bone Room, Galápagos* used in performance of *Stage* with Fiona Shaw, 2009.

The British artist Marcus Coates (b. 1968), who took up the residency in 2008, used his performance and video work to explore the iconic nature of local species. In his *Galápagos Fashions/Iconic Species* (2008; illus. 45) he poses in a shocking pink dress, sunglasses and a sunhat as the gaudy star of the island's fauna, alongside a giant land tortoise, mocking and upstaging the use of these creatures in tourist brochures. He has described the tortoise as an 'icon for the Galápagos' and the most popular subject for tourist cameras: 'In a bid to compete with their exotic appeal I purchased the most glamorous outfit available on Santa Cruz Island and planted myself in the tortoises' breeding enclosure.'[34] In his work *Human Report* (2008) he deployed a similarly playful strategy when he used the format of a filmed nature documentary to observe human behaviour on the island. Dressed in a cardboard costume as the endangered blue-footed booby (illus. 46),

Coates interviewed some of the 30,000 islanders. His report was filmed in the studio of a local news programme, Channel 9 TV – on which it also featured – and walking around Puerto Ayora. In this disguise, he presented a question to the scientists at the Charles Darwin Research Station: 'If you were an animal visiting the Galápagos, what do you imagine you would say about the human colonisation here and the societies they have established?'[35] By using mimicry, role play and provocative visual imagery, Coates raised important ecological issues without hectoring his audience.

The Irish artist Dorothy Cross (b. 1956) was the first to take up the Calouste Gulbenkian residency in 2007. Renowned for her interest in the relationship between nature, culture and ecology, she used photography and film to explore the evolution of local species. On an earlier visit to Galápagos in 1994, she scuba-dived with hammerhead sharks and swam with sea-lions. In 2007 she was accompanied by her friend the Irish actor and director Fiona Shaw, who contributed to the projects involved. Cross had been commissioned by Shrewsbury Museum and Art Gallery to create a show for the bicentenary of Darwin's birth in 2009. This included her film *Stage* (performed in the Unitarian Church that Darwin attended in Shrewsbury), which combines video footage of local animal life on the Galápagos Islands with recorded conversations between Cross and Shaw, where they discussed the role of art both on and about the island, using quotations from literature, including Shakespeare's *The Tempest* and poems by Emily Dickinson. Images include a grazing giant tortoise with a cow, and a tattoo of the map of the Galápagos Islands on a man's arm at the ferry port in Puerta Ayora, Santa Cruz. The schematic tattooed map, which will endure forever on the islander's arm, adds a sense of inevitability to the human 'occupation' of the islands. *Stage* ends with images inside a dusty repository in the Charles Darwin Research Station on Santa Cruz, including footage of Shaw sitting naked amidst whale bones and the shells of dead tortoises (illus. 47). Cross's imaginative capacity for 'making strange', which often involves the manipulation of materials and organic matter, was adapted here to aestheticize a series of troubling ecological encounters.[36] In a piece written for the Galápagos catalogue of 2012, Shaw quotes

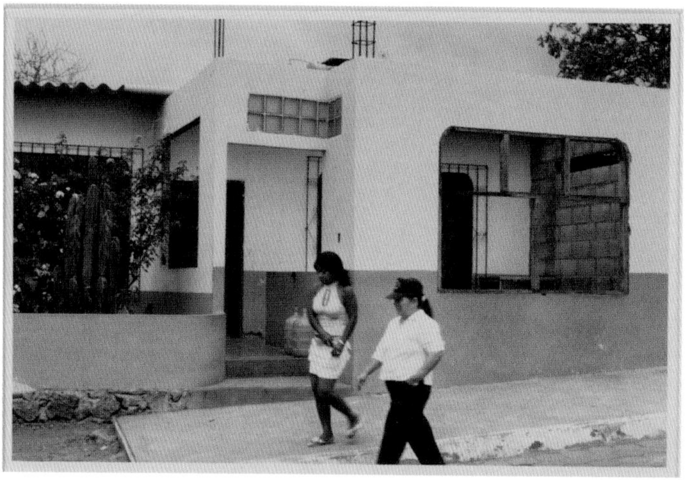

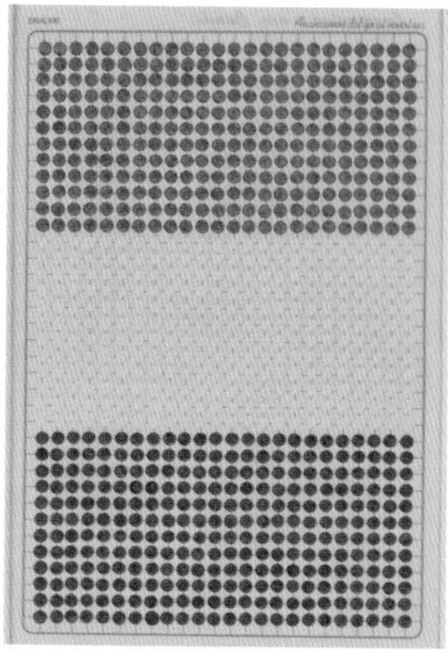

48 Alison Turnbull, *Let's Progress from Me to Us*, 2011, ink on printed paper and silver gelatin print.

Caliban's speech from Act III, scene two of *The Tempest*, which seems to foreshadow the magic of 'Las Islas Incantadus'. In it he describes an island full of

> Sounds, and sweet airs, that give delight and hurt not.
> Sometimes a thousand twangling instruments
> Will hum about mine ears, and sometimes voices
> That, if I then had waked after long sleep
> Will make me sleep again.[37]

Later in the essay Shaw looks back with some guilt and sadness after hearing about the islands' problems in seeking a tourist industry that also threatens their survival. She suggests that if people must be part of the future of the Galápagos, 'then it stops being Prospero's island. It stops being the Ancient Mariner's sea ... Art is riven with contradiction. My thoughts are informed by my visit, but the oblivious eye of a blue-footed booby tells us to stay away.' As mediated through the lens of contemporary art, Prospero's island, like the blue-footed booby, is increasingly under threat.

In 2009 the British artist Alison Turnbull (born in Colombia in 1956) took up residency. Many of Turnbull's works have drawn on scientific

49 Alison Turnbull, *Specimens*, 2012, unique archival pigment print.

BUTTERFLIES FROM THE GALÁPAGOS ISLANDS IN THE NATURAL HISTORY MUSEUM

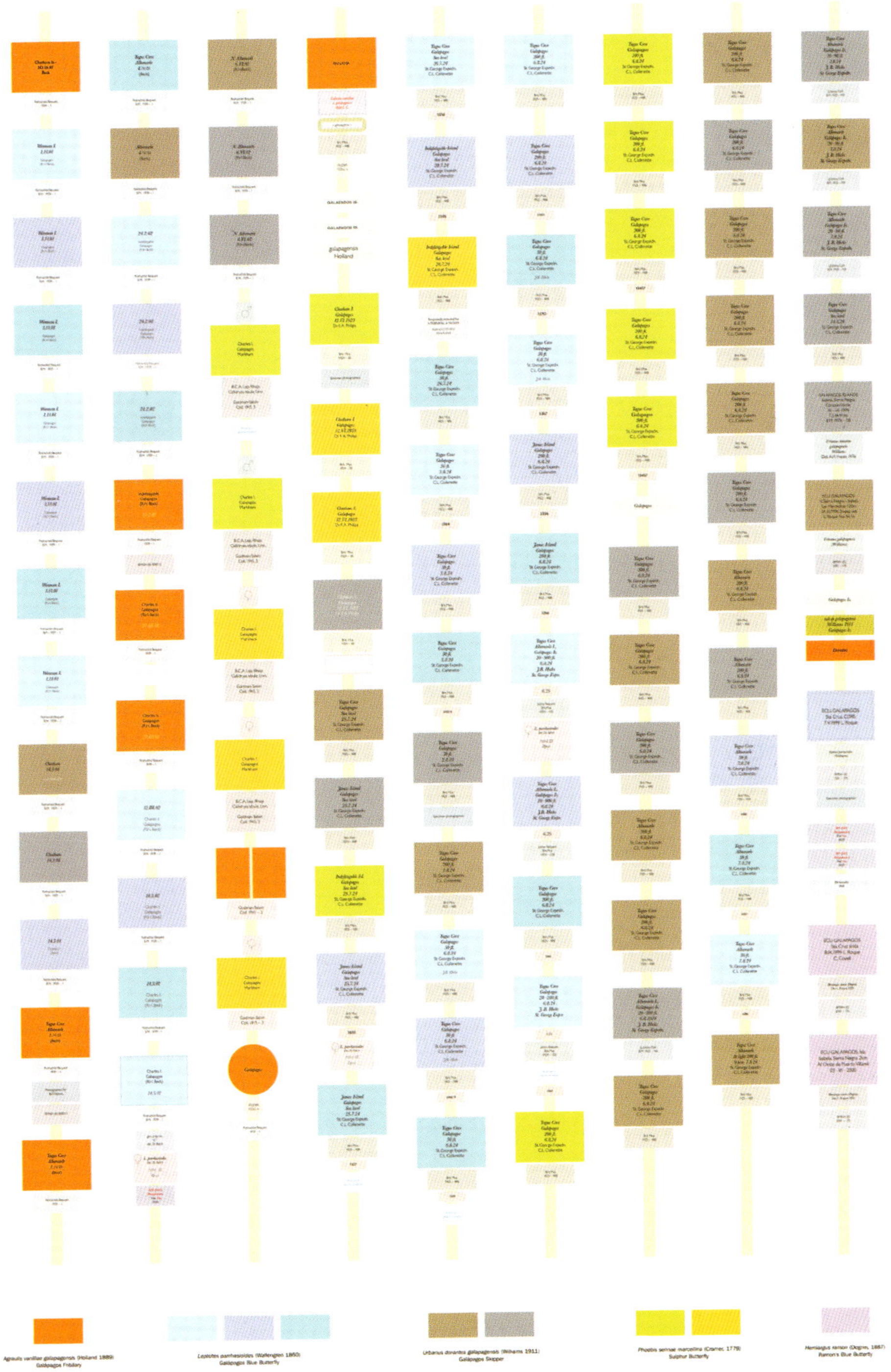

research, systems of documentation and labelling, from astronomy to biology and architectural drawings. With painstaking attention to detail, she appropriates colour to define and mediate both artistic and scientific material, creating charts, maps and deceptively decorative designs. Her discovery of *Werner's Nomenclature of Colours*, the manual that Darwin had taken on his voyage on the *Beagle*, inspired several works. The manual contains hand-painted swatches of colour that correspond to objects and creatures from the mineral, vegetable and animal worlds. In one series of Galápagos works she juxtaposes photographs of island life with grids of coloured dots drawn on notebook pages bought on Santa Cruz. Each notebook page is headed with a Spanish saying or aphorism, designed to encourage local morale and social commitment. For example, dots recreate the green, white and blue stripes of the Galápagos flag under the page heading *Let's Progress from Me to Us* (*Avancemos del yo al nosotros*), opposite a photograph of two local women walking down a street in Puerto Ayora (illus. 48). Colour (of the fauna, species, island flowers and so on) looms large in the cultural imaginary of the Galápagos; from the blue-footed booby to the yellow butterflies referenced in Turnbull's large-scale print *Specimens* (2012; illus. 49), it is a vivid signifier of local life.

While on Galápagos she explored the butterfly and moth collection at the Charles Darwin Research Station. On her return she sourced all 105 specimens of Galápagos butterflies at the Entomology Department of the Natural History Museum in London. In her print *Specimens* she translates all the information gleaned into a carefully annotated pictorial chart. Butterfly details and typographies are transformed into colour-coded, numbered and dated labels, arranged in nine vertical lines across the page. Butterflies are signified by the colour swatch, date and the named island site at which they were found. This quasi-scientific yet seductively decorative chart offers a correlation between a coloured swatch and a point on a map; the Galápagos Islands are evoked metonymically through the (partly threatened) butterfly species. Turnbull often reminds us that the Greek word for 'butterfly', or lepidoptera, is *psyche*, which also means 'soul'.[38] Her work embraces this double meaning as both literal and imaginary; her coloured labels represent far more than scientific data. As she explains: 'These tiny labels tell the story of the insect and its habitat but also stories of discovery, scientific and linguistic change and migration – even of typography and print technologies.'[39] The geography, history and entomology of Galápagos have been memorialized through colour, typography and metaphor.

PART 2: DISAPPEARING ISLANDS ON THE SOUTH COAST OF ENGLAND

Absent and Present on Portland

> G and I walk to St George's. We'd seen the guide in the church on the path earlier. I ask if he's local. Says his name is Stone (one of the island's original names) and he's lived on the island for five hundred years. He was a quarryman and his dad and dad's dad etc. A lot less quarrying going on now.
> **Katrina Palmer, *Portland Diary***[40]

In the summer of 2014 the British artist Katrina Palmer (b. 1967) spent over six months living alone near the southern tip of Chesil Beach on the Isle of Portland, researching its history, geology and geography in preparation for a multimedia commission by Artangel and the BBC in 2015. Shaped like a lamb chop or a flamingo's head, Portland reaches out into some of the most dangerous seas off the south coast of England. Crowned at its southern tip by the famous Portland Bill Lighthouse, the island is now joined to the Dorset mainland by a spectacular shingle causeway running alongside the beach (illus. 50). Stone, especially Portland stone, largely defines the island's history on the awe-inspiring, eroding Jurassic coast. The much-coveted luminous limestone has been quarried there since Roman times, and in its purest, whitest form – known as base-bed – has furnished the building blocks of many of Britain's most iconic buildings, including the Tower of London, St Paul's Cathedral, several Wren churches, the west front of Westminster Abbey, the British Museum, Broadcasting House in Portland Square and the Cenotaph, among many others.[41] The construction of these buildings, bristling with the symbolism of Britain's imperial, ecclesiastical and colonial pasts, has contributed to the hollowing out of the Isle of Portland.

Palmer's project included an audio walk titled 'The Loss Adjusters', a book, *End Matter* (illus. 51), and a radio broadcast on BBC Radio 4 called *The Quarryman's Daughters* in 2015.[42] The project revealed the artist's

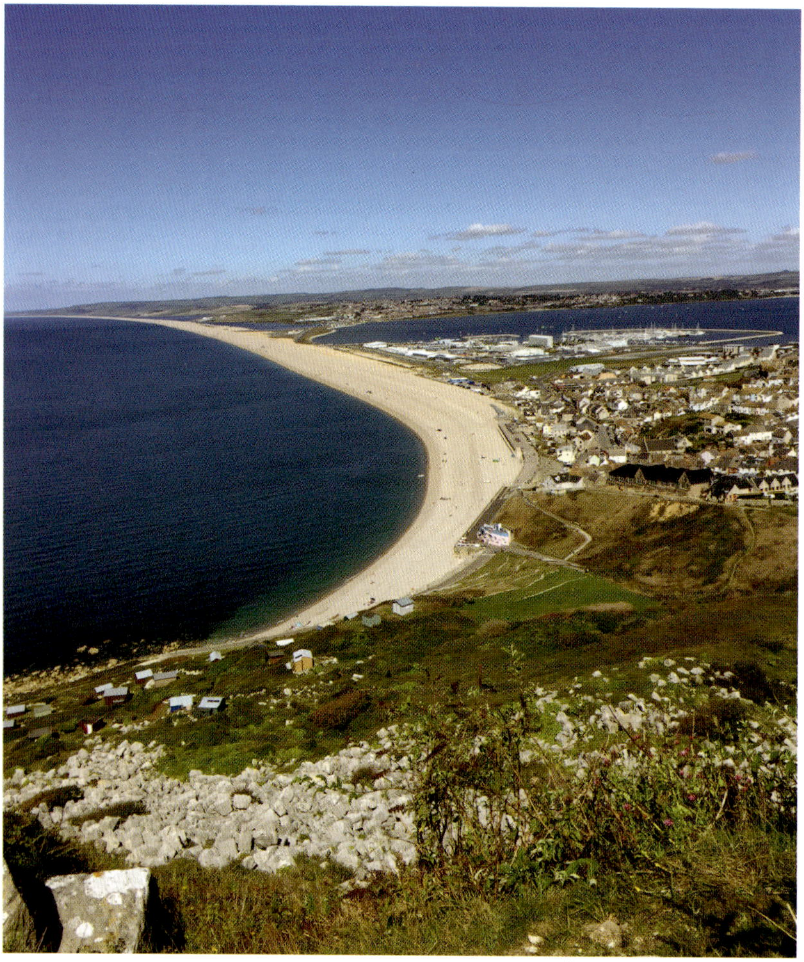

50 View of Chesil Beach and Portland Causeway.

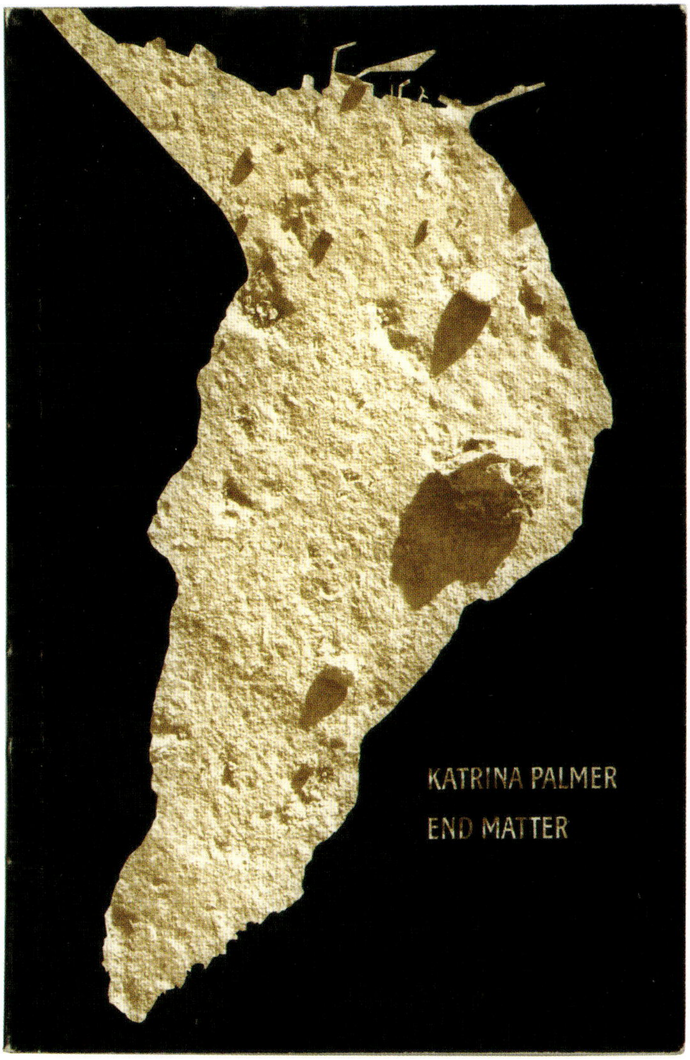

51 Cover of Katrina Palmer, *End Matter* (Book Works and Artangel: London, 2015).

ongoing interest in geological histories and the significance of place in the shaping of landscapes. Palmer's conceptual approach to landscape focuses on the loss, across the centuries, of this desirable white stone. Portland's many quarries and, more recently, underground mines have progressively emptied out the underbelly of the island. Once defined by Thomas Hardy as 'a peninsula carved by time out of a single stone',[43] in Palmer's work,

Portland becomes an inverted sculpture defined by the absence of the very stone of which it is made. Hence the literal and metaphorical significance of 'Loss Adjusters', whose protagonists are located in a windowless Portland office, at the heart of this work. As she has described it, the whole island might be conceived as 'an absent and present sculpture'.[44]

Before the Ferrybridge was built in 1839, Portland was connected to the Dorset mainland by a shingle and sand isthmus that is submerged at high tide, described by a character in *End Matter* as 'a highway to oblivion'.[45] Quarrying, fishing and smuggling were the island's main industries, helping to define a distinctive local identity. The apparent 'separateness' of Portland has informed Palmer's sense of puzzlement. She has described 'a deviance enabled by separateness'.[46] When she began researching her project, she became aware of a powerful sense of ownership and identity around the history of the quarried stone that is often conflated with the material itself. As she notes in her diary, one of the island's common family names is 'Stone'.

Those excavations of the ground below Portland also link this small island to a global history of imperialism, colonial conquests and naval and military history. Its highly prized stone furnished the building blocks for some of the highest offices of church and state in the UK and its colonies; Portland's distinctive islandness is paradoxically linked to a network of national and global power relations. Moreover, its strategic geographical position on a southern tip of the south coast of England has ensured its status as a key site for the defence of the nation. For half a century Portland Harbour was also the home of one of the UK's most important naval bases, finally closed in 1995, although Royal Naval frigates and supply ships are often moored there today. The fortified breakwater built with Portland stone was home to the Channel Fleet, and in 1944 was one of the main embarkation points for the D-Day landings. In the Cold War era the base included HMS *Osprey*, Europe's largest helicopter base. This encompassed the Admiralty Underwater Weapons Establishment, infiltrated by the notorious Portland Spy Ring, one of the most infamous espionage cases from the Cold War. KGB spies operating under false identities taken from the deceased were stealing secrets from the submarine research base. The ring was finally exposed in 1961, placing Portland firmly within a British history of Cold War espionage and devious secret agents, with a plot worthy of a John le Carré novel.[47]

The island is also home to two famous prisons. The first 'convicts' were shipped there from Weymouth in 1848, and their forced labour was used to break stone for the breakwaters that created the fortified naval harbour.[48] The original prison at the top of the eastern cliffs is now a young offenders institution, while a new category C prison, HM Prison The Verne, was established in 1949 within the island citadel (the highest point on Portland). Between 2014 and 2017 it was used as a reception centre for illegal immigrants, but following refurbishment in 2018 it now houses sex offenders, among them the British glam-rock star Gary Glitter (released – and readmitted in 2023). Although several years after Palmer's project, these events would qualify for the constantly revised 'End Matter' that she envisaged as part of her performative and published project. The book *End Matter*, as a metaphor for Portland, is missing its main body (of stone) but retains its status as a site of ongoing narratives or 'postscripts'.[49]

Palmer engaged with some of the social and geological contradictions of Portland in all aspects of her Artangel project. She consciously avoided replicating representations of island culture as hermetic or separate. Her multimedia work avoids discrete categories, instead suggesting fluid boundaries – between genres (performance, writing, sculpture), geographies (sea and land) and cultural identities (islanders and visitors) – and the wild, elemental nature of the wind-battered coastal paths and spectacular eroding cliffs has inspired a series of related works that operate on literal and symbolic levels to challenge and confuse the viewer. As her work suggests, the stone is heavy with the traces of prehistoric eras, while also metaphorically embracing 'the death of individuals and events it is shaped to memorialise'.[50] On the opening page of *End Matter* she describes this complicated sculptural heritage, formed over 150 million years in the Jurassic period, that 'became compacted and compressed under the mass of new existence until solidification preserved the remains and finally transformed them into Portland stone'.[51] She identifies the Isle of Portland as a sculpture that had absorbed 'an enormous quantity of death'.[52] As literal and metaphorical ammonites, the stones carry multiple layers of mortality. They are imprinted with histories of quarrymen and their families, of cliffs being eroded by storms and rising sea levels, of shipwrecks, death and rebirth. The lives of those Portland quarrymen and fishermen were harsh, poorly paid and dangerous. But those imprinted memories have been progressively hollowed out as the stone has been removed from the island over the centuries.

'The Loss Adjusters' begins in an abandoned former insurance office on the main street in Easton, Portland's only town. The audio walk then leads the listener past a cemetery towards Bowers Quarry, a site that reveals traces of decades of heavy, dangerous quarrying. The repetitive whirring sound of the photocopier in the Easton office is overlaid with the somewhat eerie voices of the eponymous loss adjusters, who describe themselves as 'hiding in plain sight' to 'quantify the manifold losses' of Portland's resources. Palmer's history of loss is then counterbalanced with a 'whispering gallery' of actors telling the stories of local bureaucrats, a young offender turned grave-digger, a wild horse and the Horrocks sisters, two daughters of a quarryman who live in huts on the island. In a low, quiet voice Palmer herself describes her aim to create a book of 'matter' in which 'body matter should be missing'. One reviewer has suggested that the real history that Palmer investigates – 'the poverty and violence imposed on West Dorset by capital and state – often seem obscured by the very ellipses'.[53] But Palmer's cryptic, multimedia project also functions as a multi-layered ghost story of an endlessly hollowed-out island.

Brambles and Barbed Wire on Orford Ness

Another British island haunted by military secrets and eroding traces of a previous life is Orford Ness, a bleak 16-kilometre (10 mi.) shingle spit off the Suffolk coast that can only be reached by boat. Although technically a peninsula linked to nearby Aldeburgh by a narrow strip of land, it is divided from the mainland by the rivers Alde and Ore. Before longshore

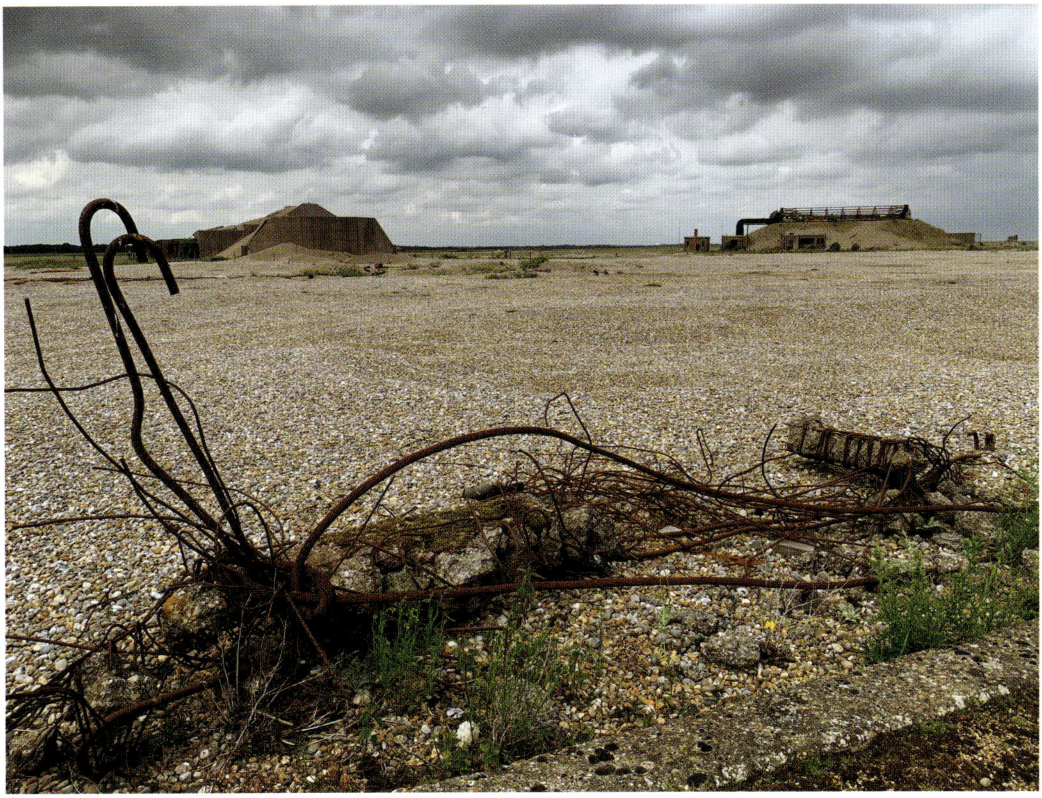

52 View of Orford Ness, 2021.

drift helped to separate it from the village it was a medieval port. Known locally as the 'Island of Secrets', it looks and feels like an inhospitable, deserted island. The windswept remains of various military structures and armouries (illus. 52) bear witness to its history; for decades Orford Ness was a laboratory and testing site for ballistics, weapon and navigation systems and nuclear projects – especially during the last two world wars and the Cold War; there are rumours that the bouncing bomb was tested on its beaches. In the 1930s it hosted the first experiments with the radar system that played a strategic war-time role in the Battle of Britain; in the post-war period it was the site of an Anglo-American experimental radar station codenamed 'Cobra Mist'.[54] The island was also used as a base for the Atomic Weapons Research Establishment and many military laboratory tests. Abandoned by the Ministry of Defence in 1971, it slowly acquired

European designations for nature conservation and was acquired by the National Trust in 1993. Weathered signs declare 'MOD property keep out', and regulated visitor numbers are expected to follow a marked path that leads past various abandoned ex-military buildings where 'for reasons of nature conservation and unexploded ordinance, this trail must not be left'.[55]

Gnarled strips of barbed wire, artillery fragments scattered among driftwood, detonation craters in the shingle and ghostly abandoned buildings seem to sit uneasily with the spectacular natural landscape. Traces of the island's past are slowly disappearing as material signs, relics and memories are battered and degraded by the elements and severe coastal erosion. The Orford Ness Lighthouse, which once stood on the shingle at the middle point of the island, was demolished in 2020 after it became vulnerable to the encroaching sea.[56] Yet many buildings remain as decaying monuments of twentieth-century warfare, provoking a heighted sense of the passage of time. Sophia Davis describes the highly visible decay in 'the palimpsest buildings repeatedly appropriated for a multiplicity of military and interpretative uses, and the juxtaposition of buildings from so many different times against one another – all of these [distance] you from the site, so the conjunction of science and warfare [appears] safely confined in the past.'[57]

The secret military history and the bleak, eroding landscape has long inspired artists, writers and filmmakers, many of whom seek to reinvigorate that elusive past and its relationship to the present. Through film, installation and writing, various forms of artistic representation have subtly challenged, or confirmed, Davis's 'distanced' viewer. Emily Richardson's film *Cobra Mist*, commissioned and broadcast by the UK's Channel 4 in 2008, explores the relationship between decaying military architecture and this eerie coastal landscape.[58] The soundtrack includes haunting recordings made by Chris Watson of gulls and howling winds. The now-demolished lighthouse appears half lost in sea mist. Over the centuries, eleven lighthouses have been built and destroyed on Orford Ness. In 2018 Robert MacFarlane and Stanley Donwood's prose poem and mystery play *Ness* provoked some impassioned responses. The writer Max Porter described the poem as resonant for our times: 'Beyond poetry, beyond the word, beyond the bomb – it is an aftertime song . . . It is a triumphant libretto of mythic modernism for our poisoned age. *Ness* is something else and always has been.'[59] 'Ness' and Orford Ness are thus perpetually positioned as dark and 'beyond', echoing through time yet eerily elusive, a status enhanced by its distinctive islandness.

This landscape offered rich possibilities for artists commissioned by Artangel to contribute a series of installations on the island in 2021. Supported by the National Trust and titled *Afterness* (inspired by a J. G. Ballard play on ideas of aftermath and emptiness), works by twelve artists were sited around and within the deserted buildings. After being closed to the public during the COVID-19 pandemic, Orford Ness was re-opened in the summer of 2021. Armed with maps and headphones, visitors followed the designated walk, which began at the ominously named Bomb Ballistics Building. *Afterness* included several sound pieces that accompanied the visitor along the prescribed route, including a series of poems by the Ukranian American poet Ilya Kaminsky titled *I See a Silence*.[60] A deaf writer, he describes sounds he is unable to hear, using words that echo the effects of Watson's earlier soundtrack for Richardson's *Cobra Mist*. This adds a further layer of strangeness to the viewing experience, inviting a synaesthetic response to the barren island landscape. Kaminsky seeks to merge visual and verbal representation to evoke sound in his short poems, including 'On This Clear Friday over the Shingle's Endless Path', which begins with the lines:

> I come to the shingle spit
> To watch
> How silence
> Hammers us
> ungrammars us
> In this morning's
> gull-white foam.[61]

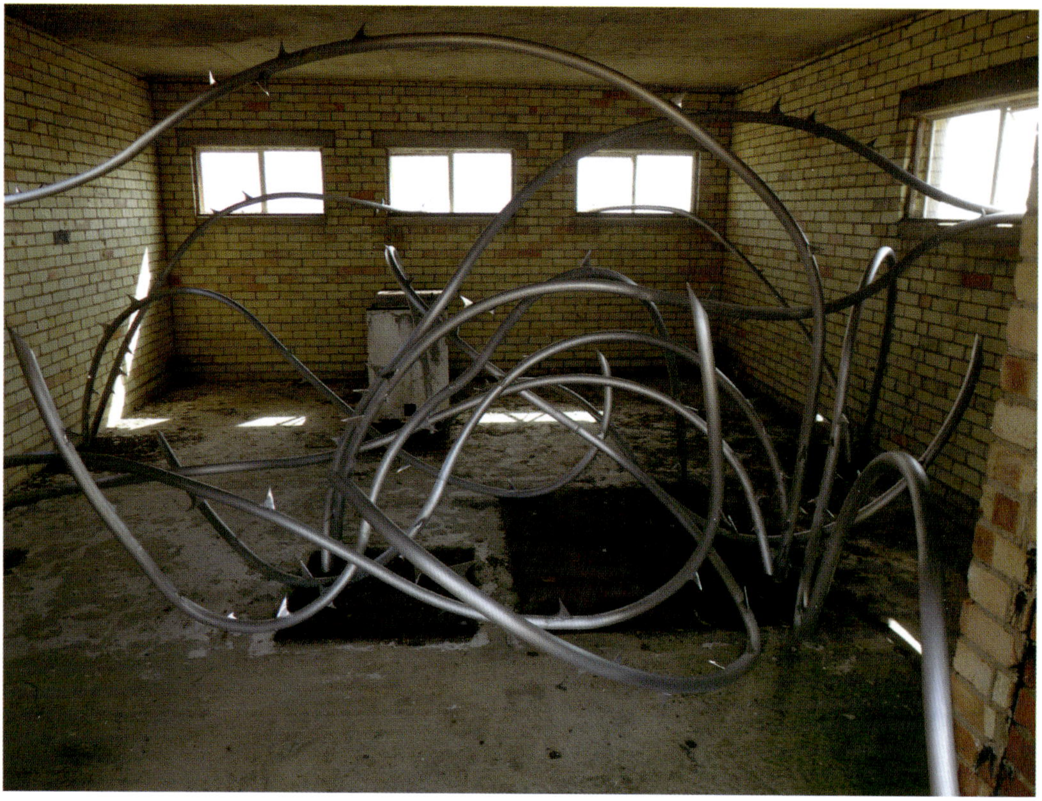

53 Alice Channer, *Lethality and Vulnerability*, exhibition view, *Afterness*, Orford Ness, Suffolk, 2021.

The British artist Alice Channer's installation *Lethality and Vulnerability*, a tangle of gigantic aluminium brambles pushing out of a decaying military shelter, evokes the surreal relationship between untamed nature and a sinister history (illus. 53). It also plays with scale, one of the most challenging spatial aspects of the Orford Ness experience. Unbroken shingle vistas can confuse our sense of size and distance. Channer (b. 1977) explodes the dimensions of her metallic brambles, welded with sharp thorns, as if to signal the contemporary relevance of these metonyms of warfare. Barbed wire carries powerful resonances of detention, reinforced by the isolation of the setting.

The 'distance from the past' evoked by eroding traces of military activity is also problematized by art projects that deploy memory through metonymic objects. The French Italian artist Tatiana Trouvé (b. 1968) took over one of the 'laboratories' built for the Atomic Weapons Research Establishment testing programme in the 1950s and '60s, filling it with household objects cast in bronze and aluminium. The site of *The Residents* was the abandoned Laboratory 1, a large, roofless structure with high cathedral-like walls. During the installation, the floor was often covered in pools of rainwater, weeds, nettles and building detritus. In this derelict space Trouvé positioned blankets, a suitcase, chairs, books and recording equipment, all cast in metal and periodically sinking into puddles (illus. 54). This tactile confusion was enhanced by diagrams of geological rock strata and scientific systems drawn onto the surface of blankets. Temporality is again confused as the viewer struggles to place the objects and their relationships with both the ruins and the wet undergrowth that seems to be slowly engulfing the installation. Trouvé carefully researched the effects of nuclear explosions on the environment and her post-apocalyptic abandoned space is approached on planks through damp, rain-soaked

54 Tatiana Trouvé, *The Residents*, exhibition view, *Afterness*, Orford Ness, Suffolk, 2021.

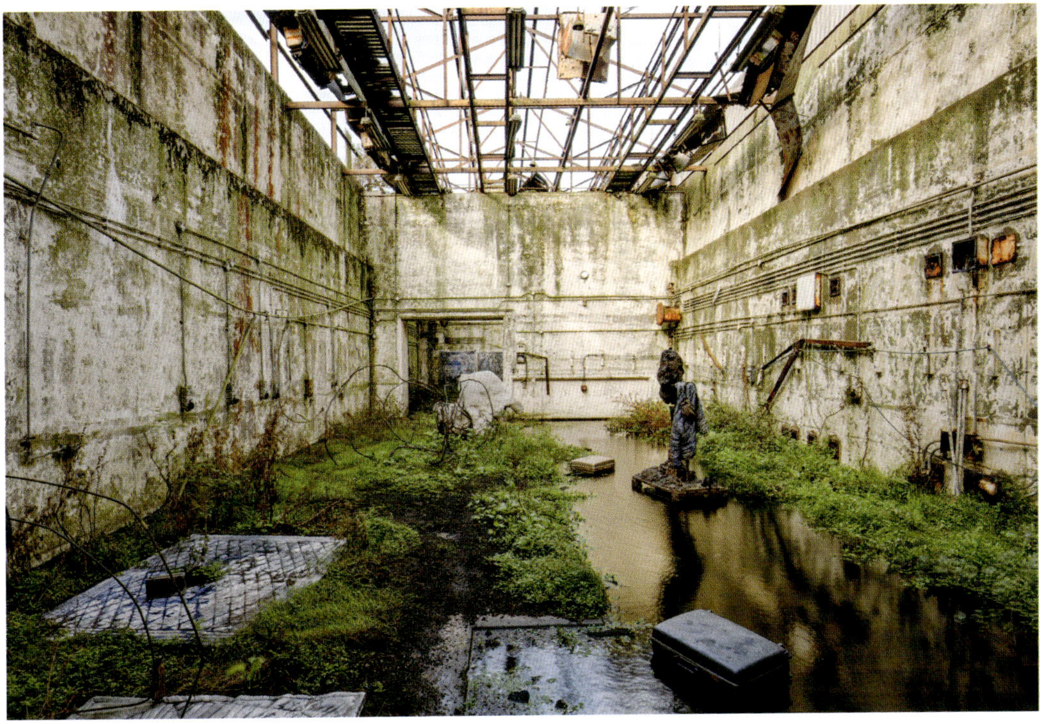

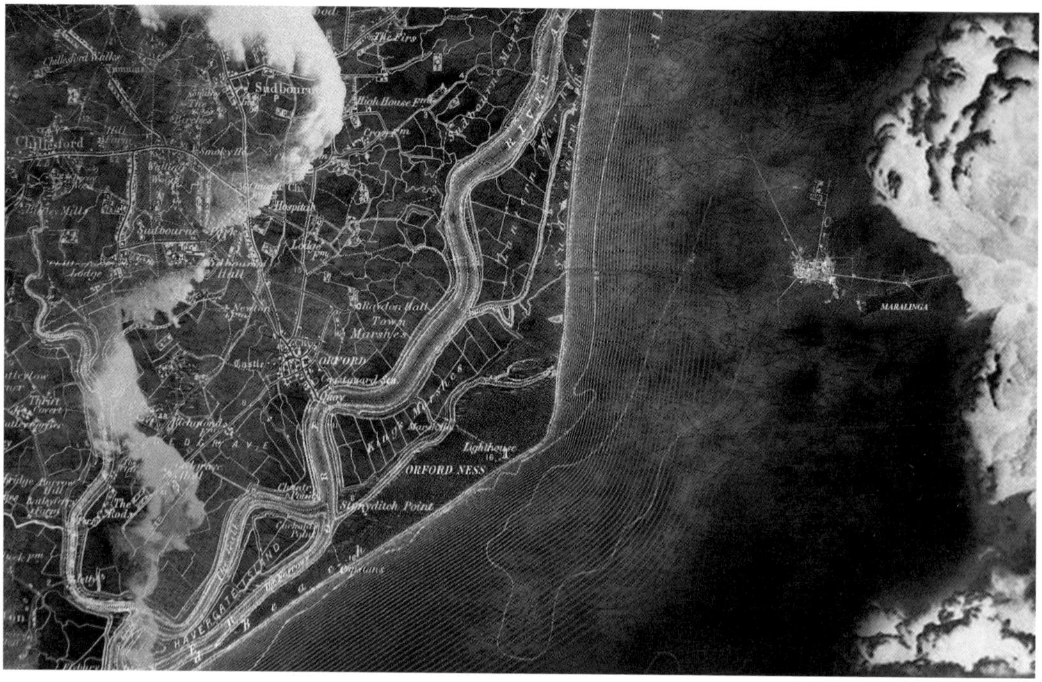

55 Emma McNally, *Untitled*, exclusive edition for Artangel, Orford Ness, 2021.

corridors, increasing an ominous sense of loss in the aftermath of some unspeakable event.

Following a path across the shingle from Laboratory 1, the visitor arrived at a hanger-like building called the Armoury, a huge, damp space once used to store armaments for atomic weapons research. In 2021 it housed a large installation by the British artist Emma McNally (b. 1969), *A river that flows nowhere, like a sea*. An immense mass of creased silvery-grey paper covered with graphite drawings, only visible by torchlight, occupied the floor space of the hanger, sitting like a rocky landmass from an alien planet. Minutely detailed drawings invoking the cosmos or geological formations cover the crumpled paper, positioned uneasily amidst walls stained with watery chemical trails from a previous secret life.

McNally's medium of graphite is a naturally occurring form of crystalline carbon, another veiled chemical reference that obliquely alludes to the role of carbon emissions in the current climate emergency. Graphite rods are also used to moderate the nuclear reactions required to manufacture

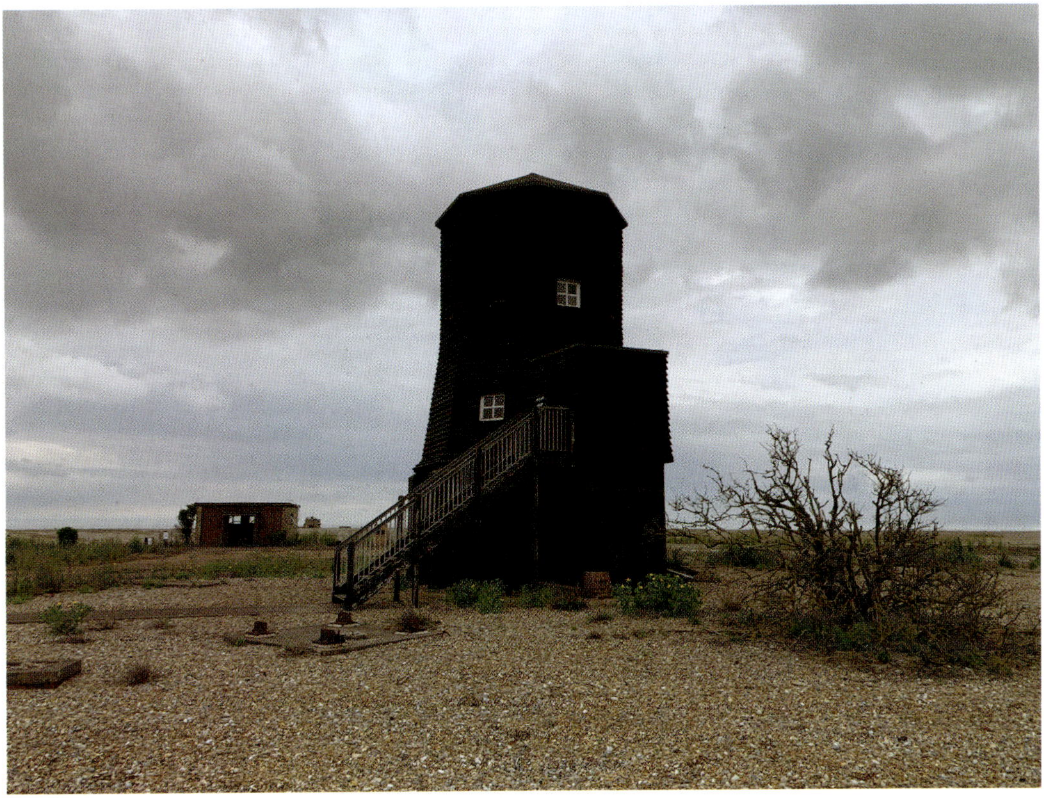

56 Black Beacon, Orford Ness, 2021.

weapons-grade plutonium. A print to accompany the installation, *Untitled*, shows a black-and-white map of Orford Ness and its Suffolk coastline superimposed with a map of Maralinga in Western Australia and images of atomic clouds (illus. 55). Dark military histories, the legacies of nuclear fall-out and the local environment are woven together to suggest an ominous contemporary relevance.

One of the most photographed landmarks on Orford Ness is Black Beacon, a wooden octagonal tower built in 1928 to house an experimental radio transmitter and develop radio navigation systems for aircraft (illus. 56).[62] Standing in the shingle like a windmill that has lost its sails, it became a library of sound for the duration of the *Afterness* project, echoing with field recordings from the island's present and secretive past, assembled by the British musicians Iain Chambers, Chris Watson and

Brian d'Souza. The sounds of skylarks and crunching pebbles, a rattling Control Room door and flapping plastic sheeting helped to envelop the octagonal space as visitors peered through viewing apertures, shaped like large letterboxes, to survey the surrounding landscape. Architectural details that suggest wartime surveillance were interwoven with sounds of shingle ridges, local wildlife and a ghostly, windswept military infrastructure. The invitation to engage with the relevance of the island's murky history to a myriad of contemporary developments (eroding coastlines, climate change, military surveillance and the experimental trials of nuclear weapons) is impossible to ignore as the visitor dutifully followed the designated path, or recklessly meandered off-piste.

The islandness of Orford Ness and the Isle of Portland, along with many other vulnerable small islands across the world, is often bound up with dark military purposes and their progressive disappearances as landmasses. Apart from impending inundation and floods, intense forms of exploitation, including tourism, mining, extractivism, pollution and military experiments, can hasten their watery demise, and the demise of their vulnerable inhabitants. Timely artistic interventions can both engage our imagination and increase our awareness of such vulnerabilities, albeit tempered by the knowledge that the future of these islands is ultimately determined by geopolitical and environmental battles on a global scale.

4 ISLAND DETENTIONS

Islands have long served as ideal locations for prisons and penal colonies. In the twenty-first century many Italian, Greek and Spanish islands in the Mediterranean have become sites for internment camps and detention 'hot spots' for migrants and asylum seekers to the European Union. Moreover, during the recent global pandemic the notion of a 'plague island' was topical; the suitability of islands as spaces for the isolation of diseased or contaminated communities, such as leprosy sufferers or the mentally ill, continues to carry resonance.

THE GEOGRAPHY OF SOCIAL CONTROL

Many famous islands, some positioned within reach of the mainland, have been used as strategic prison sites. For example, Robben Island off Cape Town on the southwest coast of South Africa, Alcatraz off the western coast of the United States and the French-owned Devil's Island (Ile du Diable) off French Guiana are among the best-known island detentions used to incarcerate political and high-security prisoners.[1] As the criminologist Jude McCulloch writes:

> The geography of the island, cut off from the mainland and by implication the mainstream of life, captures the radical separation of prisoners and prisons from outside society. The metaphorical use of island may also point back to history where literal islands were more frequently used to imprison the ill, the insane and those reproduced as criminals in societies divided along 'race', class and gender.[2]

The history and mythology that surrounds such sites is enmeshed with national and geopolitical ambitions. Islands and archipelagos often feature in critiques of power relations explored by political geographers, demonstrated by the steady growth of this discipline within Island Studies. As the geographer Alison Mountz has shown, 'the complex structures of power, territoriality, and governance on islands have captured the attention of political geographers.'[3] Criminologists are also drawn to the theme, exploring ideas of cultural isolation in the provision of spaces for the punishment of crimes.[4] The appeal of island prison sites for filmmakers, novelists and artists is often located within a more subjective spatial imaginary, rich with metaphorical and allegorical potential.

Some of the best-known prisons have inspired popular novels and cinematic dramatizations of incarceration and escape. From 1852 to 1953 Devil's Island was an appallingly harsh French penal colony for high-security and political prisoners, best known for the imprisonment of the French artillery officer Alfred Dreyfus, who was falsely accused of spying for Germany (illus. 57). The Dreyfus Affair was a scandal exposing French military and political corruption and antisemitism that rocked the Third Republic between 1894 and 1906. Although French 'convicts' were usually sent to New Caledonia, Dreyfus was sent to the more punitive Devil's Island Prison and condemned to solitary confinement. This setting was synonymous in the popular imagination with a death sentence – a horrific incarceration that only the strong could survive.[5] The Dreyfus Affair appealed to successive generations of filmmakers, including José Ferrer, who directed *I Accuse!* (1958), which also served as an allegorical commentary on McCarthyism. Roman Polanski's 2019 film *An Officer and a Spy* (French title: *J'Accuse*), based on Robert Harris's book of the same name and starring Jean Dujardin, focuses on the corrupt and fraudulent activities of the Parisian government and the political battles that ensued, with the horrors of the inescapable island prison as a background motif.[6] In contrast, Henri Charrière's modern memoire *Papillon* (1969) vividly describes – and mythologizes – the author's (now contested) periods of imprisonment on, and escape from, Devil's Island, and was adapted for cinema in

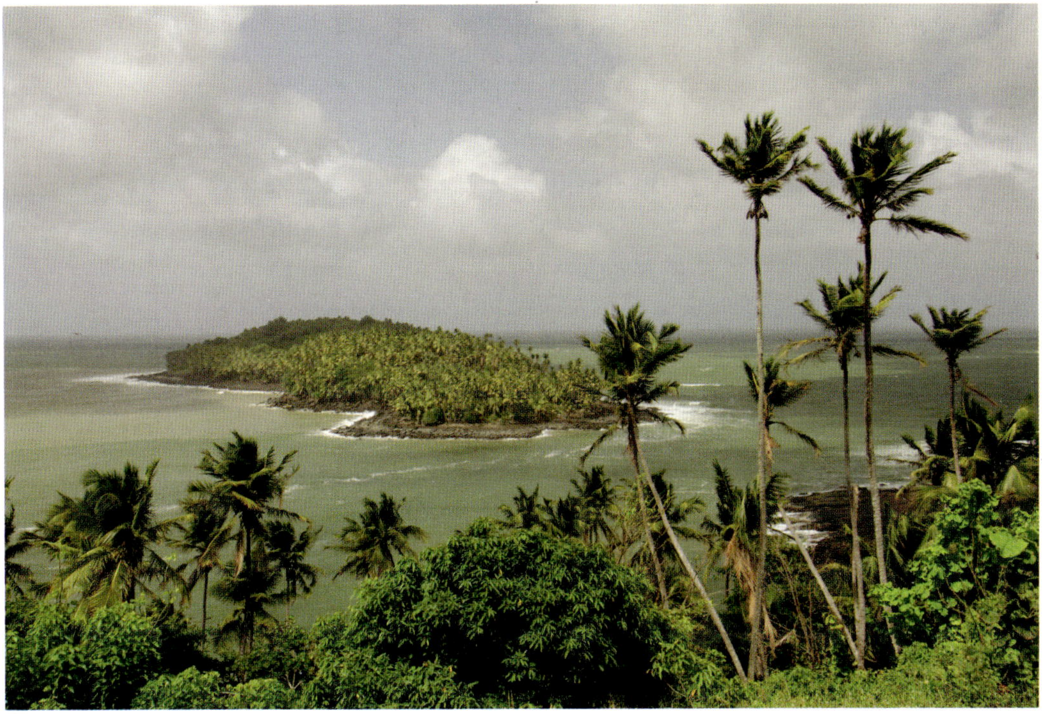

57 View of Devil's Island, French Guiana.

a popular film in 1973 directed by Franklin J. Schaffner and starring Steve McQueen (Charrière) and Dustin Hoffman (Louis Dega). After a successful escape followed by a recapture, and horrendous spells in solitary confinement echoing the experience of Dreyfus, Papillon (who bears a butterfly tattoo) makes a final escape to freedom, and lives to tell the tale.[7]

Most successful cinematic representations focus on the horrors endured and spectacular escapes from the island made by masculine heroes.[8] The triumph of the (albeit tarnished) individual against the establishment – often symbolized by the harsh island environment – is a recurring theme. In film and literature prison islands often invert the idea of the island idyll, reconceiving the space as inhospitable, inaccessible and subject to fierce institutional control. For example, Franz Kafka's novel *In the Penal Colony* of 1914 offers a deeply pessimistic meditation on justice, guilt and innocence in a space circumscribed by its unnamed and desolate island setting. A 'Traveller' is invited to witness an elaborate execution device. Through its very remoteness, the geography enables an abuse of power – the execution of a soldier who has committed a minor offence.[9] As the Dreyfus Affair demonstrated, island locations can enable such flagrant abuses.

Moreover, the powerful metaphor of the 'Gulag Archipelago' of maximum-security prisons appropriates the island/archipelago theme to represent a highly constructed and enforced isolation, often located within a prosperous state. The French cultural historian Michel Foucault explores isolation as a repressive tool often deployed by liberal democracies in his influential study of the development and workings of modern prisons, *Discipline and Punish* (1975). As he argues, power over the prisoner can be exercised through isolation from both the external world and other prisoners.[10] Island prisons are often designed to enable these multiple layers of repressive isolation. The critical power of visual art to represent such repressive island regimes is an ongoing subject of debate. As I show below, artists and filmmakers often negotiate a tricky relationship between 'documentary' and more imaginative, associative or allegorical forms of representation.

BOATS AND MEDITERRANEAN CEMETERIES

Wars and uprisings in the Middle East, widespread poverty, conflict zones and repressive regimes in Africa have led to an increase in the influx of migrants and refugees into Europe, often by boat to Mediterranean islands. What T. J. Demos has described as '*crisis globalization*, designating an era of growing economic inequality' and a rise in migration, has increased security procedures at European borders and caused a political storm within the European Union.[11] The geographers Alison Mountz and Linda Briskman have argued that the supposed remoteness of islands can be ambiguous, or even enabling, when they are the chosen destinations of migrants: 'Far from isolated, the very geography of islands means that migrants travelling by boat often land on islands as the furthest and closest bit of sovereign territory they can reach once they leave home.'[12] For example, migrants travelling from countries in northern Africa often land on islands such as Lampedusa, which although far from their sovereign mainland (Italy), are closest to the migrants' country of origin. Over the last few decades Mediterranean islands such as Lampedusa, Sicily and Lesbos have become sites of local political conflict because they are inhabited by both refugee occupants of ironically named 'welcome centres' and those who live illegally on the islands: 'the ones identified in the news as refugees, migrants, asylum seekers – as people on the move with or without legal or political rights.'[13] These 'noncitizens' often live abandoned and invisible lives. Far more visible is the trauma and tragedy that often accompanies the journey to a refugee island. After a peak in arrivals (partly from Syria and Libya) in 2015, disturbing images of such journeys were disseminated across the world's media.

Digital technology has enabled press photographs to have instant global visibility, such as the shocking image of the dead body of three-year-old Alan Kurdi tragically washed up on a beach near Bodrum, Turkey, in September 2015. Researchers at the University of Sheffield estimated that at the height of its circulation this distressing photograph reached 20 million people around the world in twelve hours.[14] It became a defining image of the Syrian refugee crisis and provoked a series of imitative art projects across the world, including the Chinese dissident artist Ai Weiwei's controversial re-enactment when he photographed himself in the same pose on a beach on Lesbos in January 2016.[15] By 2016 'the migration crisis' had become an important topic for artists, although the representation of migrant shipwrecks and ensuing deaths is vulnerable to the accusation of creating popular spectacle out of trauma. The question of how to use artistic representation to mediate such tragedies, presenting works that both enable an imaginative engagement and can challenge political orthodoxies, haunts the theme. Intensely political issues of detention, death at sea and nomadism have encouraged the evolution of new artistic strategies that do more than just document history, sometimes inviting public intervention.

A year after Kurdi's death the Chilean-born artist Alfredo Jaar (b. 1956) wrote in the *Art Newspaper* of his concern that while Kurdi's image was published on the front pages of newspapers around the world in September 2015, over the following year so many bodies were washed up on the same beach but remained invisible. In response he quotes *La Stampa* journalist Mario Calabresi, who wrote an editorial titled 'The Beach Where Europe Dies' (illus. 58). In it, Calabresi notes: 'This photograph demands that each and every one of us should stop for a moment and face what is happening on the beaches where we spend our vacations. We cannot procrastinate; dodge between our fears and impulses of compassion. This is the last chance for Europe's leaders to live up to the challenge of history.'[16] With various migrant tragedies in mind, Jaar used his project *The Gift* to invite an active collective response. At Art Basel in 2016 volunteers distributed 12,000 blue cardboard boxes, offering them as gifts, with instructions to open and refold each box inside out, turning them into both artworks and donation boxes (illus. 59). The project was organized in collaboration with the Migrant Offshore Aid Station (MOAS), a charity dedicated to saving lives at sea, established by an Italian American couple. While sailing a yacht in the Mediterranean they had encountered abandoned clothes floating on the sea, traces of refugees both drowned and rescued. They discovered that according to Italian law, it was illegal to rescue refugees without a permit issued from Rome. The encounter marked a turning point in the couple's life, and MOAS was set up to acquire drones to check for boats in distress, enabling rapid communication with Rome for the issue of permits. The project raised more than €500,000 to support this work; Jaar advocated a participatory, 'realistic' approach to what he saw as an ethical problem.[17] Unlike the more representational strategies adopted by Ai Weiwei and others, Jaar tied *The Gift* directly to that of an NGO, identifying a social and political need to use art to engage a wider public.

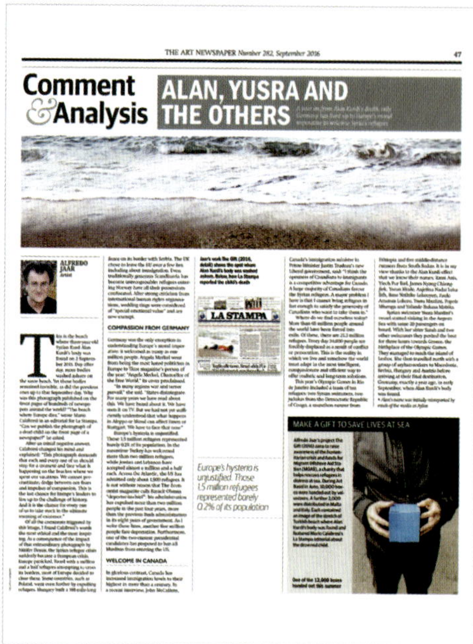
THE ART NEWSPAPER Number 282, September 2016 47

Comment & Analysis

ALAN, YUSRA AND THE OTHERS

ALFREDO JAAR

COMPASSION FROM GERMANY

LA STAMPA

Europe's hysteria is unjustified. Those 1.5 million refugees represented barely 0.2% of its population

WELCOME IN CANADA

MAKE A GIFT TO SAVE LIVES AT SEA

58 Alfredo Jaar, *The Art Newspaper*, no. 282 (September 2016).

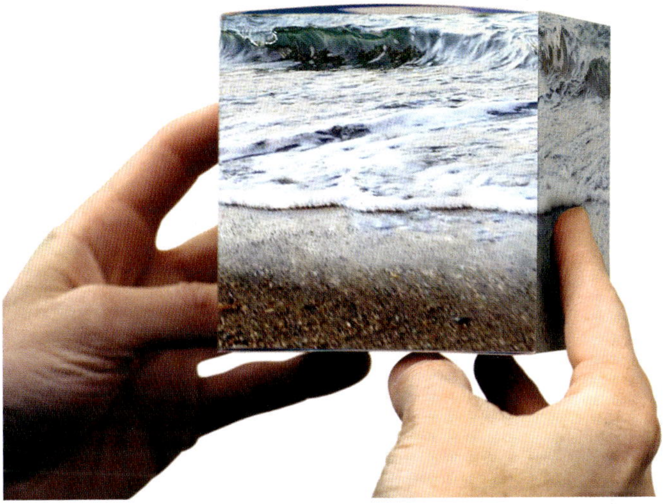

59 Alfredo Jaar, *The Gift*, 2016, public intervention, Basel.

Many Mediterranean islands have become locales for an ongoing humanitarian crisis, in direct conflict with their roles as desirable tourist havens. The Greek island of Lesbos is renowned for its idyllic beaches and mythological history as the birthplace of Sappho. Tourist fantasies were punctured when the island became a key point of entry into the European Union for thousands of refugees, especially from the Syrian civil war. A media storm followed its transformation into an immigration 'hot spot', a development not lost on Ai Weiwei (b. 1957). He set up a studio on Lesbos in 2016 to support several projects that highlighted the refugee crisis, including his installation *Law of the Journey*, first shown at the National Museum in Prague in 2017. A black 70-metre (230 ft) inflatable dinghy containing 258 oversized, faceless refugee figures was displayed in the centre of a long gallery, a direct response to the events that he had witnessed on Lesbos in 2016 (illus. 60). Deceptively literal in its subject-matter, the representation of hundreds of faceless, depersonalized Black figures references the precarity of a sea journey in such an overcrowded craft heading for an island destination. Boats (both insecure dinghies and rescue boats) have become key symbols of the migration crisis and its dependence on island 'detentions'. They are metonymic 'vessels' of migration, survival and loss. Ai Weiwei's dinghy itself appears like a long, floating island, suspended

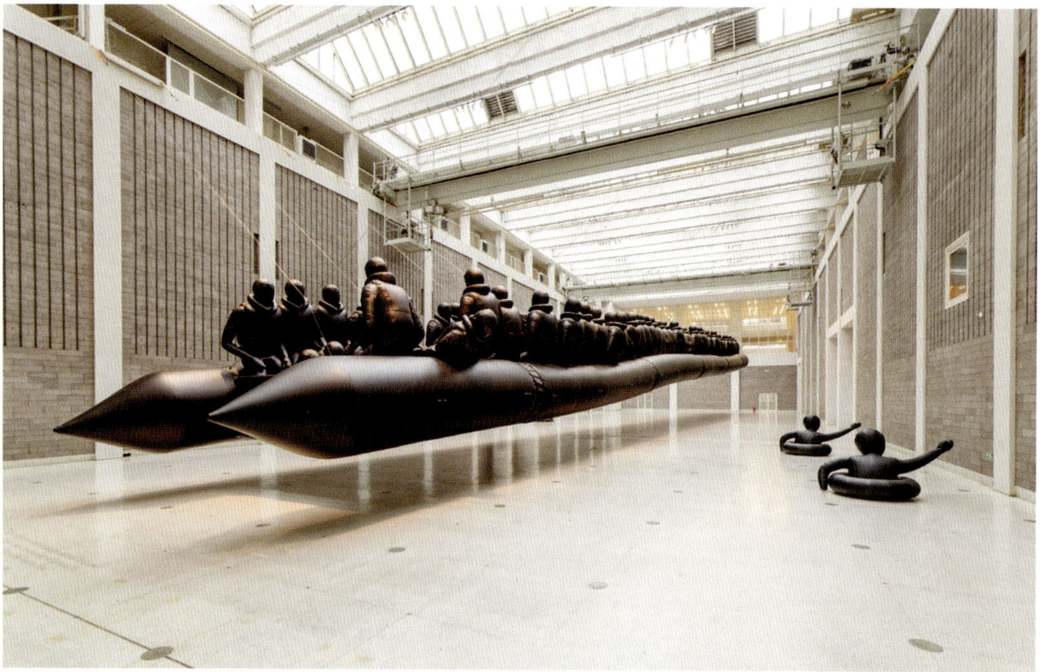

60 Ai Weiwei, *Law of the Journey*, 2017, inflatable rubber boat with 258 oversized refugee figures.

along the floor like a Noah's Ark, albeit a container that is always overloaded (literally and metaphorically). Even the Prague museum space added to its symbolic charge; the hall was a former Trade Fair Palace used in 1939–41 as a gathering point for Jews who were being deported to the concentration camp in Terezin – a resonant site of mass exodus and statelessness. Lesbos soon boasted one of the worst refugee camps in Europe.[18] Fire destroyed large swathes of the site in 2020, causing chaos and homelessness. A new camp was built in Vastria, and some refugees were evacuated to the mainland. Local protests, political pressure from the right and the increasing criminalization of refugees contributed to a social emergency on the island. Kostas Moutzouris, the regional governor for the Aegean islands, has been quoted as saying: 'The EU wants to keep the problem away, to give it to Greece . . . And Greece, they want to keep it to the islands, not the rest of the country.'[19]

This political role as both safe haven and island detention is referenced more obliquely in the work of the Irish filmmaker Richard Mosse

(b. 1980), who used a thermographic imaging camera to create unnerving, spectral scenes of migrants boarding rescue boats from rubber dinghies on and around the Greek islands in his multi-screen *Incoming* (2016; illus. 61). By deploying military-grade cameras that use heat signatures, Mosse references the technology of surveillance and control, co-opted here to reveal the victims of global inequality and political oppression. Produced in Europe, the Middle East and North Africa, his haunting monochrome film also documents the precarious journeys that precede the arrival of rescue boats on the Greek islands. Bleached-out crepuscular figures board a ship from an overcrowded inflatable dingy; in one sequence emergency workers try to revive victims of a boat disaster near the Port of Molyvos in Lesbos. Mosse's thermal imaging can be seen to echo the so-called scopic effects of modern media, in which the dispossessed subject is anonymized and politicized.[20] His work evokes the increasingly dehumanized surveillance imagery of refugees, often presented as a stateless 'problem' to be detained and marginalized – a 'noncitizen'. The title also references the growing hostility towards 'foreigners' within some increasingly xenophobic

61 Richard Mosse, *Incoming*, 2016, three-channel black and white digital video, 52 minutes, 10 seconds (looped), #293, digital C-print on metallic paper.

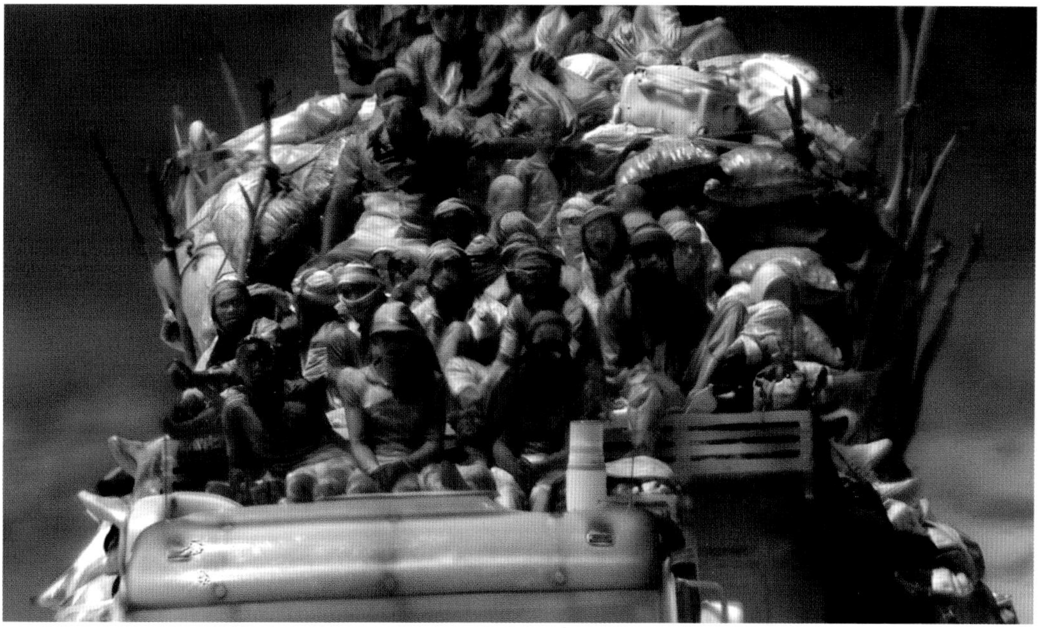

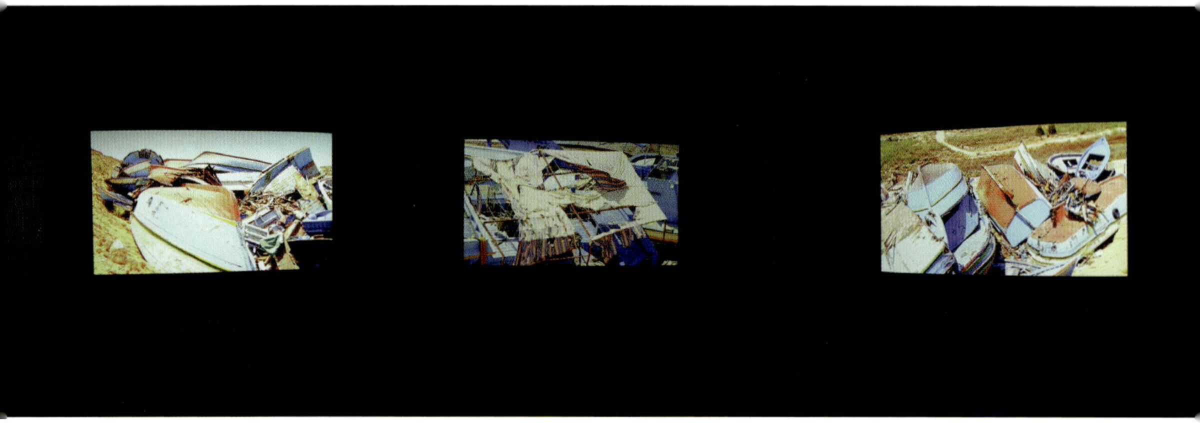

62 Isaac Julien, *Western Union: Small Boats*, 2007, three-screen projection, 35 mm colour film, DVD/HD transfer, 5.1 SR sound, 18 minutes, 22 seconds; installation view, Milwaukee Art Museum, 2012.

European communities. Mosse explains: 'I chose the title "Incoming", not only because it evokes the idea of incoming fire – prompting a defensive "little Britain" mentality of fear, currently prevalent – but also because it predicates a particular subject-object relation. The refugee is "incoming" from a European perspective.'[21] And refugees are always incoming from the perspective of those islands designated as detention centres.

Boats and their symbolic 'graveyards' on the Italian islands of Sicily and Lampedusa are key themes in works of film by the British Caribbean artist Isaac Julien (b. 1960) (*Western Union: Small Boats*, 2007) and the British artists Adam Broomberg and Oliver Chanarin (*The Bureaucracy of Angels*, 2017) (illus. 62, 63). Isaac's multi-screen film, which deploys his characteristically lavish footage, is set in both Sicily and Lampedusa and explores the global history of African migration and its impact on the individual. The film immerses the viewer in a vivid combination of image and sound and juxtaposed tableaux, with dancers playing migrants. In one sequence a Black man carries a white man over his shoulders walking over sun-bleached rocks, reversing the traditional trope of the white rescuer of Black (migrant) bodies. Tourists are filmed bathing while clothing floats in the sea, and dead bodies are shown lined up along the beach. As part of this juxtaposition of beauty and tragedy, Julien pays homage to Luchino Visconti's film *The Leopard* (1963), including footage of the opulent Lampedusa Palazzo Valguarnera-Gangi, in which the Italian film is set.

Julien also made a second single-screen version of his work: *The Leopard* (*Western Union: Small Boats*) (2007), which focuses on the Palazzo Gangi and its magnificent ballroom. Julien persistently reappropriates cinema:

> As much as I work to disentangle myself from the genre, cinema remains my home and my reference. So *Western Union: Small Boats* takes place in Italy and makes allusions to the afterlife of Italian film. Sicilian histories have been mythologised on screen for decades; I wanted to try to have a conversation with that . . . I used the same spaces in *Western Union*, but I was talking about another population [of African migrants].[22]

While some reviewers criticized the slightly incongruous quality of sensuality applied to a traumatic voyage, others welcomed this combination of opulent Lampedusa architecture with harrowing sea journeys.[23] The film provides a resonant contrast between privileged and rich visual history, and a modern Sicilian geography of fractured borders and displaced

63 Adam Broomberg and Oliver Chanarin, *The Bureaucracy of Angels*, 2017, film still.

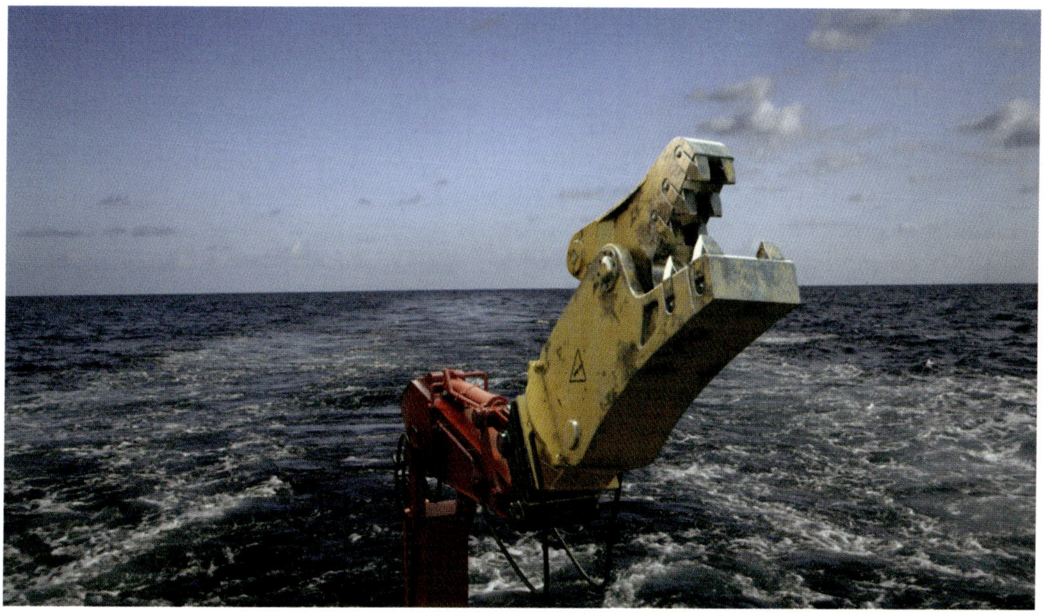

racial identities. The affective power of film is once again positioned in a fluid space of re-presentation, appropriating and juxtaposing languages that are both mythologized and powerfully 'realistic'.

Less opulent in its range of Sicilian references, *The Bureaucracy of Angels* is a single-screen twelve-minute film first shown to the transient audience at Kings Cross Station, London, in 2017. Made ten years after *Western Union*, when the tragic effects of the European refugee crisis were increasingly visible to a global audience, *The Bureacracy of Angels* records the demise of one hundred migrant boats abandoned on the concrete forecourt of Porto Pozzallo, Sicily. After being taken in by rescue boats, their desperate occupants had either been returned to North Africa or absorbed into the Italian asylum system. The film follows a hydraulic digger as it tears apart abandoned vessels in the local boatyard. The jaws of the digger are shown menacing arriving boats in a rescue operation filmed off the coast of Libya. The soundtrack is performed by a Cantastoria, or 'singing storyteller', who sings the Sicilian ballad *Terra ca nun senti* (You Unfeeling Land). Composed and recorded by the London Sinfonietta, the ballad tells of the tragedies experienced in immigration to and from Europe's islands over the last 150 years. Both monstrous and somehow playful, the menacing digger appears to dance to the rhythms of the local song, set against the landscape of a vast shipping graveyard. Using the key motifs of abandoned boats and a digger against a Sicilian soundtrack, *The Bureaucracy of Angels* performs an artful reimagining of the horrors and legacies of migration, and the metonymic forms of destruction that have redefined the island of Sicily.

The island of Lampedusa, not far from the east coast of North Africa, was the European destination of many tragic migrant voyages during the 2010s, at which point the island's beaches were transformed into fields of abandoned boats. The catastrophic fire and subsequent sinking of a fishing boat carrying migrants (originally from Eritrea, Somalia and Ghana) from Misrata, Libya, in October 2013 resulted in a death toll of more than 360. Only 155 were thought to have survived the crossing. The exploitation and horrors involved grabbed headlines in the worlds' press, but after a second shipwreck near Lampedusa that month there were impassioned cries (albeit with different objectives) from politicians and refugee charities to address the problem, including from the prime minister of Malta, who stated: 'As things stand we are building a cemetery within our Mediterranean sea.'[24] At the time, Lampedusa islanders rallied around the surviving refugees, supplying food and clothes without waiting for local authority funding. A local carpenter, Francesco Tuccio, moved by the plight of refugees he met in his church, used wood from the wreckage to make small pendant crosses for the survivors.

After witnessing this craft-based transformation of the relics of the refugee crisis, a curator from the British Museum in London commissioned a larger cross, made from the same shipwrecked wood. *The Lampedusa Cross* (2015; illus. 64) was then repositioned as a significant artwork, displayed prominently among the treasures of this prestigious national museum and anthropomorphized in a poem by Nicholas Murray as 'holding its arms outstretched' to offer comfort to survivors.[25] In 2021 the *Cross* toured various British museums, galleries and churches around the UK, where it was accompanied by a small installation of twelve miniature boats made by the Syrian-born artist Issam Kourbaj, part of a series titled *Dark Water, Burning World*. Tiny boats were made of upcycled bicycle mudguards and packed with burned matchsticks, an obvious reference to the fire on the Libyan fishing boat. *The Lampedusa Cross* helped to frame the island's recent history as a site of traumatic memory, albeit mediated by a disarmingly simple example of religious symbolism. As a metonym for Lampedusa's peculiar islandness, it is an object now (over)loaded with meaning.

In April 2015 a 27-metre (90 ft) fishing boat loaded with migrants on a voyage between Libya and Lampedusa collided with a vessel that had responded to a distress call. The tragedy remains one of the Mediterranean's deadliest disasters, in which over eight hundred people are thought to have perished. Only 28 survived.[26] In 2016 the boat was recovered by the Italian government and taken to the Sicilian naval base of Melilli, where bodies trapped inside were finally removed. The hull was eventually released to the *Barca Nostra* (Our Ship) project, a partnership between the Swiss

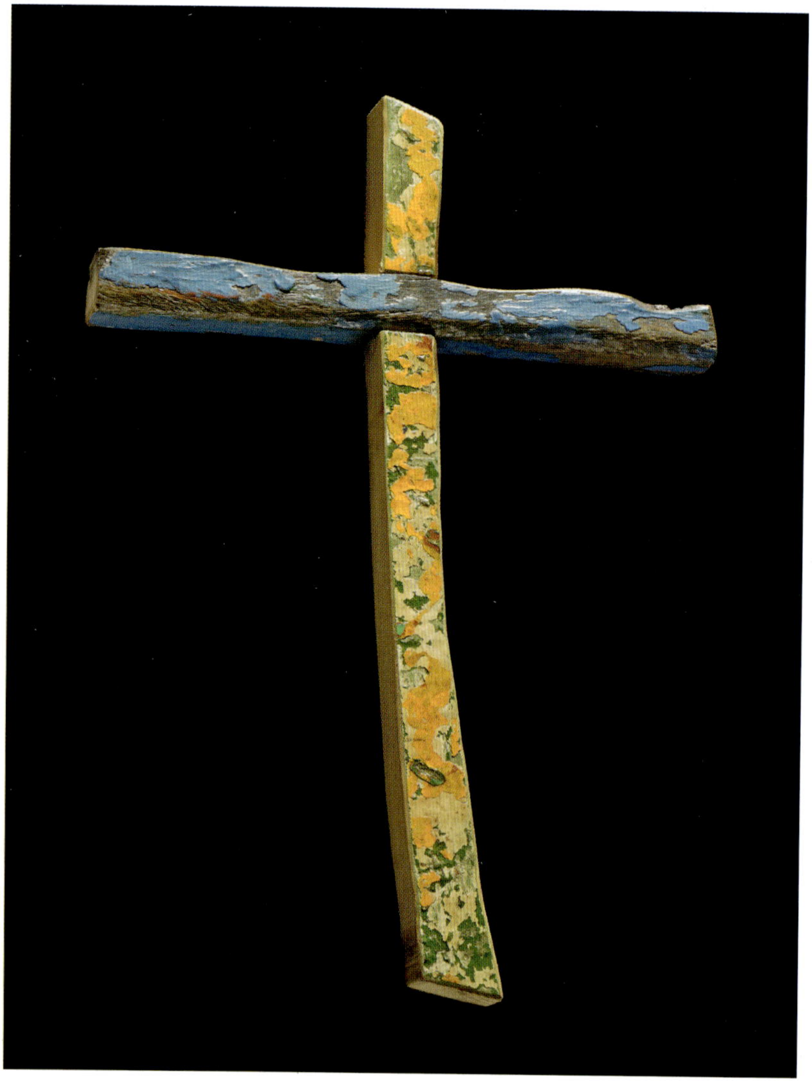

64 Francesco Tuccio, *The Lampedusa Cross*, 2015, wood.

Icelandic artist Christoph Büchel (b. 1966) and the Sicilian town council of Augusta, among others. For the duration of the 58th Venice Biennale in 2019, the ship was positioned at the city's medieval Arsenale (illus. 65). It became the Biennale's most controversial exhibit. Büchel refused all signage and interviews, denying audiences any clues as to its status as 'art'. While some attacked the lack of information on the ship's history and context, turning it into a crude spectacle for selfies, others applauded this ambiguity. Reviewer Matthew Collings described the boat as 'a sign among signs', reminding his readers that the Biennale is all 'rich and privileged fun', and that the boat also represents 'separation, the remnants of a physical object standing for those excluded from the fun. Not just the ones that died for it, but the part of the world exploited to create the extra wealth for all this fun.'[27] The Arsenale is the home of Venice's coastguard, whose tasks include policing Italian waters to keep migrants out. The *Barca Nostra* became an important signifier of a humanitarian crisis that now defines the islandness of so many Mediterranean tourist attractions. As in the histories of Pacific Oceania and the Caribbean, seagoing vessels can act as metonyms for experiences of diaspora, migration and trade. In visual representation they are a recurring motif, a 'sign of signs' rich in local and global meanings.[28]

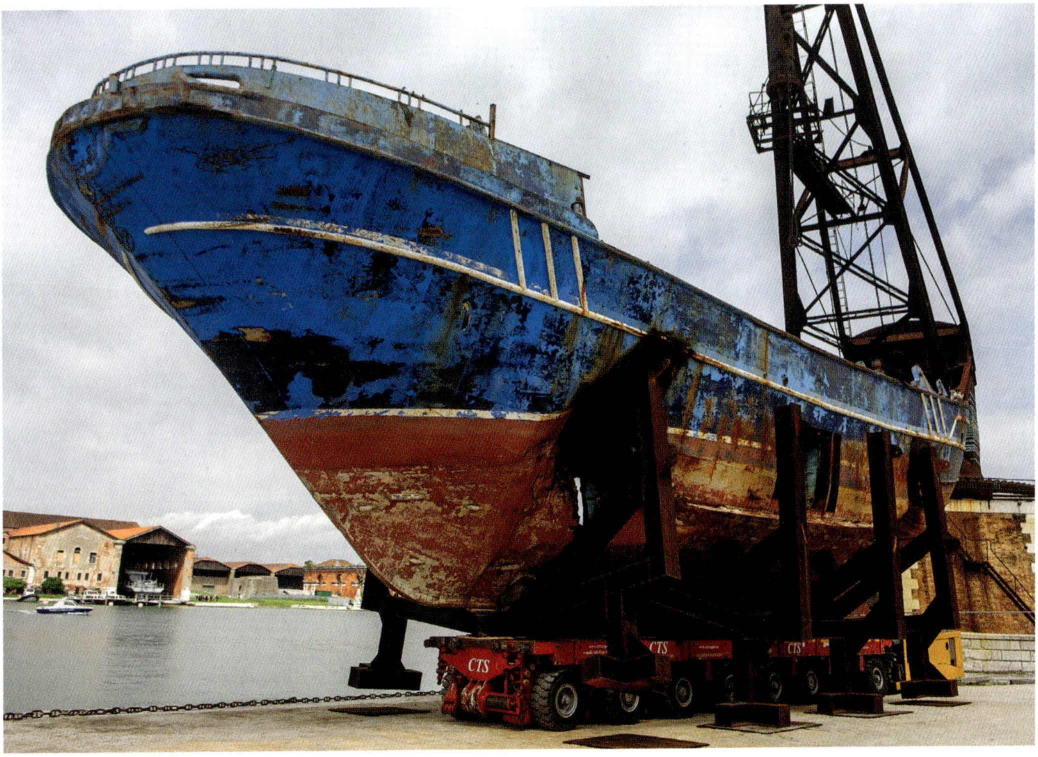

65 Christoph Büchel's migrant boat seen at the Arsenale during the 58th Venice Biennale, 2019.

PLAGUE ISLANDS AND UNDERDOGS

As a busy port of call and transit point between east and west, Venice (itself an archipelago linked by canals and lagoons) has always been vulnerable to infectious diseases, especially the bubonic plague. In the fifteenth century the city developed sophisticated systems for checking ships and isolating the sick on its network of surrounding islands. The English word 'quarantine' (allegedly the most used word of 2020–21) comes from the Italian word *quarantena*, a variant of the *quaranta giorni* (forty days) used in fourteenth- and fifteenth-century Venetian dialect and designating the number of days needed to isolate infectious patients, including those with the plague. Venice was among the first places to make provisions to control the spread of this disease, and one of the first recorded quarantine sites to include a plague hospital, or *lazaretto*, set up in 1423, was the island of Santa Maria di Nazareth.[29]

Poveglia is another famous quarantine island on the Venice Lagoon, located between the city and the Lido and known as one of the 'scariest places on earth' (illus. 66).[30] In 1645 the Venetian government began building octagonal forts on the island to protect and control entrances to the Lagoon. From the late eighteenth century it became a checkpoint for goods and people and was established as a quarantine station for the plague and other infectious diseases; sick sailors approaching Venice were allegedly forced to abandon their ships and left to die on Poveglia. In 1922 the site was converted into a mental hospital, and subsequently a long-term care facility, closed in 1968. Largely abandoned over the last few decades, the surviving buildings, including a church and an asylum, are now mostly derelict. Excavations around the island have revealed an estimated 160,000 people buried in plague pits. Poveglia is shrouded in myths of alleged hauntings by unfortunate inhabitants incarcerated by disease or mental illness, and rumours abound about the fate of victims of crude lobotomies.[31] This dark history as one of the world's most famous 'plague islands' has inspired a host of literary and cinematic references. For example, Thomas Simpson's novel *Blackened* (2020) features a group of tourists in Venice who become infatuated with the nearby island of Poveglia, to

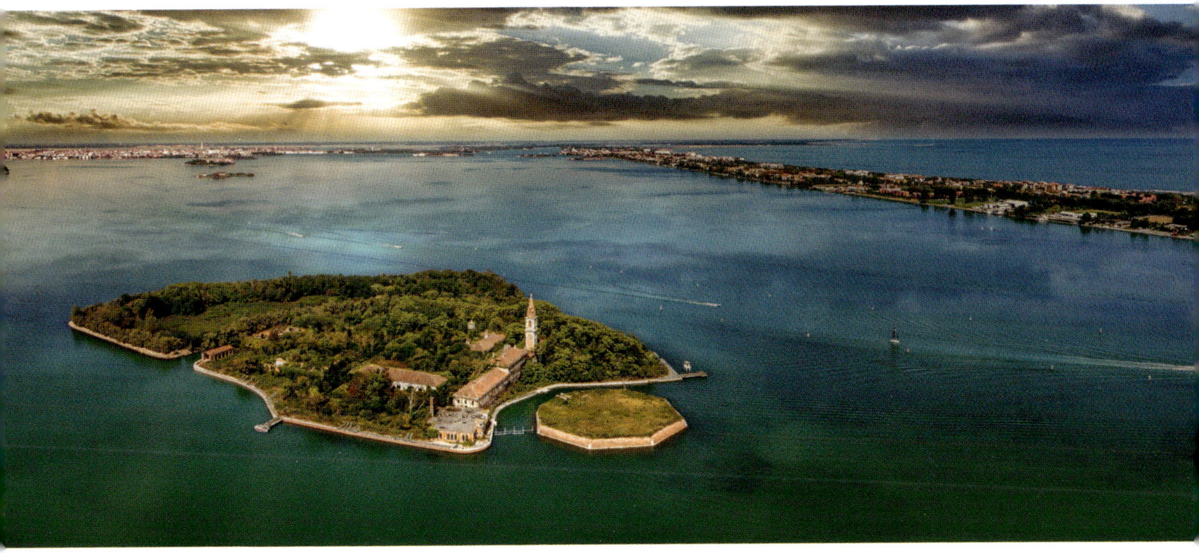

66 Aerial view of the island of Poveglia in the Venetian lagoon.

which journeys are prohibited. Determined to get there, they encounter a grisly, ghostly history. A looser association is suggested in the British writer Anthony Horowitz's *Alex Rider* series, in which the fictional island of Malagosto, just outside Venice, is the main assassin training centre for the notorious criminal organization Scorpia.[32]

The forced incarceration of mentally ill patients in an island institution is one of the themes of Martin Scorsese's psychological thriller *Shutter Island* (2010). Based on Dennis Lehane's 2003 novel of the same name, it explores the mystery of a missing patient (Rachel Solando) from the Ashecliffe Hospital for the Criminally Insane on the island, located in Boston Harbor. Deputy U.S. Marshal Edward 'Teddy' Daniels (Leonardo DiCaprio), assigned to investigate the missing person, uncovers a macabre history of incarcerated patients and experiments in lobotomy. The geography of the island, with its steep cliffs and inclement weather, frames a psychologically draining narrative of insanity, imprisonment and the abuse of disturbed patients. *Shutter Island* represents the power of the trope of the island as a space of fear and containment. Both book and film have been read as representing a Foucauldian notion of the 'docile body', as defined in *Discipline and Punish*. That is, modern human beings (bodies) that are controlled and disciplined by the power relations of the prison hospital or mental institution.[33] The inhospitable island setting frames an institution that exercises repressive disciplinary techniques.[34] Islandness is reconceived here as an inescapable space of incarceration, isolation and control.

The use of the island geography to contain disease has inspired a more playful cinematic production, described by one critic as a 'cracking canine caper'.[35] The lead characters in Wes Anderson's (b. 1969) controversial animated film *Isle of Dogs* (2018) are a band of scraggy outlawed dogs with names such as Spots, Chief, Rex, King, Boss, Jupiter and Duke (illus. 67).[36] In a dystopian Japan of the future, the mayor of Megasaki has expelled all dogs to an island filled with mainland detritus, following the outbreak of a canine dog flu. Seen as unclean and potentially diseased, the dogs are forcibly exiled to the foul garbage dump of the Japanese archipelago. The film can be seen as a bleak, if humorous, reference to the xenophobic and discriminatory tendencies of modern societies that seek to exclude and demean those deemed to have 'underdog' status. Abuse of political power and the manipulation of fake news are themes embodied by Mayor Kobayashi and his discriminatory tactics. Atari, the mayor's twelve-year-old nephew, pilots a small plane in a rescue bid to find his beloved Spots, once his loyal bodyguard. Helped by the pack of dog leaders, proudly

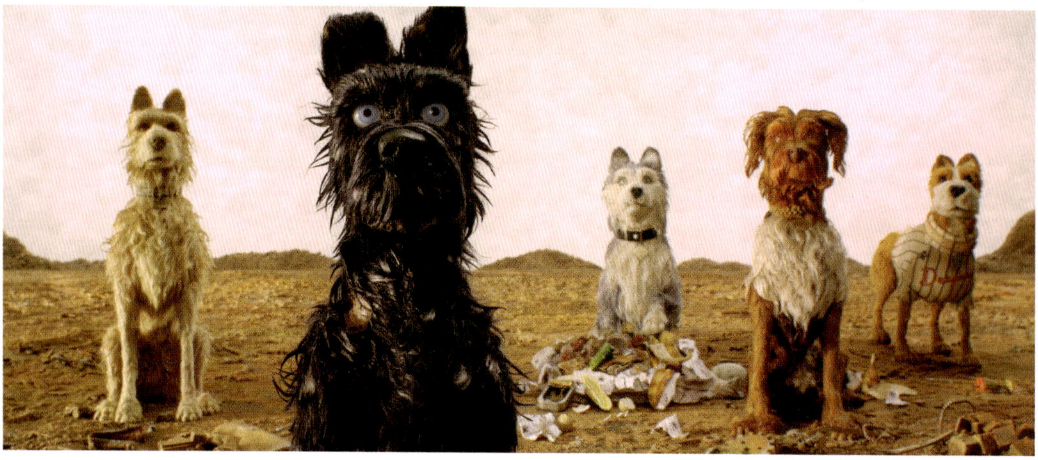

67 Animated film *Isle of Dogs* (2018, dir. Wes Anderson).

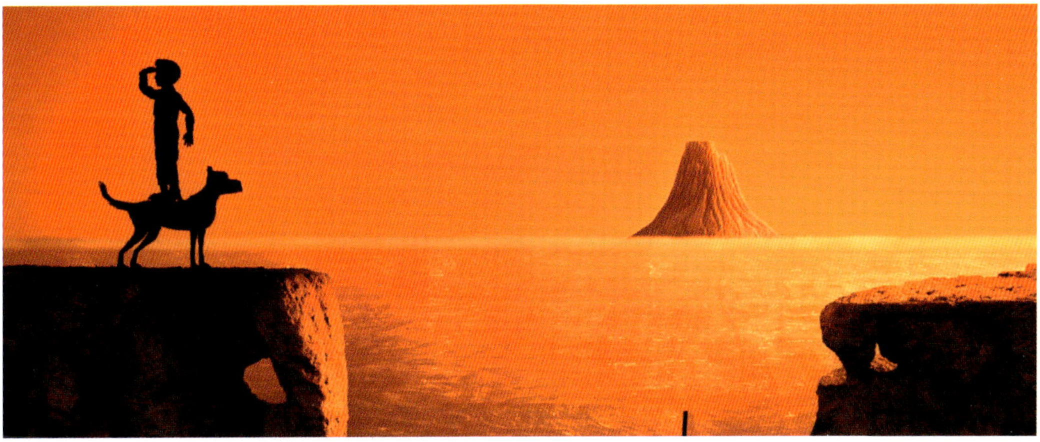

68 Animated film *Isle of Dogs* (2018, dir. Wes Anderson).

described by Chief as 'a pack of scary, indestructible alpha dogs', he finds Spots, who has become a leader of the dogs' resistance. Meanwhile an American exchange student, Tracy, discovers that the dog-hating mayor initially spread the plague and murdered a professor who discovered a cure. Kobayashi and his cat-loving followers are finally exposed. After recovering from a serious injury, and following a peculiar law of succession, Atari becomes the new mayor, and the exiled dogs are finally returned to Megasaki. No longer vilified as contagious trash, they are welcomed back from the island as loyal friends and protectors. Anderson could not resist a happy ending – perhaps a deliberate strategy that reinforces the potential playfulness of the medium of animation.

However, the cartoon-like characterizations provoked debates about the depiction of Japanese characters. Justin Chang wrote that much of the Japanese dialogue, especially Atari's, had been reduced to short statements that non-speakers can decipher based on context and facial expression, while more complicated exchanges are translated aloud by an onscreen English interpreter (Frances McDormand).[37] Most of the villainous humans speak in un-subtitled Japanese; the dogs, meanwhile, speak American English. That said, *Isle of Dogs* uses the island theme to mischievously offer up layers of meaning relevant to the failings of contemporary society and local municipal power. The title was inspired by

London's Isle of Dogs, an urbanized industrial peninsula on the River Thames, near 3 Mills Studio, where some of the film work was done. In 1597 the English playwrights Ben Jonson and Thomas Nashe wrote the satirical play *The Isle of Dogs*, a mocking attack on the government and character of Great Britain, misconceived as a single island.[38] And in an era reeling from the effects of a global pandemic, Anderson's *Isle of Dogs* holds an uncanny prescience. The island is perceived by the authorities as the necessary space of (dog flu) quarantine and detention. It is also infested with the filthy detritus of modern life, pushed out of sight from the mainland. The literal and symbolic motif of the island frames, imprisons, punishes and protects this contaminated canine army of resistance, albeit an army largely dominated by canny *male* survivors of injustice and corruption.[39] The evocative island vistas, littered with mountains of trash but perpetually bordered by an expansive and imprisoning sea, provide the dramatic leitmotif of the film (illus. 68). The geography of Japan is dominated by sprawling archipelagos; Anderson's film humorously illustrates the literal and metaphorical potential of this geography in the exercise of social control. What has been described as Anderson's 'omnivorous appropriation' in *Isle of Dogs* may reveal an animated 'othering' of Japanese culture.[40] But it is also a topical, thought-provoking exploration of the politics of islandness and its potential for abuses of power.

5 ISLANDS OF 'WHITE GOLD'

Island geographies have enabled various forms of detention and forced labour that benefited the transatlantic slave trade. On the West African coast of Sierra Leone, Bunce Island became a strategic processing centre and fortress prison for enslaved people from the seventeenth century onwards. Now abandoned, it was first settled by British traders who transported tens of thousands of kidnapped Africans across the Atlantic for work in the American and Caribbean plantations.[1] Its role as a busy transit point for the 'Middle Passage' is now enmeshed with its modern tourist appeal. It has been described as 'the most important historic site in Africa for the United States', attracting many African American tourists exploring their family heritage and encouraging the production of numerous documentary films.[2] This island in the Sierra Leone River became an unlikely symbol of hope for many seeking their slave ancestors.

Many of those ancestors ended up on Caribbean islands, which became profitable sites for sugar, coffee and tea plantations, producing valuable crops shipped back to colonial capitals. For centuries these plantations operated oppressive systems of enslaved labour as they generated huge wealth for the British, French and Spanish empires. Sugar, or 'white gold' (as the British often called it), was the most important cash crop across this archipelago. For those enslaved Africans, island life, where they endured varying degrees of incarceration, dominated their experiences – a fact that has inspired many writers and artists who are now exploring the complex histories of the area. Contemporary artists, writers and critics have used their work to mediate both the horror and the beauty of Caribbean island culture. Moreover, recent research has demonstrated the importance of the art of the anglophone Caribbean and its diaspora within a transnational geography of modern and contemporary art.[3] The cross-cultural interconnections between these islands, Europe and North America provide rich material for the study of world art history and the rethinking of colonial histories.[4] The connected archipelagos of Caribbean coastal societies and their colonial histories have enabled some imaginative art projects that carry meaning both within and between islands.

Facing Diamond Beach at Anse Cafard, on a hillside on the south-west coast of Martinique, fifteen white figures look out over the Caribbean Sea (illus. 69). Hulking stone and concrete statues (each 2.5 metres (8 ft) tall) stand with bowed heads and hunched shoulders, forming a triangle that echoes the triangular routes of the slave trade. The Anse Cafard Slave Memorial by Martinican sculptor Laurent Valère (b. 1959) was completed in 1998 as a memorial to a terrible shipwreck off Diamond Beach on 7 April 1830, when a boat carrying a cargo of shackled Africans destined for a Martinique slave market supplying the sugar plantations crashed into the rocks; 46 bodies were recovered.[5] All but four were Africans, and they were buried in a mass grave nearby. By the nineteenth century the sugar plantation, or *habitation sucrière*, was feeding a global market, generating huge wealth for its French colonial owners.[6] Valère created anonymous, near identical statues, emphasizing their dehumanized status. Fixed to the Martinique hillside with cast concrete, they have become a key landmark in the island's history, albeit heavily mediated by their tourist appeal. The role of tourism, now the economic mainstay of most Caribbean economies, is enmeshed with that of public art. Exotic beach holidays sit side by side with the artistic visualization of traumatic memories. While tourism has benefitted most Caribbean islands economically and socially, its effects are complex, and have had some controversial ecological and environmental impacts. The following chapter is primarily concerned with some of the visual stereotypes and tropes associated with these sites, and the relationship between the tourist gaze and the realities of island life, and its artistic representations.[7]

The Martinican-born writer, poet and philosopher Édouard Glissant (1928–2011) has described the dark holds of ships where captured Africans

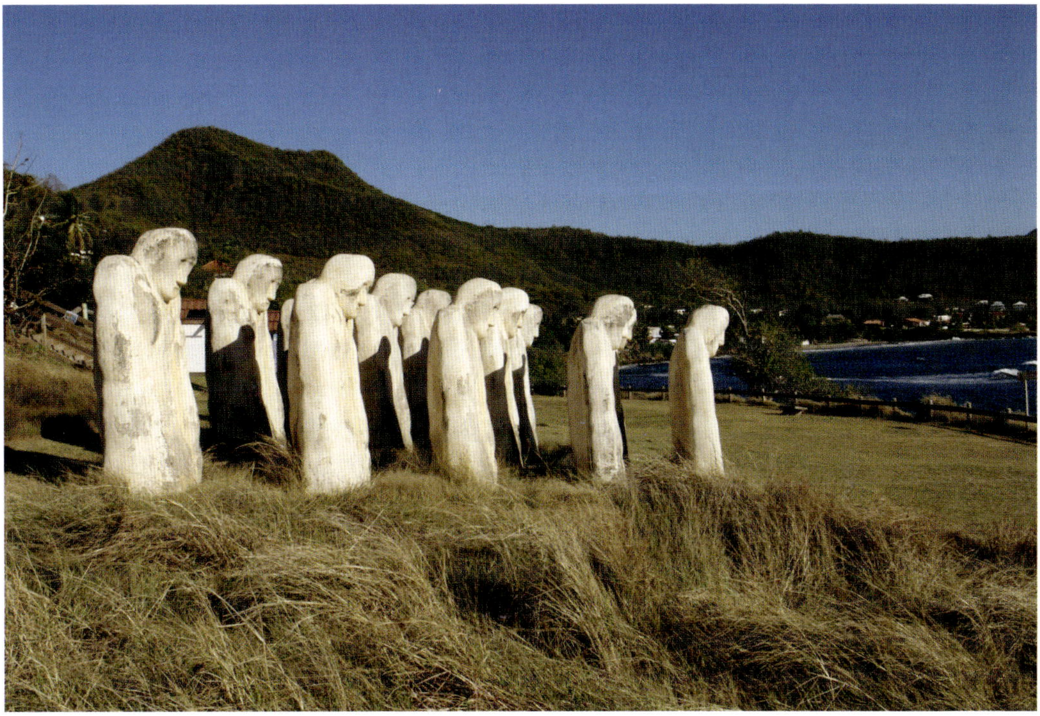

69 Laurent Valère, *Anse Cafard Memorial Cap 110*, Martinique, 1998, concrete.

were chained up as the 'womb of the Caribbean'. He has explored the post-colonial history and fractured identity of Martinique and the Caribbean archipelago in many essays and novels and is critical of the island's cultural and economic dependence on France. Throughout his writings he sought to formulate a specifically Caribbean response to what he calls the 'triple abyss' experience wrought by colonialism: the abyss that tore people away from homes in Africa; the abyss of the Middle Passage, where the captured were fettered in the holds of ships; and the abyss of arrival as 'slaves' in the so-called New World.[8] He argues that the project of locating origins is always constrained as the past is 'drowned' and all that remains is fragments, a bricolage without linear continuity. He proposes the need to understand the specificity of the Antillean context as archipelagic, both literally and as a metaphor for relational, open-ended identities, which is opposed to more insular forms of continental thinking. This involves 'creolization', a dynamic process of cultural and linguistic becoming that is fluid and cross-cultural. While the tourist industry and colonial narratives have depicted these island spaces as remote and isolated, Glissant proposes a notion of islandness that is both hybrid and creolized, that depends on relationships between and within cultures. As he said in 1973:

> Ordinarily, insularity is treated as a form of isolation, a neurotic relation to place.
> However, in the Caribbean each island embodies openness.
> The dialectic between inside and outside is reflected in the relationship of land and sea. It is only those who are tied to the European continent who see insularity as confining. A Caribbean imagination liberates us from being smothered.[9]

For Glissant, the figures of island, boat and archipelago are deeply rooted in the corporeality and connectedness of island histories. His sense of (dialectical) connections between islands has been identified in the work of many writers from the Caribbean, Indian and Pacific archipelagos. The literary and postcolonial scholar Elizabeth DeLoughrey has argued that centuries of transoceanic diaspora and settlement have helped to make islands spaces into dynamic centres of cultural exchange.[10] Using the category of 'island writers', she cites the creative possibilities of 'the oceanic imaginary' as providing an alternative model of time and space, drawing on what the Barbadian poet and writer Edward Kamau Brathwaite has called a 'tidalectics', a cyclic, repetitious movement of water, currents and tides.[11] In a similar vein, the Saint Lucian poet Derek Walcott (1930–2020) famously declared that 'the sea is history' in his poem of the same name (1979). Packed with biblical references, Walcott's poem responds to a question from colonials:

> Where are your monuments, your battles, martyrs?
> Where is your tribal memory? Sirs,
> in that grey vault. The sea. The sea
> has locked them up. The sea is History.[12]

Walcott's response is that the sea holds what the colonizer's hegemonic history cannot see or hear: 'Then came the men with eyes heavy as anchors/ who sank without tombs/ . . . where the men-o'-war floated down.'[13] In this context we might see the Anse Cafard Slave Memorial as a modern attempt to use sculpture to memorialize a previously 'locked in' or drowned past. Here I explore some less literal artistic responses to these hidden yet connected island histories. Many artists are engaged in difficult conversations with Caribbean island locations, in which the present is perpetually haunted by the past. That said, the artworks that I discuss here have also been selected on the basis of their power as imaginative visual projects. As the viewer negotiates the wealth of cultural theory and identity politics that inevitably frame our knowledge of art of the Caribbean and its diasporas, I intend to explore the way aesthetic strategies and metaphors can mediate and reframe some of those cultural and social meanings.[14]

MAPPING SUGAR

Barbados was Britain's first sugar island. Occupied by the British in 1627, it became one of the first Caribbean islands to expand a network of lucrative plantations, worked by large numbers of enslaved Africans, many shipped from Bunce Island. As Hilary McD. Beckles has described it: 'The geography of Barbados was ideally suited to sugar plantations and there were enormous fortunes to be made for British royalty and ruling elites from sugar produced by an enslaved, "disposable" workforce, fortunes that secured Britain's place as an imperial superpower.'[15] The English author Richard Ligon's map of 1657 (illus. 70) shows the huge number of named plantations along the island's coast. During the late seventeenth and early eighteenth centuries, Barbados became the sugar capital of the Caribbean and the rum capital of the world, a status reinforced by colonial map-making – the staking out and naming of plantation territory.[16] 'White gold' came to account for 20 per cent of all European imports by the eighteenth century. This profitable sugarcane and molasses industry, and the exploitative plantation system upon which it depended, have become

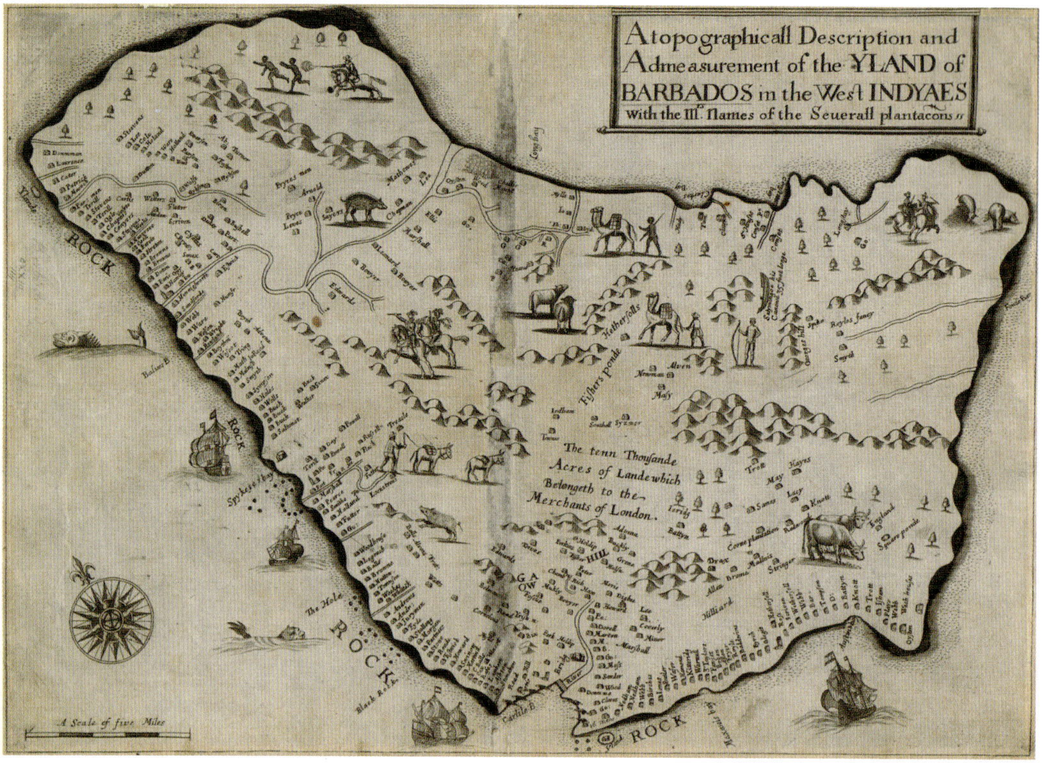

70 'A Topographical Description and Measurement of the Island of Barbados', in Richard Ligon, *A True and Exact History of the Island of Barbados* (1657).

iconic signifiers of the island's history. In his 1975 essay 'Caribbean Man in Space and Time' Brathwaite sees the plantation system as a model for understanding colonial life in the Caribbean; he developed a notion of the 'inner plantation' and the 'outer plantation'. While the latter signifies the systemic colonial order, generating wealth for the European imperial nations, the 'inner plantation' describes the subcultural, imaginary life of the Caribbean people. This is the locus of creativity and cultural expression, which he argues has been largely neglected by researchers.[17] Direct and oblique references to plantation life, and its aesthetic and political possibilities, characterize many of the artistic projects explored below.

The creative potential of reviewing plantation history is a key concern in the work of Annalee Davis (b. 1963), an artist born and working in Barbados. She spent her childhood on a series of local sugar cane plantations, where her father was a planter. In her performance and installation piece *A Walker's Diary – An Effort at Disalienation* (2021), Davis repeatedly walked around the fields behind her studio, now based in a working dairy farm that was previously a sugar cane plantation dating back to the seventeenth century. Her walks are traced on a large drawing that resembles the topography and contours of ordnance survey maps, reminding the viewer that the process of mapping the island and its plantations was critical to its representation in the dominant narratives of British colonial history (illus. 71). Across this backdrop Davis displays flowers and fauna collected on walks and recorded on ledgers salvaged from an abandoned sugar factory. She thus incorporates the geography and fauna of the Barbados plantations into a creative practice; hers is a personal diary of reconnections with land.

Her photographic series *Sweeping the Fields* (2016) documents some of the performative gestures of islanders that are designed to cleanse the land of its violent past: women are photographed literally sweeping the

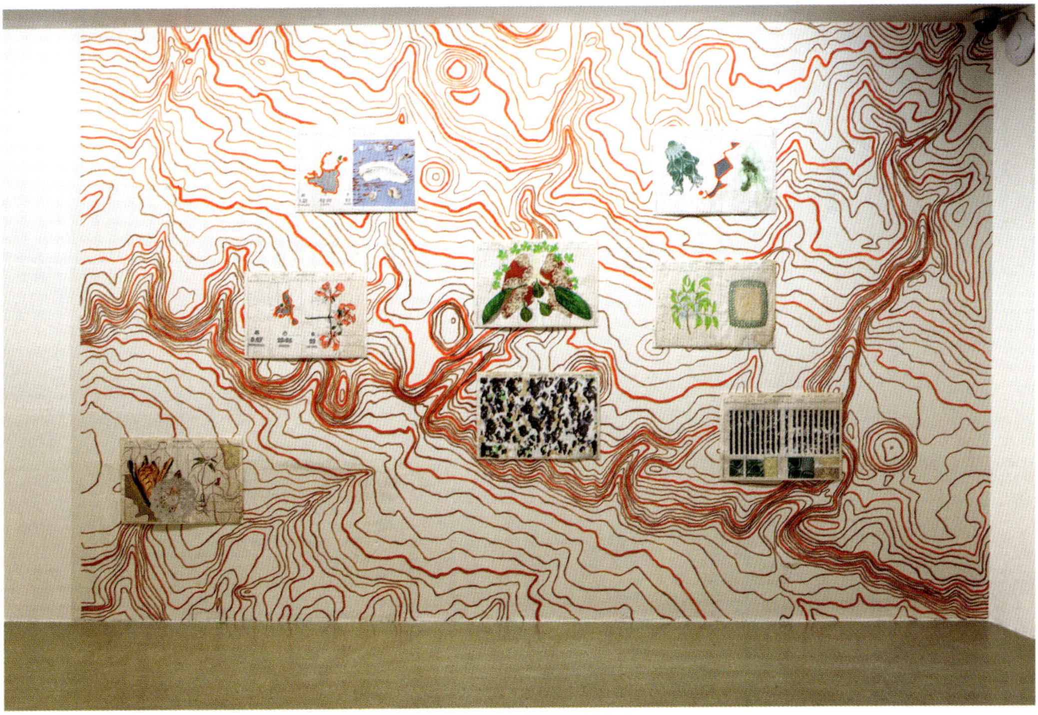

71 Annalee Davis, *A Walker's Diary – An Effort at Disalienation*, 2021, mural, Slovak National Gallery, mixed media on Daily Analysis Record sheet from Bulkeley Sugar Factory.

landscape. Centuries of sugar cane farming devastated the biodiversity of Barbados. The wild botanicals that Davis collects and illustrates are repopulating the fields; they point to the possibilities of post-plantation ecological resurgence. In a series of six drawings titled *In Defence of Beauty* (illus. 72) she uses mixed media on plantation ledger pages from the 1970s and '80s to create 'alternative landscapes or floating archipelagos'.[18] Using latex paint, pencil and occasional gold leaf, she depicts strange shadows cast by pieces of locally made crochet. These shapes appear to float across the neatly delineated rows and columns of the plantation pay list, resembling lost archipelagos, lace-like forms or even volcanic debris. Shards of clay and pieces of eighteenth- and nineteenth-century porcelain unearthed from former plantation fields contribute to the complex material history implicated here. Lace-like forms and crochet patterns also evoke the (often unpaid) labour of women, especially enslaved women, an aspect of Caribbean plantation life that is increasingly inspiring artistic research, as I show below.[19] Davis's graphic patterns are layered over the red lines and black words of the ledgers, offering a disorderly, gendered challenge to the more controlled fiscal language of columns, wages and recorded labour. She has described her artistic intentions thus:

> My inscription of non-transactional images onto the ledgers offers alternative ways of reading the plantation by repopulating, complicating and exposing gaps in shared plantation histories, while enabling different understandings of conflictingly imagined landscapes to be glimpsed. The series refers to a common need for beauty, proposing that post-colonial, post-independence spaces accommodate beauty also.[20]

Davis's 'imagined landscapes' resonate across the wider Caribbean archipelago and its plantation histories; we might even see them as reworkings of Brathwaite's imaginary 'inner plantation', which he described as 'resistant local forms; roots and stumps, survival rhythms'.[21] Her projects use performance, installation, photography, drawing and mixed media to metaphorize

72 Annalee Davis, *In Defense of Beauty*, 2017, mixed media on plantation ledger pages, one of a suite of six drawings.

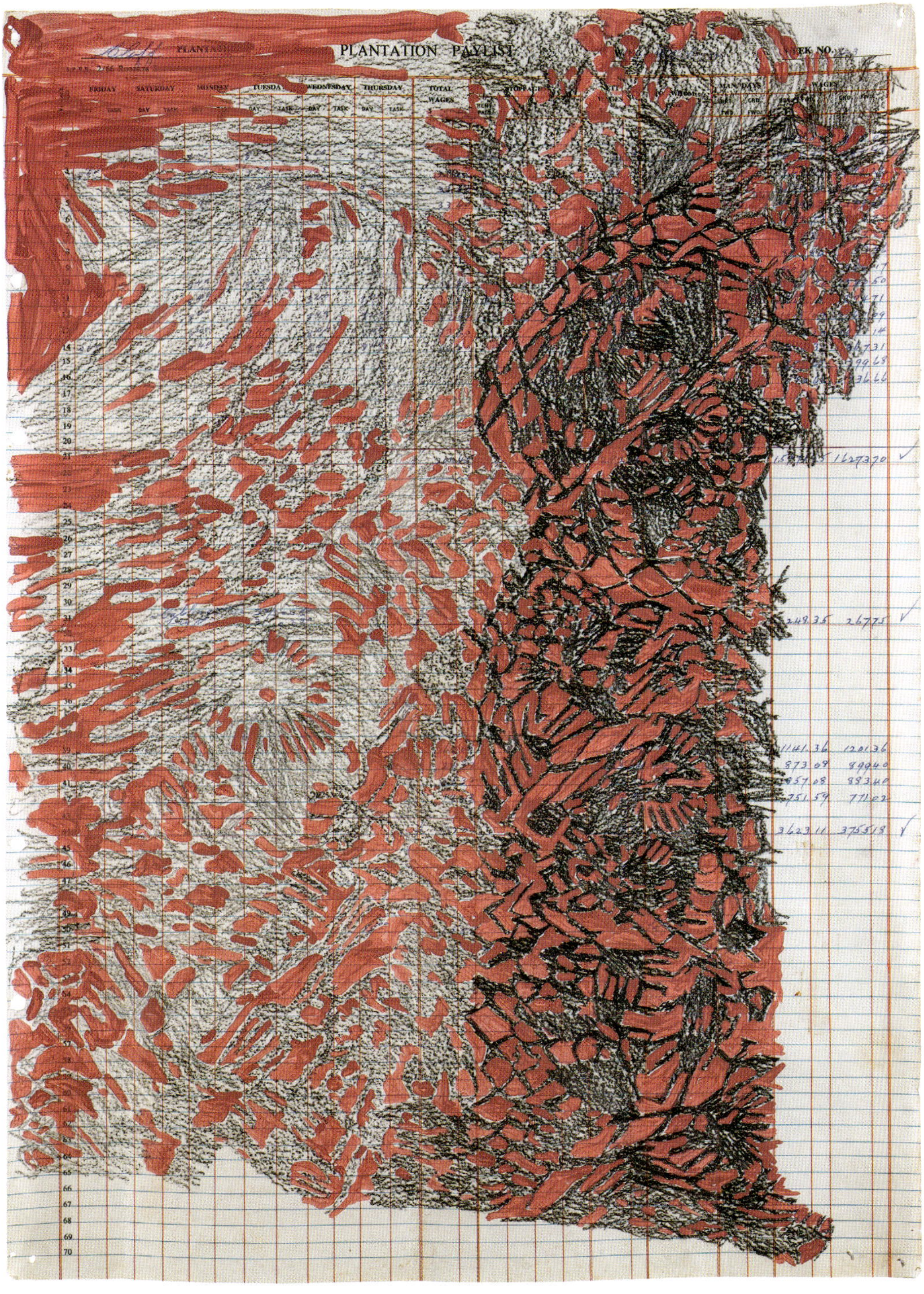
PLANTATION PAYLIST
FRIDAY
SATURDAY
MONDAY
THURSDAY
TOTAL WAGES

and repopulate those connected islands of 'white gold'. Davis's practice is grounded in a feminist ethos that engages with multiple meanings and histories of the Caribbean and its diasporas.[22] She subtly reclaims the (often hidden) work of women through multi-layered aesthetic interventions, in pursuit of her 'common need for beauty'.

The histories of sugar cane farming on Caribbean islands are also at the heart of a series of works by the Trinidadian-born artist Karen McLean (b. 1959), who has been living and working in England since 2000. In her installation *The Precariat* (2017) she suspended 28 'sugar houses' made from refined sugar solution (illus. 73).[23] They slowly dissolved into a sticky, glutinous solution, leaving puddles that crept across the gallery floor. A multi-channel sound installation evoking the everyday sounds of working the land, recorded on a Birmingham allotment, accompanied the melting houses.[24] McLean uses her work to interrogate motifs

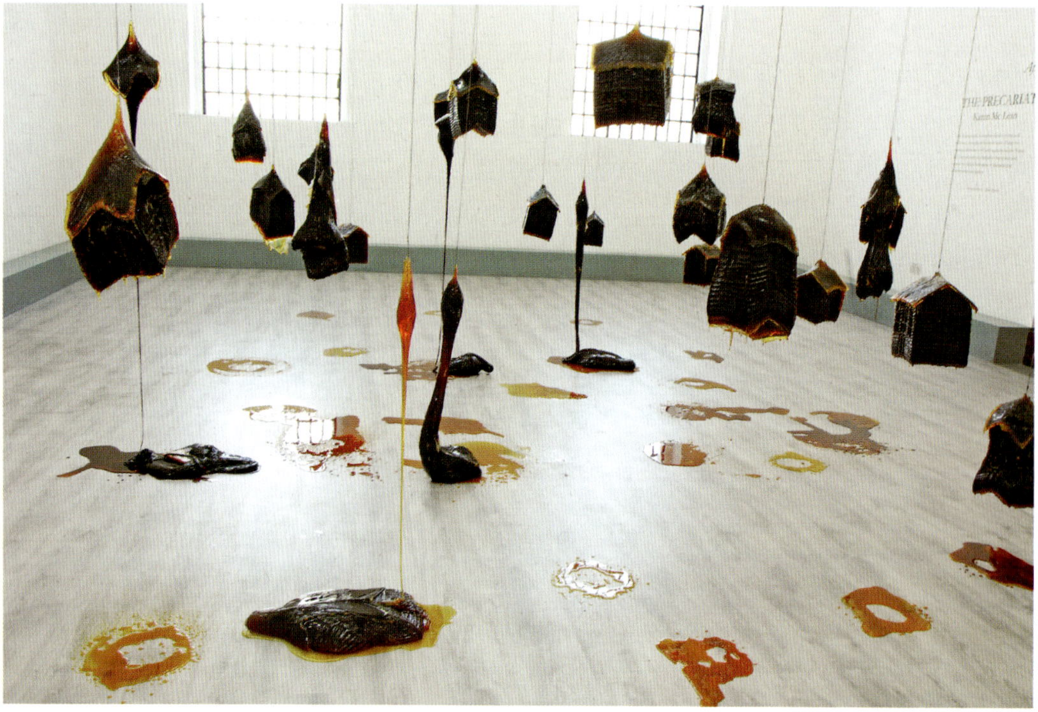

73 Karen McLean, *The Precariat*, 2017, sugar, golden syrup and water, wire rope; installation view, 163 Gallery, London.

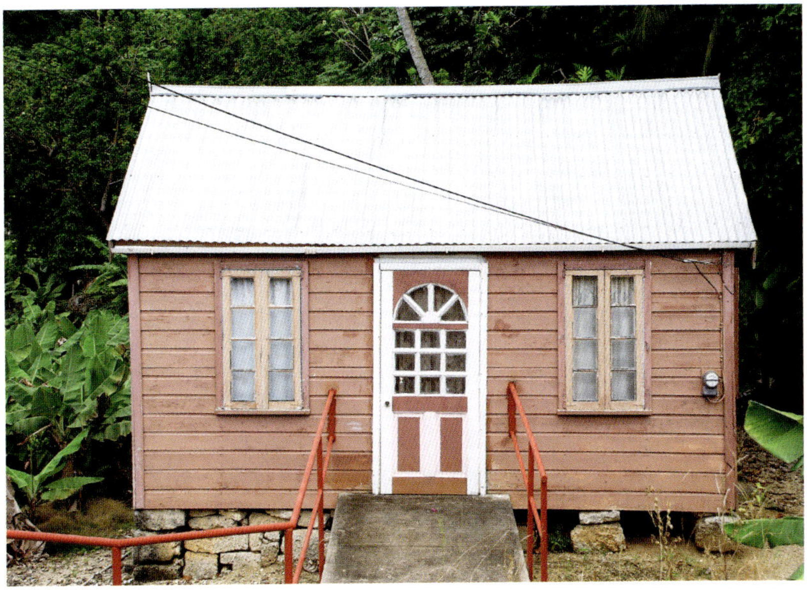

74 Barbados pink chattel house, photograph by Karen McLean.

and symbols that signify her Caribbean history; she has spent many years researching the vernacular architecture of Caribbean islands, including the 'chattel house'.[25] Tourist images of Barbados often feature small wooden houses, usually brightly coloured, raised on stone blocks or stilts and with modern extensions and verandas (illus. 74). Seen as iconic signifiers of vernacular Barbados, they are transportable dwellings with origins in the history of slavery and temporary labour. Even post-abolition, workers who did not own land could be fired easily by landowners and forced to leave the plantation. 'Chattel' signifies a moveable possession; enslaved workers were also often described as 'chattel'. The motif acts as a metonym for Barbados; it references plantation life, colonial legacies, the brutal constraints on living endured by enslaved workers and problematic issues of ownership that have plagued the island's history of housing.[26]

McLean notes the 'cuteness' and pastel colours of the Barbadian chattel house: 'they are so different to the "shacks" prevalent in other islands, which previously used similar styles of vernacular architecture in years gone by but hadn't survived.'[27] Her sugar houses mimicked the shape of small rectangular cottages found in seventeenth-century southern England blended with features of folk houses typical to areas of West Africa from which the enslaved labourers had been transported. In Barbados chattel houses were also raised off the ground to allow mobility and protect from insects and animals, and jalousies were added to shield from the wind. The 'cute' appropriation of Georgian features, such as symmetrical front facades, porches and verandas, references the island's colonial history and the plantation worker's lack of access to wealth and ownership. These diminutive archetypes are a direct response to the forced mobility that Beckles identifies as 'the building technology of the "chattel house", a stoneless castle that was sent packing from "his" land when the plantation man [owner] went mad . . . There were a million such rightless middle passages; the chattel house was the sign and symbol of their rejection by society.'[28] Even after emancipation, and the island's independence in 1966, a series of Housing Acts deprived the freed slaves of automatic rights of tenancy or ownership; the 'Located Labourer's Act' kept freed slaves attached to the plantation by a tenantry system until as late as 1980.[29] The plantation evolved as a 'total institution' that dominated the economic and social lives of workers long after slavery had been officially abolished.

Referencing this history, McLean's melting houses are without foundations. Built from the very material that determined and constrained the lives of their inhabitants, their distinctive architecture transforms into brown puddles. Their dissolving spaces represent the precarious nature of 'home' and plantation life for the local community on these connected islands. McLean deliberately sourced Tate & Lyle granulated sugar and boiled it to 300 degrees, adding golden syrup to give it the correct consistency for a slow melt, echoing the arduous labour involved in harvesting and processing sugar for the colonial markets.

In her account of the ideas behind *The Precariat* McLean cites the influence of the cultural theorist Homi K. Bhabha's theory of mimicry in both her observation and imitation of the vernacular and pseudo-Georgian styles of Barbadian chattel houses. She draws on his argument that 'colonial mimicry is the desire for a reformed recognizable Other as a subject of a difference that is almost the same but not quite.'[30] According

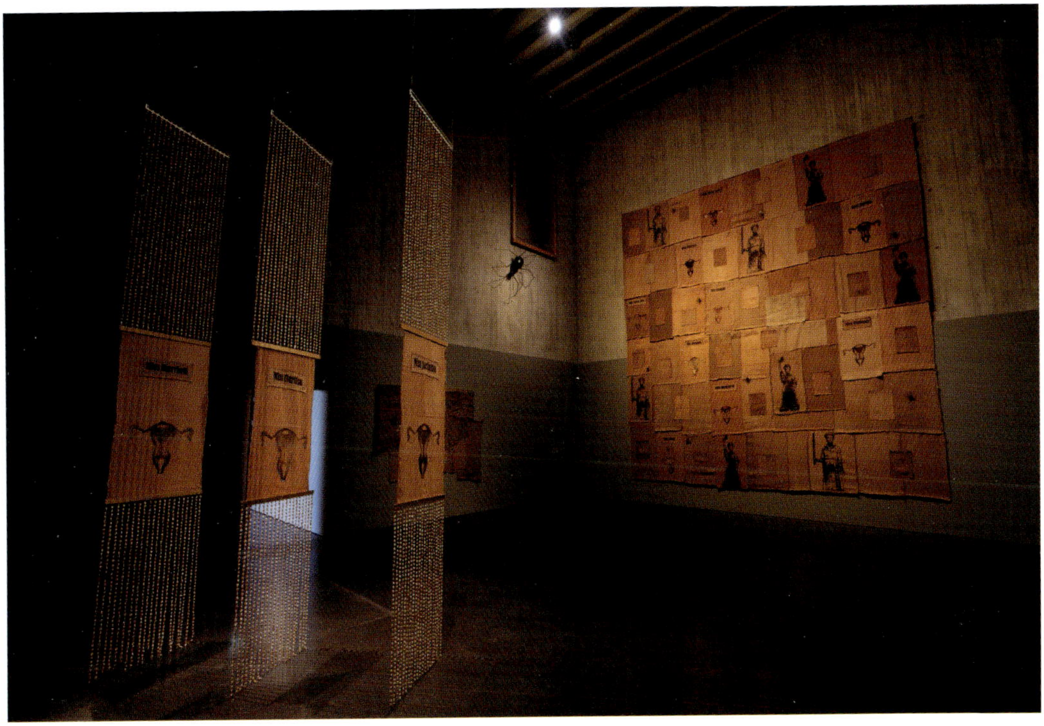

75 Karen McLean, *Ar'n't I a Woman!*, 2022, dyed hessian sacking, black/gold screen printing and branding, animal suture thread, cowrie shells; installation view, The New Art Gallery Walsall.

to this argument, the European colonizer attempts to 'civilize' the Other through the projection of religion, education, architecture and culture generally. But for colonial mimicry to work, there must be a clear difference – or slippage – between representations of the colonized and the colonizer. McLean cites these arguments in her observations of little pink chattel houses that mimic characteristics of the larger pink houses owned by the 'Buckra', or plantation master. By hanging her dissolving houses, she allows for further artistic 'slippage' and distortion. However, there are other readings that explain her artistic process. As architectural features begin to melt, they morph into new hybrids. The changing nature of the art object and its duration through time transforms the installation into performance, directed initially by the artist, but following its own slow evolution, according to temperature, gallery conditions and the thickness of the boiled sugar solution. Echoing the changing cultural and political landscape of the modern plantation island of Barbados, which gained independence in 1966, this is an unpredictable metamorphosis (perhaps beyond mimicry), subject to unforeseen developments and environmental interventions. McLean has reported that an early display of *The Precariat* at Goldsmiths, University of London, seriously damaged the floor onto which the solution was dripping, offering another layer of metaphorical meaning. The production of 'white gold' is associated with a long history of environmental damage.

JAMAICAN MAROONS AND ISLAND QUEENS

In McLean's installation *Ar'n't I a Woman!* (first exhibited in 2020 at Block 336 in Brixton, London, and then at Walsall's New Gallery of Art in 2022) two haunting images of enslaved women, one wielding a machete and the other holding an *abeng* (animal horn), are repeated across a large, stitched tapestry of hessian sacks (illus. 75). Both are composite images representing the iconic Queen Nanny of the Maroons. The Maroons were originally escaped slaves who ran away from their Spanish-owned plantations when the British took the island of Jamaica from Spain in 1655.[31] Queen Nanny of the Maroons led a community of formerly enslaved Africans called the Windward Maroons and is now a celebrated symbol of Jamaica's independent island status. During the early eighteenth century the Maroons fought for many years against the colonizers and terrorized British troops, until peace treaties were signed in 1739 and 1740.[32] In exchange for peace and the promise of some form of support for the plantation system, the Maroons were granted freedom and land. But with the expansion of the plantation complex, further wars ensued in 1795–9 that ended in the defeat and deportation of Maroons.

McLean has drawn on multiple sources, including a portrait of Nanny on the Jamaican $500 banknote, a sculpture in the National Hero Park in Jamaica and archive photographs. She has woven together various physical characteristics and metonymic objects, such as the distinctive headwrap and *abeng*, into two single figure studies. These figures are presented as powerful symbols of resistance, screen-printed in black onto dyed sacks

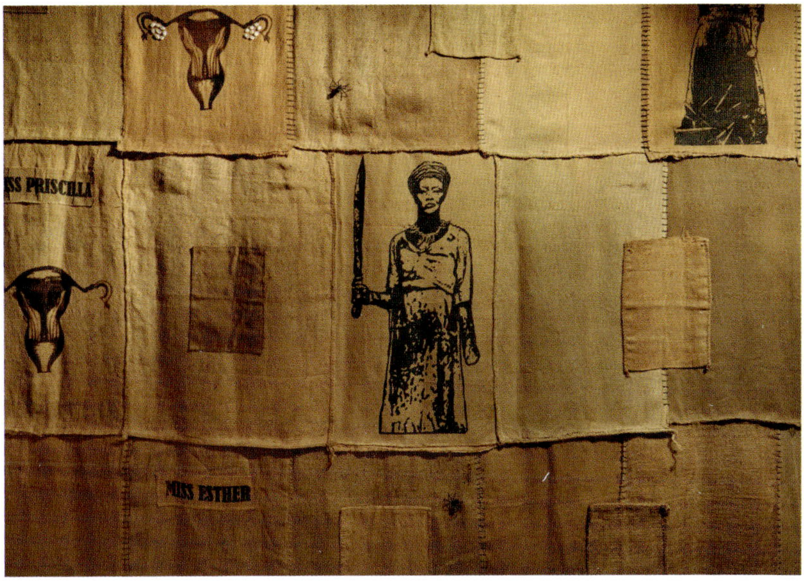

76 Karen McLean, *Ar'n't I a Woman!*, 2022, detail.

in a celebratory repetition of their struggles (illus. 76). McLean grew up saturated in folklore in which myths of the Jamaican Nanny resonated across then newly independent islands such as Trinidad and Jamaica (both achieved independence in 1962). Moreover, Nanny's symbolic status as a figure of anti-colonial struggle in Jamaica and surrounding islands was inseparable from her gender: she was consistently claimed as a brave *mother* of resistance against slavery and colonization.

The British colonized the island of Jamaica in 1655. Trinidad was visited by Christopher Columbus and claimed for Spain in 1498, and although settled by French colonists, it remained under Spanish rule until ceded to the British in 1797.[33] Abject poverty hindered resistance, and the geography of these plantation islands also enabled a system of colonial enslavement. Running away was constrained by the surrounding sea. Moreover, on smaller islands with limited uncultivated land, 'runaways' were easily caught. These islands were often harder to escape than the antebellum plantations of the American South, where the culture of runaways was aggressively policed and punished. The Windward Maroons developed their own localized strategies for escape on larger islands with

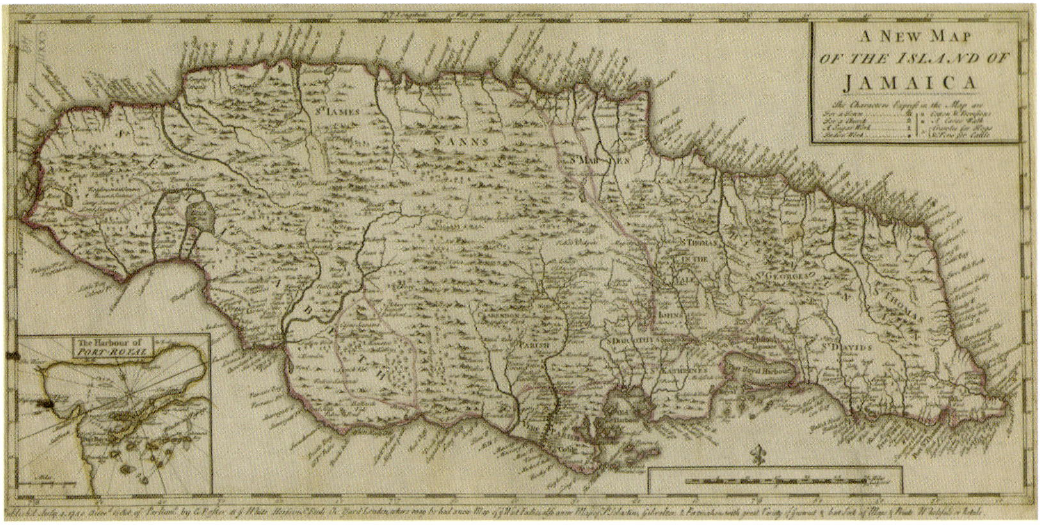

77 George Foster, *A New Map of the Island of Jamaica*, 1740, hand-coloured print.

inaccessible and less populated mountainous areas. In Jamaica they occupied a region of steep-sided limestone hollows, forests and hills known as Cockpit Country.

As with Barbados, the detailed mapping of this sugar island and its many plantations was critical to its representation in the dominant narratives of British colonial history. In the late seventeenth and early eighteenth centuries the British established sugar cane plantations throughout Jamaica, which are clearly labelled in a map of 1740 (illus. 77) by symbols on a key at the top right. From the late seventeenth century Jamaica took over from Barbados as the main sugar-producing island in the Caribbean, and by 1739 it was producing 16,000 tons of sugar for export each year. The 1740 map displays an island littered with anglicized place names for towns, parishes, ports, rivers and villages; it suggests a haven of peace and prosperity, a place rich in economic activity (cotton fields, cacao plantations and livestock pens are marked alongside sugar cane). But this mapping conceals the exploitative history of an island dependent on a brutal slave trade for its economic status and geographical shape. An expanding sugar economy transformed both its fortunes and its landscape; it put Jamaica at the heart of Britain's Atlantic empire.[34]

Despite treaties signed in 1739 and 1740, the Cockpit settlements situated in the Trelawny and Saint Elizabeth parishes are not marked on this map. More recently, the histories of many Caribbean plantation islands are being rewritten by writers, artists and academics to enable a remapping of a complex and violent history. Similarly, McLean has consistently used her installation work to explore aspects of island culture and their colonial and gendered legacies.[35] *Ar'n't I a Woman!* revisits a Caribbean island history using a multi-layered celebration of the activities of enslaved women and their strategies of resistance. The work also reveals McLean's ongoing interest in the folklore and material cultures of colonized islands, and the close relationship with the history of slavery in the antebellum South. She draws on a long tradition of female weaving, stitching and dyeing of fabrics, activities that were also deployed by enslaved women in their attempts to control commercial and social processes.[36] Through her mimicry, translation and aestheticization of such processes, McLean invites a contemporary audience to engage with a hidden history of women's practice.

The branded, printed and stitched sacks of her wall-hangings are replete with corporeal and symbolic references to the harsh lives of enslaved women and Jamaican Maroons, re-presented here as iconic figures. The sacks allude to the commercial history of slavery; hessian is an ancient material derived from jute and is famously durable. Such sacks were used to carry produce from the plantations, such as sugar, coffee and tea. They were the vehicles of distribution to the colonial capitals and symbols of the accumulation of wealth that ensued. McLean sourced hers from various UK suppliers, combining different textures, tones and weaves. Each was dyed using tea and coffee, turned inside out to hide the old lettering and cut in half. She then stitched on new hessian backs, creating her own reclaimed sacks, imbued with laborious practices that echo those of the past. Imitating the gendered activities of dressmaking and quilt-making in enslaved communities, she laced them together with animal suture thread, another corporeal reference to the wounded/sutured bodies of those who were enslaved, especially women. As Entela Bilali has argued: 'The weaving of stories into quilts became a way for Black women to defy the system of slavery and patriarchy and assert themselves . . . Black women weaved resistance into their daily lives.'[37]

McLean makes vivid use of metaphor, metonym and semiotically charged objects to explore the important role of the body in both the representation and the resistance of enslaved women or 'bondwomen'.[38] While the threatening or statuesque poses of her Jamaican Maroons speak of female resistance and escape, other symbolic objects and materials provide evocative visceral references. Black, shadowy shapes of wombs are branded onto the hessian, echoing both the violent physical abuse (of the branding iron on the body) and the 'ownership' involved. Yet McLean reinstates some status originally denied to her subjects by screen-printing the uterus in gold onto the sackcloth. Expensive and coveted, gold helps to reframe this coarse patchwork hanging and the objects that surround it. It can also serve as an ironic reminder of the plantation context – an island of 'white gold'.

Female reproduction was itself an important source of value; it insured the ongoing income of the plantation owners, hence the smaller sacks that McLean has stitched onto the wall-hanging. These break the lines of stitching and reference the plantation 'baby sacks' that would have been used for stillborn babies or those lost from infanticide. The desire to control women's reproductive and sexual functions was part of the ethos of colonial and antebellum slave owners. As the American feminist historian Stephanie Camp argues, 'the slave body, most intensely women's, served as the "bio-text" on which shareholders inscribed their authority and indeed their very mastery.'[39] Yet women's reproductive capacities were also often deployed by bondwomen as a means of resistance. McLean mediates this resistance through her use of crude hessian quietly embellished with glitter, shining with double meaning.

This installation is replete with other references that reaffirm the role of enslaved women in the history of Caribbean islands. On a row of twelve smaller sacks, laser-cut lettering spells out 'Ar'n't I a Woman!' (illus. 78). The sacks were stitched together by McLean and embroidered by a local women's collective, Walsall Black Sisters, many of whom are from Jamaican

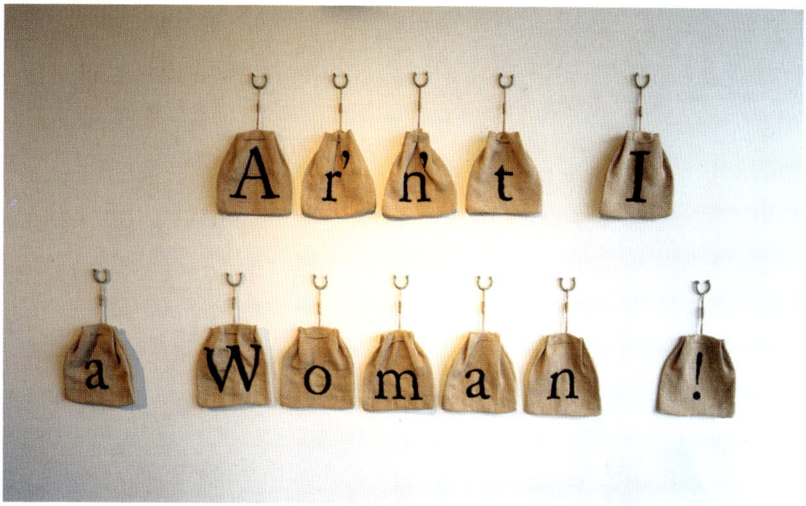

78 Karen McLean, *Ar'n't I a Woman!*, 2022, detail of small sacks.

Windrush families. Women's labour in the present post-imperial context is deployed to celebrate the struggles and achievements of their island ancestors in a colonial past. The sturdy hessian sack, reduced here in scale, evokes not only the plantation container but poignant histories of infanticide, abortion and miscarriage – events all too common in enslaved societies.[40] Tiny bodies were often buried or hidden in sacks, a powerful signifier of women's control – or lack of control – over their reproductive functions and economic 'value'. Each sack is hung with a manilla (a form of currency used in the slave trade) with a threaded loop at the top, tied closed like a lynching noose.

Other objects heavy with historical meaning also adorn – or impinge upon – the sacks. In the Walsall installation wire mesh, referencing the fettering of slave communities, obscured the view of the smaller wall-hanging. In contrast, on the large wall-hanging, small cream-coloured cowrie shells formed delicate trails, suggesting ovaries. Strings of shells also rattle gently below each of three hanging sacks branded with wombs in *Silence me not . . . me ah rise*. Partly branded black on one side, they glisten with printed gold on the other. The branding has left parts of the hessian ruptured with holes, another process that helps to aestheticize the display, rich in double meanings. Cowrie shells carry symbolic resonances as a substitute for money in parts of Africa, as currency between Caribbean islands, as jewellery when threaded into bracelets and necklaces, as charms and as symbols of the feminine. Derek Walcott has signalled this gendered association and its tragic demise in the Caribbean in his poem 'The Sea Is History': 'as the white cowries clustered like manacles/ on the drowned women'.[41] The shells were also used as currency in the eighteenth- and nineteenth-century trade for both enslaved labourers and gold, a historical elision that is neatly referenced in McLean's use of gold leaf.[42] Issues of social, economic and gendered value haunt her installation, quietly suffusing its aesthetic power and its multi-layered references to island life.

An oversized black metal spider (*Anansi*) appears to scale one of the exhibition walls. Smaller spiders also meander across the large wall-hanging. These mischievous arachnids reference the cultural symbolism of Anansi, a character from Akan folklore. In West African, African American and Caribbean folklore Anansi often takes the form of a spider and is an inventive trickster, or god of knowledge of stories. In the postcolonial Caribbean, Anansi is often celebrated as a historic symbol of individualism and slave resistance, a mythical figure that enabled enslaved communities to establish a sense of continuity with their African past.[43] As they scuttle across the hessian, the spiders remind the viewer of an oral history heavy in tales of struggle and defiance on these Caribbean islands, especially Jamaica.[44]

McLean's installation depends partly upon a lexicon of symbolic objects, rich in metaphors of resistance. She has claimed that apart from the desire for escape to Jamaican Cockpit Country that her female subjects embody, the corporeal references also signify the desire for more control over their bodies, an attempt to escape from the persistent sexual exploitation and management of female reproduction.[45] *Ar'n't I a Woman!* represents the bondwomen of Jamaican history as inhabitants of an oppressive island culture, as iconic maternal figures of resistance, relevant to all enslaved workers in the Caribbean archipelago.

Memories of Jamaican women's resistance also live on in the writings of many contemporary Caribbean writers, including Melanie Schwapp, whose short story 'Granny Dead' describes a young Jamaican girl's intense relationship with her 'half-Maroon' grandmother.[46] The latter's status as Maroon is both cherished and mocked by her younger family, as granddaughter Pearl (the narrator) listens to and muses on her 'Granny Stories'. After the sudden death of her beloved Granny, Pearl recalls her lessons in mixing medicinal potions from plants and herbs, stories of attending local festivals as a child (before Jamaican independence in 1962), and how Granny's father 'teach her how to listen for them things nobody but Maroon could hear. "We hear them plannin', Queenie," Granny tells me. "We hear them plannin' how to fight them England people. When you hear them voices, Queenie, when you hear Cudjoe talk, there's no battle you can lose in this life!"'[47]

The sense of hope and resistance embodied historically in the Jamaican Nanny and her traditions is palpable here. Granny also nicknamed her granddaughter 'Queenie', anointing her with a title inherited from the Maroon tradition; she continues the line of island queens.[48] Schwapp's story also explores social, class and gender divides – the residues of colonialism within Jamaican culture. In a recording from 2020 she argues for the shared transnational themes of islandness in her story: 'If Granny Dead were an island, I think she would be very much tied to her sister islands in *So Many Islands*: in the raw poetry of her expression, and in the vulnerability of her voice.'[49] Schwapp references the anthology *So Many Islands* in which her story was published, and which features short pieces of writing from other authors based on Caribbean, Mediterranean, Indian and Pacific islands, including Barbados, Bermuda, Antigua and Barbuda, St Vincent and the Grenadines, Trinidad and Tobago, Saint Lucia, Grenada, Malta, Mauritius, Fiji and Tonga, among others. The anthology title is taken from a verse in Derek Walcott's celebrated poem 'The Schooner *Flight*':

> There are so many islands!
> As many islands as the stars at night
> on that branched tree from which meteors are shaken
> like falling fruit around the schooner *Flight*.[50]

A sense of the connected nature of Caribbean 'islandness' is implicit in Walcott's epic poem describing a literal and metaphorical sea voyage in search of local and mythic history. His voyage between islands is also a metaphor for creativity. As he writes at the beginning of Part 3 of his poem: 'I had no nation now but the imagination.'[51]

SO MANY ISLANDS

The connectivity of life between these Caribbean islands featured in an important exhibition organized by Tate Britain, London: 'Life between Islands' (2021–2), curated by Alex Farquharson and David A. Bailey. Focusing on the work of artists of African Caribbean heritage and exploring the transnational and diasporic nature of British art in the second half of the twentieth and early twenty-first centuries, this popular exhibition revealed the ways in which generations of artists have offered a 'wellspring of inspiration for the decolonization of cultural identity and the Caribbean psyche'.[52] The ironic circumstances of being held in a London institution originally funded by the wealth of a nineteenth-century sugar baron, Henry Tate, was not lost on the exhibition organizers.[53] Inspired by the title of the cultural theorist Stuart Hall's memoir, *Familiar Stranger: A Life between Two Islands*, first published in 2017, the show featured works by artists of the Caribbean diaspora that – much like Hall, who was born in Jamaica in 1932 and died in London in 2014 – are in dialogue with their island past and the ideas of Caribbean thinkers from the post-war Windrush era to the present.[54] The effects of the Caribbean diasporic community on British art, culture and society, often in the face of hostility, cannot be understated. As Farquharson writes: 'waves of popular music and subculture – Ska, Lover's Rock, Roots Reggae, Dub, Trip-Hop, Drum and Bass, Grime, etc.' are constantly evolving reminders of these effects, not to mention the celebratory annual carnivals organized by the Caribbean community in Notting Hill and elsewhere across the UK.[55]

The exhibition revealed the important contribution of the visual arts in the social experience and cultural imaginary of the Caribbean, mediated through life in the British Isles and featuring a range of practices, including painting, installation, video and photography, by different generations of artists of African Caribbean heritage. It featured work by artists from the first generation of Caribbean migrants to Britain from the 1940s to 1960s (or *arrivants*, as Brathwaite called them[56]), such as Aubrey Williams, Frank Bowling and Donald Locke. In the 1980s there emerged second-generation artists, many of them women, including Lubaina Himid, Sonia Boyce, Veronica Ryan, Ingrid Pollard, Maud Sulter and Marlene Smith, among others, and the 1990s saw work by artists such as Keith Piper, Chris Ofili (now living in Trinidad), Isaac Julien, Steve McQueen, Hew Locke (son of Donald Locke), Michael McMillan and the Otolith Group. Most of these artists have continued to be in dialogue with Caribbean island histories, exploring themes such as carnival, domestic life, struggles for independence and ongoing links to the sugar economy and slavery.[57]

Of particular interest here are the ways in which this hybridized (British) visual culture carries memories and symbols of island life and islandness. For example, the sculptural *Plantation Series* by Donald Locke (born in Guyana[58]) provides an early example of imaginative reworkings of the island plantation theme, in which phallic, dark brown stumps are arranged in tight rows on a black rectangular base (illus. 79). As Giulia Smith has noted, such works suggest a literal relationship with Brathwaite's notion of the 'inner plantation' as 'a zone of grassroots resistance made up of "cores and kernels; resistant local forms; roots and stumps, survival rhythms, growing points."'[59] Using the medium of film, with its capacity to represent performance through time, Sonia Boyce's (b. 1962) two-screen video *Crop Over* (2007–20; illus. 80) also explores the sugar plantation economy and its 'resistant local forms' through its carnival traditions on Barbados. *Crop Over* is a form of harvest festival that marks the end of the sugar cane season, and Boyce's film represents subversive and celebratory performances – mischievous carnival rituals that are now merged with a heavily marketed tourist attraction.[60] Cross-dressing and stilt walking are among the carnival activities filmed on a plantation estate in Barbados and at Harewood House in Yorkshire. The wealth of the latter

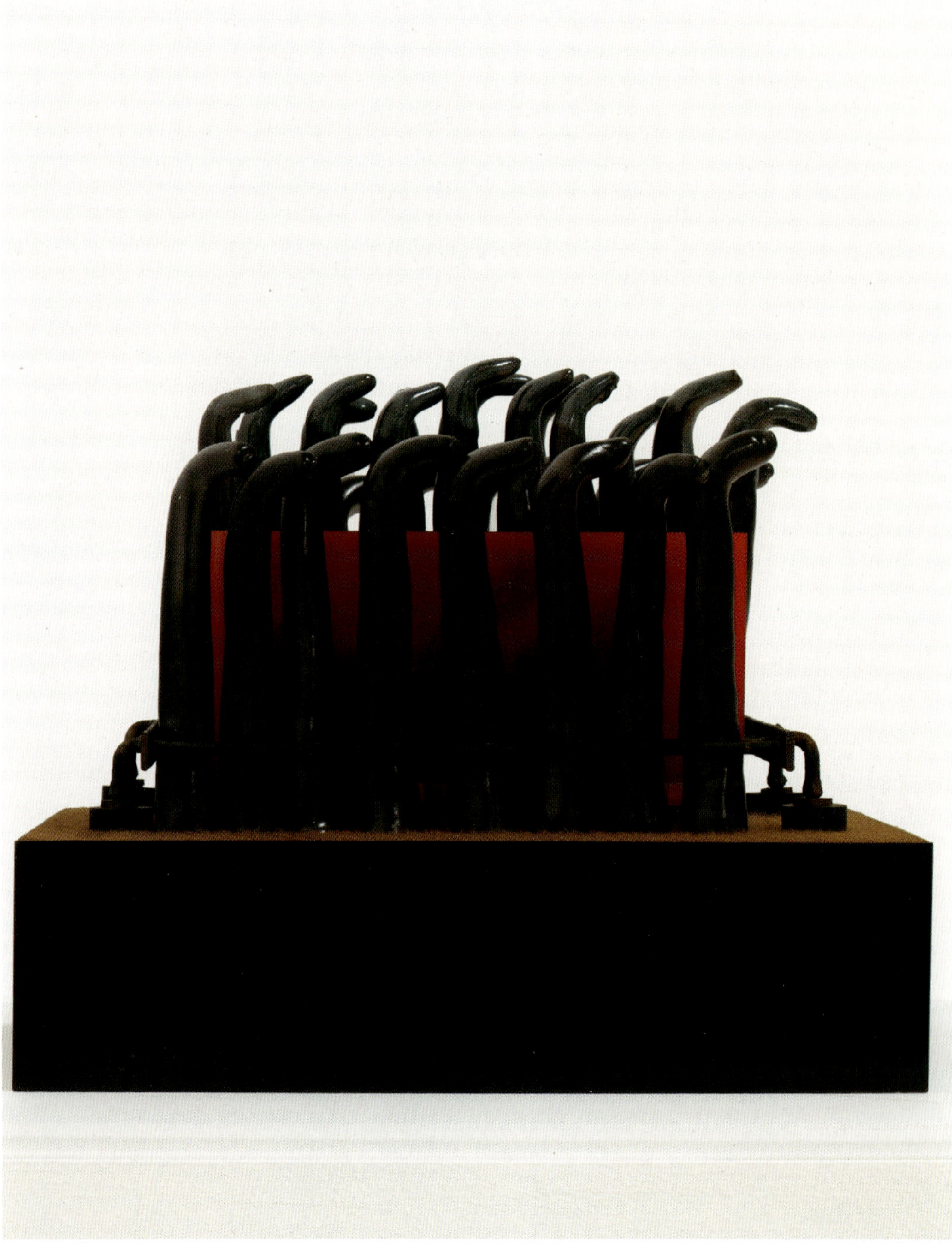

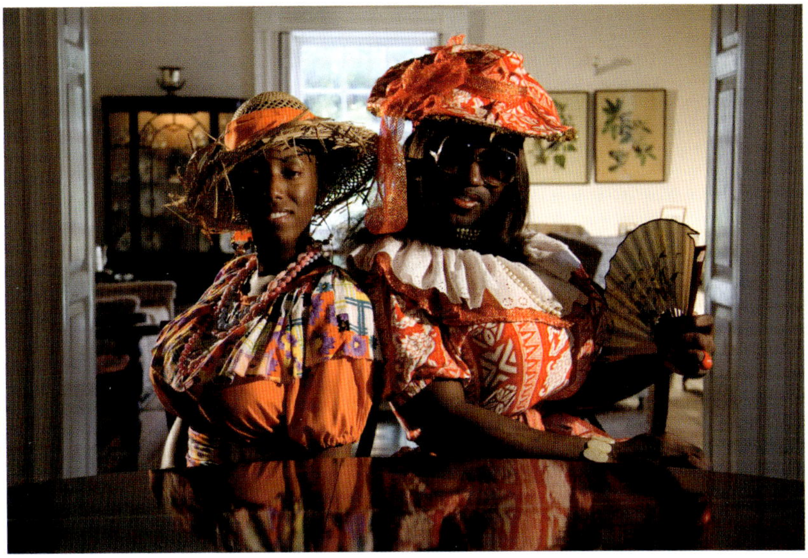

80 Sonia Boyce, *Crop Over*, 2007, still from two-channel video, colour with sound.

was originally dependent, of course, on exploitative labour in the former. As in the recent work of Davis or McLean, the representation of visual symbols and traditions of plantation island life can become critical forms of observation, or even weapons of resistance, mediated through sculpture, film and installation.

Caribbean island struggles for independence haunt the works of many artists featured in 'Life between Islands'. In her 1987 life-size collage/painting *Toussaint L'Ouverture* (illus. 81) Lubaina Himid (born in 1954 in Zanzibar) used the metaphor of breeches to compress colonial histories. L'Ouverture was a Haitian general who led the Revolution on Haiti. His breeches are tightly collaged with cuttings from British newspapers from the early 1980s that reveal racist headlines. To the right of his breeches Himid has written: 'This news wouldn't be news if you had heard of Toussaint L'Ouverture', drawing parallels with the latter's fight for independence against a colonial power. As suggested in my reference to Captain Cook's breeches in Chapter One, as an emblem of eighteenth-century masculine, colonial clothing, breeches can offer the artist a multi-layered metaphor, rich in trans-historical associations. Here they also contain a collaged palimpsest of oppressive stereotypes. Born enslaved in

79 Donald Locke, *Plantation K-140*, 1974, ceramic, wood, steel, acrylic sheet, carpet and laminate.

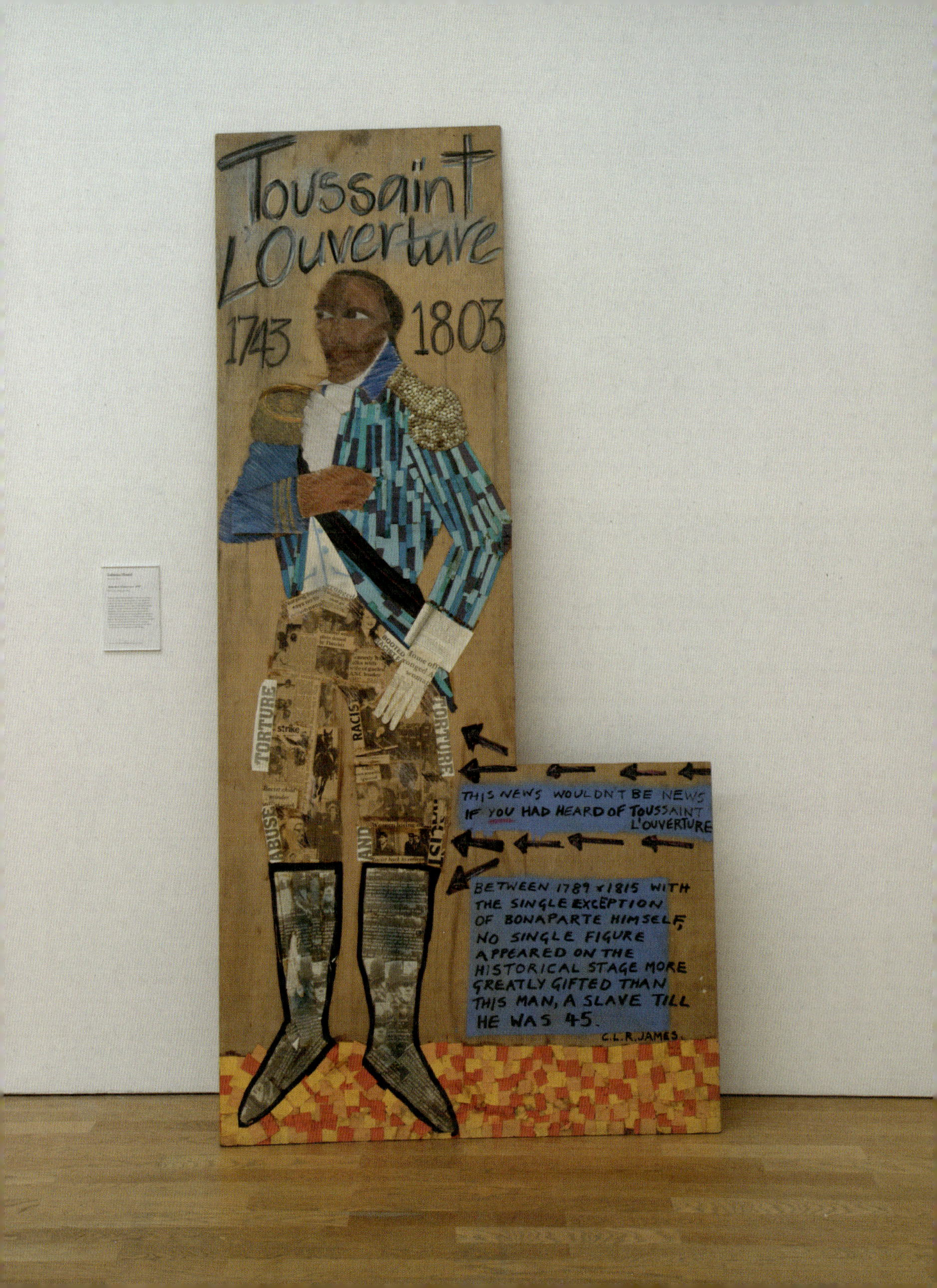
Toussaint L'Ouverture
1743
1803
THIS NEWS WOULDN'T BE NEWS IF YOU HAD HEARD OF TOUSSAINT L'OUVERTURE
BETWEEN 1789 & 1815 WITH THE SINGLE EXCEPTION OF BONAPARTE HIMSELF, NO SINGLE FIGURE APPEARED ON THE HISTORICAL STAGE MORE GREATLY GIFTED THAN THIS MAN, A SLAVE TILL HE WAS 45.
C.L.R. JAMES.
TORTURE

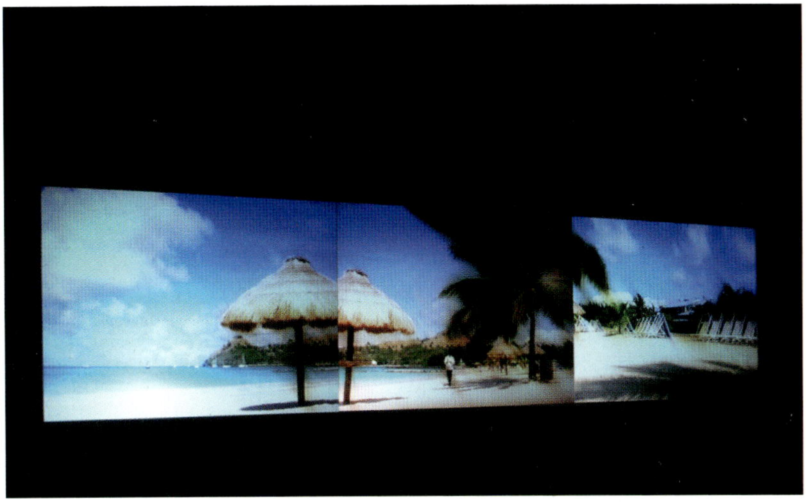

82 Isaac Julien, *Paradise Omeros*, 2002, triple DVD projection, 16 mm film transferred to DVD, 20 minutes, 29 seconds; installation view, Victoria Miro, London, 2003.

Haiti and later granted his freedom, L'Ouverture's French military training enabled him to gain influence and dominance over his colonial rivals; it helped to liberate the island of Haiti.

Isaac Julien (born in London in 1960 to St Lucian parents) and Steve McQueen (born in London in 1969 to a Grenadian mother and Trinidadian father) have both used the medium of film/video to engage directly with problematic ideas of identity, racism and 'islandness'. Isaac Julien's three-screen, 16 mm film *Paradise Omeros* (2002, included in the 'Life between Islands' exhibition) takes its title from Walcott's poem *Omeros* (1990), loosely based on Homer's *Odyssey* (illus. 82). Based on St Lucia and London in the 1960s, Isaac's film is a cryptic exploration of creolization, the complex mixing of languages, cultures and identities that characterize life between cultures and islands. The male protagonist, a waiter called Achille, is shown working in a smart St Lucia Beach Hotel. After encountering a trickster-like character, he walks into the sea, suggesting a drowning (during a Middle Passage voyage?), but re-emerges in a concrete estate in 1960s London. Scenes from a post-Windrush Caribbean house party are combined with violent interruptions, and evocative sea views are juxtaposed with those of burning buildings. Walcott reads from his poem *Omeros* on the soundtrack and is filmed gazing over the

81 Lubaina Himid, *Toussaint L'Ouverture*, 1987, paint and collage on wood.

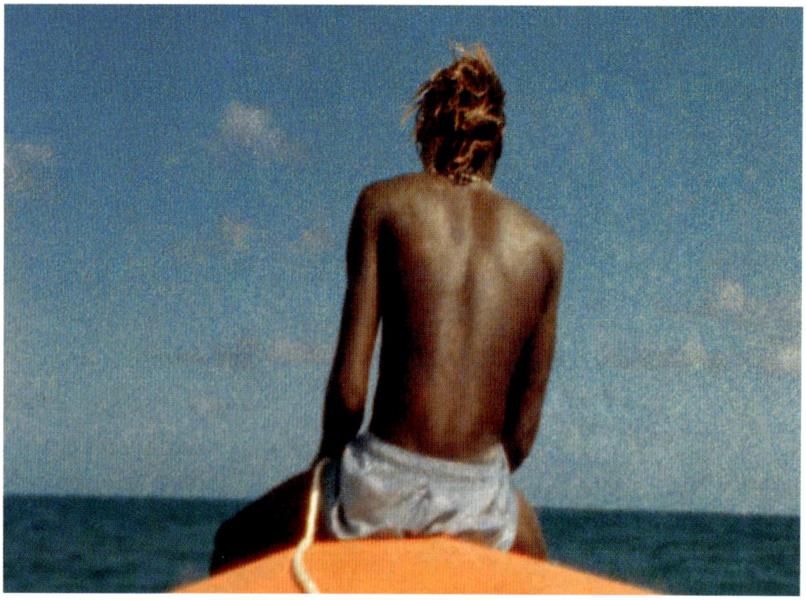

83 Steve McQueen, *Ashes*, 2002–15, still, super 8 and 16 mm colour film, transferred to HD, 20 minutes, 31 seconds.

ocean from his native St Lucia. The ending features an amorous embrace between Achille and a white man, an uneasy fusion of cultures and identities. Imagery of the sea recurs throughout the film, a visual 'tidalectics' that encourages meditation on the tense ebb and flow of a life between islands and cultures. The Caribbean islandness of *Paradise Omeros* is both fluid and hybrid, a visualization of historical trauma and tourist paradise. The idea of the journey between islands (as recounted by both Homer and Walcott) merges memory with diasporic encounters.

Steve McQueen's two-channel video installation *Ashes* (2002–15) was made on two separate visits to the island of Grenada (his mother's birthplace), a former French and British colony that gained independence in 1974. The eponymous protagonist is a smiling Grenadian boy, filmed lounging on his boat on McQueen's first trip in 2002 (illus. 83).[61] When the artist returned to the island in 2015, he looked for Ashes and was told by two local men of his tragic demise. Their account, with the sound of the sea in the background, is played over the earlier footage. Ashes discovered a stash of drugs on a local beach, and when dealers came looking for the loot, they shot him several times as he tried to escape. The juxtaposition of a playful Grenadian boy messing around in a boat on a glorious sunny day with the account of his brutal death represents the contrasting experiences for descendants of enslaved Africans on Grenada. The visual power and resonant repetitive sounds of the Caribbean sea frame a disturbing tale of modern island life enmeshed with poverty and crime.

ISLAND OF BLUE DEVILS

One of the most distinctive and potentially subversive aspects of the Caribbean imaginary is carnival. Many islands have developed exuberant forms of display and traditional folk characters, echoing slave traditions of masquerade and forbidden dances, and demonstrating a vivid cosmopolitan imaginary.[62] Much has now been written about carnival, and the capacity of masquerade to distort social and cultural distinctions. Notwithstanding its importance for the modern tourist appeal of Caribbean islands, carnival has enabled some contemporary artists to blur the boundaries between performance, participation and aesthetic intervention.

Modern Trinidad hosts one of the largest carnivals in the region, much trumpeted in tourist reviews. With its complex social and colonial history, combining French, Spanish and British influences, the island boasts a strong festival tradition that has evolved from the Canboulay festivals of the 1800s. The first 'modern' form of carnival is thought to have been introduced into Trinidad and Tobago in the late eighteenth century by French colonials when settlers brought with them the *mardi gras* masquerades. Although enslaved communities were banned from these events, they would often hold mini carnivals in their backyards, mocking the behaviour of their owners and drawing on their own rituals, folklore and religious histories. Following emancipation in 1834, these African and creolized communities embraced such festivals as expressions of their newly found freedoms and subcultures. Christian religious customs were syncretized with Yoruban customs and folk characters reimagined. The famous Trinidadian Blue Devil is one such character, with its origins in the figure of Jab Molassies, freed slaves from the sugar plantations who disguised themselves with sticky sugar molasses, carried farm implements and allegedly ran around persuading people to give them money. 'Playing the Blue Devil' has become one of the most vivid signifiers of modern creolized Trinidadian culture. Originally played by masqueraders from the Trinidadian hill village of Paramin, the Blue Devils and their carnivalesque traditions are enmeshed with the island's folk history and have informed the work of several artists born or working in Trinidad, including Chris Ofili, McLean, Peter Doig and Lisa Brice. Blue is a colour loaded with local significance; apart from its association with the working man, blue carbolic 'cake soap' was used for washing white linen, as a skin lightener and was hung above doorways to protect against unwanted spirits and omens. Often adopted by island artists and musicians, this unique performance as *Blue Devils*, replete with multi-layered cultural symbols, is rich in subversive potential.

After moving from London to Trinidad in 2005, Chris Ofili (born in Manchester in 1968 to Nigerian parents), painted several large-scale blue canvases. In his *Blue Devils* (2014; illus. 84) an almost monochrome blue space reveals ghostly carnival figures, perhaps British soldiers/police, all set in a forest at night. Ofili's saturated colour reduces the figures to menacing silhouettes. He recalls: 'I'd seen the blue devils, and the power of dark blue, and I realized it was more than a color – it had a strength other than color strength.'[63] Ofili also suggests a menacing reference to the 'boys in blue', signifying both the local police and the oppressive policies of the British police, especially stop and search. Matthew Ryder has suggested that Ofili has effectively 'subverted the famous Trinidadian Carnival reference, transposing it to the streets of London, Manchester or New York'.[64] Moreover, the painterly flatness of the dark indigo washes, itself a modernist trope, seems to contribute to its 'exotic' camouflaged effect.[65] Leon Wainwright suggests that Trinidad is an essentially hybrid space of production, in which 'tourism and the tropics collide at the locus of vision and the painted, printed and photographic image'.[66] Ofili's *Blue Devils* might be seen as a paradigmatic example of this complex collision enabling multiple levels of meaning.

84 Chris Ofili, *Blue Devils*, 2014, oil paint and charcoal on canvas.

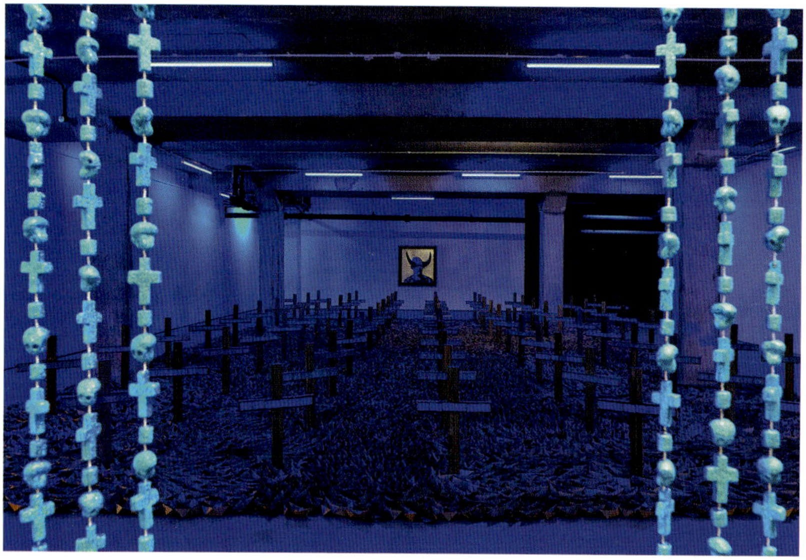

85 Karen McLean, *Blue Power*, 2021, carbolic soap, plasterers' laths, 12,000 paper boats; installation view, Block 336, Brixton, London.

In 2021 Karen McLean filled a basement room at Block 336, Brixton, London, with eighty wooden crucifixes bathed in a field of saturated blue light. *Blue Power* (previously exhibited at the Ort Gallery, Birmingham, in 2018) appeared like a memorial site of war graves (illus. 85). The visitor entered through a curtain of blue soap (washing away bad vibes) and encountered a field of crosses made of plasterer's lathes and cross bars of blue soap, and 12,000 hand-folded paper boats. At the back of the installation sat a plywood Blue Devil, painted with beeswax, Reckitt's Crown Blue and ultramarine blue pigment, framed in a bed of 22-carat gold leaf. In this eerie space, McLean's value-laden Blue Devil appears to be mimicking the religious icons of his predecessors. The artist asks: 'have we become so oblivious to the murder statistics that we are like the carnival bystander: just willing to pay the price of losing a generation of young men – pay the devil and avoid contact with the issues?'[67] Despite relatively low levels of unemployment on Trinidad, violent crime and drug trafficking have plagued the island.[68] McLean activates visual symbols from history and the popular imaginary to become agents of her Caribbean island projects and their decolonial ambitions. Her Trinidadian Devils, Jamaican Nannies and Barbados sugar houses mix historical and modern references, using messy artistic processes of sculpture, embroidery, bricolage, branding and repetition to create metonymic signifiers of islandness. Throughout this chapter, Caribbean islandness has been explored as a weighty palimpsest, a creative compression of multilayered cultural symbols, hybrid histories and interrelationships between different racialized identities.

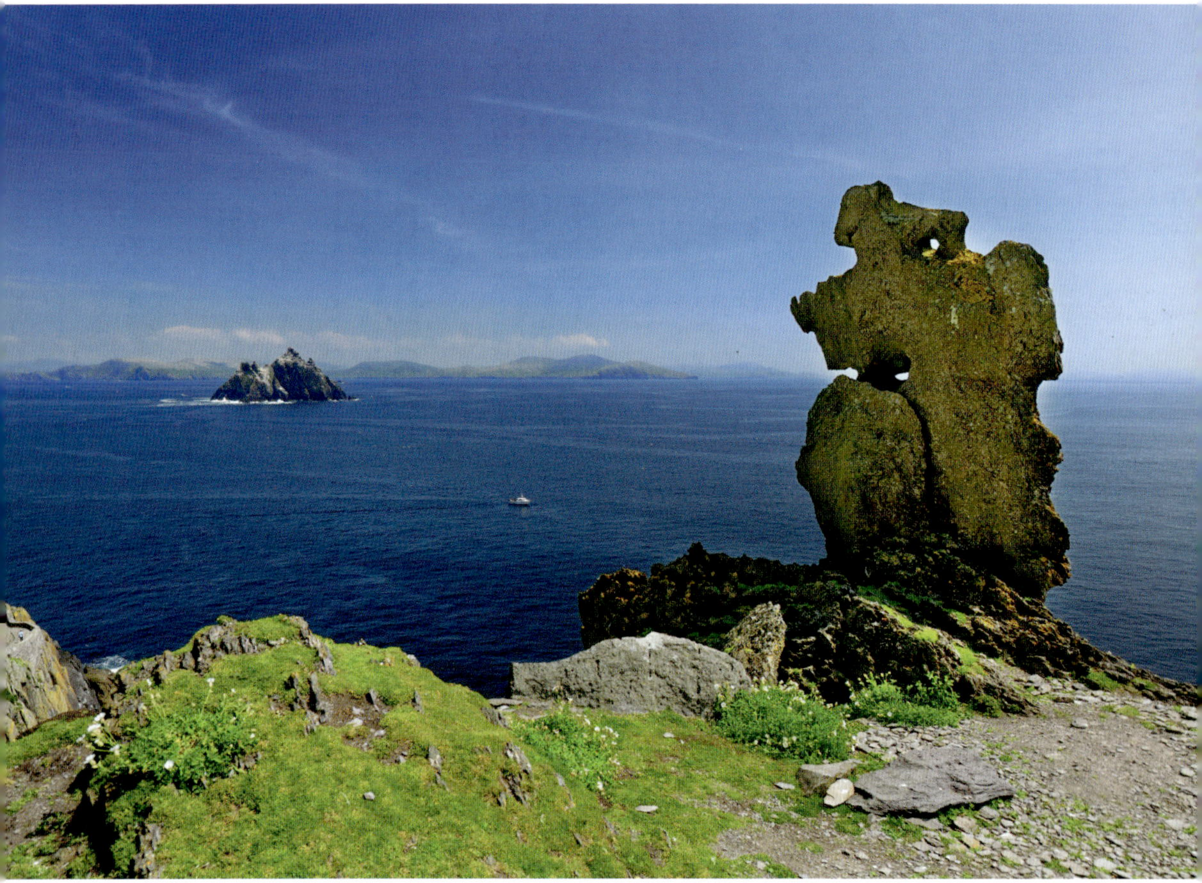

86 View of Skellig Michael with the Wailing Woman Rock and Little Skellig, County Kerry, Ireland.

6 IRISH ISLANDS: OF MYTHS AND MAPS

One of the hardest islands to reach on the Irish Atlantic coast is Skellig Michael, an uninhabited outcrop of pyramidal rock about 11 kilometres (7 mi.) off the Iveragh peninsula of County Kerry. Home to sea birds such as gannets, puffins and razor bills, and a colony of grey seals, this inhospitable site also hosts an ancient Celtic monastery, founded between the sixth and eighth centuries, a ruined medieval church and an oddly shaped natural landmark called the Wailing Woman Rock. The Skelligs, along with some of the Blasket islands, make up some of the most westerly parts of both Ireland and Europe – the 'Atlantic edge' (illus. 86).[1] The rock of Skellig Michael features at the beginning of the art historian Kenneth Clark's renowned BBC series *Civilisation* of 1969 as one of the most remote and remarkable outposts of medieval 'civilization'. He claimed it is hard to believe that 'Western civilization survived by clinging on to places like these'.[2] Early Christianity often established religious communities on islands, believing that the physical isolation enabled a more direct channel to God. More controversially, its landscape has also featured in the two most recent *Star Wars* films. Its bleak 'islandness' has entered the modern cultural imaginary, encouraging an (often unwelcome) increase in tourism.

Over the centuries literary and artistic representations of these weather-beaten islands of the Irish archipelago, especially the West Coast, have contributed to a legendary sense of a hardy, self-sufficient Celtic identity. In Seamus Heaney's celebrated poem of 1966, 'Storm on the Island', an island dweller describes how squat houses, built into rock, and sparse trees protect inhabitants as gales ravage the landscape and the sea 'explodes' down the cliffs:

But no: when it begins, the flung spray hits
The very windows, spits like a tame cat
Turned savage. We just sit tight while wind dives
And strafes invisibly. Space is a salvo,
We are bombarded with the empty air.[3]

The poem can be read on many levels, and as a Northern Irish poet, Heaney was adept at deploying natural metaphors to convey multiple meanings. Island is a homophone for Ireland and the 'Storm' is code for Stormont, the seat of the Northern Ireland Government, also spelled out by the first eight letters of the title. Heaney's metaphorical storm alludes to the Northern Irish Troubles, bubbling up at the time. He often concealed references to contemporary Irish politics, a strategy adopted less obliquely, through use of visual imagery and metaphor, in the work of several contemporary women artists that I discuss below. The poem also provides a powerful representation of the fierce weather that batters the barren landscapes on those Irish Atlantic islands.

MOTHER IRELAND

That 'strafing' wind is the most familiar visitor to Skellig Michael and its remaining landmarks. Significantly, perhaps, Clark did not mention Skellig's Wailing Woman Rock, visibly strafed and eroded by storms. She commands a lofty, exposed position in the centre of the island overlooking a smaller, inaccessible and uninhabited Little Skellig and the Irish mainland beyond, from where she speaks symbolically of the trials and tribulations of centuries of local history – and Irish history more broadly. As such she could be seen to represent a different approach to Irish history to that taken by Clark in the 1960s. Her status as an expressive, grieving woman and a piece of natural, weathered rock encapsulates her mythical Irishness. Symbols of these islands, and the nation, are often gendered feminine.

Ireland's complex historical and political identity (encompassing both the Irish Republic and Northern Ireland) has long been enmeshed with its geographical and mythical status as a large island within its own archipelago, bounded and separated by sea from its colonial neighbour. Relationships with that neighbour have inevitably affected different perceptions of an 'island nation'. In Northern Ireland, for example, some unionists still refer to Britain as 'the mainland'.[4] That said, the landscape and culture of the archipelago that make up the Irish Republic are steeped in gendered histories. In her famous 1976 memoir *Mother Ireland* the Irish writer Edna O'Brien mapped a history of invasions and 'infiltrations' from the end of the Ice Age, arguing that despite the armies and delegations that 'tried to subdue her, Ireland was never fully taken, though most thoroughly dispossessed'.[5] Tracing the many invasions from across the Irish sea, O'Brien describes centuries of 'colonisation, decimation, rebellion, counter-rebellion, laws, impaling, statutes . . . Ireland has always been a woman, a womb, a cave, a cow, a Rosaleen, a sow; a bride, a harlot and, of course, the gaunt Hag of Rosaleen'.[6] While narratives of exploration and discovery have been dominated by male storytelling and masculine activities, symbolic identifications of the nation and its geography have more often been feminine. Colonial bids to conquer and control a land often gender it as feminine. The colonial feminization of Ireland and the Irish was adapted and reworked within both religious and Irish nationalist discourse.[7] This sense of Ireland as an archipelago rich in mythical and gendered histories and separated from its colonial 'master' by a watery border has informed some of the most interesting artworks produced on and around these islands.

Mother Ireland has a complicated history in literary and visual representation. As O'Brien suggests, she has enjoyed a range of personifications, including My Dark Rosaleen (Róisín Dubh), Kathleen Ni Houlihan, Deirdre of Sorrows or Mother Eire.[8] She is often depicted as an amalgam of various Celtic goddesses and Catholic fantasies, including Danu, not to mention Queen Maeve (Medb in Old Irish), a strong-willed warrior queen from Irish mythology. Her symbolic possibilities are also rooted in Catholic mythology and sometimes merged with the Virgin Mary, Mary Magdalene and a 'Wailing Woman'. Anne Crilly's film *Mother Ireland*

(1988) reviews this complicated and controversial iconography.[9] Given the complexity of these multiple representations and their political implications, Mother Ireland can also reveal a deep-seated fear of, and resistance to, women's sexual, political and religious emancipation. As an imaginary, romanticized vision of a nation, she can be both a protective mother and a mother/woman in need of protection. Such tropes have presented generic, simplified images of women as either oversexed or desexualized. The Irish poet Eavan Boland sought to rewrite and reclaim this mythology inherited from a male literary tradition. Although vulnerable to accusations of a revised form of essentialism, Boland's poems such as *Mise Eire*, *The Making of an Irish Goddess* or *Mother Ireland* align some traditional female personifications of Irish nationalism with women's lived experience.[10] *Mother Ireland* opens with the metaphor of woman as an embodied Irish landscape:

> At first
>   I was land
> I lay on my back to be fields
> and when turned
>   on my side
>   I was a hill
> under freezing stars.
>   I did not see.
>   I was seen.

But Boland soon tells us that she, as a woman poet, is reclaiming her story, which is different from 'the story told about me'.[11]

It is no coincidence, then, that many visual artworks and projects on the Irish island theme are by women artists. Like Boland, they have struggled to reclaim some of the gendered allegories, religious metaphors and essentialist tropes that have infused Irish landscape and culture both north and south of the border. Irish art practice has undergone some major shifts since the 1980s; artists are increasingly adopting installation, film, mixed media and performance art, and contributing to a wider, connected

87 Jesse Jones, *Tremble Tremble*, 2017, production image, 57th Venice Biennale performance, 2017.

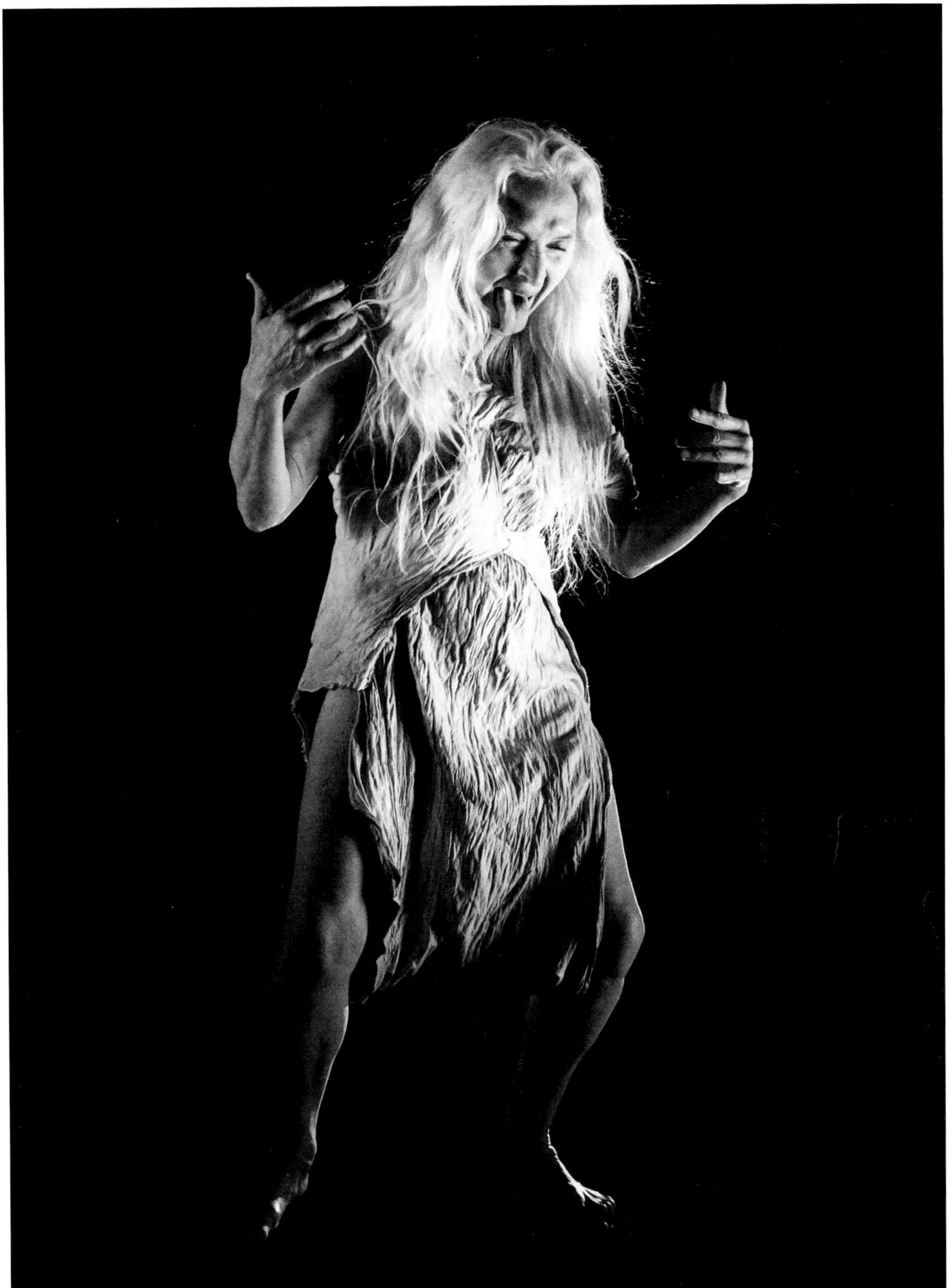

(global) field of art practice. The exhibition 'Elliptical Affinities: Irish Women Artists and the Politics of the Body' at the Highlanes Gallery, Drogheda, in 2019–20 directly addressed the intense engagement of so many Irish women artists from the period with the island's symbolic history as a woman, often embodied and visceral. Curated by the art historian Fionna Barber and the gallery director Aoife Ruane in the wake of the successful 2018 referendum to repeal the Eighth Amendment of 1983 in the Irish Republic, it traced the generational struggles of women artists and the interconnectedness of feminist art and politics.[12] The exhibition explored the frequent conflation of Irish geography and culture with the representation of women's bodies. Barber identified associations and affinities between Irish women artists and their use of the theme of the (female) body that enabled some vivid forms of art practice 'that defy the silencing strategies that still persist within art history, both in Ireland and elsewhere'.[13]

Works in the exhibition by Irish artists such as Alice Maher, Rachel Fallon, Jesse Jones, Dorothy Cross, Pauline Cummins, Amanda Coogan and Kathy Prendergast (among others) revealed that a critical engagement with tropes of the body and domesticity as allegories of 'Irishness' are recurring features within recent Irish art by women. For example, video and performance are widely used, enabling an emphasis on the profoundly corporeal and temporal nature of performance, especially when enacted by a woman's body, with its heavy allegorical baggage of Mother Nature/ Mother Ireland. Jesse Jones's powerful film installation *Tremble Tremble* (illus. 87), commissioned for the Irish Pavilion of the 57th Venice Biennale of 2017, deployed the figure of the witch as a potentially disruptive feminine archetype, with a visceral performance by Olwen Fouéré as Temperance Lloyd, whose gigantic white-haired maternal body performs the 'bodily territory of the woman', and in the process '[peels] away layers of patriarchy', as described by Jones (b. 1974).[14] Although Temperance Lloyd was allegedly one of the last witches to be hung in England, Jones's archetype also stands for all the Irish witches, hags and goddess-like figures that have embodied both national histories and their symbolic landscapes.[15]

88 Kathy Prendergast, *To Alter a Landscape*, 'Body Maps Series', 1983, mixed media on paper, unframed.

TO ALTER A LANDSCAPE

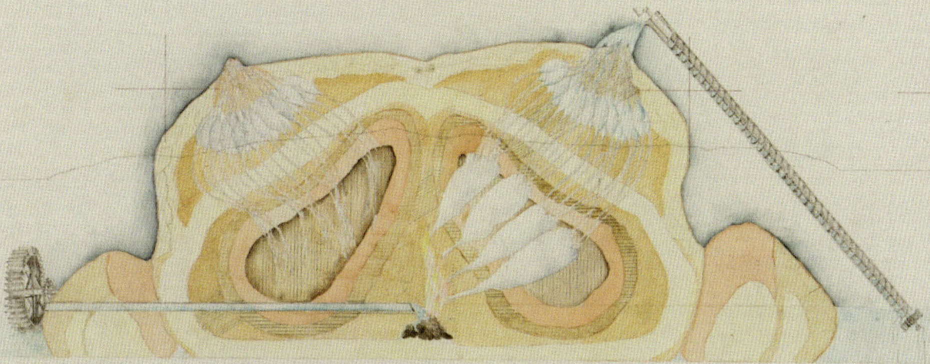

Volcanic Mountain: To quench a Fire

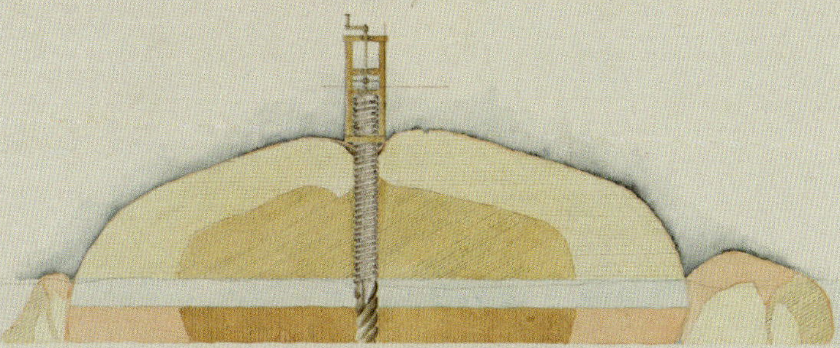

Desert: To find a Well

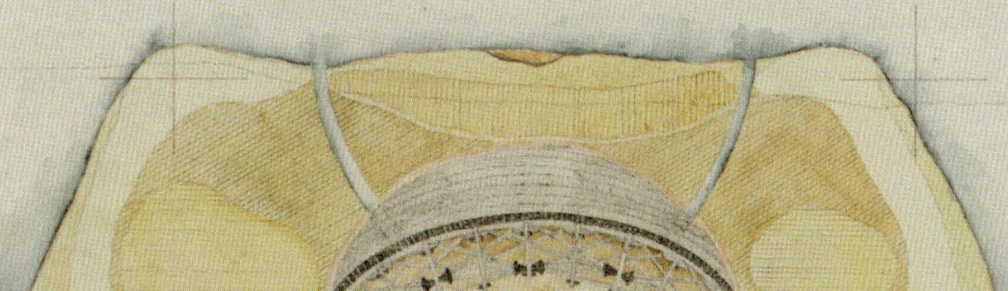

Cavern: To mine a Passage to the Harbour

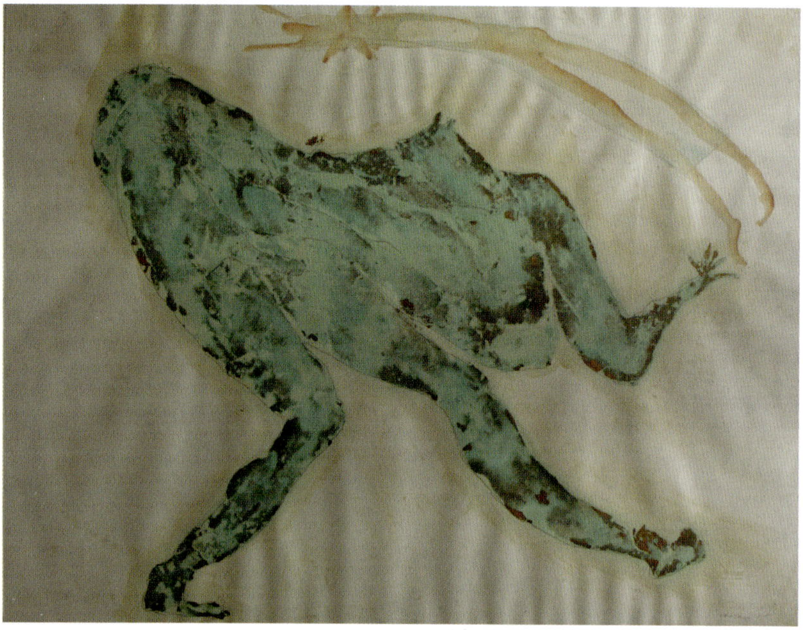

89 Kathy Prendergast, *Untitled*, 1985, watercolour.

This theme is developed further in Jones's recent work *The Tower* (2022), an immersive film installation that reclaims the lives of women who were burned as heretics even before the first witch trials in the seventeenth century, and explores the Christian mythologies of figures such as Mary Magdalene (discussed below).[16]

More direct references to Ireland as a corporeal landscape – as a feminine geography – are addressed in the work of Kathy Prendergast (b. 1958). In the 1980s Prendergast produced a series of 'Body Maps' that combine representations of landscape with the female body to explore issues of ownership and the colonization of Ireland. In one series of three drawings from 1983, parts of a woman's body are imaginatively drawn in pen and ink in a somewhat surreal, pseudo-cartographic form under the title 'To Alter a Landscape' (illus. 88). This technique recalls both the British Ordnance Survey's mapping of a colonized Ireland in the early nineteenth century and the styles of gynaecological diagrams, evoking a connection between colonial control of both lands and female sexuality.[17] In works such as her *City Drawing Series* of 1997 Prendergast has continued to explore the relationship of cartography with practices of power and knowledge.[18] Mapping is perceived as a complex form of mediation, rich in imaginative possibilities and visual puzzles.

Prendergast has also used watercolour to signal a slippery ambiguity between both female and male bodies and ideas of (Irish) landscape. In her *Untitled* watercolour series (1985), female and male bodies appear to morph into inchoate connected forms. These watery, amorphous limbs also suggest undulating landscapes – or strange islands. In several images the female (or male) limbs appear with or against a green patina, a more literal reference to the green grass of land – and, by implication, the 'Emerald Isle' (illus. 89). Such elliptical references to a problematic Mother Ireland in her various mythological and geographical disguises continue to inform many aspects of recent and contemporary Irish art.

ON THE ATLANTIC EDGE

Small islands in the Irish archipelago are also implicated in these fluid, gendered meanings. The geographer and cultural historian Catherine Nash has argued that traditional representations of Irish landscape 'are imbued with conceptions of both national and gender identity, most significantly in the imagery of the West of Ireland'.[19] The three Aran Islands at the mouth of Galway Bay on the west coast have long attracted the interest of artists and poets. Steeped in Irish history, these islands boast some of the country's oldest archaeological remains, including Bronze Age and Iron Age forts. Ancient stone walls criss-cross the land and enclose fields of grazing sheep and livestock, alongside traces of pre-medieval Christian landmarks; the largest island, Inishmór, was once home to twelve monasteries.

Representations of Aran as revealing an earlier stage of Irish national culture, somehow frozen in time, abound within art, film and literature. Concerns about the preservation of cultural purity and national identity were often focused on the west of Ireland, a region that offered the strongest contrast to the colonial landscape of 'Englishness'.[20] In the first few decades of the twentieth century the visual iconography of those west-coast islands on the 'Celtic Fringe' was often seen to represent an archetypal Irish landscape, saturated in what Nash describes as a 'primitivization of the West and of women'.[21] In the early twentieth century the work of the Irish painter Paul Henry (1877–1958?), who lived intermittently on Achill Island, was widely seen to visualize this perceived Irishness. He and his wife Grace were painters influenced by European modernism, and developed modern 'primitivized' languages for the representation of local peasant women and men of the west coast of Ireland.[22] But this reworking of late nineteenth-century French Primitivism, reminiscent of both Gauguin and Van Gogh, was double edged in its application to Irish culture. While it challenged existing sentimental representations of Irish peasantry off the western seaboard, offering a positive representation of its strong, cohesive community, it could also feed into debates about the ideal Celtic feminine. Mother Ireland has offered artists and writers a shifting set of signifiers for both the national character and its island geography. As Nash has argued, the supposed instinctive and unselfconscious sexuality of the 'primitive', 'had to be reconciled with the use of women by cultural nationalists as signifiers of moral purity and sexual innocence'.[23] This sense of the necessary moral purity of Irish femininity has left its own contentious legacy, a theme explored by many of the contemporary Irish women artists featured in this chapter.

Despite its artistic appeal, Achill Island does not share the distinctive remoteness of the Aran Isles. Further from the west coast, Skellig Michael and the Aran Isles are more often seen as part of the windswept, inhospitable 'Atlantic Edge' (a term used to describe Ireland's rugged, most western coast and archipelagos). A strongly masculine Irish identity was depicted in the influential fictional documentary *Man of Aran* of 1934, directed by the American filmmaker Robert J. Flaherty (illus. 90). Here the inhabitants of the three Isles of Aran are shown struggling to survive, fishing off steep cliffs, farming poor soil, fighting gales and hunting for basking sharks; the film finishes with a dramatic storm that destroys the protagonist's boat. Flaherty set up a studio on Inishmór in 1931 and shot his footage over the next two years using local subjects. As a silent film,

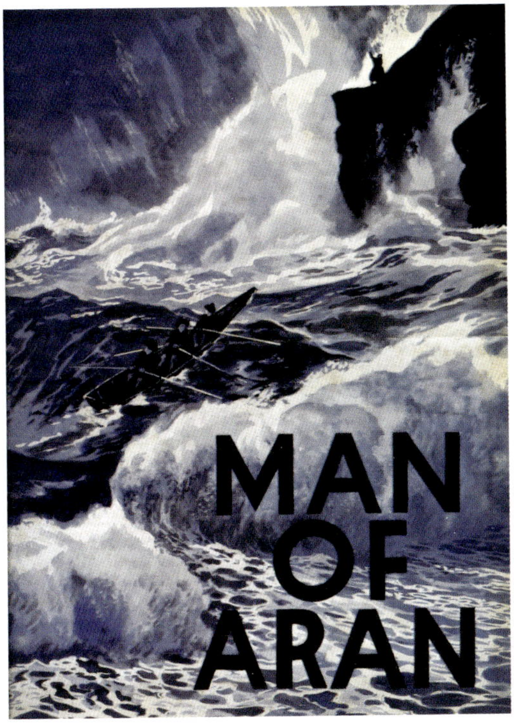

90 Poster for the film *Man of Aran* (1934, dir. Robert J. Flaherty).

it used a lengthy caption to set the scene for a fiercely independent masculinity. It describes vicious winter storms and gigantic seas: 'In this desperate environment the Man of Aran, because his independence is the most precious privilege he can win from life, fights for his existence, bare though it might be. It is a fight from which he will have no respite until the end of his indomitable days or until he meets his master – the sea.'[24]

Although mired in controversy about the accuracy of the events depicted (including shark-hunting, which at that time had died out on Aran), and subsequently accused of romanticizing its subjects, down-playing the important roles of women and avoiding the harsh social and economic reality of life on these islands, the film opened to major publicity and various awards in London and Dublin in 1934.[25] In the Irish capital the film's traditional image of a resilient Irish island community was enthusiastically received by the ruling party Fianna Fáil and its president, Éamon de Valera. The controversies inspired the American filmmaker George Stoney's 1978 documentary *How the Myth was Made*, now marketed on DVD with the original film. Stoney visited the islands, exploring the island life and culture, and concluded that *Man of Aran* had significantly contributed to the myths surrounding this notion of islandness on the Atlantic Edge. Debates linger on regarding the value and historical relevance of Flaherty's film, and have informed some evocative works of contemporary art.

In 1997 Dorothy Cross implicated this mythical history when she integrated a scene from *Man of Aran* into her first video work, *Teacup* (illus. 91). Film footage of wind-tossed curraghs and savage seas is projected onto a piece of inherited porcelain. The historical Irish 'memory' of

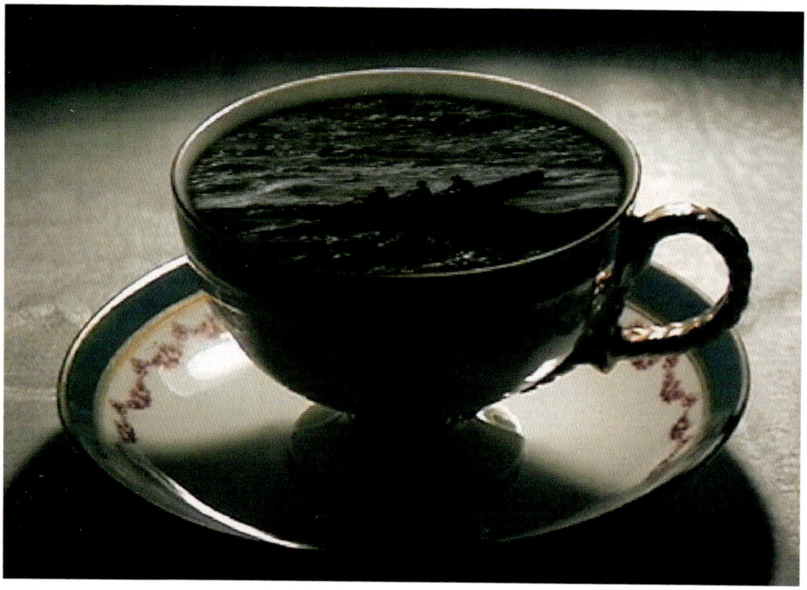

91 Dorothy Cross, *Teacup*, 1997, porcelain, video still.

harsh subsistence living on the island is juxtaposed with a fragile symbol of Irish bourgeois refinement. The cup and saucer, inherited from Cross's mother in Cork, are both decorated with garlands of delicate pink flowers, contributing to what Marina Warner has described as 'competing nostalgias, for civility on the one hand, for salt-of-the-earth authenticity on the other'.[26] Such 'competing nostalgias' haunt the written and visual histories of so many Irish islands.

Over the last few decades aspects of Aran's local history have also been reclaimed for what is loosely labelled 'salvage ethnography'. The writer, artist and cartographer Tim Robinson (1935–2020) used his map-making skills to reinscribe Aran's Irish history into visual representation. In his redrawn map of the Aran Islands at a scale of 2.2 inches (5.5 cm) to the mile, *Arainn* (1968), he meticulously translates and lists place names in Irish, adding layers to the original ordnance survey maps. He moved to the West of Ireland in 1972, having noticed that maps of the local areas were anglicized, bland and inaccurate. He set about walking around the local landscape, recording every place and track in minute detail in drawings made with ink on paper, and these works are included in his series *Folding*

Landscapes (1980). Viewing from above, he used a downward-facing splay to list and name every landmark, presenting a visual meditation on the history of place. Somewhere between a drawing and a map, Robinson's *Arainn* reclaims the landscape from the postcolonial cartographers, creating what Declan Quirke has described as an 'encyclopaedic novel spread over a single page'.[27]

Today the Aran Isles are probably best known for the thick, high-quality wool that weatherproofs its sturdy, storm-resistant breeds of sheep. An online search for Aran wool sweaters usually leads to a host of fashion outlets, many of them advertising jumpers for men. Yet those famous patterned fishermen's jumpers are enmeshed in myths of 'Irishness' and, of

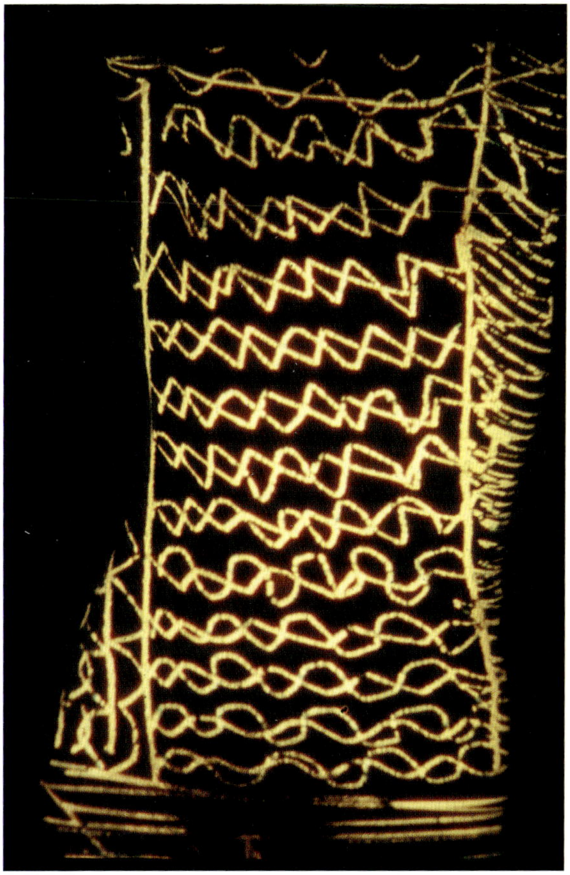

92 Pauline Cummins, *Innis t'Oirr/Aran Dance*, 1985, slides, sound.

course, traditionally spun and knitted by women, work that is now increasingly mechanized. In a slide-tape work of 1985, *Inis t'Oirr* (Aran Dance), the artist Pauline Cummins projected her sketches of local knitting patterns (now thought to originate as late as the 1930s) onto an eroticized male body (illus. 92), a deliberate confusion of the relationship of both the male and female body to notions of Irishness.[28] Behind the chevron and zigzag patterning, the rugged Aran fisherman has been replaced by a sensuous and anonymous male body, an object of female desire. Cummins presents another reworking of Flaherty's prototype that is merged with a female gaze. The traces of women's work – their local island patterns – are interwoven with a memory of their erotic desires.

The retrieval of women's history on islands along the Irish Atlantic Edge has featured in recent works by women artists. Drawing on her characteristic 'bricoleur's ingenuity', Dorothy Cross has explored the work of a notable woman botanist based on another west-coast island.[29] In 2001 the artist visited Valentia Island, off the Iveragh peninsula, southwest of Kerry, to research the life of Maude Delap (1866–1953), who first bred jellyfish in bell-jars in her father's house on the island in 1902. Jellyfish, and their metaphorical potential, are recognizable themes in Cross's oeuvre, revealing her capacity for 'making strange'.[30] During her visit to Valentia Island she also came across a remarkable grotto in a slate quarry that had been dedicated to the Virgin Mary in 1954 (illus. 93). That year the men and women of the island had offered their wedding rings and other valuables to crown statues of Mary with gold; this spectacular slate grotto was infused with the visibly sparkling cult of the Virgin Mary. In the process, Ireland's symbolic women were enmeshed with the natural and industrial history of Valentia Island. As Cross wrote: 'The Grotto contains statues of the Virgin Mary and Saint Bernadette located above a gaping hole of sliced rock leading into the mountainside. It is a place of overlapping elements: an excavation into the earth, an amphitheatre, an industrial slate quarry and a shrine.'[31] Inspired by the possibilities of the site, Cross suggested setting an opera there and the Opera Theatre Company, directed by James Conway, staged Pergolesi's seventeenth-century arrangement of *Stabat*

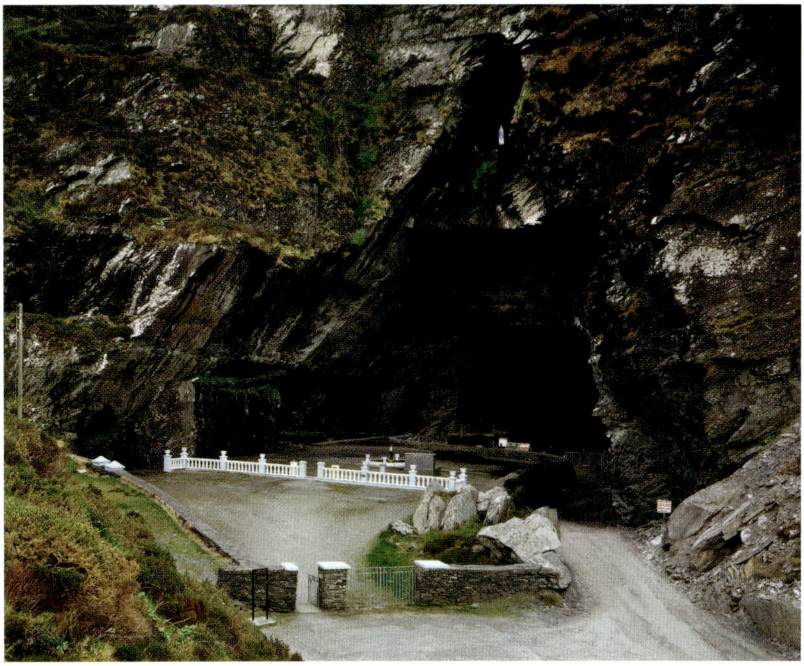

93 Dorothy Cross, *Valentia Island*, 2005, entrance to grotto, photograph.

Mater in 2005. A soprano, counter tenor and nine baroque players emerged from the back of the cave dressed in dirty miner's clothes. As the performance ended, they returned into the bowels of the quarry. Meanwhile a large video screen emerged from the cave displaying an open mouth and blasting out industrial sounds. The dramatic effects of this Wagnerian-style performance, which showed over three nights, were accentuated by the weather. Cross recalls that the prevailing winds, which usually blew in from the southwest, turned to the north and blew straight into the cave: 'Sheets of horizontal rain soaked the singers, drops pouring down their faces like tears.' The performers retreated further and further back into the cave to protect their instruments. As Cross notes, 'the elements added a power that could not be faked.'[32] Seamus Heaney's violent, strafing wind, that elemental force of west-coast islandness, enriched the aesthetic power of a modern multimedia spectacle in which even the cultural power of the Virgin Mary seemed overshadowed – or perhaps overwhelmed.

MYTHICAL AND MYSTICAL

The history of the Irish archipelago is replete with tales of mystical islands and voyages of discovery that were often driven by fantasies of a Celtic Elysium. No myth is perhaps better known than that of Hy-Brasil, a long-lost land supposedly located beyond the Aran Isles, 322 kilometres (200 mi.) southwest of Galway Bay, and represented in the poem 'Hy-Brasail: The Isle of the Blest' by Limerick-born Gerald Griffin (1803–1840). The poem tells of a peasant who set sail from Aran in search of this fabled island.

> ON the ocean that hollows the rocks where ye dwell
> A shadowy land has appeared, as they tell;
> Men thought it a region of sunshine and rest,
> And they called it Hy-Brasail, the isle of the blest;
> From year unto year, on the ocean's blue rim,
> The beautiful spectre showed lovely and dim;
> The golden clouds curtained the deep where it lay,
> And it looked like an Eden, away, far away![33]

However, this 'rash dreamer' searched in vain and died at sea. A persistent Atlantis-like mythology developed around the island, drawn on maps as early as 1325 (illus. 94). Fourteenth-century Mediterranean mapmakers marked it on nautical charts, and a dubious cartographic history turned a myth into a presumed reality (a cultural tendency that Smithson exploited in his *Hypothetical Islands* series, featured in Chapter Three). The travel writer Philip Marsden, who has explored mythical islands along the west coast of Ireland and the Scottish Hebrides in his book *The Summer Isles* (2019), has claimed that his own home in Cornwall was once owned by a family who lost all their money in the sixteenth century searching in vain for Hy-Brasil.[34] That said, according to Irish legend, in 1674 Captain John Nesbit from County Donegal came across the island of Hy-Brasil on a voyage from Ireland to France. As he approached the Irish coast on his return from France, Nesbit and his crew allegedly found themselves close to an unknown rocky coastline; they decided that it was most likely Hy-Brasil

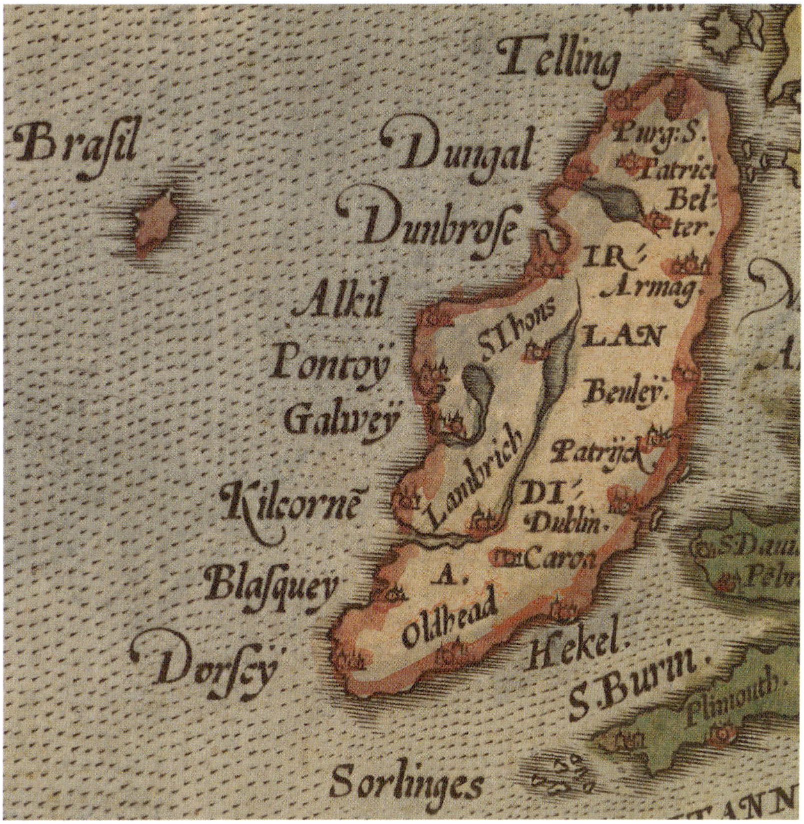

94 Map of Ireland showing Hy-Brasil, from Abraham Ortelius, *Theatrum Orbis Terarrum* (1570).

and went ashore.[35] Reports recount that they found a fertile land with grazing cattle, horses and sheep, and a castle, but no people around. Locals had allegedly been imprisoned in the castle by a 'the malicious, diabolical art of the great Negromancer [*sic*]' who had cursed the island. Nesbit's fire had broken his spell, and they were freed.[36] According to this unlikely tale, Nesbit sailed back to Killybegs laden with gold and silver given by grateful islanders. A few days later another expedition sailed to Hy-Brasil and returned to Ireland claiming to have been generously entertained by the islanders and confirmed the stories.[37] As Barbara Freitag has summarized it, Hy-Brasil metamorphosed from 'Cartographic Error to Celtic Elysium'.[38]

However, like many island tales, evidence and sightings of Hy-Brasil as a landmass became more elusive over the centuries. Not until the studies

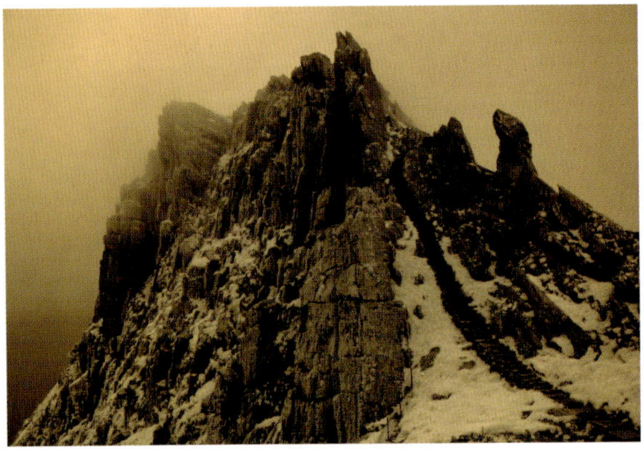

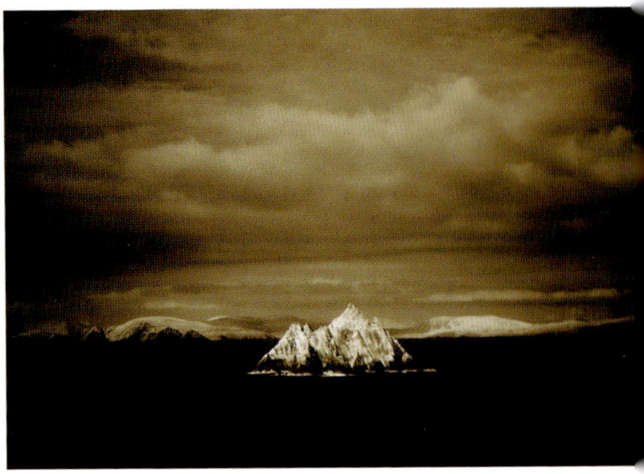

of nineteenth-century cartographers was the existence of this Celtic 'land of enchantment' finally questioned. It disappeared from cartographic records in 1865. Unlike many phantom islands, it seems to have maintained roughly the same location and physical shape (oddly circular crossed by a central river). One theory posited for its strange disappearance is the effects of subsidence in the shallow banks and cold-water reefs west of Ireland. The many legends of Hy-Brasil provide further evidence of the rich and self-perpetuating potential for island mythology, especially on Ireland's Atlantic Edge. Throughout Western (and global) histories we find a recurring need to construct fantasies of alternative societies and geographies sited on elusive landmasses surrounded by sea and awaiting discovery by the intrepid (male) explorer. As Griffin's poem tells us, myths of Hy-Brasil as a 'beautiful spectre' or an 'Eden far away' abound in Irish legend. Celtic myths in which heroes, beckoned by the mirage of 'gold-roofed towers and domes that glistened from beneath the waves', set out to sea towards the land of magic are common.[39]

Hy-Brasil is a recurring trope in Irish writing, and has continued to inspire various forms of written and visual art, including some modern practices concerned with the global effects of the Anthropocene, enabling imaginative reinterpretations of Irish islandness.[40] For example, Galway's TULCA Festival of Visual Arts in winter 2015 titled 'Seachange' sought to explore 'the ways in which the myths associated with this island reflect

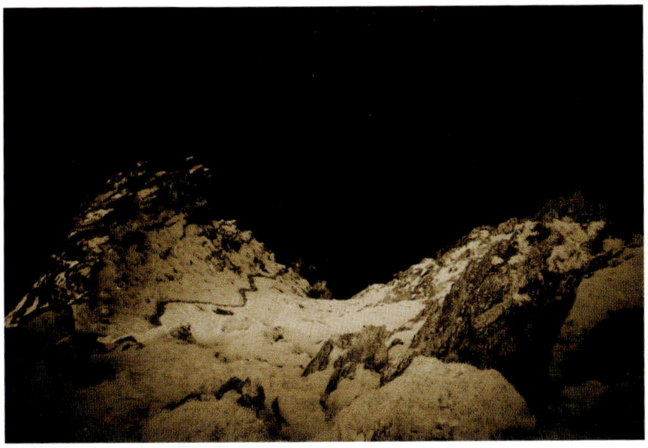

95 Clare Langan, *The Floating World – Skellig Triptych*, 2013, three screen film installation, archival pigment print.

the changing landscape of our environment'.[41] Curated by Mary Cremin, it featured more than thirty international artists. The elusive nature of Hy-Brasil's history enabled various imaginative reappropriations of the island theme. The Irish artist Clare Langan's film triptych *Floating World* (illus. 95), shot in three locations, features the uninviting snow-covered cliffs of Skellig Michael as a symbolic substitute for Hy-Brasil.[42] Footage includes the traces of human intervention in the dizzying causeway of stone steps that trace the route to the rocky summit and isolated monastery. Once a remote site of Christian fervour, Skellig Michael appears here as an alien, even surreal space, incompatible with human life. Two other locations are featured on other screens: high-rise buildings in Dubai that seem to float like metaphorical islands on a sea of clouds, and the 'exclusion zone', an area of abandoned housing swallowed up by volcanic ash on the Caribbean island of Montserrat, which has a complex relationship with Ireland. Irish indentured servants and prisoners sent out by Cromwell were among the first European settlers on the island and Irish entrepreneurs set up plantations with enslaved Africans, leading to Montserrat's label as 'the other Emerald Isle'.[43] As Langan (b. 1967) describes it: '*The Floating World* goes from the remote and extreme landscape of the Skellig [islands] to Dubai's futuristic cityscape in the sky, to Montserrat, a modern-day Pompeii with completely devoured interiors.'[44] Symbols of nature's elemental history are viewed next to modern skyscrapers, buildings that represent the (debatable) triumph of the Anthropocene. *Floating World* presents a series of island homes in surreal juxtaposition: abandoned, floating and submerged. It has been suggested that these landscapes move us beyond comfortable understanding, 'as the light and effect of Langan's lens illuminates a dark and chaotic reality'.[45] As legends of Hy-Brasil suggest, island histories are often chaotic and contested – an ideal vehicle for artistic reimaginings.

OFF AND ON THE MAP

Hy-Brasil's identity was dependent on the perpetuation of myth and some questionable early map-making. Developments in cultural geography have encouraged the modern viewer to understand maps as complex forms of social construction: visual expressions of power relations and national identities, rather than irrefutable data, as was vividly illustrated in the famous redrawn nations and continents of the Surrealist map of the world of 1929 (illus. 96).[46] As Ireland's history and identity have been persistently redefined, we have seen that several Irish artists have adopted creative forms of cartography in which knowledge is also redrawn. Moreover, feminist cartography is now a recognized academic subdiscipline in which researchers and scholars explore the ways in which data and mapping processes may reveal inequalities, misrepresentations and issues of patriarchal power and control. It is hardly surprising, then, that many women and feminist artists have sought to redraw imaginary maps of Irish cultural history.[47] While Prendergast's series of *Body Maps* conflate and combine cartographic and gynaecological techniques of description, the Irish artists Alice Maher (b. 1956) and Rachel Fallon have mischievously reimagined the landscape of Ireland 'as its own world in the universe, filled with an annotated topography that challenges the official narrative of the detention of Irish women since the formation of the state in 1922'.[48] They have created a monumental textile installation that has been sewn, embroidered, appliqued, felted, crocheted, printed and painted. Following historical cartographic conventions that flattened out the world into a fan-shape, *The Map* (2021; illus. 97)

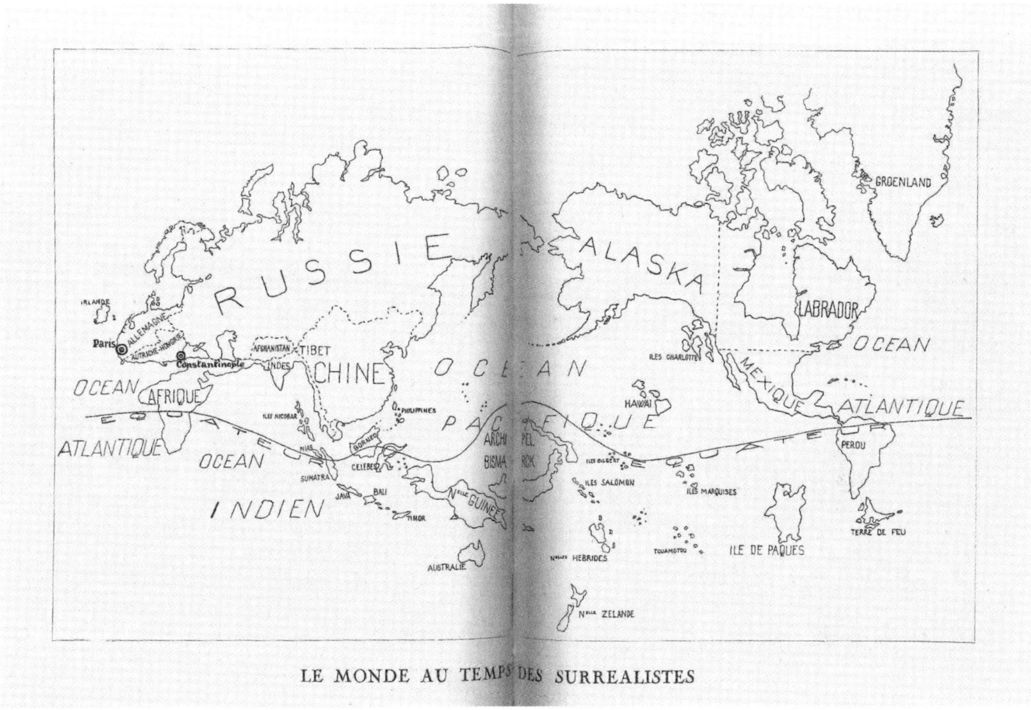

96 'The World in the Time of the Surrealists', 1929, in *Variétés – Le surréalisme en 1929* (June 1929).

is an archipelago of embroidered islands that explore and reframe the multiple narratives of Mary Magdalene. Standing at 6.5 metres high and 4.5 metres wide (21 × 15 ft), *The Map* formed part of 'The Magdalene Series', a programme of radical exhibitions, performances and events curated by Maolíosa Boyle at Rua Red, South Dublin Arts Centre, in 2021–2.[49]

According to the Christian Gospels, Mary Magdalene travelled with Jesus and witnessed his crucifixion and resurrection.[50] Cast as a prostitute from the sixteenth century onwards when Pope Gregory I conflated her with Mary of Bethany and the (unnamed) 'sinful woman' who washed Jesus' feet (Luke 7:36–50), she supposedly spent her last days in the wilderness in prayer and self-castigation. She has been associated with tales of prostitution, morality, shame, reparation and penitence – a moveable feast of Christian femininity. As Boyle writes, 'She is a binary creation: conflicted and mysterious, noble and humble, strong yet morally weak, beautiful and haggard, passionate yet penitent, erotic and unreserved,

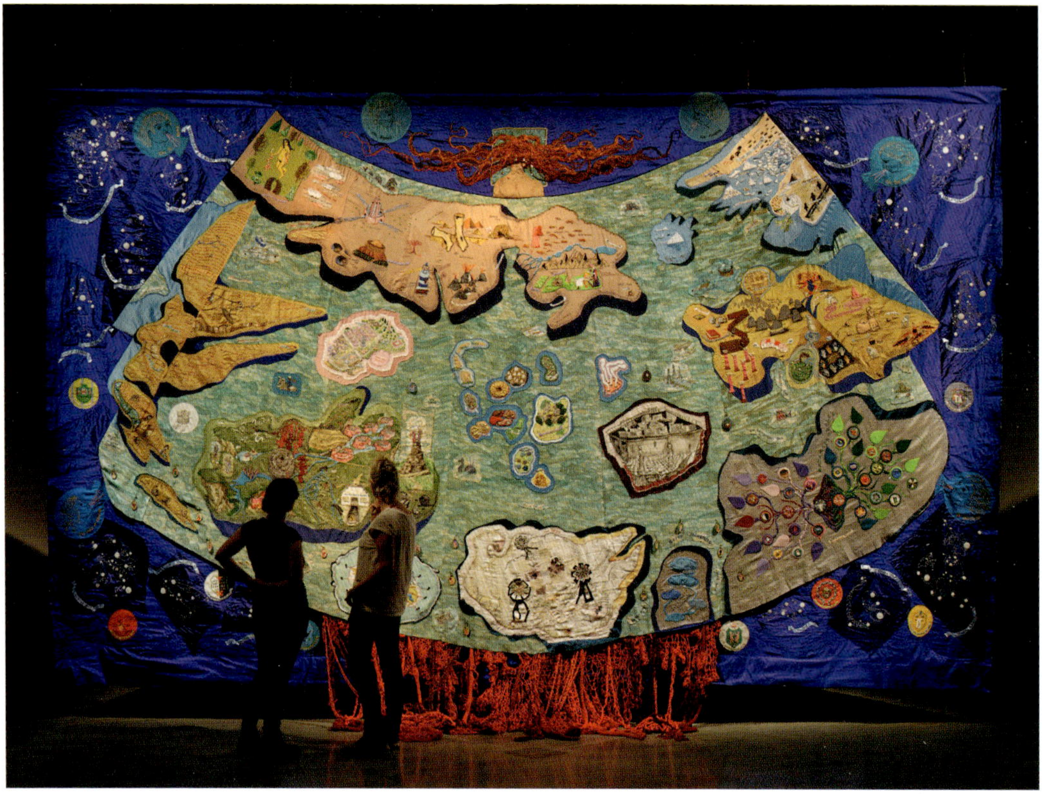

97 Alice Maher and Rachel Fallon, *The Map*, 2018–21, installation of fabrics, thread, canvas, wool, acrylic paint, found objects and felt.

reclusive and solitary.'[51] Such contradictions, folkloric associations and gendered myths are carefully stitched into a vast patchwork of imaginary islands, dispersed across a mottled green sea.

Several commentators have noted that the shape of the sea suggests a bishop's wide, flowing cape, a possible reference to the popular tale of St Brigid's cloak.[52] Born around AD 450 in County Louth, Brigid (recently made an official Irish saint) requested unsuccessfully that the king of Leinster give her land in Kildare to build a monastery. According to legend she asked again, requesting only as much land as her cloak would cover. Seeing how small it was, he granted her request, and she instructed her helpers to take four corners and walk in opposite directions. Allegedly, the cloak began to grow, eventually covering many acres, where she built the abbey of Kildare.[53] This expansive, embroidered ocean references Irish legends and feminine traditions of sewing and embroidery, connected archipelagos and the potential transformative magic of a woman's clothing. It is no coincidence that transformation and metamorphosis are strategies elegantly deployed in work over the last few decades by several Irish women artists, including Maher and Fallon.[54] The sea-cloak, heavy with its layered mythical baggage, sits on a wider stretch of dark blue silk, stitched with constellations of stars, banners and portrait lockets.

Any idea of a peaceful surrounding cosmos is disturbed by coiling locks of flame-coloured hair that emerge from the top of the cape and appear to rage across the dark blue firmament while also crowning *The Map*. In many medieval and Renaissance images, Mary Magdalene is depicted with flowing red hair, often so long that it covers her body, protecting her modesty and signalling her 'penitence'. In *The Map* her tresses appear both dishevelled – wild, even – but under her command. Similar coils and crocheted sections of vivid red yarn fringe the bottom of the sea-cloak and fall along the gallery floor. Maher has described this excessive and disorderly continuation of the work as 'eviscera', an oblique reference to notions of bodily excess so often associated with women's bodily functions and emotions. As such, it could also reference feminine hair.[55] The haptic and symbolic potential of hair – whether flowing, braided, coiled or in tresses – has been creatively explored in Maher's work since the 1990s. As she has acknowledged, it is a material rich in evocative associations; it appears often in fairy tales, carries many cultural connotations and can hold a liminal or borderline position on the body,[56] hence its relevance in a work that maps a host of Irish femininities associated with women's corporeal histories. In traditional illustrations Mary Magdalene is often depicted weeping, a reference to the biblical account of her crying in sorrow by Jesus's tomb. But in this reclaiming of her legacy, stitched tears are falling from a flowing, faceless mass of hair. She is necessarily anonymous, and the 'wailing woman' is no longer depicted as actually wailing. As a metonym for femininity and its excesses, these flaming tresses and 'eviscera' do not conform to religious myth; they appear rather to be both supporting and escaping from an ocean of islands, as if leading the way out of the myth. Much like Mary Magdalene herself, these disorderly coils encompass many of the gendered contradictions that inhabit *The Map*.

Every carefully stitched and embroidered island references some state of womanhood, its contested mythological and religious histories and/or social status. For example, Slag Island, or Oileán Olc (illus. 98), has a fleshy pink border – or is it a beach? – and is embroidered with monuments, roads and houses named after mythological women and 'sluts' from Western and classical history. Medea Drive, Strumpet City, Circe Roundabout, Petronella Place, the Fields of Salome, Slutside, Mother Shipton Row and Hecate Road are among the many women whose histories are celebrated through place names. One side of the island even boasts a large black spider, labelled 'LB Monument', a tribute that the French-born artist Louise Bourgeois, with her love of stitched and embroidered projects, would surely have approved of. She would most likely have been amused by the mischievous audacity of this pink islet. A long, meandering island, dotted with bleak landmarks, dominates the top of the pale green cloak. Hell's Point (and kitchen) marks the eastern end, along the coast from

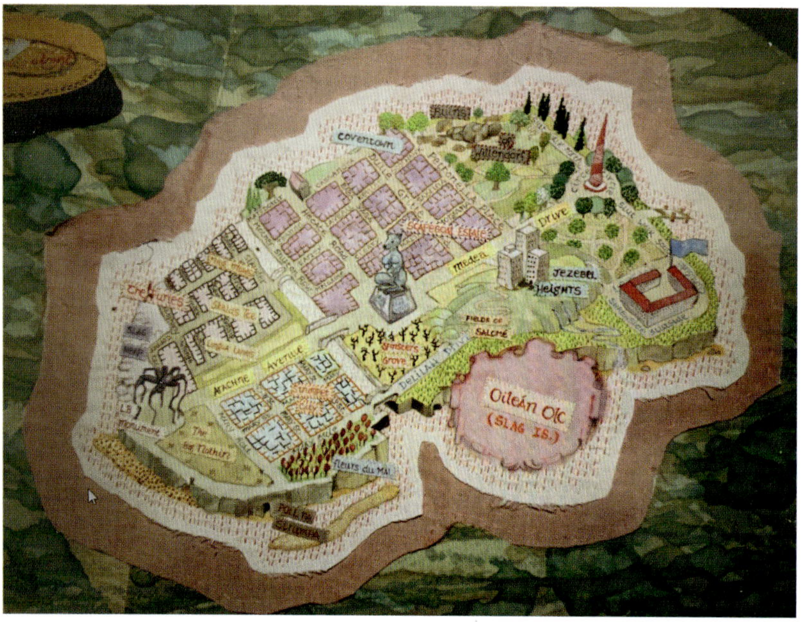

98 Alice Maher and Rachel Fallon, *The Map*, 2021, detail of Slag Island.

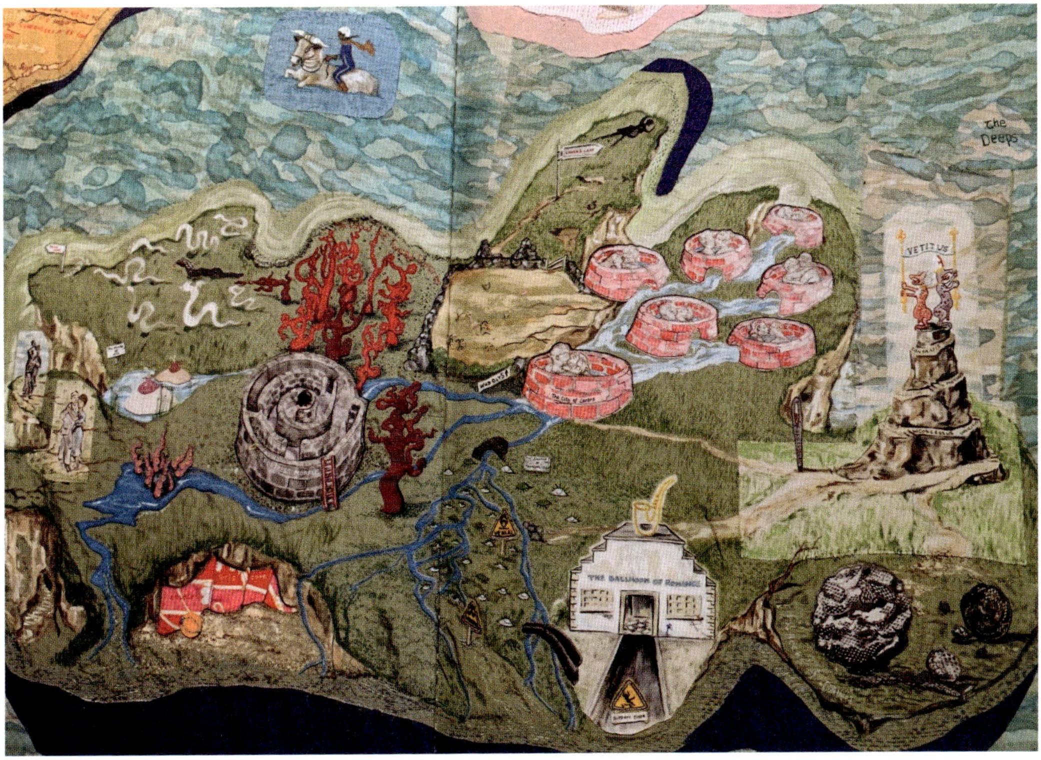

99 Alice Maher and Rachel Fallon, *The Map*, 2021, detail of island with field of wild oats and ballroom of romance.

Bone Yard and Bloody Point. Acts of violence and abuse against women are referenced across *The Map*, as are sinful acts and 'sluttish' behaviour, for which 'fallen' Irish women were persistently punished by a hypocritical Church. Another island is peppered with embroidered labels that perpetually remind us of women's sins, committed in, for example, a field of Wild Oats, the Ballroom of Romance or the City of Lovers. On the same island the fallen woman is imprisoned in a tower labelled Fortress Moralis and surrounded by the trees of Twisted Desire. She is never far from Sinner's Cove (illus. 99).

As part of 'The Magdalene Series', Boyle invited the poet Sinéad Gleeson to compose a poetic response to *The Map*, which was read by multiple readers in a sound installation *We Are the Map*, presented in a room alongside the work. The opening section of Gleeson's poem presents a list of collective feminine experiences referenced on *The Map*:

You do not need to know my name but:

I am *Mary, Amina, Penelope, Brigid,*
Persephone, Frida, Maebh, Makeda,
Sojourner, Granuaile, Cassiopeia, Nan

I am *Hecate, Rosa, Lakshmi, Aphra*
the X-Case Girl; the women given letters not names,
Sappho, Marsha, Maura, Edna,
Green Tara, Black Madonna
I am *the first girl child they put in the septic tank*
Come to the loud, feral
Herland, Sheland, Theyland.
A Queenopolis, Cisopolis, Transopolis
A Republic of personhood.

I am the Map
We are the Map[57]

DIRTY WASHING

Apart from her famous weeping – or wailing – Mary Magdalene was known for the act of washing the feet of Jesus. One of the most shameful fates for Irish girls and women in the period from the 1920s to the late 1990s was to spend their days washing dirty clothes as a 'Magdalene laundress'. All over Ireland, dozens of high-walled institutions run by nuns were called Magdalene Laundries, where oppressive regimes imprisoned 'fallen' girls and women, condemned to perform the literal and metaphorical act of washing. Often on the instructions of a local priest, such women were 'deemed "fallen" (pregnant or having had sex outside marriage) or even simply "in moral danger" – which may mean nothing more than being on the brink of marrying a Protestant or going to the cinema too often with a boy or for any reason that the local priest put forward, real or imagined'.[58] By 1996 more than 10,000 girls and women had been imprisoned in Magdalene Laundries. Many of their babies were illegally adopted and paid for by wealthy couples.[59] Some stillborn babies met an even more disturbing fate, as cited by Gleeson: 'I am the first girl child they put in the septic tank.'

In the right-hand corner of *The Map* a constellation of stars flickers around an embroidered woman hanging out washing, labelled 'The Little Laundress', while one of the smaller islands that float across the green-blue sea is peopled with labouring laundresses, three of whom appear to work an enormous mangle. Praying Virgin Marys metamorphose into pillars, supporting a largely monochrome 'Architecture of Containment' that frames the toiling women (illus. 100). The brutal nature of their work and the culture of 'containment' experienced in these profit-making laundries was exposed following investigations in the 1990s and ongoing historical research. The writer Lynn Picknett has described a system that 'was geared to extract the last drop of slave labour, while inculcating in the girls a crippling sense of their unworthiness, of self-hate – often reinforced by the endemic sexual abuse by the priests who were their spiritual confessors'.[60]

Islands provide the ideal contexts for the (embroidered) depiction of such brutal regimes, offering suitable spaces in which to imprison 'offenders' or socially undesirable women. Those grey, high-walled institutions closely resembled, and were managed as, spaces of incarceration. References to the punishments enforced by the Eighth Amendment and illegal abortions are written and embroidered across *The Map*. On the right-hand side, a naked woman 'sinner' is being dragged by a cleric, pulled by her hair across a brown landscape overwritten with the words conviction, confession and penal servitude for life. Echoing the treatment of enslaved communities, the nuns often gave their laundresses new names (usually after saints) as a means of controlling them mentally and spiritually. Renaming was an attempt to change and deny a former identity and a confirmation of the power of the nuns. Maher and Fallon challenge this process by a sometimes ironic deployment of naming. Notorious women, their 'sins', histories and resistances, are carefully labelled and re-presented in tapestry-like form.

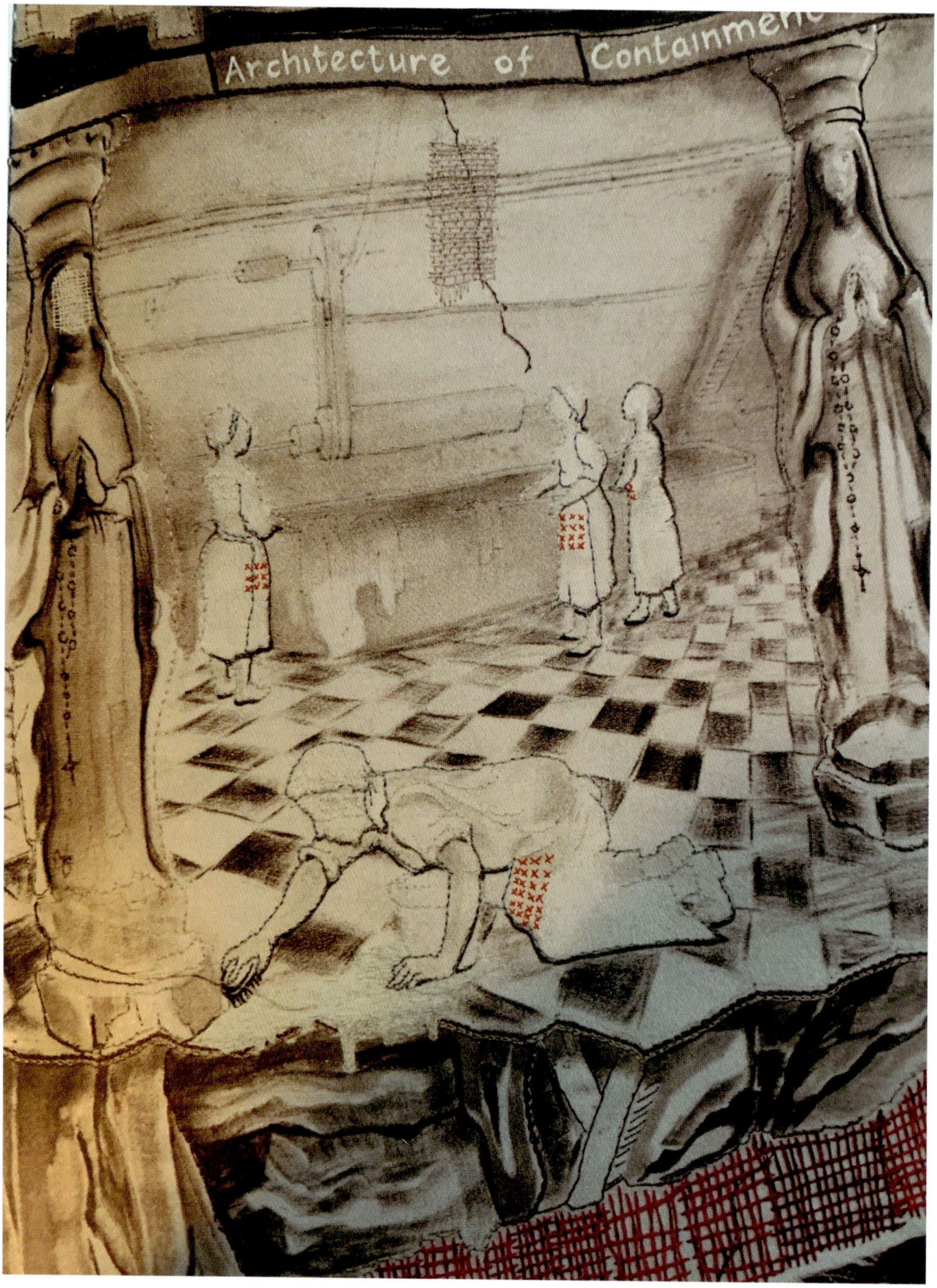
Architecture of Containment

Humorously named islands and constellations remind us of the power of language – and typography – to help frame our readings of visual material. Moreover, this work is conceived not just as a group of islands and continents but as a network of related landmasses – an archipelago connected by fluid oceans and a shared lexicon of visual references. Despite the wealth of names and associations referenced in *The Map*, Maher and Fallon decided not to supply a key – the more traditional cartographic device.[61] As a 'new kind of map', without coordinates, it invites the curious viewer to scrutinize its complex layered surface, seeking out the many labels and playful renamings.

The Map involved a lengthy three-year process of research, preparation and collaboration. Limited by the constraints of the COVID-19 pandemic in 2020–21, Fallon and Maher worked separately but in constant communication, building on the productive collaboration they enjoyed when they were both making striking banners for the Irish Artists' Campaign to Repeal the Eighth Amendment, led by Maher, in 2018. Through the appropriation of embroidery, appliqué and crochet – traditionally feminine techniques loosely described as *femmage*, combined with painted and found material – Fallon and Maher mapped an intricate new archipelago. Maps and knitting had been successfully combined in the large gallery installation *The Knitting Map* in the Glucksman, University College Cork, in 2015. A collaborative work involving local Irish knitters, it staged a woolly participatory spectacle, and was described by Barber as having 'an inability to lie quietly, to acquiesce in a seamless stitching into historical categories of Irish art'.[62] By contrast, *The Map* of 2021 is an epic work of multiple textiles and narrative complexity, albeit with a shared denial of traditional categories of Irish art history – a refusal 'to lie quietly'.

Each island has (what appears to be) a surrounding beach, cliff face or clear boundary neatly delineated with an appropriate textile. Fabrics and stitching were carefully chosen to represent the complex histories embodied in the work. For example, for the island in the centre-bottom of the cloak, labelled The Napery, the artists sourced old fabrics, linens and materials, echoing the medieval definition of 'napery' as the household

100 Alice Maher and Rachel Fallon, *The Map*, 2021, detail of Architecture of Containment and laundresses at work.

space where linen was washed. The cosmos, studded with stars, is made of blue silk. To remind us of the labour-intensive process of stitching, the work has been hung to be viewed front and back, revealing the painstaking network of stitches that hold the fabrics together. A network of bright red stitches resembling blood vessels is visible across the back, a self-conscious reappropriation of the medium of embroidery. As Rozsika Parker famously explained in 1984, the medium 'evokes the stereotype of the virgin in opposition to the whore, an infantilising representation of women's sexuality . . . Embroidery has become indelibly associated with stereotypes of femininity.'[63] It is precisely those infantilizing and degrading stereotypes of female sexuality that *The Map* seeks to undermine, exemplifying Parker's famous 'subversive stitch'.

This epic installation of textiles and stitching speaks to women's histories of misogyny, religious oppression and institutional abuse. At the heart of this critical engagement with persistent myths of femininity lies the theme of the island and its archipelagos. *The Map* provides powerful visual evidence of the rich aesthetic and symbolic potential of this theme, used to critique and explore so many aspects of Irish political, cultural and gendered history. 'Island' is not merely a homophone for Ireland (and vice versa). It embodies a web of shifting associations and meanings that have helped to shape and redefine what it has meant, and means, to be Irish.

7 FLOATING ISLANDS

Many island tropes that haunt the modern literary and artistic imaginary have their origins in ancient classical literature. One of the first floating islands found in literature is Aeolia, home of Aeolus, god of the wind, visited in the *Odyssey* (Book 10). Homer described 'the floating island of Aeolia' surrounded by steep cliffs and 'a wall of unbreakable bronze'.[1] He represented Aeolia's islandness as magical and other, along with the many other ports of call on his famous voyage. Aeolus gave Odysseus a favourable west wind and a pouch containing unfavourable winds to enable his journey home. When he fell asleep close to the shores of Ithaca, his island home, his curious crew opened the pouch, releasing the winds and causing the ship to be blown off course.[2] As a floating signifier, the island could both enable and disable the journey home to safety. The floating island is rich in metaphorical possibilities; its potential for the representation of utopias, dystopias, diasporas and nations has been widely explored in literary and cultural criticism.[3] Within the visual arts the metaphor of 'floating' identities (for which islands, water and boats can provide visual surrogates) has gained popularity. For example, the Lyon Art Biennale of 2016 was titled 'Mondes Flottantes' (Floating Worlds), and the Venice Art Biennale regularly includes projects that foreground themes of fluid geographies, identities and oceans. The 'floating city' is one of many labels attached to Venice, made up of 118 islands connected by canals and bridges. Within an increasingly global culture marked by inequalities and imminent ecological disaster, an unstable, floating place that can move around and defy political and cultural orthodoxy offers a metaphor for mobile international creativity.

FLOATING LEGACIES AND MAKING ART

Literary history reveals the powerful metaphorical baggage of the floating island. In 1673 a satirical novel by Richard Head was published under the title *The Floating Island*, a spoof travel narrative recounting the adventures of its debt-ridden protagonist, Captain Robert Owemuch, in supposedly distant lands. In fact the voyage turns out to be a faintly disguised crossing from the south to the north bank of the Thames and results in a scatological tour of the City of London.[4] In the nineteenth century Jules Verne's novel *The Floating Island* of 1896, first published in French as *L'Île à hélice* (Propeller Island) in 1895, constructs another nautical fantasy in which a French string quartet is abducted to an immense constructed island reserved for the super wealthy that travels around the Pacific Ocean.[5] Verne's original French version contained some overt social commentary deemed critical of the Americans and the British, which was cut by his British publishers. Although separated by centuries, for both Head and Verne the floating island theme enabled some pertinent observations on contemporary society. More recently visual artists have also used the theme to transform some traditional notions of both landscape and islandness. In the Introduction I explored arguments for the representation of landscape as an active, cultural process 'by which social and subjective identities are formed'.[6] When appropriated by artists, the floating island theme has often been reconceived as an evolving, performative project, as in the work of Robert Smithson in the 1970s and projects by the American artist Andrea Zittel (b. 1965) since the 1990s.

In 2005 Smithson's *Floating Island* was launched off Manhattan Island. Never executed in his lifetime, it was constructed from a single sketch drawn in 1970 and a few notes. For two weekends in September 2005 a 27-metre (90 ft) barge landscaped with trees, rocks and shrubs was towed around a part of Manhattan Island (illus. 101). Many of Smithson's preferred sites were those 'that had been disrupted by industry, reckless urbanisation or nature's own devastation'.[7] Although this stretch of the Hudson River hardly represents the devastation inflicted on some of his other urban sites, the work consisted of an artificial and displaced island,

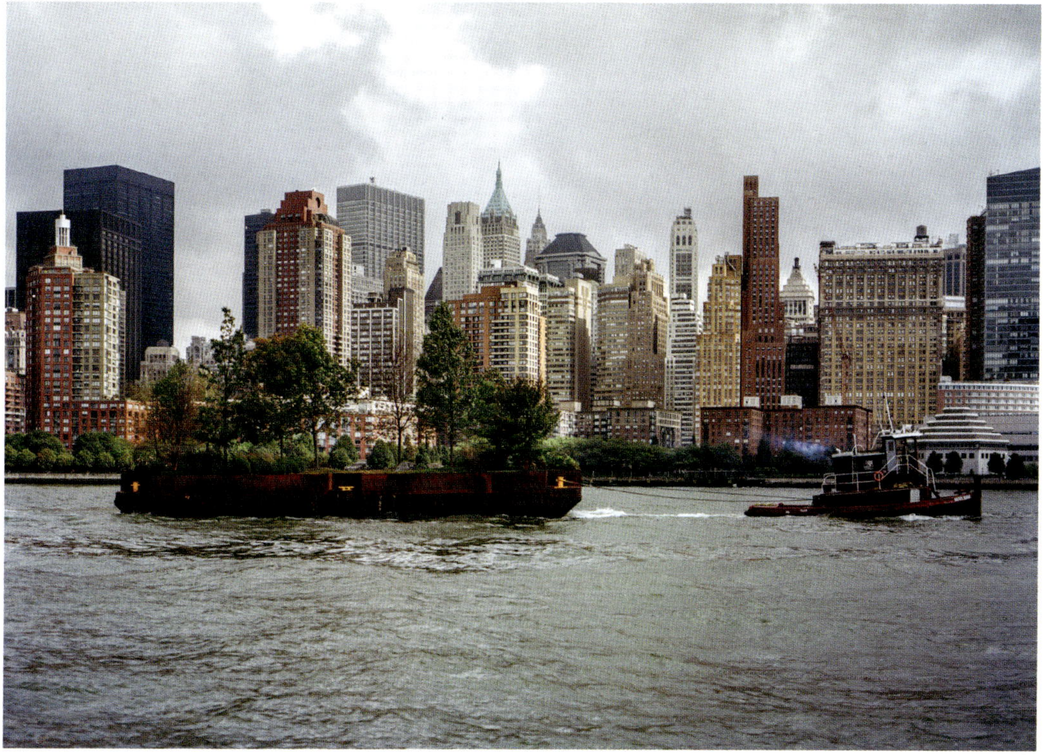

101 Robert Smithson, *Floating Island to Travel around Manhattan Island*, 1970, produced by Minetta Brook in collaboration with the Whitney Museum of American Art, on view 17–25 September 2005.

a counter to the relative rootedness of Manhattan, itself both an island and a symbol of ruthless and 'reckless' modern urbanization. As it travelled along the Hudson, the island was highly visible to New York's residents and commuters. It drew attention to our tenuous relationship to land and place and reminded its audience that the space of Central Park, from which Smithson took his trees and rocks, was itself a carefully constructed urban landscape.[8] Although this celebrated modern voyage redefined the nature of both islandness and place, we cannot be sure that Smithson would have approved of this posthumous public performance and the media attention involved. It created the kind of spectacle that he usually sought to avoid in his choice of 'Nonsites'.

Some similar questions around place, identity and performance have been raised in the work of Andrea Zittel (b. 1965), who has long been fascinated with the theme of floating islands. In the 1990s she constructed

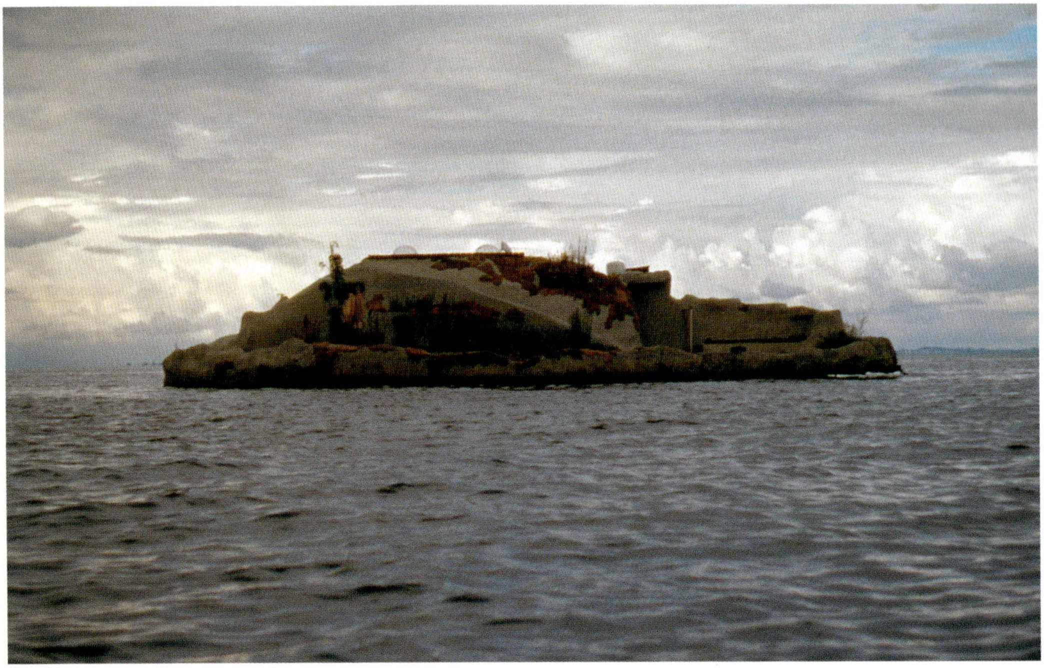

102 Andrea Zittel, *A-Z Pocket Property*, 1998, concrete, steel, wood, dirt and vegetation.

her *A–Z Pocket Property* (1998–9), a 44-ton concrete island anchored off the coast of Denmark (illus. 102) and lived on it for a month as an experiment in escapism and isolation.[9] While Smithson repurposed bits of his local New York landscape, Zittel produced a self-conscious fabrication that mimics natural landscape. Her work involved an exploration of how we construct and define ideas of place and dwelling, and the title references a series of housing projects by Zittel that explore the modern tendency for 'pocket' living in small urban spaces.[10] Ironically, this small-scale habitable island eventually had to be destroyed as it was too large to be maintained.

Zittel has created other floating island projects, including her *Island in 100 Acres* (2010) in the Virginia B. Fairbanks Art and Nature Park at the Indianapolis Museum of Art. This was more obviously artificial in appearance – a dome-shaped igloo made from polystyrene foam coated with fibreglass resin and floated on a dock structure. Developing her interests in how we construct our dwellings and create identities for them, Zittel invited people to volunteer to become temporary residents of the island in the summer, and to personalize the space. Through this performative, interactive process, the boundaries between art and life were deliberately blurred. In an interview given at the time of this work, she described her interests:

> The idea of an island appeals to me as a representation of many of the values that we strive for in our 21st-century culture: individualism, independence, autonomy, and self-sufficiency. Yet at the same time, these are the same desires that isolate us and lessen collective social and political power. I am fascinated at how the things that set us free are also the same things that oppress us; you could say that the concept of the deserted island is both our greatest fantasy and our greatest fear.[11]

Zittel addresses one of many paradoxes of the island motif, which can liberate us from social or political control yet separate us from an enabling collective social process. Her *Island in 100 Acres* explored various forms of social and economic exchange and collective dwelling. It became its own fantasy, with perpetually blurred boundaries between identity, inhabiting and art-making.

NOW HERE IS LAND?

In the summer of 2012 holidaymakers relaxing on beaches along the south coast of England were intrigued to see a strange rocky island approaching from northern waters, towed by a tug (illus. 103, 104). It proceeded around the southwest coast, arriving at Weymouth at the end of July and continuing along the Devon coast, stopping off at various holiday resorts.[12]

Conceived by the British artist Alex Hartley (b. 1963), this carefully planned nautical journey coincided with the opening of the Olympic Games. The floating construction was called *Nowhereisland*, also pronounced as Now-here-is-land, and was partly made up of soil and rocks taken from an island that had appeared in the Norwegian archipelago of Svalbard in the High Arctic (illus. 105). The land was revealed as the result of the retreating Sonklarbreen glacier, a direct effect of global warming. Hartley claimed to have discovered the island, which was absent from all existing maps and charts, in 2004 on a Cape Farewell Arctic expedition (see Chapter Eight). There followed a lengthy correspondence with the Norwegian authorities and the governor of Svalbard in which Hartley sought to name and claim the island as a secessionist micronation with multinational citizens and its own system of government.[13]

This is part of a much longer, drawn-out story, in which Hartley's claim on the island was refused by the Norwegian government. He eventually won permission to remove a small part of Nymark (as he named it) and towed it south in 2012. He declared its independence and established it as an island-nation seeking citizens from around the world. Just over 23,000 people from 135 countries signed up to be citizens of *Nowhereisland* on its website and through its mobile embassy. In the wake of the 2016 Brexit vote to assert the UK's separate island status, reduce immigration and supposedly 'take back control', it is hard to ignore the political and ironic potential of this ambitious project. This floating island was perpetually moving its geographical coordinates, and its borders were open to all to claim citizenship. As a mobile, transitory landscape, it challenged many tropes not only of nationhood and islandness but of the idea of a stable relationship between place and landscape. As a participatory project, it also clouds the boundaries between representation and the real. Moreover, access to the event is now entirely through photographic and filmed records and materials.

Nowhereisland sought to combine a natural resource (the Norwegian rocks revealed through the effects of climate change) and a manufactured or sculpted object that represents an island. In this process Hartley acknowledges the influence of Smithson's Manhattan project. Both islands were dependent on a messy, sculptural process of making a floating structure. Both artists took fragments (rocks, stones, soil) from their respective sites and transplanted them, changing their narrative histories. And both involved a performance through time which (it was hoped) would engage local spectators, whose responses would complete the artwork. As a mobile,

103 Alex Hartley, *Nowhereisland* being towed by a tug off the South Coast of England, 2012.

104 Alex Hartley, *Nowhereisland* approaching the Devon coast, 2012.

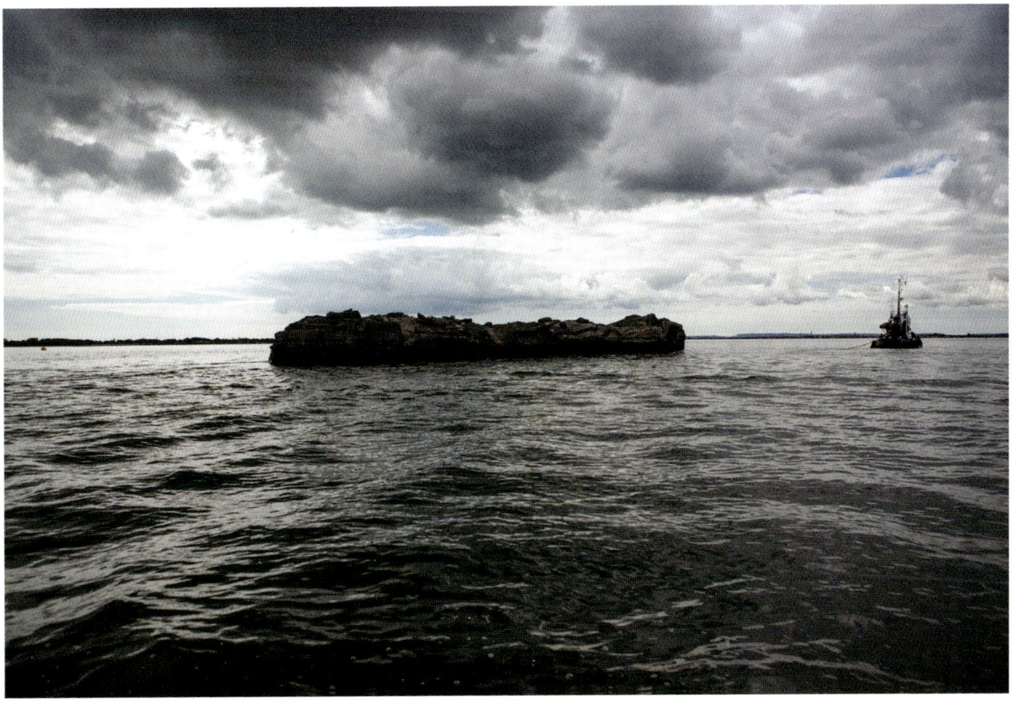

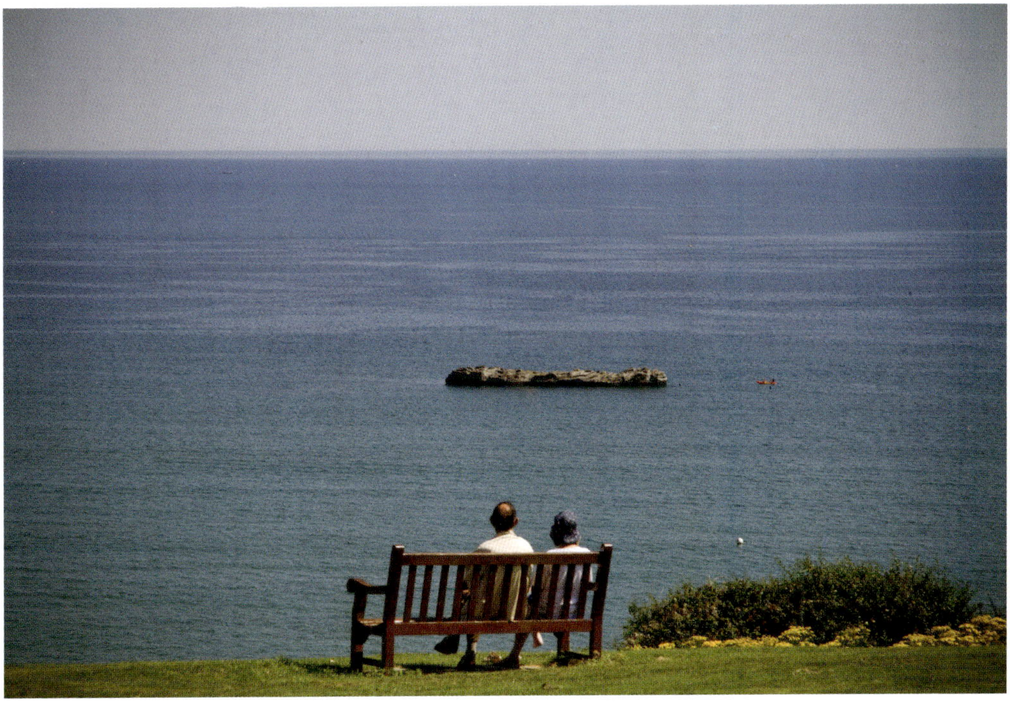

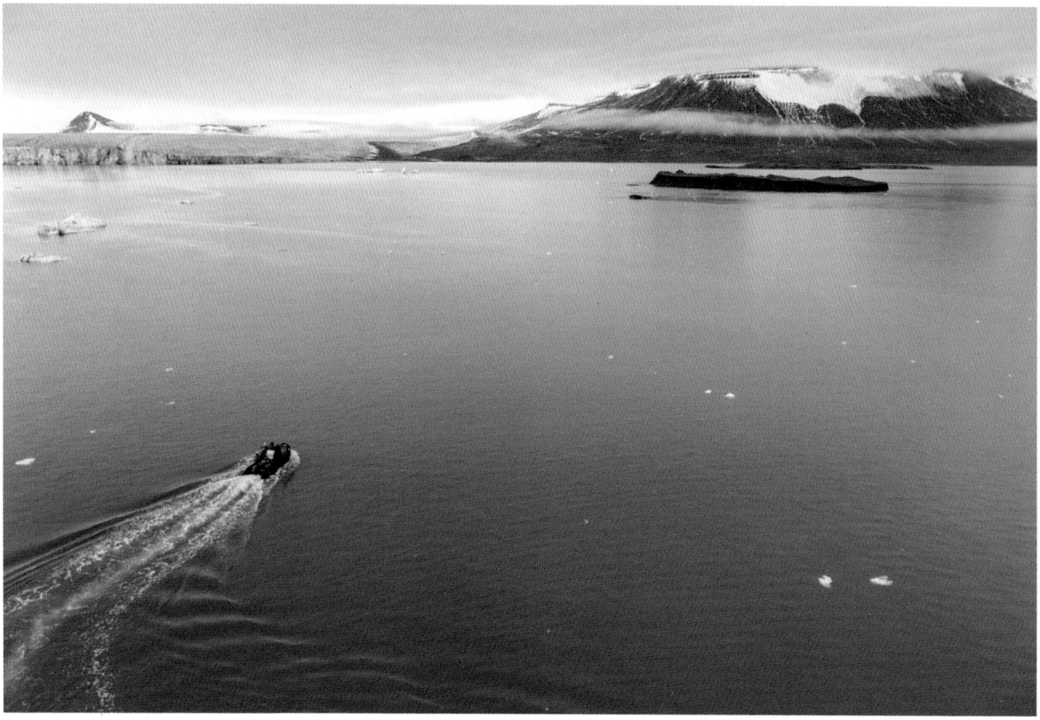

105 Alex Hartley, *Nymark in the Arctic*, 2010, expedition team revisiting the island.

durational project *Nowhereisland* undermines any sense of both landscape and place being apparently 'natural' and fixed. Hartley's landscapes were re-presented to subsequent audiences through filmed and photographic images, reorganized into artworks that can substitute for, or reference, the original performance.[14]

Hartley's 'discovery' of the island on his first trip to the Arctic in 2004 was documented and exhibited in 2006 as part of the group show 'Art and Climate Change' at the Natural History Museum, London. The exhibition included photographic records and new works inspired by several Cape Farewell expeditions that took artists and writers to the High Arctic (see Chapter Eight). Hartley's installation *The Ship/Undiscovered Island* (named after the ship they had travelled in when they found the island) was also included in the Liverpool Biennial of that year (illus. 106). *The Ship* includes photographs of the discovery and the Cape Farewell expedition, the remote Arctic landscape, and framed letters to the Norwegian

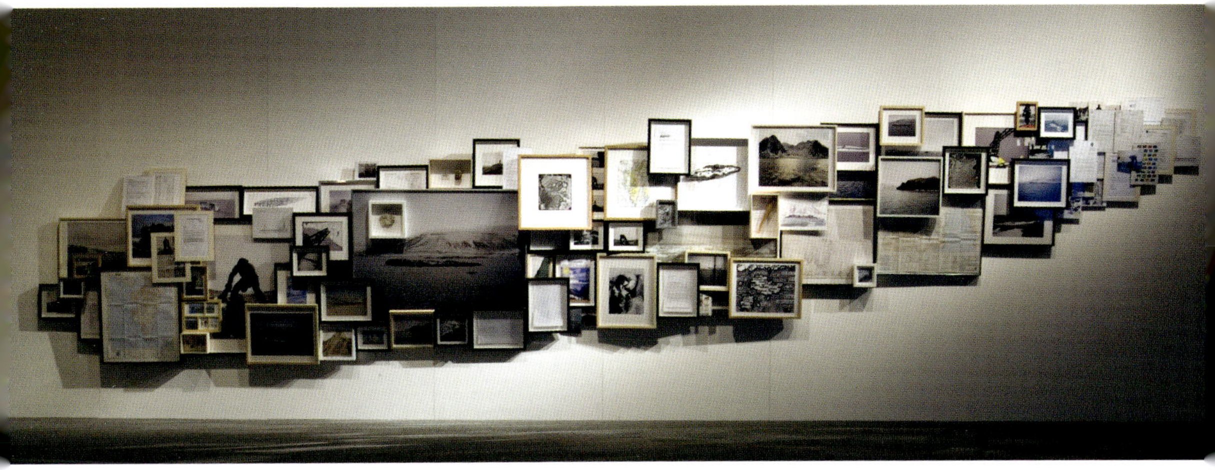

106 Alex Hartley, *Undiscovered Island*, installation exhibited at the Liverpool Biennial as part of *The Ship: The Art of Climate Change*, a collaborative exhibition by Cape Farewell, the Natural Conservation Centre and the Natural History Museum, 2006.

government requesting that they secede the island from the Kingdom of Norway. As the artist intended, these documents used landscape and text to chart what Clare Doherty called 'a deliberate act of colonisation'.[15] Several photos of Hartley staking his claim on Nymark are mischievously transgressive and mock the heroics of colonial conquest. The Liverpool installation provides a vivid example of the photographic archive being orchestrated by the artist to become part of a multi-layered, ongoing work.

ISLANDS, NATIONHOOD AND CITIZENSHIP

By 2010 Hartley's project was selected as one of several major art commissions supported by the Arts Council and other funders of the 2012 Olympics. This helped to finally persuade the Norwegian government to allow him to remove part of the island, sail it out into international waters and tow it around the southwest coast of England. In 2010 he set sail to the Svalbard archipelago with a seventeen-strong expedition team, retracing the earlier voyage. Instead of the more scientific team of geologists and climate-change scientists who accompanied the earlier Cape Farewell trip, this time people were selected who might form the foundations of a 'new nation': these included a human geographer, a psychologist, a linguist, a feminist journalist, an environmental activist, a constitutional lawyer, an

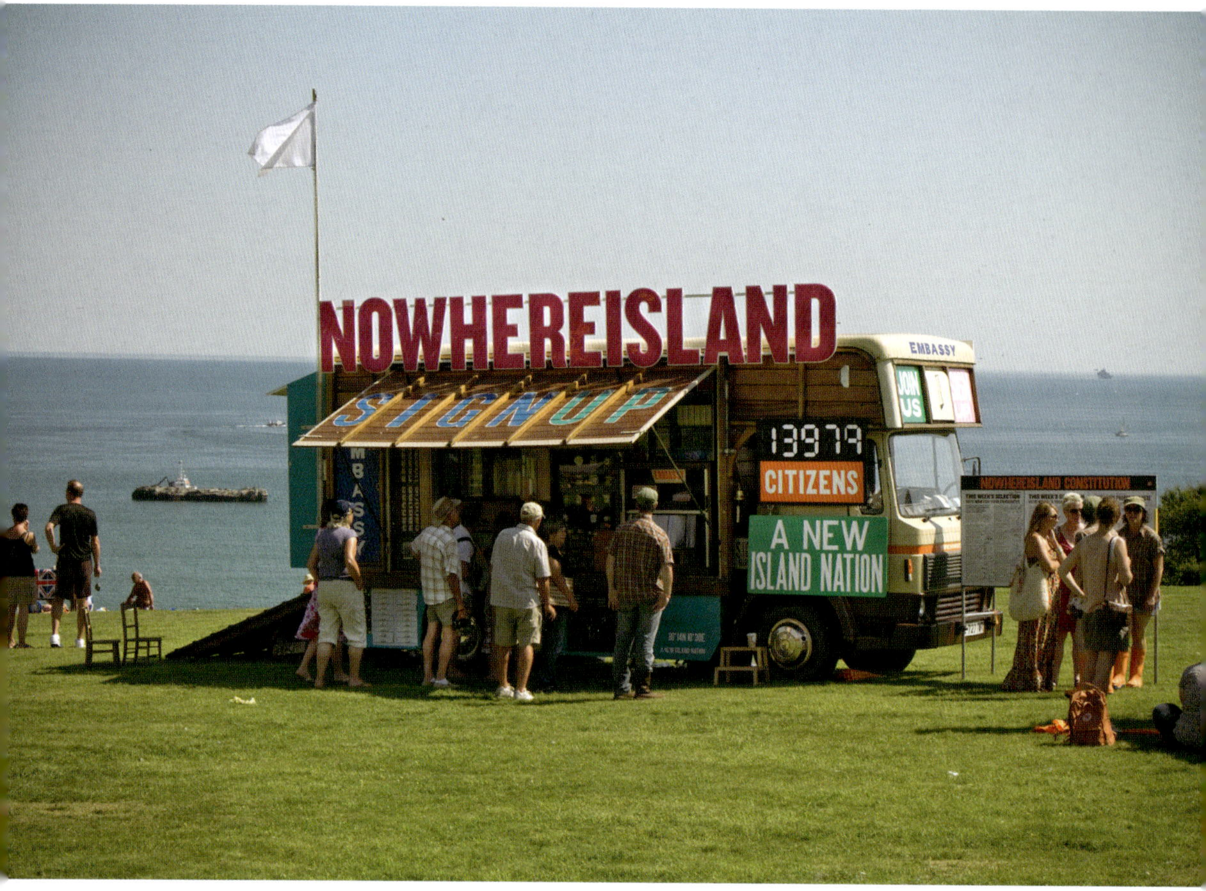

educationalist and a magician. Once they had broken off sections of rock and soil and installed them on floats, the work was towed into international waters. A declaration of independence was made, along with an invitation to citizenship, which could be claimed online or at the mobile embassy opened at each subsequent port of call (illus. 107). *Nowhereisland* arrived in Weymouth on 25 July 2012, four days before the Olympic sailing races took place at Weymouth Bay. It continued its slow journey around the southwest coast as an open visiting nation, hosted by Devon and Cornwall's famous ports and cities. It ended up in Bristol, leaving the port on 9 September to be broken into pieces, which were sent to each of its 23,003 citizens all over the world.

107 Alex Hartley, *Nowhereisland* mobile embassy, near Plymouth, 2012.

Many of the Olympic commissions were designed to affirm the UK's status as an internationally esteemed creative hub, and London as a site for Olympic (and Olympian) display. Much better known is the monumental tower that is the Indian-born British artist Anish Kapoor's *Orbit*, completed in 2016 with the world's longest tunnel slide by the artist Carsten Höller. Thought to be the tallest sculpture in the UK (114 metres (374 ft) high), it is nearly 7 metres taller than the Statue of Liberty. Its £23 million cost was largely financed by the steel corporation ArcelorMittal. Praised by some as an awe-inspiring feat of modern engineering and critiqued by others as a vanity project pursued by then Mayor Boris Johnson, it has transformed the east London skyline, reshaping the landscape in a brazen celebration of its Olympic past (illus. 108). What has since happened to housing in the surrounding Olympic Village is more controversial.[16] In some respects the Olympic Park mimicked the form and status of an island community, clearly separated from the surrounding area of east London and subject to its own regulations.

Orbit and *Nowhereisland* could be seen as diametrically opposed commissions in what they sought to represent. *Orbit* was partly defined by its fixed position and rose hubristically to the skies like a cathedral, creating

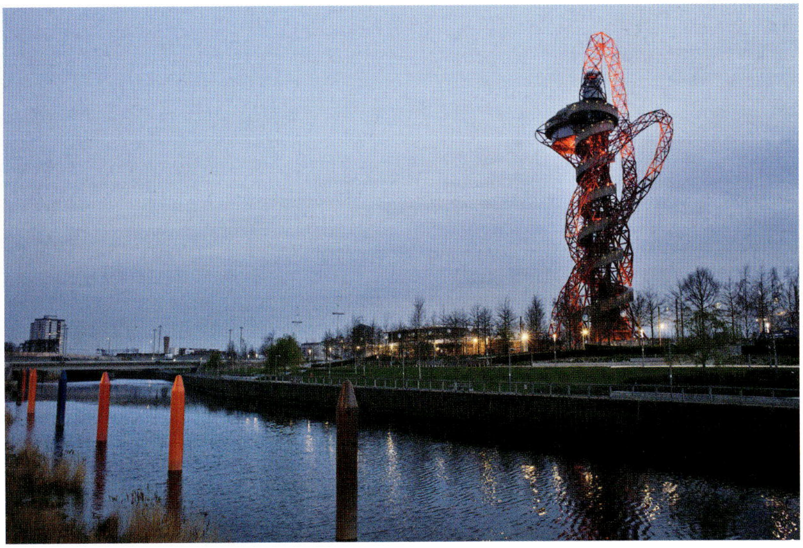

108 View of Queen Elizabeth Olympic Park showing the *Orbit*, London, 2014.

and celebrating new London landscapes, especially the highly symbolic Olympic skyline. In contrast, *Nowhereisland* suggested an inhospitable Arctic topography – barren, rocky and icy. This was an anti-nation island, perpetually mobile, against ideas of exclusive national identity, and paradoxically uninhabited, despite the mobile embassy following it on land. While *Orbit* twisted and turned as it reached to the skies like a tower of Babel, *Nowhereisland* was bleakly horizontal.[17] But Hartley's project was also creating new, transitory landscapes: as it was towed around the south coast it transformed some of those Devon holiday landscapes. No one was more surprised than Hartley when the Arts Council agreed to sponsor his provocative project. It caused controversy: in 2011 the right-wing British newspaper the *Daily Mail* pronounced angrily that the British Arts Council was spending 'a staggering £500,000 on floating a huge piece of Arctic rock more than 2,000 miles [3,218 km] from Norway to England ... But critics have branded it a complete waste of public money.'[18]

Claire Doherty has described the evolution of *Nowhereisland* from the artist's studio-based, photographic and sculptural practice into a socially engaged 'post-practice' (which I take to mean an evolving, performative project) with significant political, territorial and economic implications: '*Nowhereisland* was not simply an island sculpture on the move – but to see it, to really *see* the work as a whole, you had to engage with the propositions, exchanges, disagreements, desires and demands of the *Nowhereisland* citizens.'[19] The project both issued a utopian call for open and unrestricted citizenship and promoted (a loose notion of) open governance. Hartley referenced Thomas More's *Utopia* on his website, acknowledging Philip Hoare's observation that 'the island, real or fictional, aspires to Utopia'.[20] It also had a constitution of sorts. Following the Declaration of *Nowhereisland* as a new nation on 20 September 2011, Hartley and the expedition team suggested that the constitution should be an ongoing collaborative document written by its citizens using digital technology. They devised an online tool by which propositions of 120 characters (that is, suitable for Twitter/X) could be put forward for the constitution, and in turn retweeted or disliked. Through a system of continuous ranking, the less popular proposals sank to the bottom of the list.[21]

Nowhereisland was never intended to offer a literal political form of 'citizenship' – itself a much-debated notion.[22] That said, Hartley was using mimicry and metaphor to address a contemporary preoccupation with national identity, 'sovereignty' and what might be called the resurgence of the nation state. Performance art often functions as metaphor or allegory, encouraging us to reflect on our relationship with 'the real world'. Inevitably, many contemporary writers and theorists are engaging with the problem of the nation state in rather more complex ways, among them the novelist and essayist Rana Dasgupta. In his book *After Nations* he argues forcefully that the nation state is no longer capable of rising to the challenges imposed by an increasingly internationalized world; he claims we need new global conceptions of citizenship, democracy and financial regulation.[23] I would add new global environmental regulations (beyond those supposedly signed up to). Hartley's artistic practice can take us into areas of complex political and economic debate – all of them topical.

Hartley is one among many contemporary artists who have referenced ideas of international citizenship in island projects on unstable or floating landscapes that deploy multimedia activities. For example, the artists Lucy and Jorge Orta (who work in London and Paris) directly engage with the theme in their ongoing *Antarctica Project*. In 2007 they went on an expedition to the Antarctic, itself a large, increasingly unstable archipelago, aided by the team of scientists stationed at the Antarctica base on Seymour (Marambio) Island. Here they found a site for their temporary encampment comprised of fifty domed tent dwellings (illus. 109). These were hand-stitched with sections of flags and clothing fragments from countries around the world, designed to symbolize the multiplicity and diversity of peoples, and reminiscent of images of refugee camps. The flags and fragments were emblazoned with silkscreen motifs referencing the right to freedom of movement upheld in the UN Declaration for Human Rights. The artists hoped that this could represent a physical embodiment of (or a metaphor for) a new 'Global Village'. Although not staged

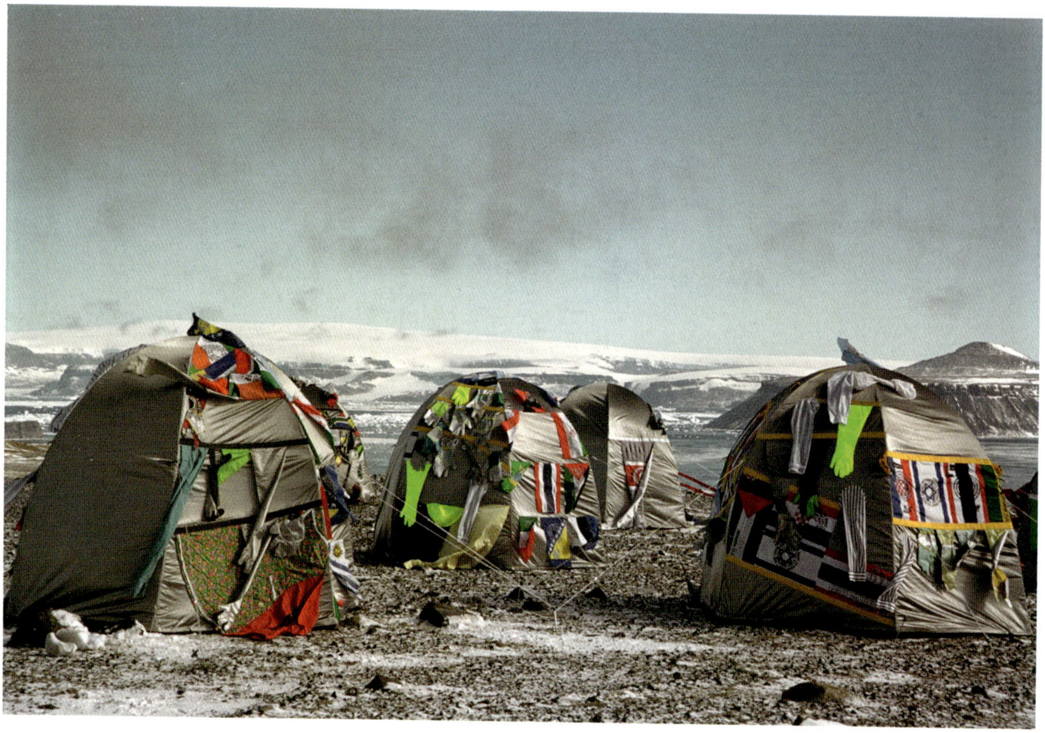

109 Lucy and Jorge Orta, *Antarctic Village – No Borders*, 2007, ephemeral installation across the Antarctic Peninsula consisting of 50 dome dwellings, hand-stitched nation flags, fragments of clothing, webbing, silkscreen print.

on a visibly floating island (although polar icebergs are, in effect, floating islands), there was a sense in which this was a mobile global village. Tents, of course, are infinitely mobile.

The artists conceived this Antarctic Village project as a symbol of the plight of those struggling to cross borders to escape political and social conflict. The project evolved to include further Antarctic installations and the issue of 'Antarctica World Passports'. The contents of the passport are a kind of manifesto for a borderless form of citizenship, for which Antarctica is seen as a symbolic model.[24] In signing up for one of these passports, the viewer is (in theory at least) signing up to support their Amendment to Article 1.3 of the Universal Declaration of Human Rights, which reads: 'Everyone has the right to move freely and cross frontiers to their chosen territory. No individual should have an inferior status to that of capital, trade, telecommunication, or pollution that traverse all borders.'[25] The fact that you could obtain one of these passports for free at another mobile embassy at the London Frieze art fair of 2017 comes with its own ironies and reminds us of the difficult relationship with the market that is often part of contemporary performative art practice. The artists' Antarctic landscape is perceived as a mobile and potentially political zone. Mock passports were issued (like Hartley's invitation to sign up for citizenship) in a bid to encourage art visitors to symbolically transfer their individual national identity into that of a collective world citizen.

Nowhereisland has much to contribute to the debates that surround notions of 'place' – traditionally a major concern of geographers. Place, like 'home', is a contested, interdisciplinary notion, much debated by scholars of art history, visual culture and geography. Landscape is often seen as an intensely visual concept, and a material topography. The geographer Tim Cresswell (who was part of Hartley's Arctic expedition) argues that '[in] most definitions of landscape the viewer is outside of it', a quality that differentiates it from place.[26] Place is often seen, then, in contrast with landscape, as a lived experience – a social construction around an identifiable neighbourhood, geographical area or nation. Place can be a spatial imaginary tied to a landscape; it is heavily invested with meaning that is social, political, cultural and so on. But Hartley's work suggests that landscape – that is, the visual project – can be equally fluid and unstable. It is both literally and metaphorically a floating signifier, a verb rather than a noun. The aesthetic and political economies of *Nowhereisland* are explicitly linked.

A sculptural exploration of place, made from fragments of Norwegian rock and debris, is integral to the *Nowhereisland* project. Rocks, pebbles, walrus bones and other local objects found on Nymark were displayed in the mobile land-based embassy that followed the floating island around the south coast of England. These included a small piece of moon rock, which constituted a part of both the larger work and the official archive (the objects and fragments displayed in the mobile embassy). The artist Tania Kovats (b. 1966), who was part of the expedition, has described the fluid – even global – function of this archive: 'One of the objects in the *Nowhereisland* embassy was a tiny fragment of a lunar meteorite. This object was the smallest item in the archive, yet it added the most to reflections on the nature of mobile territories. Nothing you could touch could bring you closer from something further away.'[27] At the same time, these objects can be perceived as evidence of the distinct islandness of the project; fragments provide evidence of its particular geological characteristics as part of the bleak, rocky formations of the Arctic Circle. Fragments constitute further evidence of the deliberate contradictions at the heart of this floating island. It could be argued that Hartley was deliberately trespassing on, and damaging, Norwegian territory, since his initial claim on the island was rejected by the Norwegian government. As we saw in Chapter Two, Hartley's island projects often involve some kind of mischievously aggressive act that serves to de-romanticize the associations of specific places and landscapes.

Through their part in the ongoing performance, the engaged citizens of *Nowhereisland*, alongside the artist, helped to create and develop the narrative of the journey and sea voyage. I have argued that representations of the island theme have been significantly enriched by developments in the expanded field, enabling participatory and interdisciplinary engagements with visual material. Hartley's floating island was perpetually changing its landscape and its performative history as it travelled from the High Arctic to southwest England. It leaves little sculptural trace (apart from the fragments dispatched to citizens). As such it also reminds us that topographies of landscape are constantly evolving; they are enmeshed with our shifting ideas of both place and space. As the geographer Doreen Massey writes in a fitting quote from her 'Reflections on Moving Mountains' of 2006: 'bearing in mind the movement of the rocks, both space and landscape could be imagined as provisionally intertwined simultaneities of ongoing, unfinished stories.'[28] *Nowhereisland* offered its audiences the unfinished story of an evolving island landscape, rich in imaginative possibilities and ongoing tales of social collaboration.

STRUGGLING WITH PLURALS

Hartley's project was underpinned by shifting notions of both landscape and national identity. As I write, British art institutions are struggling with the harsh economic effects of the 2016 Brexit referendum, and cultural debates have blossomed around controversial ideas of our 'island nation'. 'Britishness' is increasingly 'coming apart at the seams', producing contradictory allegiances.[29] The recent Brexit-related collusion of geography, history and politics to reclaim an identity steeped in self-determination and separateness has enhanced the relevance of the island theme. The notion that islands have immutable borders – that is, the sea – and uncontested geographies is increasingly being challenged across disciplines and artistic practices. The writer Madeleine Bunting argues that being part of an island has been a central part of English nationalism. She points out that generations of children (including former prime minister David Cameron) learned their history from H. E. Marshall's *Our Island Story* (1905), despite the fact that the title is based on some obvious mistakes:

> England shares an island with two other nations, and the UK is actually an archipelago of about 6,300 islands. English nationalism struggles with plurals, and for writers the island trope has offered an easy way to pluck the heartstrings of English sensibility.[30]

Englishness and Britishness have long been conflated, with a mythical 'Englishness' at the heart of some pro-Brexit narratives. England is not, and never has been, an island. Except, perhaps, in some erroneous nationalist fantasy. This historic inability to see England – and Britain – as part of a connected archipelago, has informed the work of several contemporary British artists who have reimagined ideas of both nationhood and islandness. According to Hartley, during the development of *Nowhereisland* 'we always talked about the idea of an island as a node of connectivity rather than a place alone and separated.'[31] This connectivity is also central to the work of the British artist Tania Kovats. Her *All the Islands of All the Seas* (2016; illus. 110) consists of 36 works, each containing up to ten

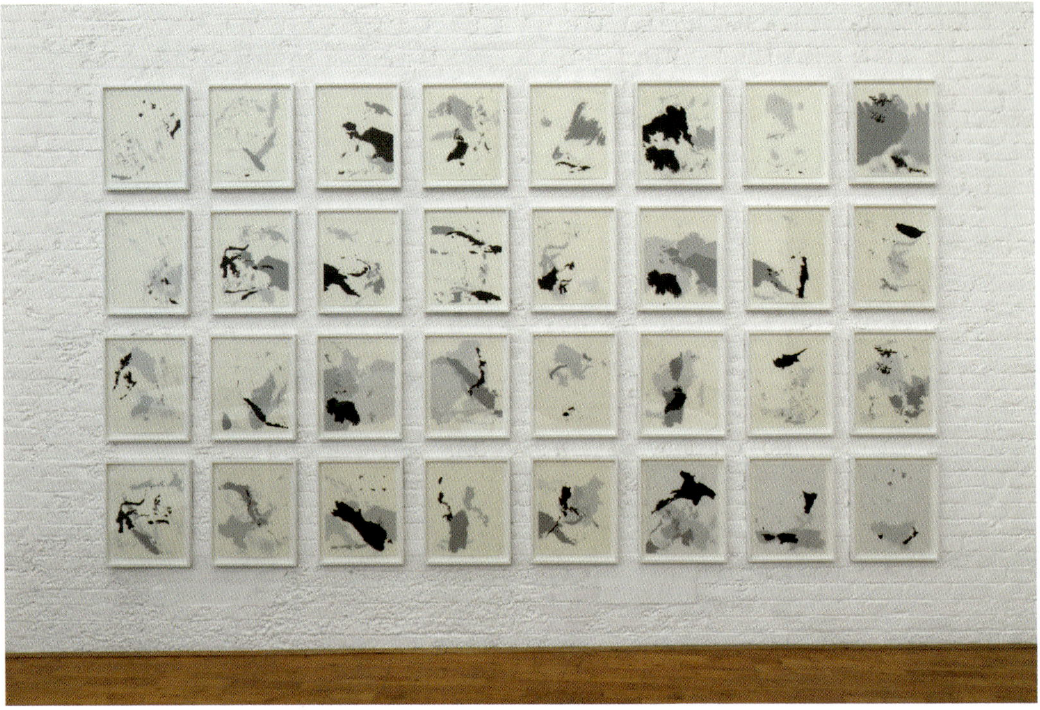

110 Tania Kovats, *All the Islands of All the Seas*, 2016, ink on layered matte acetate, 196 drawings, 32 parts.

different layered drawings of landmasses. Traced from atlases onto translucent paper, Kovats's islands are never static. They float across each other, giving up their geographic, cartographic and cultural certainty – a system of plurals. One year before the Brexit referendum Kovats made *Only Blue (British Isles)* (2014), which uses obsolete atlases of the archipelagos of the British Isles but blots out the land in each map with white gesso (illus. 111). National identities and place names are thus erased, leaving mottled areas of blue ocean to define a strange, overlapping geographical identity.

We saw in Chapter Five that the label 'island writers' is often used to identify a body of postcolonial writing from former British colonies in Caribbean, Indian and Pacific archipelagos. These writers (including the St Lucian poet Derek Walcott) 'have rendered island spaces as vital and dynamic loci of cultural and material exchange'.[32] As a series of small nations connected by the sea, these archipelagos have profited from fluid transcultural, diasporic and regional alliances. Glissant has described the

111 Tania Kovats, *Only Blue (British Isles)*, 2014, eight altered atlases, acrylic box.

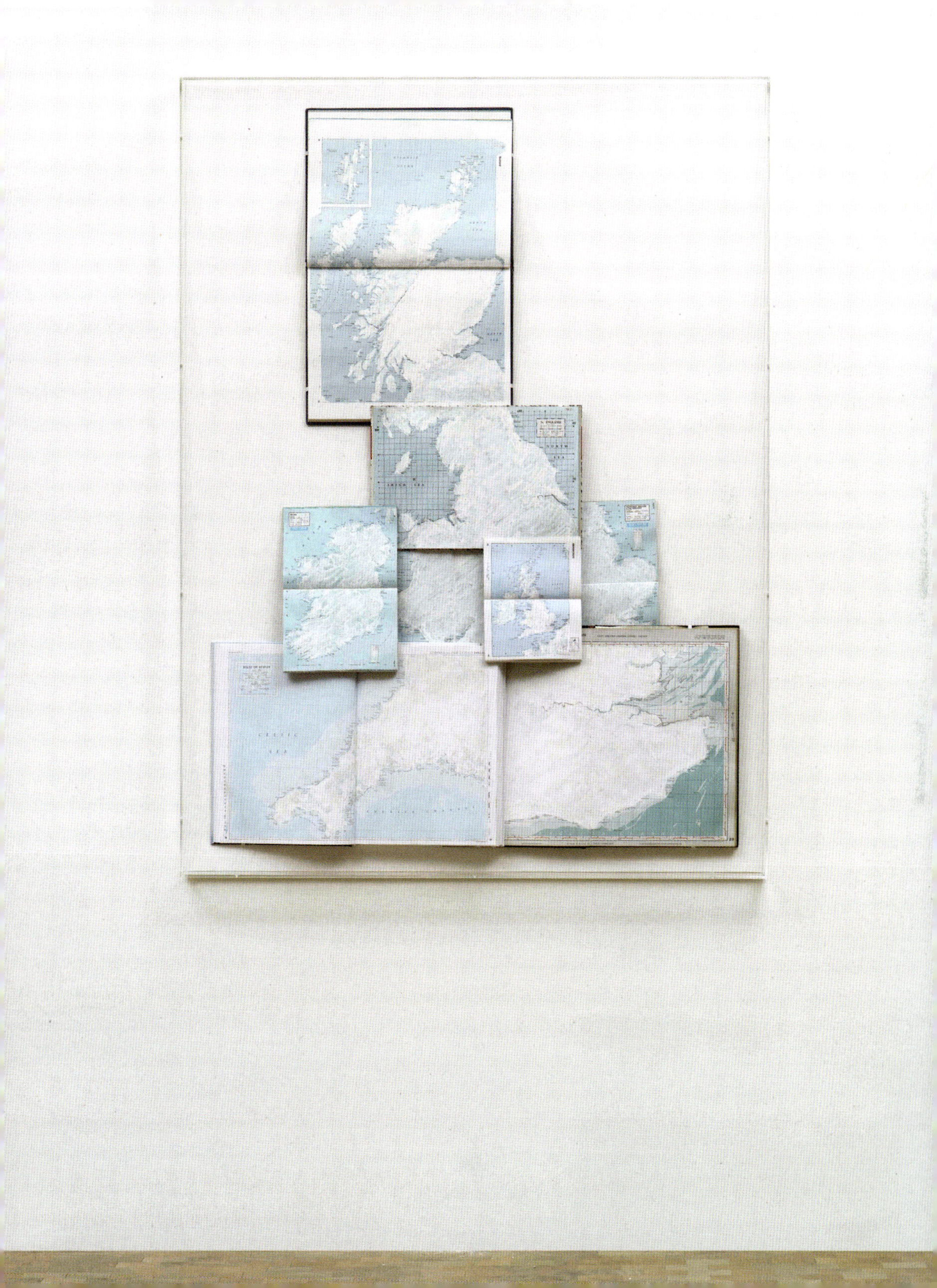
N. ENGLAND
NORTH SEA
CELTIC SEA

'openness' embodied by these islands: 'the dialectic between inside and outside is reflected in the relationship between land and sea.'[33] For Kovats, Hartley and other contemporary British artists (including, for example, Tacita Dean) the sea is vital to the spatial scale of island imagination, enabling my parallel designation of 'island artists'. In their work the sea can act as a metaphor of connectivity within and beyond archipelagos. It can defy colonial and pro-Brexit narratives of separate island status and affirm the important role of art, and its floating signifiers, in the ongoing 'struggle with plurals'.

8 GOING NORTH AND MELTING ICE

The island.
The ocean surround.
The going north.
The light.
Roni Horn, 'Island Zombie'[1]

The Scandinavian and Northern archipelagos have long attracted tourists seeking remote ice-capped landscapes with elemental scenery and volcanic geology. These sites are rich in myths and legends that contrast with what Baldacchino has described as the 'warm water branding' of tropical island tourism. While the latter is more often associated with desert island and castaway myths, Northern and Arctic islands often involve tales of endurance amidst glaciers and freezing seas, not to mention more recent explorations of the devastating effects of climate change on the polar regions.

Jules Verne's famous science fiction novel *Journey to the Centre of the Earth* (first published in French as *Voyage au centre de la Terre* in 1864), set in Iceland, has helped to fuel its own brand of cold-water tourism. It adopts the trope of the journey in island literature to frame spectacular adventures and their parallel psychic journeys. An eccentric German geologist, his nephew and an Icelandic guide begin their exploits in the crater of the island's inactive volcano Snæfellsjökull, from where they travel through volcanic tubes to encounter prehistoric creatures, collapsing caves and sub-polar tornadoes, among other subterranean events. The party are finally spewed up by an active volcano, Stromboli, on the Italian island of the same name.

The volcanic Icelandic landscape and its elemental weather frame this extraordinary tale, which ends on another (much warmer) island. Even the name Ice-land suggests a remote, bitterly cold place, which some have mistakenly presumed to be close to the North Pole.[2] The island has inspired a string of films and TV series, and some vivid examples of performance and installation art.[3] These include the American artist Joan Jonas's *Volcano Saga*, first performed live by Jonas (b. 1939) in 1985, when she narrated a thirteenth-century Icelandic folktale about a young woman called Gudrun. It was later adapted into video, with roles played by actors (Tilda Swinton played Gudrun) superimposed onto shots of elemental Icelandic vistas (illus. 112). In the film Jonas describes an Icelandic storm that suddenly blew her car off the road while she was gathering footage. The event (it is implied) connects her to the elemental vicissitudes of Iceland and its myths. Northern and Arctic islands have provided dramatic stages for the creation and curation of some recent art projects, many of which reference personal journeys and the all too visible climate emergency. Moreover, melting glacial ice has become a ubiquitous symbol of that emergency, and a material increasingly deployed in contemporary art.[4]

WATERY WEATHER AND ICELANDIC ICE

The American conceptual artist Roni Horn (b. 1955) first visited Iceland in 1975 and returned three years later as a postgraduate, roaming the island for six months. In her collection *Island Zombie: Iceland Writings* (2020) she wrote that she returned there 'with migratory insistence and regularity. The necessity of it was part of me.'[5] Since her postgraduate sojourn she has spent lengthy periods living and working in Iceland, gathering material for many works, including her series of artist's books *To Place* and her photographic installation *You Are the Weather*, displayed in the show *My Oz* at the Museum of Modern Art, Reykjavik, in 2007.[6] *My Oz* ran parallel to her multifaceted arts project *Vatnasafn/Library of Water*, commissioned by Artangel and installed in a former library in the western coastal village of Stykkishólmur in the summer of 2007. Horn's artistic production has

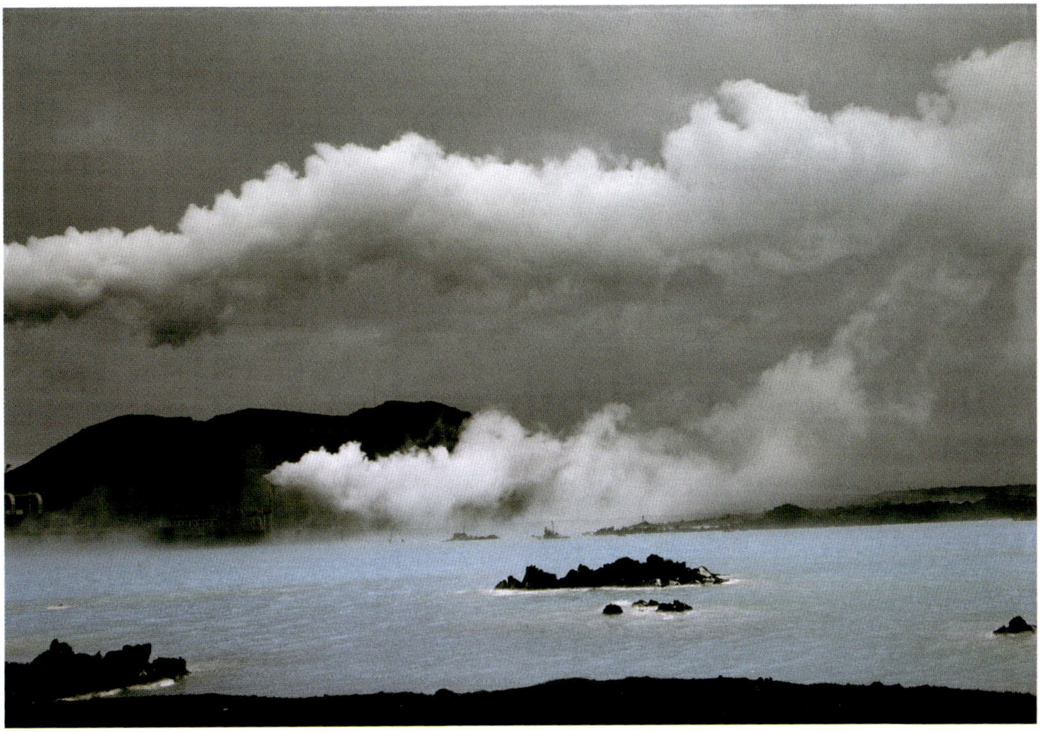

112 Joan Jonas, *Iceland Photo for Volcano Saga #3*, 1985, digital C-print.

been intimately engaged with the island's dramatic landscape and meteorology. She has described Iceland as her 'open-air studio of unlimited scale and newness', comparing it with an artist's use of marble as 'the substance' of the work.[7] Moreover, in Iceland Horn redefined the word 'place' as a verb – a landscape in process, echoing ideas mapped out throughout this book. Identifying an island of 'young geology' – 'an act, not an object, a verb, never a noun', she argues for a dialectical relationship between the viewer and the place being viewed.[8] Icelandic geology and weather have been artfully woven into her *Library of Water*, conceived as a permanent installation and community arts centre.

The Stykkishólmur library stands on a rocky mound overlooking the port and its watery inlets. Its rounded art-deco windows and sea views evoke lighthouses and ocean liners as it appears to ride the waves and the weather (illus. 113). When Horn heard of plans to move the library to

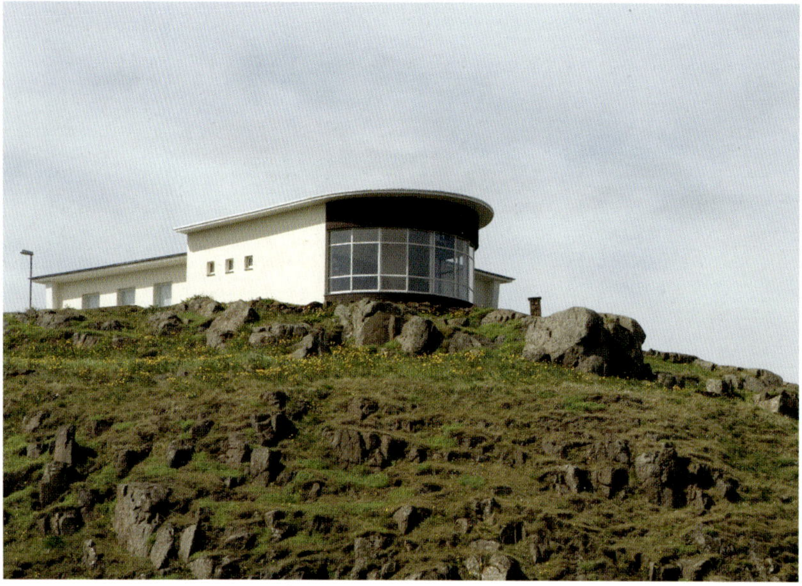

113 Stykkishólmur library, the site of Roni Horn's *Library of Water*, 2007.

another building, she approached the mayor offering to create an 'umbrella work' in the disused library that would be intimately involved with the life of the local community. Her project, which was approved by the mayor, involved enlarging west-facing windows to produce a light gallery space leading into the glazed, apse-like north end overlooking the Stykkishólmur Lighthouse, an orange, bell-like structure that dominates another rocky mound. Horn embraced the associations of lighthouse iconography, which holds emblematic status around the rugged Icelandic coastline, providing dramatic landmarks and visual metaphors for the islanders' taste for solitude and resistance to dangerous weather. In her collection of local memories *Weather Reports You*, produced as part of the *Library of Water* project, a retired lighthouse keeper at Hornbjarg in the Westfjörds, which could only be reached by sea, recalls: 'When I was at the Hornbjarg lighthouse everything revolved around the weather . . . I could feel it all.'[9] In the first of her series of books *To Place (Bluff Life)* (1990) Horn included a series of drawings made in the Dyrhólaey Lighthouse on a sparsely inhabited stretch of the south Icelandic coast. Here she spent two months living alone and described an inspirational space for making art: 'I wanted to go to a distant and solitary place and be there . . . I knew that whatever came out of it would be about who I was and about what this place was . . . I was wagering that I could find intimacy in this isolated, pared-down way of life.'[10]

This sense of inspirational 'intimacy' contrasts with the wilder, masculine 'lighthouseness' explored in Chapter Two. Horn compares the *Library of Water* to a lens that reflects and refracts the lights and colours of different weather, describing the space as a 'lighthouse in which the viewer becomes the light'.[11] Dispersed around the main room are 24 floor-to-ceiling glass columns, each 30 centimetres (11 in.) in diameter, containing water collected from Iceland's major glaciers (illus. 115). Her experience of weather becomes a cipher for self-knowledge, encouraging metaphorical musings on identity, climate, ecology and place. The extremes of Icelandic weather and their effects on the lives of Icelanders are referenced here in multiple ways. Watery columns have replaced the stacks of books, providing lenses through which light, landscapes and human figures are reflected. Ice from glaciers with evocative names such as Tungnaájökull or Köldukvíslarjökull, and Verne's glacier-capped volcano Snæfellsjökull, was installed in March 2007 (illus. 114). After the installation, mineral deposits rendered some

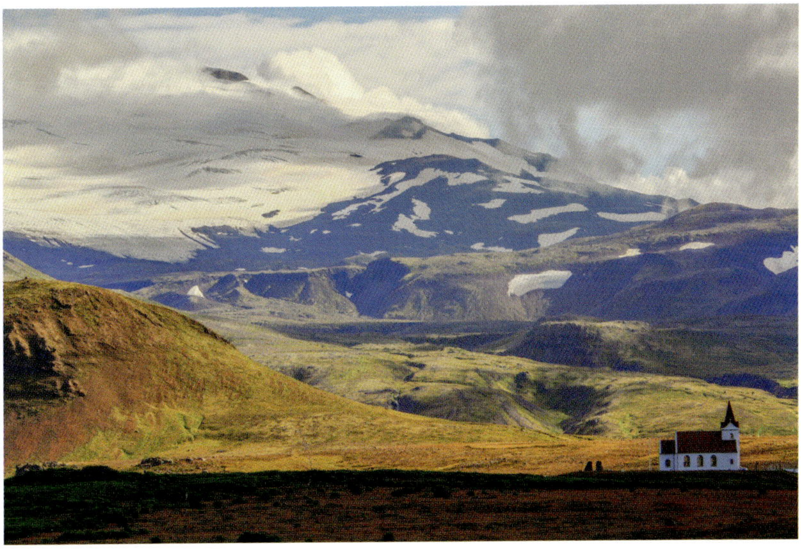

114 Extinct Snæfellsjökull volcano with glacier view.

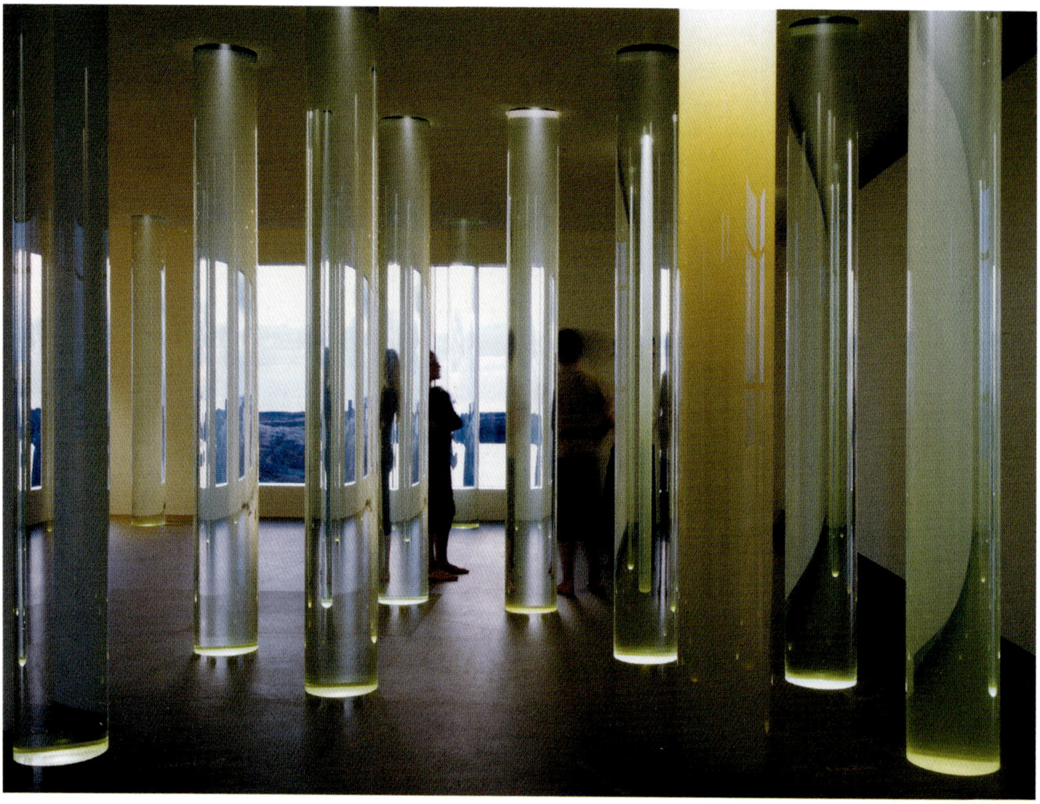

115 Roni Horn, *Vatnasafn/Library of Water*, interior, 2007, installation at Stykkishólmur. Each cylinder contains water from one of 24 Icelandic glaciers.

columns opaque, while others reflected figures and landscapes from inside and outside the space, reversed as if mirror images. As the deposits settled, little mountains of sediment formed at the bases of the tubes, combining miniaturized landscapes with reflected ones.

Horn refers to her edited collection *Weather Reports You* as a 'Collective Self-Portrait', describing shared immersive experiences that have 'enabled us to merge into a single, global us: each passing day we can watch as the weather actually becomes us'.[12] Whatever the ontological power of this claim, testimonies in this collection bear witness to the effects of climate change on the lives of islanders. In 2006 the Hornbjarg lighthouse keeper recalled that one winter in his childhood the family had to dig themselves out of the snow from their upper floor window: 'Imagine that snowfall!! That's unknown these days.'[13]

Nowhere on earth has warmed as quickly as the Arctic. Since 1980 its ice sheet has decreased by more than 50 per cent. All three hundred of Iceland's glaciers are melting; the smallest, Okjökull, has disappeared. At the time of writing, just over 10 per cent of Iceland's total area is covered by glacial ice caps (approximately two-thirds of Iceland is almost completely devoid of vegetation). When Horn installed her *Library of Water* in 2007, it was 11 per cent. Some recent studies have claimed that Iceland's glaciers could lose about two-thirds of their current volume within decades.[14] Horn's installation references such ecological issues obliquely, but with gentle persuasion. The accompanying Artangel print, *Water, Selected*, is a map of Iceland with each of the 24 glaciers labelled in an orange-brown font (illus. 116). These labels appear to float across white, black and grey contours that trace the complex geography of this archipelago, echoing the emblematic colours of Icelandic lighthouses.

Horn has often expressed her concerns for Iceland's future and the growth of its global economic interests: 'Iceland is no longer an island: economically, chemically, climatically and even psychologically speaking.' She has cited climate change, economic expansion, pollution and political pressure as urgent concerns, arguing that these issues necessitate 'a new approach to maintaining the integrity of Iceland's land, water and culture'.[15] Several decades ago the Icelandic air was so pure that the Kyoto Protocol of 2005 gave the country permission to increase its carbon emissions by 10 per cent from 1990 levels. Controversial plans were then pushed through for many geothermal and hydroelectric power plants, alongside several new aluminium smelters that were allowed to emit 1.6 million metric tons of carbon dioxide (one-third of Iceland's CO_2 emissions). Given the island's rich natural resources, it has been claimed that a network of hydroelectric dams would provide a large amount of cheap 'green' energy to the world.[16] However, environmentalists have argued that much of this energy source is now used by the new aluminium smelters owned by the major global corporations Alcoa, Alcan and Rio Tinto, and that 'an aggressive industrialisation policy' pursued by the Icelandic government has used the country's renewable energy sources 'to prop up other

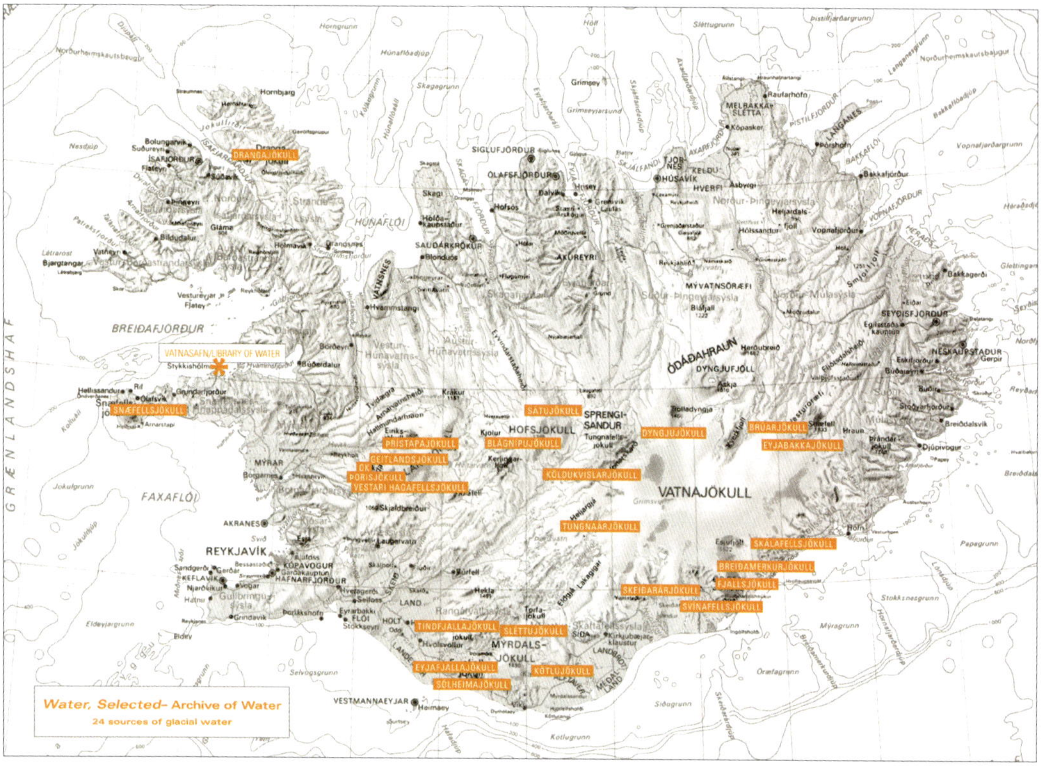

116 Roni Horn, *Water, Selected*, 2007, Artangel print.

environmentally damaging industries'.[17] Heated debates that rage on the effects on Iceland's remarkable ecosystem were topical at the time that Horn produced *Library of Water*, and have informed her recent statement of 2020 that 'islandhood is over'.

Present trends suggest accelerated increases in glacial melting and rising sea levels. Iceland is located at the junction of cold and warm air and ocean currents and shifts in ocean circulation could have a dramatic effect on the island's vital fishing industries. Given the harsh environment of treeless tundra, lava and ice fields, even small climatic changes in the future could affect the delicate seasonal balance between erosion and regrowth. *Library of Water* mediates these issues to a local and wider audience, using the site-specific art installation to seduce and provoke the viewer. While these aspects of Horn's project do not necessarily constitute a practice that could be labelled 'activism', they do reveal the artist as engaged with the literal and symbolic potential of artworks to raise ecological awareness.[18] We have seen that issues of 'material' (for example, waste, finite resources and changing geologies) are often highlighted by artists concerned with ecology; Horn's ongoing preoccupation with Icelandic weather and water – especially glacial water – can prompt viewers to think critically about their relationship with a threatened environment. Moreover, her concerns with 'the loss of islandhood' due to global pollution, corporate exploitation, geopolitical expansion and digital surveillance, as expressed in her essay 'On the Obsolescence of Islands', can colour our understanding of such evocative works.[19]

Horn's Icelandic projects have also provoked metaphysical musings on identity and solitude. In her catalogue essay for *My Oz* Fríða Björk Ingvarsdóttir explores some Icelandic notions of place and solitude which, as she argues, Horn has appropriated in her aesthetic practice. Most Icelanders who have grown up on this sparsely populated island (the current population is just over 300,000) are all too familiar with isolation as a necessary part of experience. Ingvarsdóttir claims that by gathering material from these vast open spaces, Horn has found a kind of refuge from 'the alienation of the inhabited world'.[20] Horn herself has used the term 'inner geography' to describe her experience of nature as a mirror, as a means of gathering a kind of common sense: 'I have always understood Iceland as being big enough to get lost on, but small enough to find oneself.'[21] The British art historian Briony Fer has suggested a notion of 'psychogeology', adapting the *derive* of Situationist 'psychogeography' as a framework for understanding Horn's practice.[22] Horn's geographical and psychic wilderness is populated with sometimes bleak, yet compelling, images of Icelandic geology, which often appear to merge into abstraction. Many of the photographic and lithographic works in the books that make up her series *To Place* represent Icelandic lava, folds, pools, tundra and glaciers. Book v of the series, *Verne's Journey* (1995), includes vivid images of the tempestuous waters, extraordinary rock formations and aerial photographs of Snæfelsjökull, where Verne's protagonist, Sir Oliver Lindenbrook, began his descent. Horn's journey merges psychogeology with compelling ecological and aesthetic concerns.

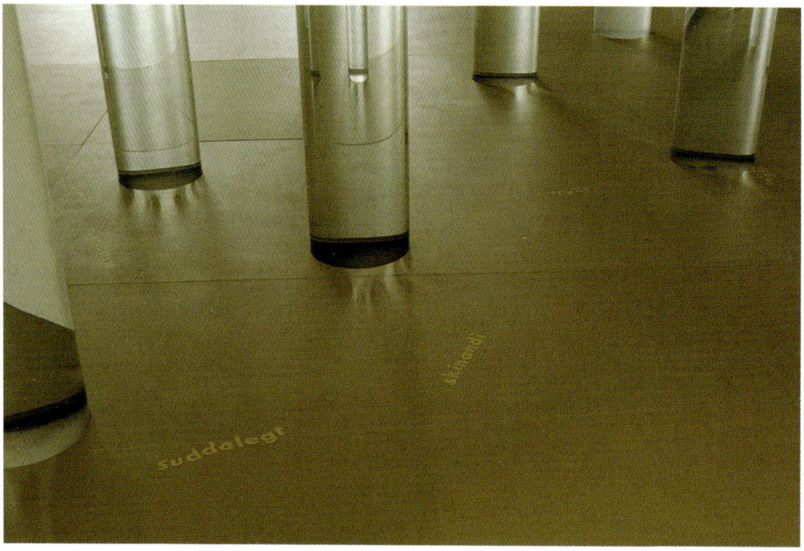

117 Roni Horn, *Vatnasafn/ Library of Water*, 2007, detail of floor.

The watery columns in *Library of Water* can stand as melting glaciers, miniature landscapes, reflective lenses, ecological weathervanes and aesthetic sculptures both transformed and transformative. These columns are also positioned amid a sea of words, titled *You are the Weather (Iceland)*. Embedded in the vulcanized rubber floor is a field of English and Icelandic adjectives that have been used to describe the weather, suggesting the slippery connections between words, images and meanings (illus. 117). English words that evoke both weather and human emotions, such as 'oppressive', 'violent', 'serene', 'frosty' and 'cruel', are scattered among their Icelandic equivalents. Human emotions appear to be refracted through weather conditions and vice versa, echoing Horn's ongoing concern with the fluidity of both language and identity. The suggestion that art itself can provide a space for creative enquiry is echoed in its role within the Stykkishólmur community. The building is used for local and international events, including musical performances, yoga, environmental groups, literature readings and writers' residencies. It also offers a space for young girls to learn to play chess, traditionally an integral part of Icelandic male culture.[23]

As a travelling artist who has spent long periods living on Iceland, Horn is well aware that her engagement with the country is partly that of a tourist in danger of romanticizing its 'otherness'. At the same time, debates around hybridity and transnational artistic practice have perhaps enabled her to stake a claim, not simply as the American Conceptual artist who discovered the spectacular aesthetic possibilities of the Icelandic landscape, but rather as what she calls a 'permanent tourist', an oxymoron that allows her to comment on and embrace this island and its culture while also maintaining a certain distance. Throughout her work and writings she has embraced contradiction, describing the weather as 'the key paradox of our time', confusing and deceiving us with warmer weather patterns that are 'wrong'.[24] In terms of cultural migration and its aesthetic effects, it could be argued that Horn has enabled some paradoxes and elisions that allow us to salvage her own brand of 'cosmopolitanism'.[25] The increasingly global, geopolitical transformations of the contemporary art world and its relentless pursuit of international art fairs and corporate capital should not necessarily be conflated with the migratory patterns and hybrid aesthetic concerns of some of its 'travelling' artists. Thus Horn's work could also be interpreted as a form of critical interplay between an artistic repertoire developed initially within the Conceptual art movement, but reworked and refocused through her engagement with the geology of Iceland and its future as an island.

Library of Water was enthusiastically supported by the local community and the Icelandic parliament and has significant personal connections with the artist. The art historian Claire Bishop has posited a model of successful site-specific installation art that goes beyond the decentred viewing 'experience' to include more critical forms of engagement. She has argued for an installation art 'which does not exist outside of historical memory, but draws connections between the individual and the cultural, the past and the present'.[26] *Library of Water* is such a project; it stands as a modern Gesamtkunstwerk signalling local and global concerns, comprising a sculptural installation, an arts centre and an accumulation of oral histories. With a sense of threatened northern islandness at its heart, *Library of Water* gently reminds us that 'Weather that is nice is often weather that is wrong.'[27]

ARCTIC MELTS AND MYTHS

A concern with glacial ice melts has also been visualized in the work of artists who have made sea journeys to the Arctic to observe at first hand the effects of the climate crisis. In 2001 the British artist, curator and film-maker David Buckland set up the *Cape Farewell* project, bringing together scientists, artists and educators on expeditions designed to encourage artistic production that draws on scientific research, and to change attitudes towards the climate emergency.[28] On several Arctic expeditions between 2005 and 2010 Buckland projected texts onto crumbling icebergs, often photographed in low light, creating haunting *Ice Texts* (illus. 118). Each melting iceberg resembled a floating island, dramatically labelled with scaled-up, ironic or portentous words.

Other artists have incorporated ice harvested from northern archipelagos into their work, involving journeys to new (often incongruous) sites. Between 2004 and 2008 American-based artist Tavares Strachan (b. 1979) (who grew up in the Bahamas) worked on *The Distance between What We Have and What We Want (The Arctic Ice Project)*. He sent a

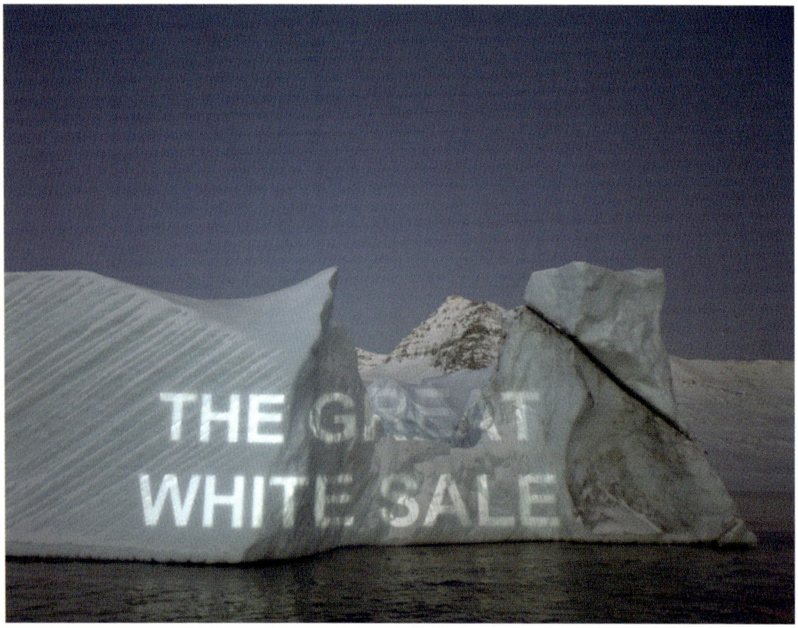

118 David Buckland and Amy Balkin, *The Great White Sale*, from 'Ice Texts', 2009.

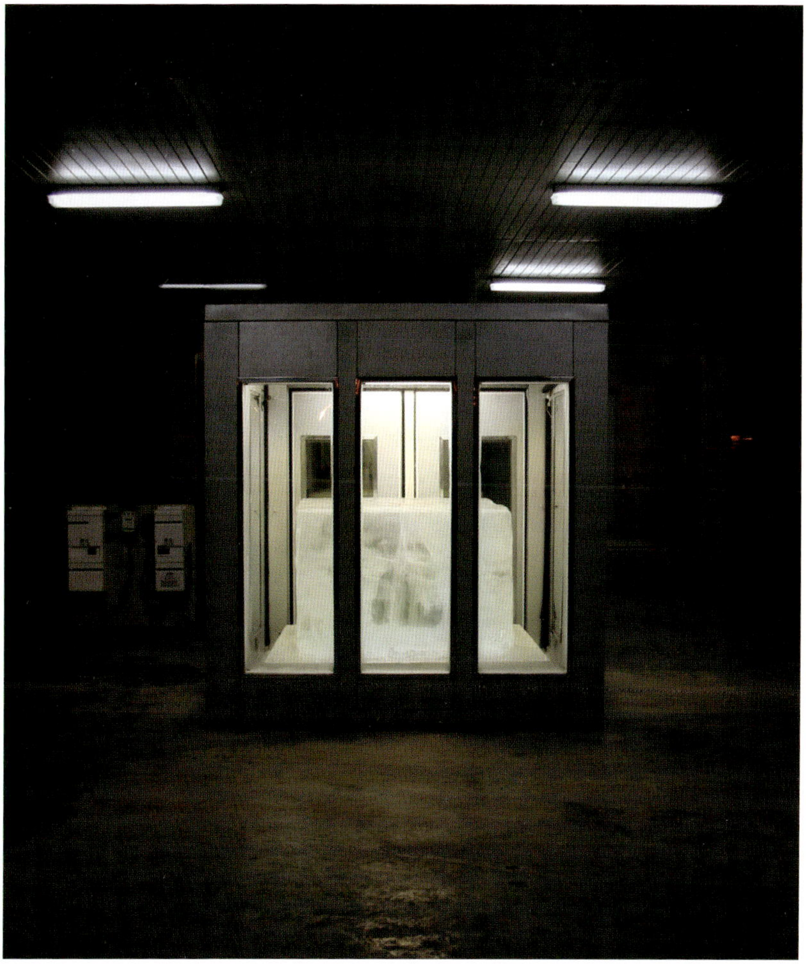

119 Tavares Strachan, *Chamber with Ice: Elevator for the Reversal of Up and Down*, 2006, ice, refrigeration unit, solar panels, fans, flags, battery system.

4.5-ton cube of ice from the Alaskan Arctic back to his former elementary school in Nassau in the Bahamas, and then on to be exhibited in the Brooklyn Museum, using a solar-powered refrigerated glass case (illus. 119). Evoking themes of geographical, cultural and artistic displacement (as discussed in earlier chapters), the relocated ice block was displayed as something 'exotic and rare, a specimen reminiscent of moon rocks brought back to earth by astronauts'. As Julie Reiss argues, this piece of ice becomes a 'stand in for the artist'.[29] A similar strategy of oblique self-representation might be identified in Horn's reflective tubes of glacial ice.

The local economy of the Lofoten Islands in the Arctic Circle in Nordland, northern Norway, is supported by a different form of Arctic travel, 'art tourism'. Renowned for its Northern Lights and Midnight Sun, this archipelago of dramatic mountain peaks, sheltered bays and the world's largest deep-water coral reef enjoys a relatively temperate ocean climate for its Arctic location (illus. 120). Its tourist appeal has encouraged investment in the visual arts: the Lofoten International Art Festival (LIAF) is a biennial of contemporary art on and around the islands, without a single set venue.[30] Dramatic island sites are deployed for a range of experimental and site-specific work. The official LIAF website describes its mission to acknowledge the complex nature of 'place' and to provide a 'discursive, engaged and social platform for different positions creating dialogue between the local and the global'.[31] Such dialogues inevitably implicate

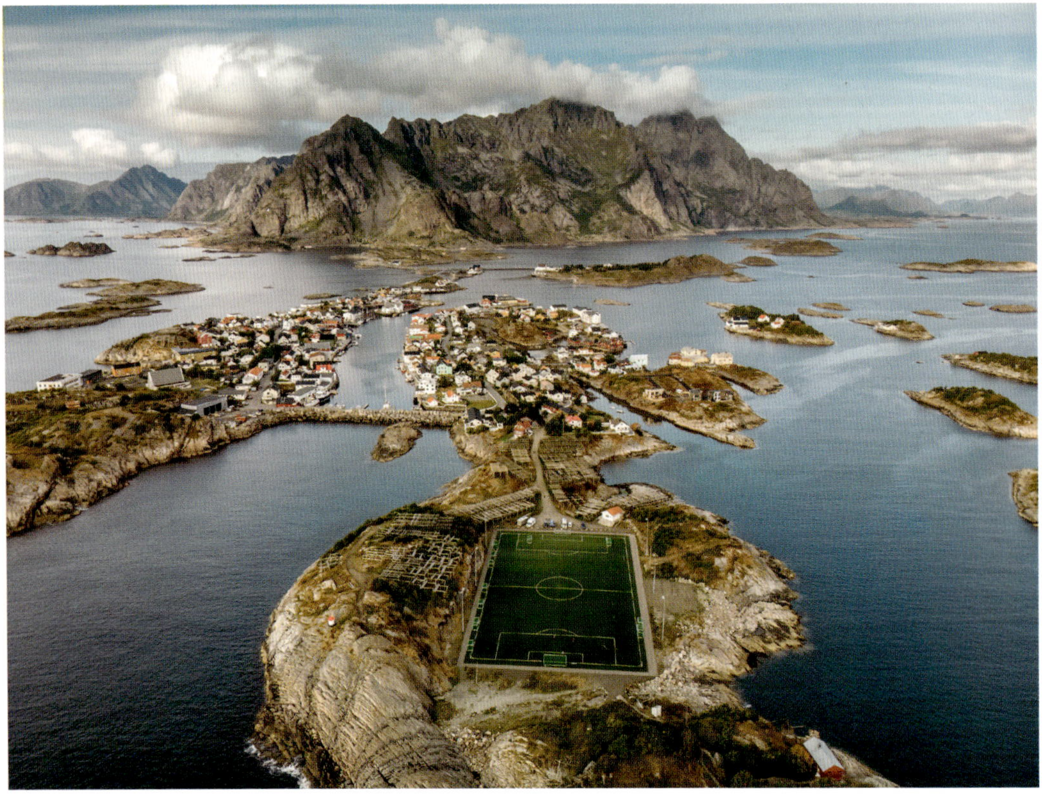

120 View of the Henningsvaer fishing village, Lofoten Islands, with football stadium in the foreground.

the effects of the climate crisis that are hard to avoid when commissions are positioned on vulnerable northern islands. In August 2017 the Lofoten Declaration, an international manifesto signed by six hundred organizations from 76 countries, called for an end to hydrocarbon exploration and further expansion of fossil fuel reserves 'for the purposes of climate change mitigation'.[32] Public lobbying from the Lofoten archipelago successfully prevented some offshore development of petroleum reserves. The varied, sometimes oblique ways in which art practices can mediate difficult political and environmental issues, yet also inform a 'tourist gaze', are set into sharp focus in these ambitious art biennials. In 2015 the eighth festival was titled 'Disappearing Acts', curated by Matt Packer and Arne Skaug Olsen. A review by critic Oliver Basciano underlines the problem of how we relate the works exhibited to stated artistic intentions. In it, he argues that the show's title and location in the small Lofoten town of Svolvær, 186 kilometres (115 mi.) above the Arctic Circle, inevitably reveals ecological concerns. But in place of 'hand-wringing', there is 'an acceptance that the end of the world is coming, an apocalypse consequential of technology and the burning of fossil fuels that drive our psychotic obsession with progress'.[33]

Basciano's pessimistic reading would most likely be confirmed by some of the 2015 exhibitors. For example, the Swedish artist Anna Ådahl's (b. 1973) mixed-media installation *Impossible Image* (illus. 121, 122) explores our notions and experience of landscape – and the idea of the sublime – in an era of increased awareness of the negative effects of the Anthropocene. She combines three types of landscape imagery: Arctic landscapes found through an online search, which are superimposed on top of each other; a silent video portrait of the Norwegian landscape painter Christian Krohg (1852–1925); and a microscopic live feed of sand collected from a Lofoten beach. In the middle of these screen projections is the pile of sand. During the exhibition performers intermittently interacted with the installation to reinforce a sense of the contingency of the human figure with these fluid landscapes. Drawing on the ideas of the French philosopher Bruno Latour, Ådahl sought to reframe ideas of the 'sublime' in the (contaminated)

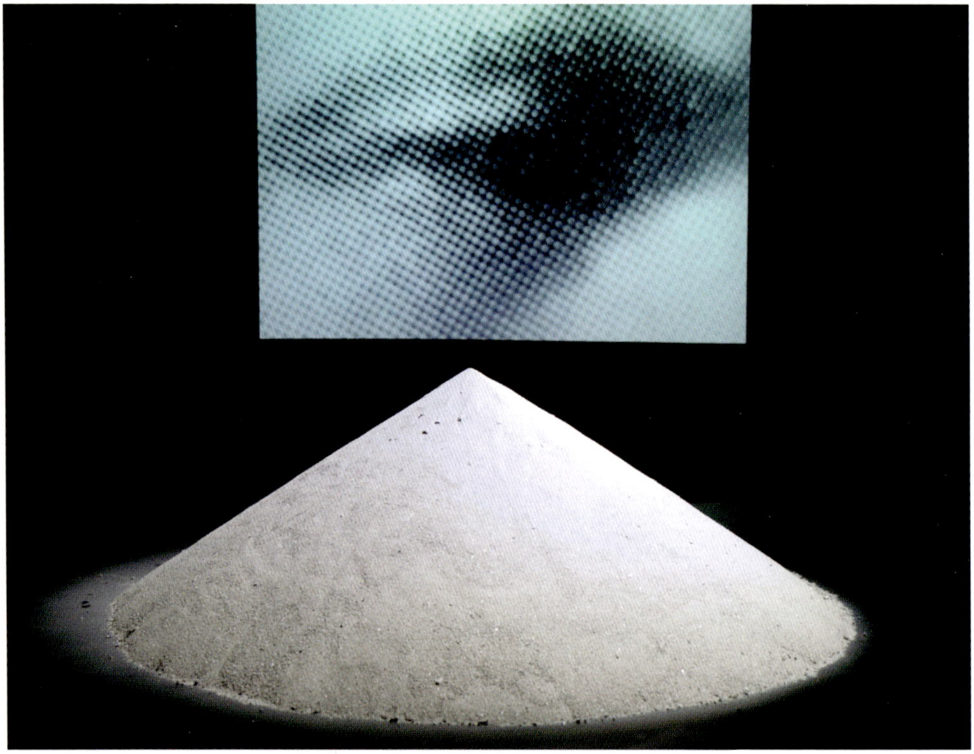

modern landscape. On her website she quotes from Latour's lecture of 2011, 'Waiting for Gaia': 'But what has become of the sublime lately, now that we are invited to consider another disconnect, this time between, on one side, our gigantic actions as humans, and, on the other side, our complete lack of a grasp on what we have collectively done.'[34]

The title 'Disappearing Acts' embraced a rethinking of the idea of the sublime and the worrying possibility of dystopian futures within the Arctic and beyond. Related topics have inevitably informed the themes of subsequent LIAF biennials. In 2017, the year of the Lofoten Declaration, the exhibition, curated by Heidi Ballet and Milena Hoegsberg, was titled 'I Taste the Future', and addressed topical themes of climate change, oil, trade and technology. Sited largely in Henningsvaer, a small fishing village with a population of under five hundred in the Lofoten Islands, landscape loomed large. The Japanese/Norwegian artist Daisuke Kosugi's (b. 1984) 2017 sound piece *Good Name (Bad Phrase)* was set in the local football stadium in Henningsvaer (illus. 120).[35] This well-maintained symbol of modern sport and leisure sits in a spectacular archipelago. It appears incongruously framed by picturesque peaks and Arctic seas; it looks like a field at the end of the world. Headphones instructed the viewer to stand at the goal line 'or a place where you can see the entire pitch'. Various narratives were then played to the listener, including a Japanese folktale and stories written by the artist, and one, by Walter Benjamin, in which a mountain restaurant-owner's livelihood is threatened by the picturesque location's appeal for suicides.

Contradictions and incongruities abound within this field of art tourism and are perhaps a necessary part of its appeal. The tensions between the awe-inspiring island landscapes and their local traditions and the burgeoning effects of the climate emergency and global technology are difficult to ignore, be it as a tourist or as an artist. The curators of LIAF 2017 speculated on the future of the tiny islets of Henningsvaer and the surrounding sea if global warming stopped the fish coming down from the North Sea to spawn, suggesting that 'the idea of the sea as a territory that cannot be owned is really under pressure'. They invoke the ideas of the

121 Anna Ådahl, *Impossible Image*, 2015, installation in the 8th Lofoten International Art Festival (LIAF), mixed media; commission for the 2015 biennale Disappearing Acts.

122 Anna Ådahl, *Impossible Image*, 2015, composite of fused images, poster for installation in the 8th Lofoten International Art Exhibition (LIAF).

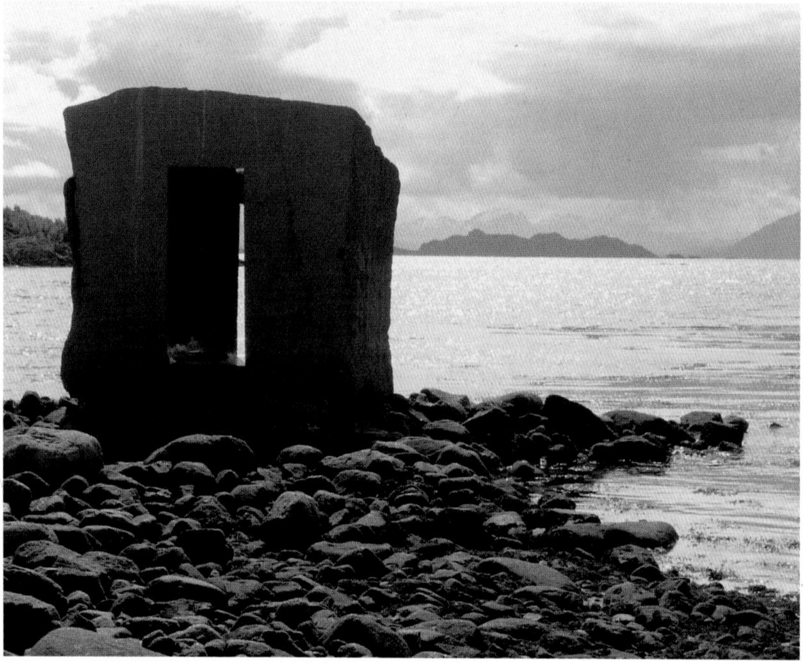

123 Anish Kapoor, *The Eye in the Stone*, 1998, granite, *Artscape Nordland*, Lødingen, Norway.

Fijian scholar Epeli Hau'ofa (cited in this book's Introduction), suggesting that his idea of 'oceanic identity and the connectivity of the ocean between islands could be applied to Lofoten in a global perspective'.[36] How this might be enacted within both political and artistic practice poses many difficult questions. Ideas of connectivity and the positioning of artworks next to water and oceans, where they are vulnerable to the effects of climate change, is a recurring theme of such archipelagic projects. Watery metaphors abound.

Conceived in the late 1980s by the Norwegian artist A. K. Dolven, a network of 36 site-specific sculptures by 33 international artists have been commissioned on sites across the north of Norway, collectively titled *Artscape Nordland* (also known as *Skulpturlandskap*). Completed in 2015, these public artworks are sited both above and below the Arctic Circle and usually positioned next to areas of water, enabling artists to exploit changing light sources and their metaphorical (and ecological) potential. Many well-known international artists took up commissions, including Dan Graham

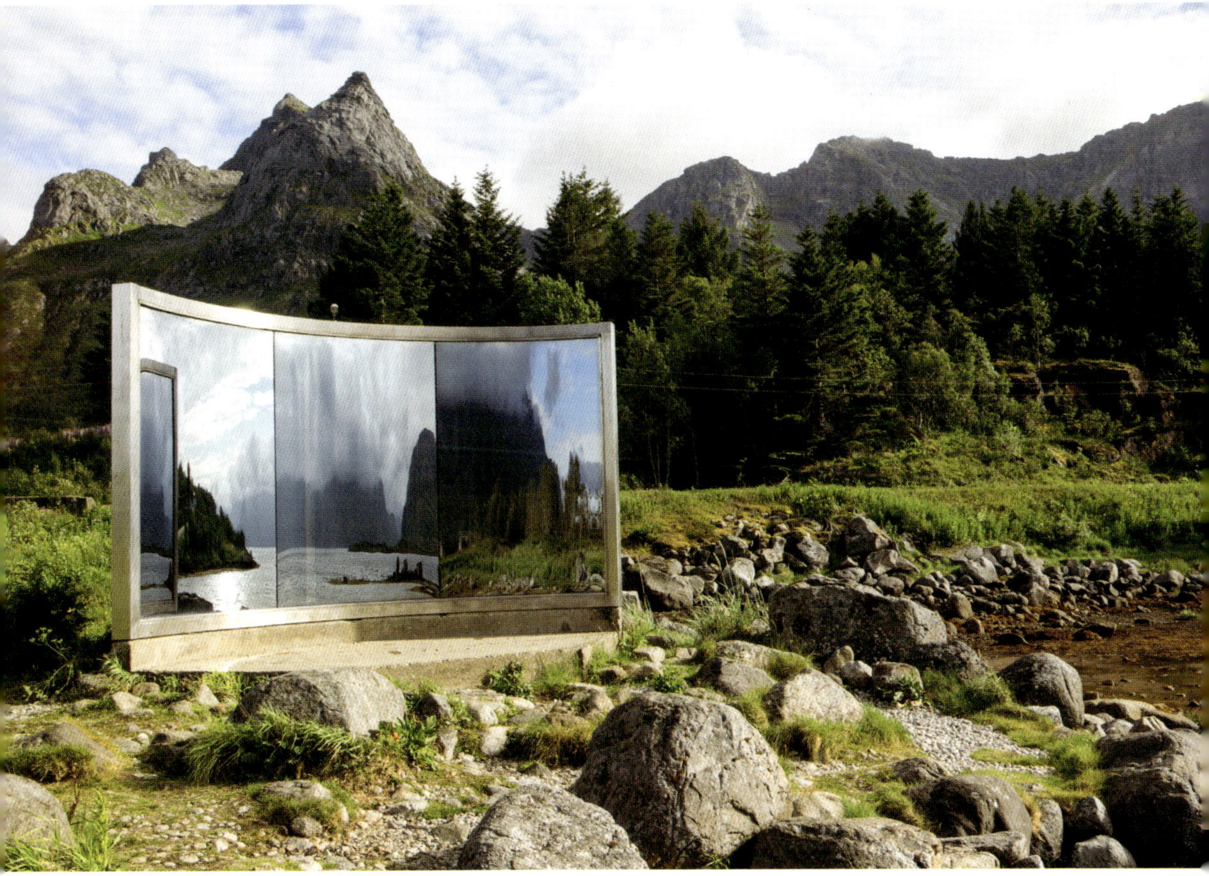

124 Dan Graham, *Two-Way Mirror Triangle with One Curved Side/Nordscape Pavilion*, 1996, *Artscape Nordland*, Lofoten Islands, Norway.

(United States), Waltercio Caldas and Cildo Meireles (Brazil), Per Barclay (Norway), Jan Håfström (Sweden) and Antony Gormley, Tony Cragg and Anish Kapoor (UK) (illus. 123). There was sustained consultation with the island communities; the negative effects of local tourism (such as increased foot and road traffic, damaged habitats and so on) were raised, but the economic advantages for the local economy have often been cited.[37]

On the Lofoten island of Austvågøya, the American Conceptual artist Dan Graham (1942–2022) created a large, steel-framed two-way mirror construction. Known for his sculptural 'pavilions', in 1996 Graham designed *Two-Way Mirror Triangle with One Curved Side/Nordscape Pavilion*, sited just off the main road in the municipality of Vågan. It offered a

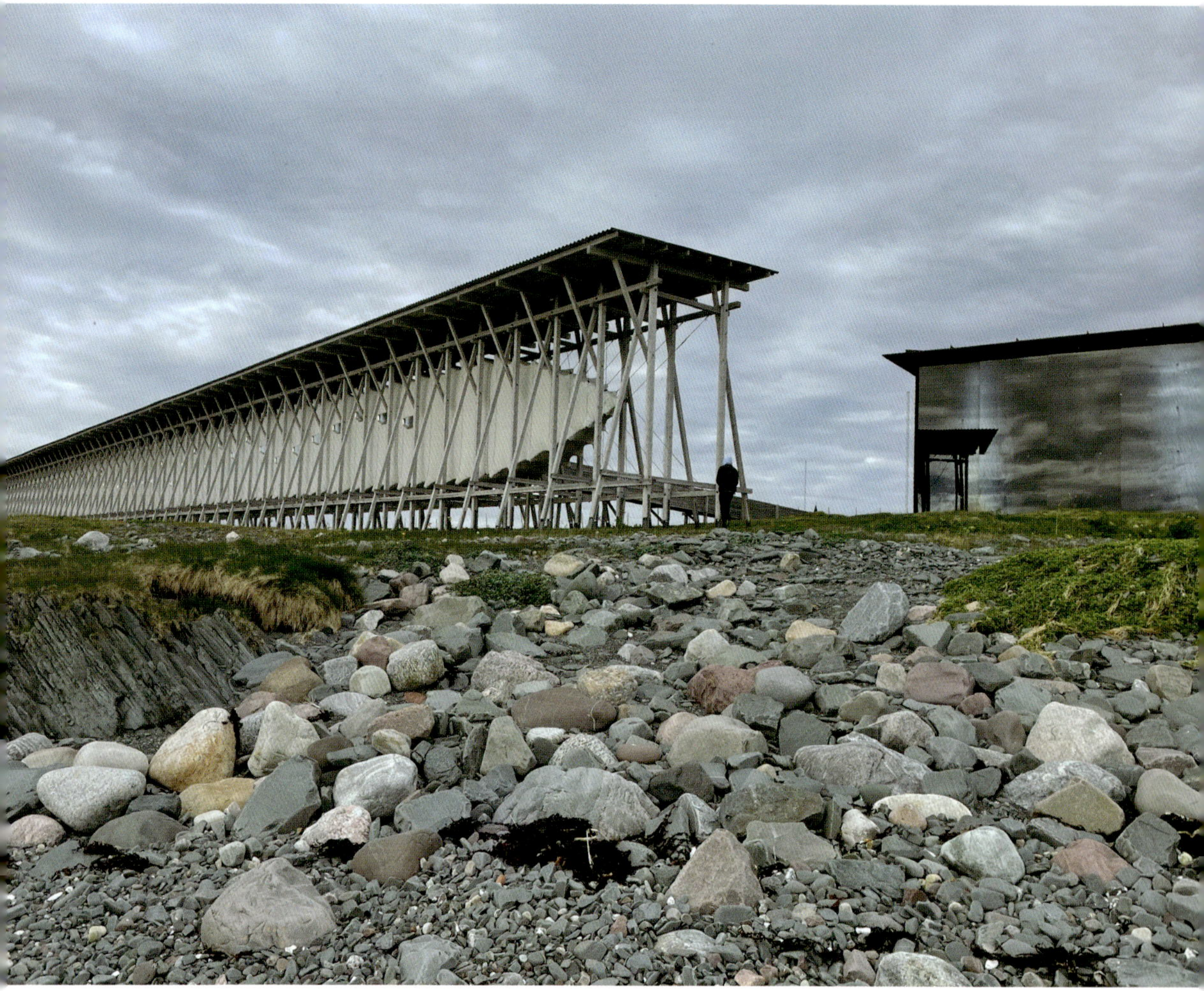

125 The Steilneset Memorial on the island of Vardø on the northeast coast of Norway, designed by Louise Bourgeois and Peter Zumthor, completed 2011.

dramatic, reflected encounter with the island's craggy peaks and clear waters (illus. 124). At 2.5 metres (8 ft) high, the large concave glass mirror and pavilioned glass walls invite the viewer to participate in the process of deciphering landscape. A persistent theme in Graham's work is the way in which our environment helps to structure how we see, exemplified in this site-specific work. The concave mirror facing the water seems to offer a panoramic view worthy of a nineteenth-century Romantic painting, which can be broken by the viewers' reflection, as both become

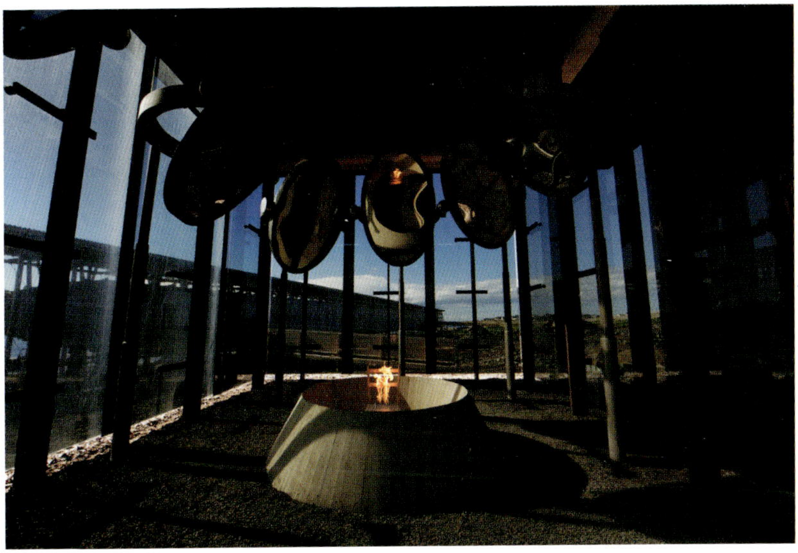

126 Louise Bourgeois' sculpture *The Damned, the Possessed and the Beloved* installed inside the Glass Pavilion designed by the architect Peter Zumthor, alongside his Memorial Building for the Steilneset Memorial to the 17th-century Witch Trials in Finnmark in Vardø, Norway, 2011.

part of the artistic representation. The Nordic island landscape is thus re-presented as an active process of image-making, subject to the mediating roles of both artist and spectator. Unlike a fixed scene, Graham's modern landscape is infinitely changing. The re-presented island has effectively absorbed the tourist's gaze.

Island histories are often celebrated by strategically positioned public monuments. One such spectacular edifice stands along the rugged coastline of the Barents Sea in Finnmark, on the island of Vardø, on the northeast coast of Norway, in the Arctic Circle. The Steilneset Memorial (2011) by the Swiss architect Peter Zumthor (b. 1943) and the French-born artist Louise Bourgeois (1911–2010) commemorates the seventeenth-century trial and execution of 91 local people for witchcraft (illus. 125) and was jointly commissioned by the town of Vardø, the Varanger Museum and the Norwegian Public Roads Administration. During a dark period in local history, 77 women and fourteen men were accused of witchcraft and burnt at the stake. According to the Norwegian historian Liv Helene Willumsen, Finnmark and Scotland were among the worst hit European areas to suffer high numbers of witch persecution.[38] The dangerous weather conditions around Finnmark and its effects on the vital fishing industry around these northern archipelagos encouraged misogynistic myths about local women secretly working with the Devil. European history is replete with stories of witches as disruptive female archetypes, as is highlighted in my discussion of Irish myths in Chapter Six. The island of Vardø was the site of many summary trials, and about one-third of these deployed the notorious 'water test'. If guilt was in doubt, the accused was thrown into the sea; if she floated, she was confirmed as a witch.[39] Northern islandness, with its associations with bleak isolation, harbours many dark histories of the persecution of the supposedly aberrant behaviour of local women.

The memorial comprises two buildings. Zumthor's long structure, resembling an island pier, is made of a pine scaffold. Between supporting poles hangs a 38-metre-long (125 ft) cocoon-like corridor, lit by 91 windows and decorated with 91 plaques; on each plaque Willumsen has summarized the surviving information from the victims' trials. Bourgeois' sculpture, titled *The Damned, the Possessed and the Beloved*, is housed in a black smoked-glass cube (illus. 126). A perpetual flame projects through a steel chair, placed inside a hollow concrete cone. Seven circular mirrors surround and reflect the flames, illuminating a memory of destruction, and suggesting observers, or reflections, of that shameful history. The women of the Steilneset Memorial are evoked through architectural associations, archival information and sculptural metaphor. With two months of darkness every winter, this site now holds a flame of commemoration, vividly illustrating the roles of both art and architecture in reframing and memorializing some of the hidden mythologized histories of Arctic islands.

CONCLUSION
ART ISLANDS, FUTURE ISLANDS AND END GAMES

Given the important role that contemporary art can play in the display and accumulation of wealth and cultural status, it is hardly surprising that spectacular island landscapes have become increasingly popular sites of display. Such sites can also offer exciting curatorial opportunities. The curator Laura Mansfield has suggested that the creative possibilities of the literary or poetic island can be applied (metaphorically) to the staging of 'critical relations' in curatorial practice in the visual arts. She draws parallels between the island, which is separated from the mainland, and the situated artwork and its surrounding context.[1] Mansfield argues that the spatial geography of islands can enable experiments and innovation in the visual arts (as in the literary arts). They can provide sites for both experimental works of art and curatorial practice, and they offer opportunities for the presentation of works that involve 'relational' art – that is, they use the social sphere to engage or interact with an audience.[2] Alfredo Jaar's *The Gift*, Hartley's *Nowhereisland* and Horn's *Library of Water* illustrate different aspects of this relational model. Both constructed and performative, each work engaged local audiences, destabilizing and exploring notions of islandness.

Over the last few decades many real and artificial islands have become sites for the construction of some spectacular edifices to modern and contemporary art, often sponsored by large corporate and private donations, sometimes supported by government funding. In 1990 the art critic Rosalind Krauss described such awe-inspiring projects as the triumph of 'starchitecture', a visual expression of the increasing privatization of funding for institutions of contemporary art.[3] Such architectural wonders have significantly helped to increase a global appetite for both art and island tourism. Denmark, for example, boasts a bold architectural design in the Arken Museum of Modern Art, built on its own constructed island, south of Copenhagen. Initially designed to mimic a shipwreck located on a beach, it was moved inland for conservation reasons and then landscaped and surrounded by water, creating an archetypal 'art island' (illus. 127). Partly funded by corporate sponsorship, it was designed by an architecture student, Søren Robert Lund, and completed in 1996. The structure houses a huge indoor gallery shaped like a ship's hull, sited to ensure that this edifice would act as a landmark in Danish cultural life. The museum houses a major collection of Scandinavian contemporary art, and includes work by high-profile international artists such as Ai Weiwei, Damien Hirst, Elmgreen & Dragset and Olafur Eliasson. Coastal maritime metaphors are enmeshed with the cultural ambitions of both the gallery and its national sponsor.

Other notable 'art islands' that house major international collections include (among many) Artipelag, near Stockholm, Sweden, and

127 Aerial view of the Arken Museum of Modern Art, Ishøj, Denmark.

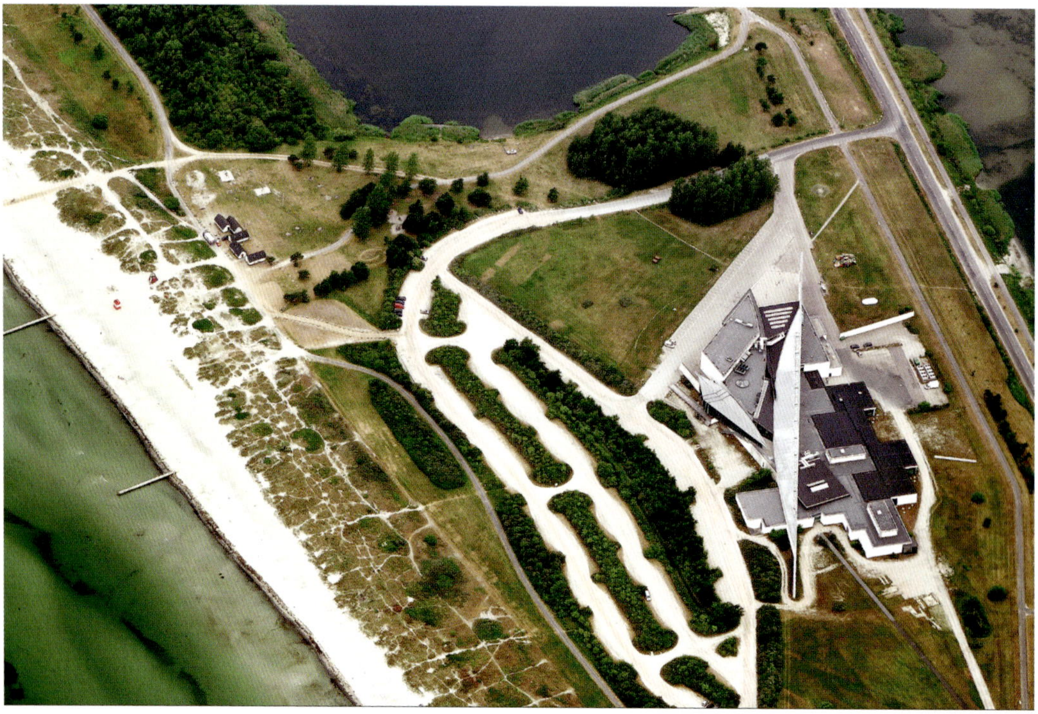

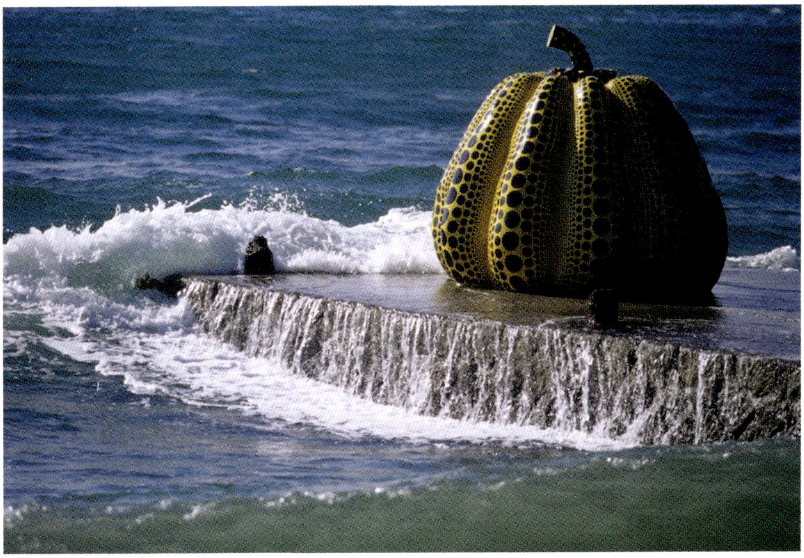

128 Yayoi Kusama, *Yellow Pumpkin*, 1994, fibre-reinforced plastic and metal, Benesse Foundation, Naoshima.

the archipelago around the island of Naoshima in the Seto Inland Sea, southwest Japan. Artipelag, a pun on the Swedish word for archipelago, is represented on the museum site as a fusion of 'Art, Activities and Archipelago'. Described as the 'brainchild' of its founder, Björn Jakobsen, and funded by money from his Swedish baby-care products company Babybjörn, it declares the ambition to 'expand and enrich' the idea of an exhibition, responding to increasingly diverse modern audiences.[4] The fundamental tension between being sited on a separate island yet being part of a connected (cultural) archipelago is built into the self-representation of these art-island museums.

On 9 August 2021 the Japanese island of Naoshima was battered by a typhoon. One of the casualties was a giant yellow-and-black polka-dotted pumpkin made of fibre-reinforced plastic, which sat majestically at the end of the pier (illus. 128). Conceived by the Japanese artist Yayoi Kusama (b. 1929) and installed in 1994, it has become an iconic symbol of the island's status as a centre for contemporary art. Waves dislodged the pumpkin from its metal fastenings and it broke into three main pieces.[5] *Yellow Pumpkin* – a recognizable motif in Kusama's oeuvre, along with her polka dots – announced the island's relationship with modern and contemporary art. This oversized, brightly coloured gourd is a sculptural installation that offers a riposte to the commemorative statues (usually of male figures) that often overlook national ports. It is also mischievously over-decorated with Kusama's signature motifs. Next to the port of Naoshima, another large half-pumpkin, painted red with oversized dots, survived the storm. A more playful work, which the visitor can enter, it also announces the participatory tourist appeal that characterizes many aspects of contemporary art, and that can thrive in an island setting.

Most of the island's art museums and installations, and those on neighbouring islands of Teshima and Inujima, were commissioned and owned by Benesse Holdings, led by businessman Soichiro Fukutake and supported by his self-declared philosophy of 'public capitalism'.[6] He positioned both this 'natural' environment and the art displayed there as 'a counter to the waves of modernism'.[7] In the early stages, the Japanese architect Tadao Ando was commissioned to design a series of museums on Naoshima, including the Benesse House Museum, the Chichu Museum and several site-specific projects (illus. 129).[8] Buildings were commissioned to blend interior and exterior space, and Japanese artists are shown alongside works by international artists such as the British artist Richard Long and the American artists Jackson Pollock, Bruce Nauman and James Turrell. The partly underground Chichu Museum also houses a collection of Monet's *Water Lilies*.

Given the range of works displayed, Fukitake's proclaimed 'anti-modernist' ambitions are hard to define in aesthetic terms, since many of the artists exhibited qualify as 'modernist' or 'postmodernist'. However, the site was chosen and designed to enable a blending of viewing spaces with a natural landscape. Some of the contradictions that plague the viewing of contemporary art on islands are addressed (if not resolved) in these 'art islands' in the Seto Inland Sea. Works have been commissioned that integrate with, and enable the futures of, these island communities, including villages that have suffered the loss of local industries. For example, in the ongoing 'The Art House Project', which began in 1998 in Naoshima's Honmura district, artists were invited to take abandoned houses in the

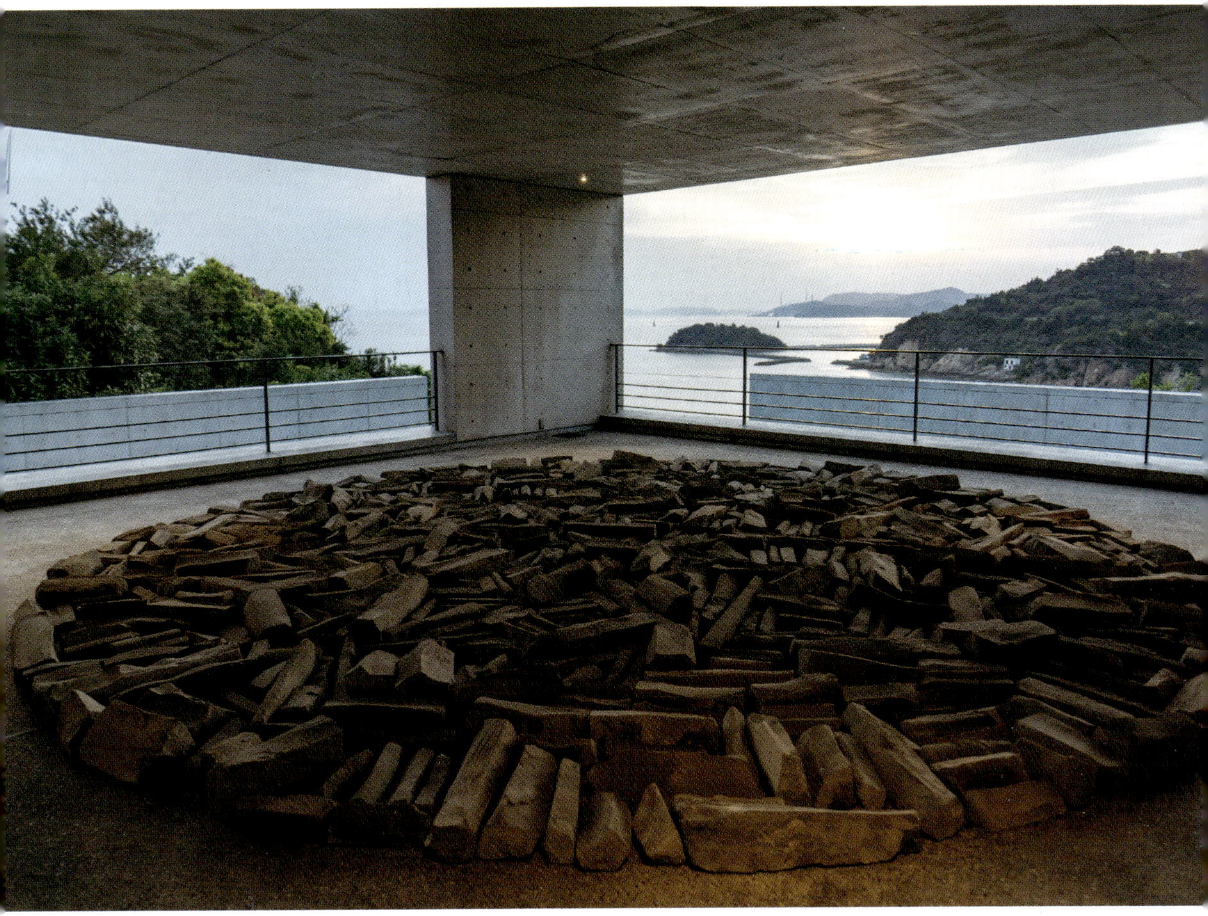

129 Richard Long, *Full Moon Stone Circle*, 1997, stone, Benesse Museum, Naoshima, Japan.

residential area, turning each space into a work of art that weaves together history, memory and artistic practice, usually involving the participation of local residents.[9]

Whatever their participatory, environmental, architectural or cultural ambitions, many of these spectacular 'art islands' can also be seen as vivid signifiers of a modern globalized art world that is structured around international art events in glamorous locations. The seemingly idyllic or 'natural' environment of the 'art island' site can contribute value and meaning to the works displayed within them, and such destinations often feature on the itinerary of a jet-setting global elite. The search for cultural capital (in the form of the ownership and display of contemporary art) and the art market are often merged in these itineraries and linked to the activities of international art biennials, which draw crowds of curators, gallerists, critics and wealthy buyers.[10] Well-funded private galleries with international profiles are increasingly attracted to island sites for the display of their expanding collections. For example, in 2021, the successful international art business Hauser & Wirth (known for its galleries in London, New York, Hong Kong, Los Angeles, Zurich, Monaco and the Somerset town of Bruton in the UK) opened their Menorca site in converted ancient buildings on the 40,000-square-metre (47,850 sq. yd) Isla del Rey (Illa del Rei), a short boat ride from the capital, Mahón (illus. 130). This island now boasts eight galleries, an education workshop, landscaped gardens and an outdoor sculpture park including work by internationally renowned artists such as Louise Bourgeois, Camille Henrot, Eduardo Chillida, Joan Miró, Martin Creed and Franz West.

The inaugural exhibition, *Masses and Movements* by the American artist Mark Bradford (b. 1961), used the island location to explore the geopolitics of the global immigration crisis. An installation of globe sculptures,

130 Hauser & Wirth Menorca, Illa del Rei.

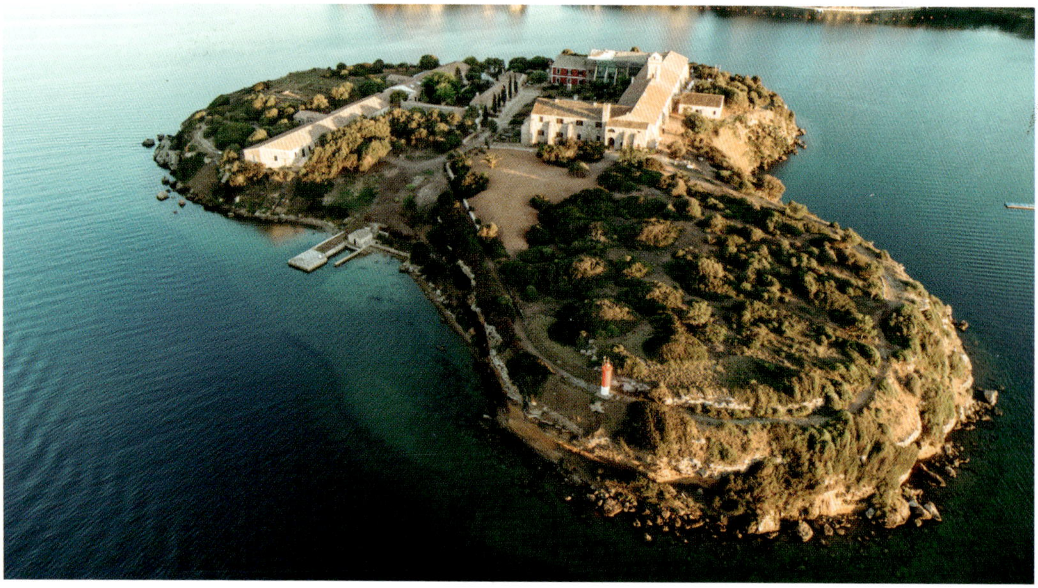

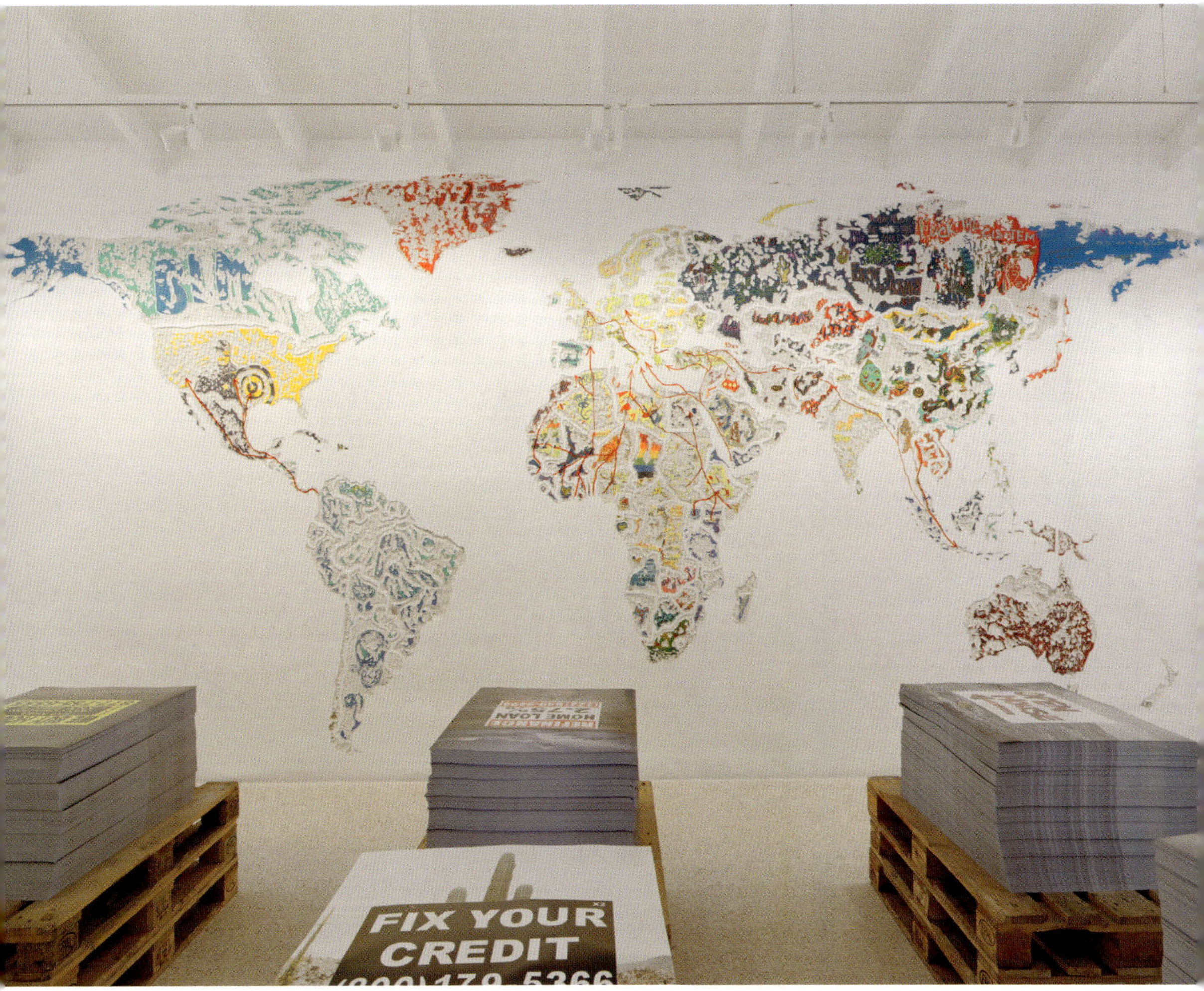

131 Mark Bradford, *Masses and Movements*, 2021, wall painting and posters, installation view, Hauser & Wirth, Menorca.

vividly coloured maps of cities and trade routes and a reworking of the 1507 Waldseemüller world map, described as 'archaeological abstraction', was designed to unpack 'the embedded biases that define the barriers and boundaries we inhabit' (illus. 131).[11] Waldseemüller's oddly Eurocentric map (which contrasts nicely with the Surrealist Map of the World (see illus. 96)) was dominated by sixteenth-century knowledge of European landmasses, with ill-defined islands and continents around its boundaries. Across the Atlantic, 'America' was written over an area now known as

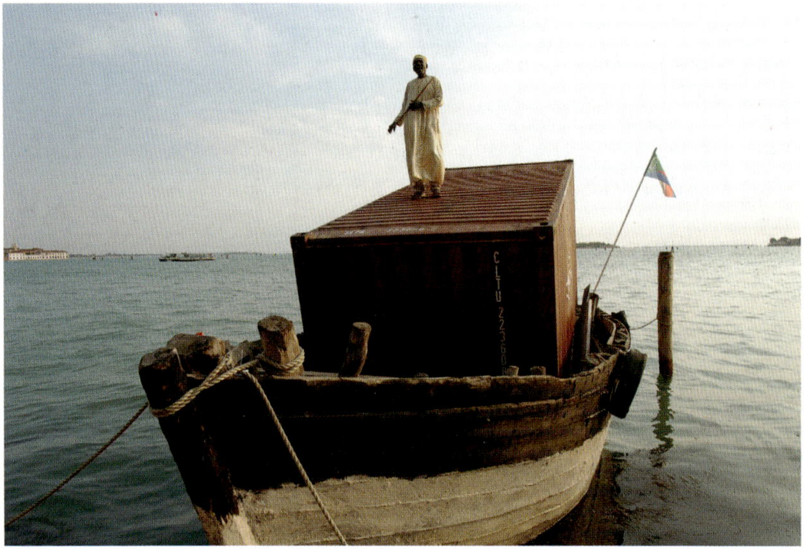

132 Paola W. Tamburella, *Djahazi*, moored by the Arsenale, Venice Biennale, 2009.

Brazil. Echoing Mansfield's claim for the innovative curatorial potential of island sites, Bradford's exhibition positioned Isla del Rey as a cipher for global histories of immigration and trade. The artist invited local students to collaborate in the production of 'marginalized stories', adding a relational dimension. One of its key themes is central to this book: the relationship between map-making and the manipulation of power, origin myths and nationhood in island geographies. As Bradford puts it: 'Maps have always been shady. So much of what we understand about landmasses comes from cartographers and their relationships to power.'[12]

Art islands can set into high relief the complex and sometimes controversial relationship between island economies, cultural self-representation and art tourism. The Venice Art Biennale, sited on islands in the Venetian lagoon, is one of the best-known events in the international art-world calendar. Contributing artists often play on local associations with islands, boats and trade routes, themes that carried multiple meanings in the debut participation of the Comoros Islands in the 53rd Biennale in 2009. In collaboration with the Italian artist Paolo W. Tamburella (b. 1973), the Comoros Islands project *Djahazi* deployed the classic wooden boat of the same name, used for centuries by the Comoros people for commercial transportation through the Mozambique Canal (illus. 132). After the opening of the Suez Canal in 1869 the importance of the *djahazi* for international transportation decreased. Yet these vessels continued to be used until they were replaced by modern sea freight in 2006. After modernization of the Comoros port of Moroni, many *djahazi* soon littered the sea floor.

In 2008 Tamburella resurrected and restored one of these sunken boats with the help of local Comorians. The renovated *djahazi*, containing a modern shipping container, was then exhibited in 2009 by the waterfront entrance to the Venice Giardini, the park that hosts the international art pavilions and exhibitions. Representing a nation of islands that had previously been largely invisible to the art world, *Djahazi* referenced many issues confronting an international art fair in an island setting. In his introductory essay for the Biennale catalogue, Octavio Zaya summarizes some of the tensions implicated. He argues that the restoration was not a gesture of 'nostalgic affection'. Loaded with a container used in modern global trade, it '[stands] as a metaphor for an ambivalent globality, bringing together hope and despair, hyper-rationalization and avant-garde extravagance, anti-modern nostalgia and exuberant narratives of progress, emergence and emergency, in a sort of cautionary tale about the new forms of the expendable in a world of uncertainty and transition'.[13] Like Bradford's re-presented maps and trade routes, the Comoros *Djahazi* reminds us of the difficult relationship of island histories with some modern narratives of progress. Throughout this book I have explored artistic representations of boats as possible metonyms for floating islands, trade routes, migration, colonial exploration and myths of progress. Tamburella's restored vessel spoke vividly of both the routes and the roots of Comoran histories.

ECOLOGY AND 'A LOSS OF ISLANDHOOD'

I have also considered ways in which a pressing climate emergency has informed art on the island theme, especially in chapters Three and Eight.

Many artists have used installation, performance and community engagement to draw attention to urgent ecological issues, as in the work of Jetñil-Kijiner, Enomoto, Moscher and Kihara, among others. They have shown how imaginative practices can extend and inform a loosely labelled 'eco-art' or 'eco-criticism'. Some artists have also used their writings to bemoan 'the loss of islandhood' associated with Roni Horn's sense of 'the ever-growing transparency of social, cultural, and economic exchange', and the global effects of pharmaceutical, industrial and technological pollution on remote archipelagos.[14] Such effects have influenced the photographic projects of artists such as Hartley, Horn and Buckland, among many others cited.

Many artists have also addressed the future implications of such problems on islands close to, and managed by, the mainland. For example, the American photographer Mitch Epstein (b. 1952) spent many years photographing sites around the United States where electricity is made, including fossil fuel, nuclear, hydroelectric and solar. Epstein selected sites that reference notions of political, economic and cultural power, such as oil refineries, rigs and cooling stations, reflecting on 'the American dream gone haywire'.[15] His *Ocean Warwick Oil Platform, Dauphin Island, Alabama* (2005) is a haunting image of a degrading oil platform, perched off Dauphin Island, known as 'the sunset capital' of Alabama (illus. 133). Corporate power and the capitalist desire for growth at all costs are vividly symbolized in this mini-island dystopia.

Other photographers have sought out future possibilities in the visibly damaged ecologies around us. In 2022 the British artist Mike Perry (b. 1960) used a large format Phase One digital camera to photograph a seemingly anachronistic uninhabited island he had encountered while travelling around the Scottish Highlands (illus. 134). His large-scale *Island* offers a misty view of a strangely verdant, overgrown landmass amidst a bleaker, depleted Highland landscape in the Flows at Strath Halladale, a vivid counter to Epstein's oil platform. While the surrounding land has been over-grazed by vast deer estates managed for hunting, Perry's small island is out of reach for both deer and their predators. He has voiced

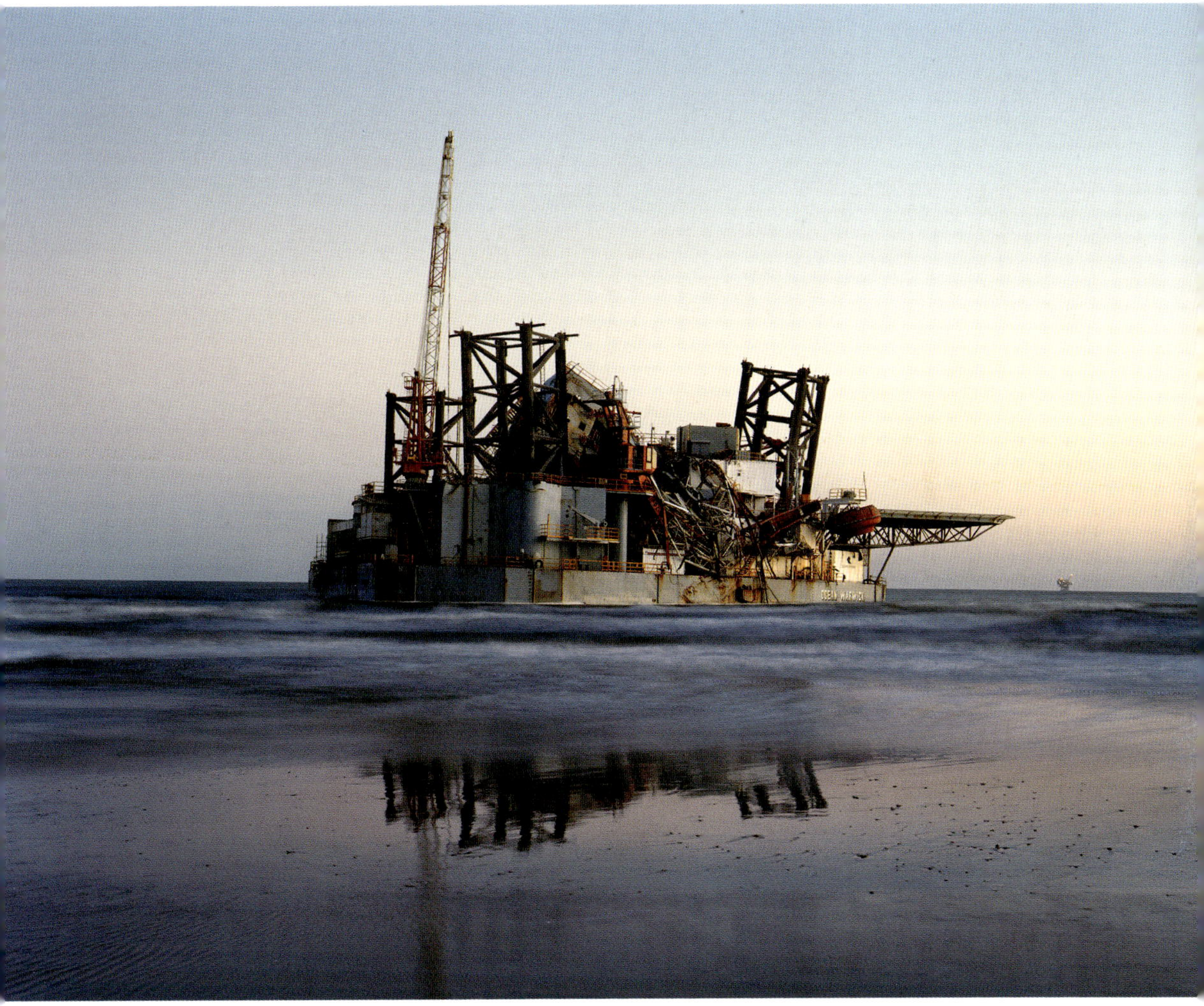

133 Mitch Epstein, *Ocean Warwick Oil Platform, Dauphin Island, Alabama*, 2005, chromogenic print.

concerns that 'Britain is one of the most depleted biodiverse nations in the world.' His eery, muted light envelops an almost mystical biodiverse Scottish island, perceived as a symbol of hope for the rewilding movement. With a sardonic pessimism, he has suggested the work might also be 'an illustration of the inevitable power of nature to reclaim the planet once we've destroyed ourselves'.[16]

Strategies for envisioning 'future islands' for survival, and the ecological issues involved, are also increasingly addressed in the fields of architecture

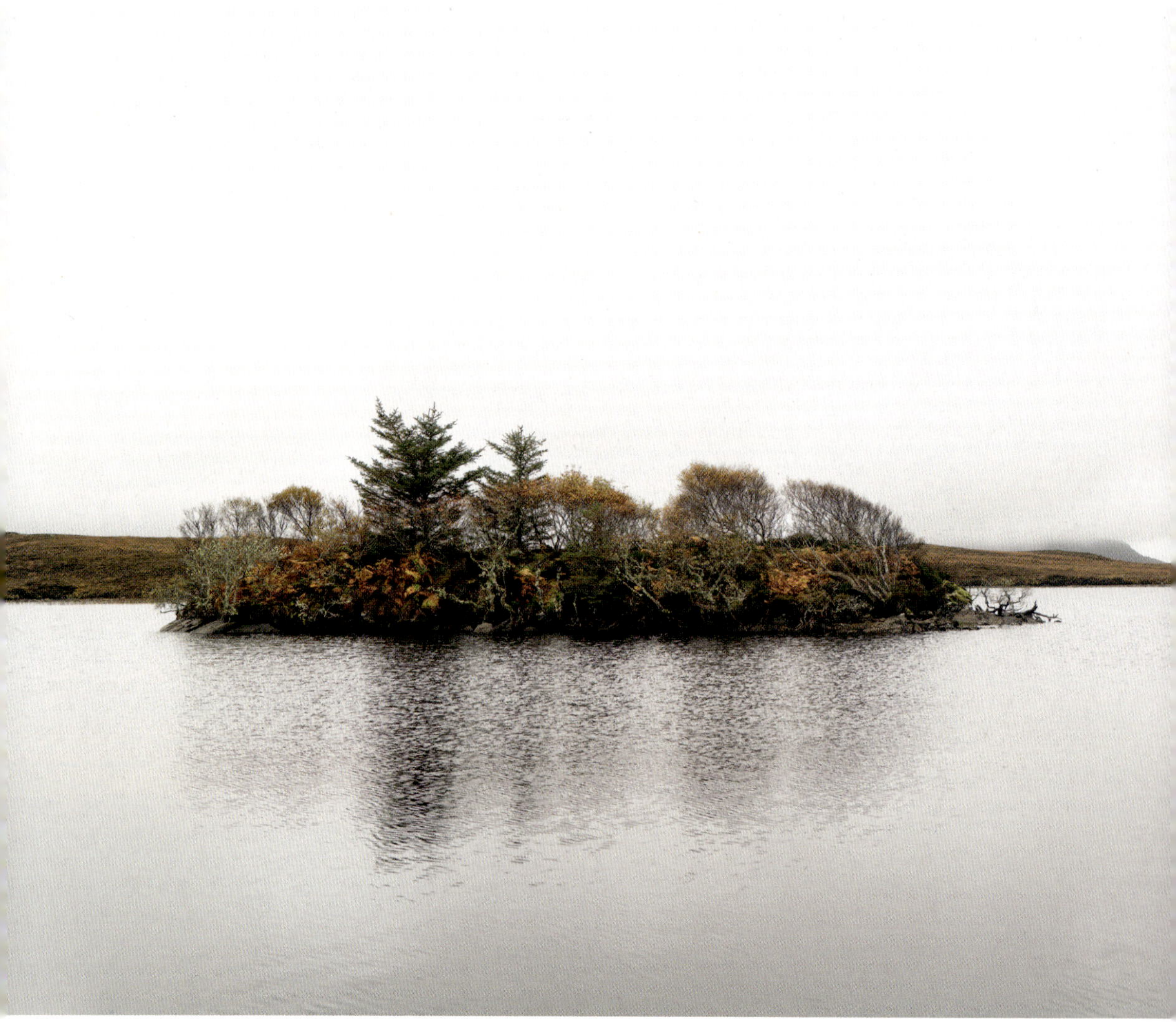

134 Mike Perry, *Island*, Highlands, Scotland, 2022, chromogenic print.

and design. Although these areas are largely beyond the scope of this book, discipline boundaries within the visual arts are inevitably blurred, and collaborations proliferate. For example, since 2017 Swedish architectural practice OOZE has managed a public art project 'Future Island' on the Albano University Campus (led by Eva Pfannes and Sylvain Hartenberg and the artist Marjetica Potrč). Described as 'a pioneer landscape in evolution over the next 100 years', this island of stones is a micro-ecosystem

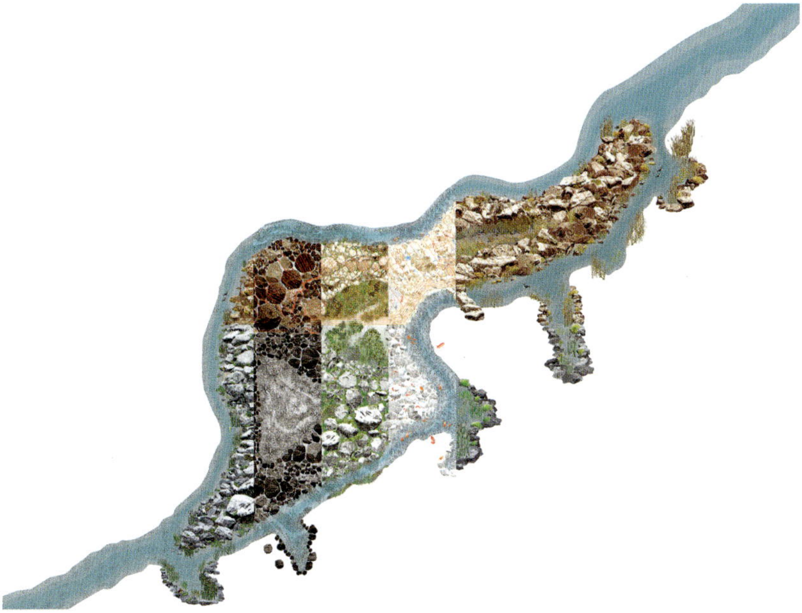

135 OOZE architects design for Future Island, Albano Campus, Sweden, prototype in the Venice Architectural Biennale in 2021.

of plants and animals that constantly adapts to changing conditions.[17] Divided into north and cold zones that create environments that correspond to current global warming, it tracks likely changes in our ecosystem and biodiversity. A prototype was exhibited at the Venice Architecture Biennale in 2021 (illus. 135); like many projects that straddle arts and science disciplines, it is designed to educate and alert its audiences to the worrying changes in our ecosystem.

ART, VISIBILITY AND END GAMES

I have argued that representations of the island theme have been significantly enriched by developments in the expanded field of contemporary art. Fluid concepts of islandness, space, place and nation and the transnational, and the critical relationship with oceans and water, have been seen as vivid, engaging topics for visual artists, including those who seek to reframe and decolonize the theme. I have addressed the difficult question of how some complex island themes can be effectively mediated through the medium of visual art. The messy material processes of making involved in the production of art, including sculpture, installation, film and participatory events, can help to create compelling, multi-layered island projects. I have selected many works for discussion that seem to me to have an affective power that can engage sensory and/or participatory responses; I have been drawn to works that deploy imaginative aesthetic strategies, including metaphor, allegory and metamorphosis, to mediate and reframe cultural, social and political meanings. My designation 'island artist' describes those practitioners who use such strategies to represent oceans and landscape as fluid nodes of connectivity rather than isolated landmasses. Increasingly, artists, along with other scholars, are viewing islands and archipelagos as part of a fluid 'oceanic space'.[18] Some artistic processes studied here have taken place outside the conventional museum display space; they may involve forms of performance that depend on film, photography and archiving for wider visibility. It is my hope that this book will play a role in enabling visibility for some innovative works of modern art on the island theme, many by women.

The work of women practitioners has featured prominently in my study and within my category 'island artists'. Reasons for their notable and developing interest in the island theme have been addressed throughout my study and include a fascination with the persistent cultural associations of goddesses, witches and female leaders with ideas of islandness. From Circe and Sycorax, to Mother Ireland, to McLean's Jamaican Nanny or Bourgeois' *The Damned, the Possessed and the Beloved*, such figures have been reassessed in recent times, enabling a rethinking of some potent myths that have dominated Western culture for centuries. For example, Maher and Fallon's epic archipelago *The Map* can be seen as a complex reworking of such myths and their gendered histories through the imaginative use of a traditionally feminized medium of embroidery. Moreover, *The Map* also reveals some of the mischievous and playful strategies adopted by contemporary women artists that can challenge dominant cultural tropes of islandness.[19]

Increasing opportunities (educational, economic, curatorial and academic) available to women artists since the 1960s and '70s, and their energetic participation in the varied modern practices of the expanded field, have also contributed to an increasing boldness in installation art, performance and film.[20] I have suggested that these proactive developments have been encouraged and enriched by the dissemination of evolving feminist and gender theories in the visual arts and across disciplines, including so-called eco-feminism, hydro-feminism, island feminism and transnational and decolonial feminisms. Within the contemporary sphere, I have explored women as dynamic co-creators in the field, and visual art as a fluid set of practices that intersect with film, photography, geography and the literary arts. Despite their (often) heavy theoretical baggage, feminist and gender theories developed across and within disciplines have both informed art-making and sometimes revealed looser or divergent relationships.[21] For example, explorations of gendered ideas of 'home', place, space and nation, and their important ecological and cultural implications, have enriched both the production and the viewing experience of work on the island theme.

I have argued that as a medium that deploys largely visual, rather than verbal or written signifiers (although text has a role to play in some works), art has a special capacity to convey meaning through association and metaphor. Although landscape (as both process and topography) has featured in some of the artworks discussed, many have deployed more oblique forms of reference and symbolism, signifying different ideas of islandness, nation or place. A recent work by the British artist Cornelia Parker (b. 1956) epitomizes this use of allegory and visual surrogates. *Island* (2022; illus. 136) was installed in its own room at the end of her retrospective at Tate Britain in 2022. A greenhouse, an emblem of 'Englishness' and the country's much-touted passion for gardening, sits on a floor of worn encaustic tiles removed from the Houses of Parliament in London. Their designs have been worn away by the footfall of Westminster politicians since 1847. The glass panes are covered with white brushstrokes from the chalk of the White Cliffs of Dover, a drawing material that has featured prominently in Parker's work.[22] Her strokes are also reminiscent of the mark-making on prison walls, chalking time. The greenhouse appears enclosed and claustrophobic – as Parker calls it 'a little England with a cliff-face veil'. It was also a much-loved space in Parker's childhood on her family farm. She describes *Island* as 'our own, in our time of Brexit, alienated from Europe'.[23] Parker thus presents an allegorical model of 'little Englandness'. The greenhouse (a glass house), with its visibility clouded by white chalk, stands in for the nation, grounded by its historic faith in the parliamentary system, represented synecdochically (that is, as part of the whole) by the worn floor tiles from the Houses of Parliament. Unlike a recognizable landscape, Parker's island is allegorized to represent a dystopic, inward-looking future.

As utopian or dystopian spaces, quarantine and prison sites, slave plantations, ex-colonial lands, enchanted isles, sites for rehabilitated witches, goddesses or maroons, cartographical enigmas, endangered and exploited landmasses, stations for lighthouses or military secrets, exotic tourist destinations and spectacular stages for the display of contemporary art, islands are deeply entrenched in national and cultural ambitions – and in the popular imaginary. Such a contradictory character, which has itself become a recognized trope of islandness, also helps to explain the wide appeal of the subject for the visual arts. Acknowledging its important relationship to connected archipelagos, I have identified the island theme as a locus of creativity, cultural critique and aesthetic innovation.

Many scholars have drawn attention to the centuries-long interweaving of the literary arts with geographical, biogeographical, political and eco-social issues within island histories. As the environmentalist Heidi Scott has written: 'Long before the beak of the finch revealed the epistemological power of island biogeography, Shakespeare imagined a native species, embodied as Caliban, come under attack from a native species, led by Prospero . . . This terrifically exciting [island] habitat has animated fiction as well as evolutionary science.'[24] She argues that within a span of five hundred years of fiction we can find evidence of islands being perceived as 'evolutionary laboratories', from Thomas More's *Utopia* (1516) to Jeff VanderMeer's *Annihilation* (2014). I argue that this interweaving of

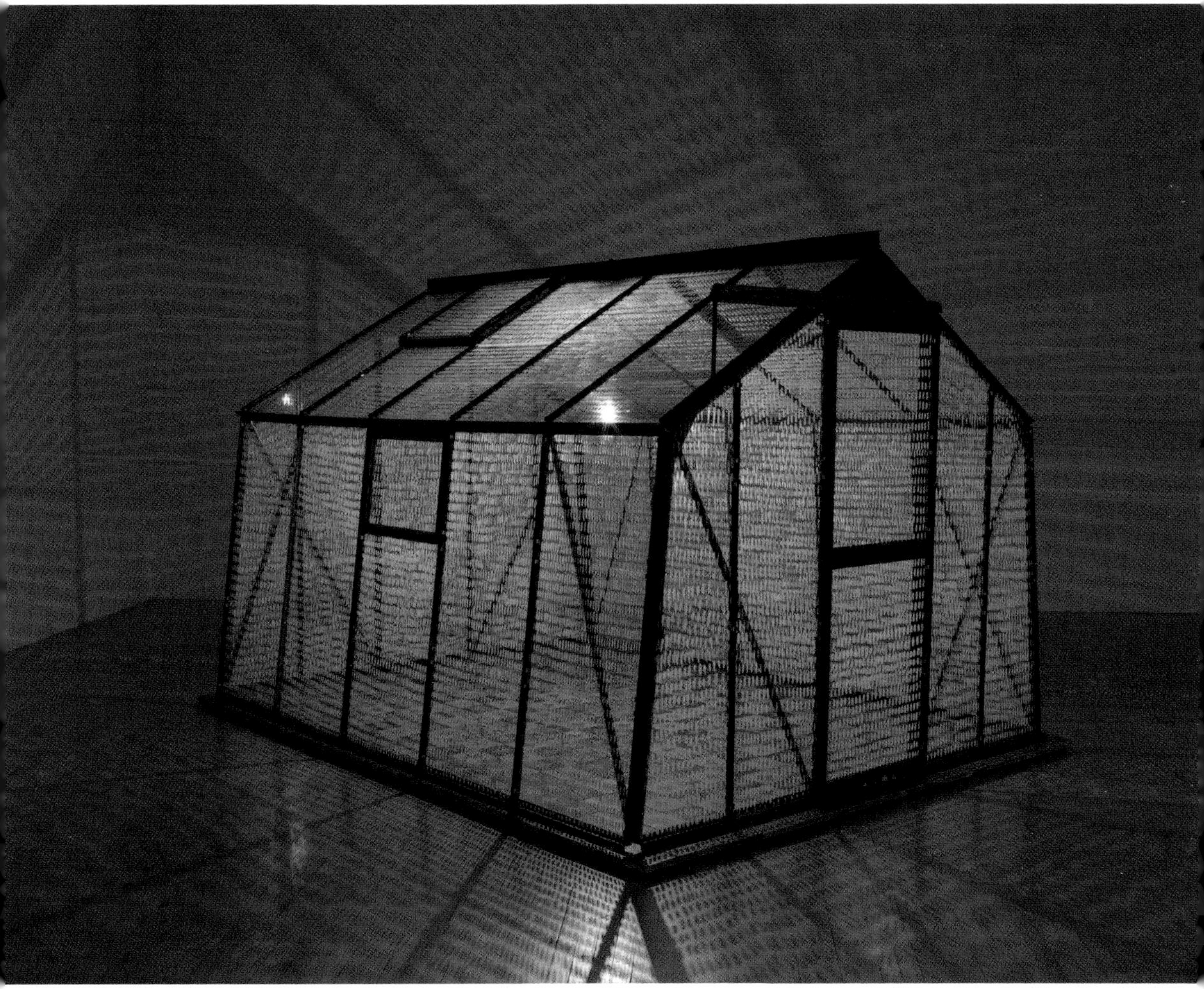

136 Cornelia Parker, *Island*, 2022, domestic greenhouse, pigment made from chalk of the White Cliffs of Dover, storm light; installation view, Tate Britain, London.

disciplines has become equally pronounced in the practices of visual artists working around the British archipelagos, the Arctic, the Caribbean, Pacific Oceania, the Atlantic and beyond. From Robert Smithson's transnational fascination with cosmology to the passionate engagement with geopolitics, ecology and history in, for example, the work of artists on the Marshall Islands, Pacific Oceania or the Arctic, the creative rewriting of colonial history by artists of the Caribbean diaspora or the memorializing of threatened species and entomologies in the work of artists on the Galápagos Islands, these island sites have inspired some remarkable aesthetic journeys.

I am, however, aware of the dangers and tensions inherent in my necessarily interdisciplinary project (albeit one that continues to inspire my curiosity as a researcher based in the visual arts). As an art historian I have cautiously woven together some different disciplinary approaches, causing shifts in tone. I have sought to blend a range of historical, ecological and contextual detail on my chosen themes with relevant theoretical approaches derived from visual culture, art history and related disciplines. Above all I have learnt that for the student of visual culture, the field of Island Studies is immense, diverse and challenging. I have only scratched the surface of a rich, interdisciplinary seam.

The last verse of Andrew Sant's prescient poem 'End Game' of 2009 muses somewhat cynically on possible future/s for islands. This book was written over a decade after his 'End Game', during some of the most challenging times in my living memory, including a climate emergency, the COVID-19 pandemic, economic crisis and dangerous political and military developments in Europe, the Middle East and beyond. It leaves open the (remote) possibility suggested by Sant that 'There are days on the island/ when it might seem appealing to imagine/ the last of the species/ will survive here, albeit wearily.' Clearly, in an era of late capitalist globalization there are major geopolitical and ecological problems to be addressed before any such vague fantasy might be contemplated. That said, I have tried to show that the innovative, multimedia and imaginary possibilities of modern and contemporary art can play a pivotal role in our critical understanding of this 'terrifically exciting habitat'.

END GAME

Always, there must be a threat.
What's the ratio of babies
named David to those praising Goliath?
No contest. Hundreds
to the one blunder

while trouble across the water
to the north, thundered –

replaced now by nature
hell-bent on revenge, in keeping
with the way continentals
don't pay back what they're lent.
They've upset her. Terrible weather.

Consequence on the island:
appeasement, co-operation,
a horror among politicians
of excess, an amply
broadcast lesson
for all – a plan to spin
electricity from the plentiful wind.

Turbines, say the continentals,
of the mind, since one has yet
to be imported or
on their coastline
tested, an observation
about to generate
a lot of energy.

There are days on the island
when it might seem appealing to imagine
the last of the species
will survive here, albeit wearily.

Andrew Sant, from *The Lives and Times of the Islanders*

REFERENCES

INTRODUCTION: **PARADISE OR PRISON?**

1 Godfrey Baldacchino, 'Islands, Island Studies', *Island Studies Journal*, I/1 (2006), p. 5.

2 The Kingdom of Tonga is a Polynesian archipelago southeast of Fiji and northeast of Aotearoa New Zealand, comprising more than 170 islands, of which 36 are inhabited. The main island is Tongatapu, a former British protectorate that acquired independence in 1970.

3 Rutger Bregman, *Humankind: A Hopeful History* (London, 2020).

4 Rutger Bregman, 'The Real Lord of the Flies', www.theguardian.com, 9 May 2020.

5 Another American version, loosely based on Golding's novel, was released in 1990, directed by Harry Hunt.

6 With the Californian company New Regency. See 'Tongan Castaway Story to be Made into a Hollywood Film', www.youtube.com, which features a recent interview with one of the surviving castaways, accessed 2 January 2022.

7 Scott Hamilton, 'The Curious Case of the Castaways on an Island in Tonga', www.newsroom.co.nz, 19 May 2020.

8 Ibid.

9 Epeli Hau'ofa, *We are the Ocean: Selected Works* (Honolulu, HI, 2008), p. 32.

10 Philip Hoare, *The Sea Inside* (London, 2014), p. 282.

11 Micronesia, Melanesia and Polynesia make up Oceania; these names were originally a racialized set of European designations that have been adopted by peoples of the region. See David Armitage and Alison Bashford, eds, *Pacific Histories: Ocean, Land, People* (Basingstoke, 2013).

12 John Connell, 'Island Dreaming: The Contemplation of Polynesian Paradise', *Journal of Historical Geography*, XXIX/4 (2003), pp. 554–81.

13 Fowles's description of the Scilly Isles from his novel *Shipwreck* (1974) is cited on the cover sleeve of John Fowles and Fay Godwin, *Islands* (London, 1978), photographs Fay Godwin.

14 Fowles, *Islands*, p. 12.

15 See Jill Franks, *Islands and the Modernists: The Allure of Isolation in Art, Literature and Science* (Jefferson, NC, and London, 2006).

16 See an influential article by Grant McCall, 'Nissology: A Proposal for Consideration', *Journal of the Pacific Society*, XXVII(2–3)/63–4 (1994), pp. 1–14.

17 *Island Studies Journal*, www.island studies.org. The founding editor of *Island Studies* was Godfrey Baldacchino, currently Professor of Sociology at the University of Malta; *Shima: The International Journal of Research into Island Cultures*: https://shimajournal.org. For a useful review of the status of Island Studies see Adam Grydehøj, 'A Future of Island Studies', *Island Studies Journal*, XII/1 (2017), pp. 3–16.

18 McCall, 'Nissology', pp. 2–3. Some of these issues are discussed by Richard Sharpley, 'Island Tourism or Tourism on Islands', *Tourism, Recreation, Research*, XXXVII/2 (2012), pp. 167–72.

19 Barney Samson, *Desert Islands and the Liquid Modern* (London, 2020), p. 3. I am indebted to Samson for his suggestions and helpful exchange of ideas.

20 Godfrey Baldacchino, ed., *Bridging Islands: The Impact of Fixed Links* (New Brunswick, NJ, 2007).

21 See, for example, Jonathan Pugh, 'Island Movements: Thinking with the Archipelago', *Island Studies Journal*, VIII/1 (2013), pp. 9–34; and 'Relationality and Island Studies in the Anthropocene', *Island Studies Journal*, XIII/2 (2018), pp. 93–110.

22 Pugh, 'Island Movements', p. 11.

23 For example, island metaphors are often used in descriptions of isolated gene pools and closed ecosystems in biology. See Thomas Hylland Eriksen, 'In What Sense

Do Cultural Islands Exist?', *Social Anthropology*, I/1b (1993), pp. 133–47.

24 John Fowles, *The Magus* [1965] (London, 2004).

25 Angeliki Mitropoulu, 'Islands beyond Tourism: Interview with Godfrey Baldacchino', www.enainstitute.org, 20 January 2022.

26 Peter Hay, 'A Phenomenology of Islands', *Island Studies Journal*, I/1 (2006), pp. 19–42. See also Philip Conkling, 'On Islanders and Islandness', *Geographical Review*, XCVII/2 (2007), pp. 191–201.

27 For a useful article that explores the concept across disciplines, see Aideen Foley et al., 'Understanding Islandness', *Annals of the American Association of Geographers*, CXIII/8 (2023), pp. 1–18.

28 Pugh, 'Island Movements', p. 11.

29 Julie Reiss's edited collection *Art, Theory and Practice in the Anthropocene* (Wilmington, DE, 2019) explores the relevance of the concept for the visual arts. Debates around its use in the visual arts are clearly explored in Samuel Shaw, ed., *Visions of the Anthropocene* (Milton Keynes, 2024), pp. 1–35. The art historian T. J. Demos has published some thoughtful critiques of the concept in relation to visual art: *Against the Anthropocene: Visual Culture and Environment Today* (Berlin, 2017). For the role of allegory in artistic engagements with the Anthropocene, see Elizabeth DeLoughrey, *Allegories of the Anthropocene* (Durham, NC, 2019).

30 'Jonathan Pugh: Interview with L. DeAngelo and E. Angliker: The Power of Thinking with Islands', *Mare Nostrum*, XXII/2 (2021), pp. 265–77. These arguments are also developed in Jonathan Pugh and D. Chandler, *Anthropocene Islands: Entangled Worlds* (London, 2021). For a critique of the explanatory powers of the 'Anthropocene' in relation to decolonization see Elaine Stratford et al., 'Islands, The Anthropocene and Decolonisation', *Antipodes*, LV/4 (2023), pp. 1255–74.

31 See Adam Grydehøj and Yaso Nadarajah, 'Island Studies as a Decolonial Project', *Island Studies Journal*, XI/2 (2016), p. 438. For an introduction to the current decolonization of art history, see Catherine Grant and Dorothy Rowe, 'Decolonising Art History', *Art History*, XLIII/1 (2020), pp. 8–66.

32 Professor Devi Sridhar, chair of Global Public Health at the University of Edinburgh, quoted in Linda Geddes, 'Island Life', www.theguardian.com, 6 February 2021.

33 Several UK newspapers used the term, and in December 2020 a website titled 'Welcome to Plague Island' appeared, admonishing the UK government for its management of the virus and lax border controls: www.plagueisland.co.uk, accessed 2 January 2021.

34 Gilles Deleuze, *Desert Islands and Other Texts, 1953–1974* (Paris, 2004), p. 9.

35 Ibid., p. 10.

36 Stephen Orgel, ed., *The Tempest: The Oxford Shakespeare* (Oxford, 2008), p. 11.

37 Made into successful films in 1949 and 2016.

38 D. H. Lawrence, *The Man Who Loved Islands*, in *Love Among the Haystacks and Other Stories* (London, 1960), p. 100.

39 John Mack, *The Sea: A Cultural History* (London, 2001), p. 30.

40 Ibid., p. 30. Mack shows how such conventions have led to many taboos, including among Scottish trawlermen: women were forbidden to come on board or touch the guard rails of a boat that was about to embark on a dangerous fishing voyage.

41 Charles Boyle [Jack Robinson], *Good Morning, Mr Crusoe* (London, 2019), p. 49.

42 Robin Cohen, ed., *Island Societies* (Oxford, 2017), p. 3. See also Gillian Hewitson, 'Deconstructing Robinson Crusoe: A Feminist Interrogation of "Rational Economic Man"', *Australian Feminist Studies*, IX/20 (1994), pp. 131–49.

43 See, for example, Vivien Morgan, *Cross-Dressed to Kill* (London, 2021) and Rebecca Alexandra Simon, *Pirate Queens* (Barnsley, 2022).

44 Marina Warner, *Indigo; or, Mapping the Waters* (London, 1993).

45 See Judith Yarnall, *Transformations of Circe: The History of an Enchantress* (Urbana, IL, 1994). For a modern rereading of Circe's history, see Madeline Miller, *Circe* (London, 2018).

46 Yarnall, *Transformations of Circe*, p. 4.

47 Michel Tournier, *Friday and Robinson* (London, 1971), p. 28.

48 Edna O'Brien, *Mother Ireland: A Memoir* [1976] (New York, 1999), p. 1.

49 *The Annals of Ulster* (AD 431–1540) record a woman in Scotland around AD 891 who was allegedly 60 metres (195 ft) tall. Cited by 'Angusfolklore' in 'Island Queens: The Hebridean Tradition', www.abctales.com, 26 May 2018.

50 The eighth-century Irish myth 'Voyage of Bran' describes an Odyssean voyage around various Celtic islands, including a visit to the 'Land of Women', where Bran and his party spend several years happily living with the resourceful female inhabitants. See Séamus Mac Mathúna, ed., *Immram Brain: Bran's Journey into the Land of the Women* (Tübingen, 1985). Recent scholarship has explored stories of the courage and resilience of Hebridean women over the last two centuries: Joni Buchanan, *Women of the Hebrides: Stories of Strength and Courage* (Stornaway, 2024).

51 The Gaelic name for the Isle of Eigg is Eilean nam Ban Móra, or 'The Island of the Big Women', derived from a legend about an intrepid group of Pictish warrior women. See John Francis Campbell, *Popular Tales of the West Highlands*, 4 vols (Edinburgh, 1860–62).

52 Marina Karides, 'Why Island Feminism?', *Shima*, xi/1, (2017), pp. 30–39.

53 See, for example, Firouz Gaini and Helene Pristed Nielsen, eds, *Gender and Island Communities* (London, 2021).

54 W.J.T. Mitchell, ed., *Landscape and Power* (Chicago, il, 1994).

55 Robert Smithson, 'The Spiral Jetty (1972)', in *The Collected Writings*, ed. Jack Flam (Berkeley, ca, 1966), pp. 143–53.

56 Smithson, 'Entropy Made Visible', ibid., pp. 301–9.

57 Craig Owens 'The Allegorical Impulse: Towards a Theory of Postmodernism', *October*, xii (Spring 1980), pp. 67–86.

58 Pandora Syperek and Sarah Wade, eds, *Oceans: Documents of Contemporary Art* (London, 2023).

59 Bergit Arends and Siân Ede, eds, *Galápagos*, exh. cat. Calouste Gulbenkian Foundation (London, 2012), p. 18.

1 DESERT ISLANDS AND MYTHS OF PARADISE

1 Charles Boyle, 'Empire of the Sun', *Guardian Review*, No. 66, 20 April 2019, p. 33. This article draws on material from Jack Robinson (a pen name of Charles Boyle), *Good Morning, Mr Crusoe* (London, 2019).

2 Ibid., p. 33

3 In *Good Morning, Mr Crusoe*, Boyle argues that the sense of entitlement 'that propelled the Western colonial and then the imperial enterprise, and the dismissal of the powerless as inferior beings, are conspicuous in Robinson Crusoe: "I looked upon these savages as slaves, and people who, had we any work for them to do, we would ha' used them as such, or would ha' been glad to have transported them to any other part of the world"' (pp. 104–5).

4 Boyle, 'Empire of the Sun', p. 33.

5 Robin Cohen, ed., *Island Societies* (Oxford, 2017), p. 3.

6 For a humorous, tongue-in-cheek re-writing of the (masculine) desert island myth, conceived in a German colonial context, see Christian Kracht, *Imperium: A Fiction of the South Seas* (New York, 2012).

7 Jean Giraudoux, *Suzanne and the Pacific*, trans. Ben Rya Redman (New York and London, 1923).

8 Ben Lucien Burman, 'The Lady of the Island', *The Nation*, 13 June 1923, p. 701.

9 Gorham B. Munson, 'A Specimen of Demi-Dadaisme', *New Republic*, 18 April 1923, pp. 219–20.

10 Ibid., p. 220.

11 Awards include 'Best Actor' at the 2001 Academy Awards and 'Best Actor in a Leading Role' at the 2001 Baftas.

12 Recounted in an 'Actor Roundtable' with Stephen Galloway, *Hollywood Reporter*, 30 November 2017.

13 Samson draws on the theories of the Polish sociologist Zygmunt Bauman, who coined the term 'the era of liquid modernity' to describe modern consumerist culture. See Barney Samson, *Desert Islands and the Liquid Modern* (London, 2020), pp. 1ff and 88–9. See also Bauman, *Liquid Modernity* (Cambridge, 2006).

14 Gilles Deleuze, *Desert Islands and Other Texts, 1953–1974* (Paris, 2004) pp. 10–11.

15 Tom Neale, *An Island to Oneself* (London, 1966).

16 See 'An Island to Oneself', www.goodreads.com, accessed 10 February 2021. The book was written with Noel Barber, a British author who visited Tom Neale on the island.

17 Rodney Graham, 'Siting Vexation Island', in *Island Thought*, ed. Rodney Graham, i/1 (Summer 1997) (Canada xlvii Biennale di Venezia) (Ghent, 1997), p. 15.

18 Rodney Graham, interview with Robert Enright: 'Graham Cracklings: Rodney Graham's Conceptual Energy', *Border Crossings*, 113 (March 2010), p. 10, www.bordercrossingsmag.com.

19 For a discussion of the role of looping in Graham's work, see Vanessa Smith, 'Rodney Graham: Temporality and Looping in Video Art', *aln/nt2 e-journal* (2018), https://nt2.uqam.ca. See also Dorothea Zwirner, *Rodney Graham*, Du Mont Literatur und Kunst (Cologne, 2004); and Mark Godfrey, Susie Boyt and Bob Stanley, *Rodney Graham* (Oxford, 2017).

20 Graham explained: 'I also wanted to exploit the rustic-hut characteristics of the Canada Pavilion. When I first encountered it in Venice, it was boarded up and looked quite different from the pavilions on either side, German and its fascist architecture and the neo-classical style of the British Pavilion.' Enright, 'Graham Cracklings', p. 8.

21 This was confirmed in my interview with the artist, 4 March 2021. I am immensely grateful to Graham, who generously provided information that has supported my study.

22 Enright, 'Graham Cracklings: Rodney Graham's Conceptual Energy', p. 2.

23 Loretta Yarlow, 'Editorial', in Graham, ed., *Island Thought*, pp. 3–4.

24 See Jack Liang, *Rodney Graham: Vexation Island and Other Works: Another Day in Paradise*, exh. cat. Art Gallery of York University (Toronto, 1998); and Alexander Alberro, 'Loop Dreams', *Artforum* (February 1998), p. 98, www.artforum.com.

25 Gonçalo Sousa Pinto explores this 'feeling lost' in 'Rodney Graham: Wandering through Unmapped Land', *D'ARS Magazine*, 200 (Winter 2009), www.darsmagazine.it.

26 Graham, ed., *Island Thought*.

27 Ibid., pp. 16–17.

28 Ibid., p. 19. Walter de la Mare's *Desert Islands*, first published in 1930, is an anthology of notes and quotations.

29 See Peter Suchin, 'Antti Laitinen', www.nettiehorn.com, accessed 21 January 2022.

30 'Interview with Antti Laitinen', https://fotografiskcenter.wordpress.com, accessed 21 January 2022.

31 The high filming costs on location in Hawaii contributed to it being one of the most expensive series ever made for television. During its first series in 2004 it had an estimated 16 million viewers per week on ABC.

32 Sampson, *Desert Islands*, p. 97.

33 Nathalie Olah, 'Cruel Voyeurism: Why Reality TV Shows are Inherently Bad for Contestants' Mental Health', www.newstatesman.com, 5 June 2019.

34 Another popular programme in this genre is *Temptation Island*, an American reality TV series broadcast intermittently on Fox and USA Network between 2001 and 2020.

35 Samson, *Desert Islands*, p. 125.

36 John Connell, 'Island Dreaming', p. 555.

37 The changing historiography of the Pacific is explored in Armitage and Bashford, *Pacific Histories*. Historical anthropologist Nicholas Thomas has also explored many myths of Pacific settlement, advocating a nuanced approach to Pacific history. See *Islanders: The Pacific in the Age of Empire* (New Haven, CT, and London, 2010).

38 Waldemar Januszczak reviewed it enthusiastically in *The Times* and posted on his own review page: 'The best artwork at the Biennale? That will be Lisa Reihana's *in Pursuit of Venus*, in the New Zealand pavilion . . . Where most panoramas present a fixed viewpoint, this one moves and unfolds in a riveting animated sequence that took 10 years to complete.' See 'Venice Biennale: June 2, 2017', www.waldemar.tv, accessed 16 November 2018.

39 See John Hurrell, 'Reihana's Infected Pursuit of Venus', *Eyecontact*, 12 May 2015.

40 Commissioned by the French wallpaper manufacturer Joseph Dyer. It comprised over 1,000 woodblock prints illustrating stories of exploration by the French explorer Louis Antoine de Bougainville, among others.

41 See Judith Ryan, 'Lisa Reihana: in Pursuit of Venus', www.ngv.vic.gov.au, accessed 17 November 2018.

42 Quoted in Anna Della Subin, *Accidental Gods: On Men Unwittingly Turned Divine* (London, 2021); see also Gananath Obeyesekere, *The Apotheosis of Captain Cook: European Mythmaking in the Pacific* (Princeton, NJ, 1997).

43 Etan Smallman, 'Why I Made Captain Cook Lose His Breeches: Lisa Reihana on Her Colonial Epic Video', www.theguardian.com, 15 October 2018.

44 Ibid.

45 Nicholas Thomas has eloquently described the 'contradictory' nature of Gauguin's Polynesian work, identifying tensions between his 'exoticism' and his sense of place and local cosmologies. See *Gauguin and Polynesia* (London, 2024).

46 Kihara is currently living and working on Upolu Island, Sāmoa.

47 Natalie King, 'Camping Paradise: I Am What I Am', in *Paradise Camp by Yuki Kihara*, ed. Natalie King, exh. cat., New Zealand Pavilion, Venice Biennale (Creative New Zealand, Toi Aotearoa and Thames and Hudson Australia) (Wellington and Melbourne, 2022), p. 18.

48 Nicole M. Nepomuceno, 'Yuki Kihara – Trouble in Paradise', *ArtAsiaPacific*, 129 (July/August 2009), p. 44, www.artsasiapacific.com.

49 In her interview with Nepomuceno Kihara points to the proactive roles of the Fa'afafine community as some of the 'first responders' after the devastating 2009 tsunami. Ibid., p. 45.

2 ISLAND HOMES

1 'Incredible Island Homes for Sale', iCountrylife, 31 May 2020. *Countrylife* describes itself as 'the quintessential English magazine . . . read by people who live the real country house lifestyle', www.countrylife.co.uk, accessed 20 June 2021.
2 See 'Private Island Properties', www.sothebysrealty.com, accessed 5 December 2022.
3 Nicholas Shaxson, *Treasure Islands: Tax Havens and the Men Who Stole the World* (London, 2011).
4 I discuss the concept of 'home' in the visual arts in *Playing at Home: The House in Contemporary Art* (London, 2013). See especially, 'Introduction', pp. 6–31.
5 Several British artists have also turned the geography of Scottish Islands into complex aesthetic projects. For example, Alison Turnbull's works on the Scottish Cape Farewell project of 2011–12 (see Chapter Three) chart the activities of clouds and planets over island maps, as in *North and South*, which shows stars over a map grid of Barra Island.
6 See Alex Hartley, *Not Part of Your World*, exh. cat., Fruitmarket Gallery (Edinburgh, 2007), pp. 10–11.
7 Marcarena Gómez-Barris and May Joseph, 'Coloniality and Islands', *Shima: The International Journal of Research into Island Cultures*, XIII/2 (2019), p. 4.
8 Gómez-Barris and Joseph cite Godfrey Baldacchino's influential essay 'The Coming of Age of Island Studies', which explores misconceptions of the ideas of 'isolation' in the then emerging field of Island Studies (*Tijdschrift voor Economische en Sociale Geografie*, XCV/3 (2004), pp. 272–83).
9 Several of these *cleitaen* have recently been restored, and one is now a museum. See 'St Kilda World Heritage Site', www.nts.org.uk, accessed 21 June 2021.
10 The title *The Edge of the World* is a reference to the expression *ultima Thule* used by Virgil (*Georgics* 1:30), which prophesied that the emperor Augustus might one day rule this extreme 'edge of the world'. Much of the film consists of the reminiscences of a former islander, Andrew, who revisits the island as crew for a yachtsman and his wife.
11 Frank Uekötter, 'War, Peace and Guano', in *Dinh Q. Lê, The Colony*, ed. Jonathan Watkins and Jenine McGaughran (Manchester, 2016), p. 4.
12 Ibid., p. 5.
13 'The Toll of Human Desire: Zoe Butt in Conversation with Dinh Q. Lê, ibid., p. 25.
14 Ibid., p. 27.
15 However, fertilizer shortages caused by the Ukraine war have caused a recent revival in guano collecting on Peruvian islands. See Dan Collyns, 'Worldwide Fertiliser Shortage Prompts Peru to Turn to Bird Poo', www.theguardian.com, 4 October 2022.
16 Dinh Q. Lê, 'The Toll of Human Desire', p. 26.
17 Virginia Woolf, *To the Lighthouse* [1927] (London, 2004), p. 209.
18 James Ducat, Thomas Marshall and William MacArthur.
19 Christopher Nicholson, *Rock Lighthouses of Britain: The End of an Era?* (Caithness, Scotland, 1995), pp. 168–79.
20 R. W. Munroe, *Scottish Lighthouses* (Stornaway, 1979), pp. 170–71.
21 Nicholson, *Rock Lighthouses of Britain*, p. 171.
22 For a review of the film, see 'Gerard Butler's Lighthouse Mystery Movie Hits the Big Screen', www.bbc.co.uk, accessed 4 March 2021.
23 The track was recorded while the group were working on their first album in 1968, but it was not released until 1998, in their album *Genesis Archive 1967–75*. See 'Genesis – The Mystery of the Flannan Isle Lighthouse (1967)', www.youtube.com, accessed 4 March 2021.
24 Tom Nancollas, *Seashaken Houses: A Lighthouse History from Eddystone to Fastnet* (London, 2019). The title is taken from Dylan Thomas's 'Prologue' of 1952: 'In my seashaken house/ On a breakneck of rocks'.
25 See Nicholas Royle, 'Top Ten Lighthouses in Fiction', www.theguardian.com, 16 October 2019.
26 Nels Pearson, 'Recovering Islands: Scotland, Ocean and Archipelago in *To the Lighthouse*', *Twentieth-Century Literature*, LXIV/3 (2018), p. 347.
27 'Tacita Dean: Selected Writings', in *Tacita Dean*, 6 vols (Paris, 2003), vol. 1, n.p.
28 See 'Visiting Bamburgh: Grace Darling', www.bamburgh.org.uk, accessed 13 March 2021.
29 Several books and films have retold the extraordinary story of Crowhurst's voyage around the Atlantic. See, for example, Nicholas Tomalin and Ron Hall, *The Strange*

Last Voyage of Donald Crowhurst (New York, 2003), and the films *Crowhurst* (2017, dir. Simon Rumley) and *The Mercy* (2017, dir. James Marsh).

30 See Dean's account of seeking out the abandoned trimaran on Cayman Brac in Jean Wainwright ed., *Ship to Shore: Art and the Lure of the Sea*, exh. cat. John Hansard Gallery (Southampton, 2018), pp. 48–53.

31 J. G. Ballard, 'Time and Tacita Dean', in Tacita Dean and Claire Walliseds, *Tacita Dean* (London, 2001), p. 33.

32 Ibid. There are many versions of the Tristan legend; I am following here the version cited by Dean.

33 Ibid.

34 Clarrie Wallis, 'Introduction', in *Tacita Dean* (London, 2001), p. 9.

35 Dean published a book of her photographs: *Tacita Dean: Teignmouth Electron* [1999] (Steidl, 2009). The film, *Teignmouth Electron (*2000), is seven minutes long (16 mm colour film).

36 Wainwright, *Ship to Shore*, p. 49.

37 Cited in 'The Teignmouth Electron (19 years after Tacita Dean)', National Gallery of the Cayman Islands, www.nationalgallery.org.ky, accessed 6 December 2022.

38 Sir Francis Drake came across the island on a voyage in 1586, when he used the name *Caymanas*, from the Carib name for crocodiles. Many now believe that he mistook the local rock iguanas for crocodiles.

39 For images, see 'The Teignmouth Electron: 19 Years after Tacita Dean', National Gallery of the Cayman Islands.

40 Wainwright, *Ship to Shore*, p. 80.

41 Ibid.

42 Quoted in a Lelong Gallery press release, February 2012. Yass filmed on 35 mm film, transferred to video; see *Lighthouse*, www.vimeo.com, accessed 8 March 2022.

43 As explained by Yass in Wainwright, *Ship to Shore*, p. 82. She works with a 1950s Graflex film camera and analogue film.

44 Michel Pastoureau, *Blue: The History of a Colour* (Princeton, NJ, and Oxford, 2001), p. 11. See also Chapter Five of this book.

45 Woolf, *To the Lighthouse*, p. 7.

46 Around the British Isles automation began in the 1950s and '60s with the introduction of helicopter reliefs, but most lighthouses remained staffed by keepers until the 1980s and '90s.

47 Nicholas Barber, 'Film Review: *The Lighthouse*', www.bbc.com, 4 October 2019.

48 The tale has been retold by many writers and journalists, including Nicholson; see *Rock Lighthouses of Britain*, pp. 58–9.

49 'The Disturbing Tale of Death and Insanity at Wales' Most Remote Lighthouse' is the title of an article by Robert Harries: www.walesonline.co.uk, 12 April 2020.

50 It was developed into a BBC play by Alan Harris in 2011: 'The Lighthouse: Drama on Four', www.bbc.co.uk, accessed 10 December 2021; and a British psychological thriller/drama, also titled *The Lighthouse* (2016, dir. Chris Crow).

51 Rodney Graham in conversation with the author, 6 April 2021.

52 See 'Minot's Ledge Lighthouse MA', www.lighthousefriends.com, accessed 10 December 2021.

53 Rodney Graham in conversation with the author, 6 April 2021.

54 Donald Graham published two overlapping books on this theme: *Keepers of the Light: A History of British Columbia's Lighthouses and Their Keepers* (Vancouver, 1990) and *Lights of the Inside Passage: A History of British Columbia's Lighthouses* (Vancouver, 1986). For the review above, see www.goodreads.com/book/show/4437982-keepers-of-the-light, accessed 21 April 2021.

55 Rodney Graham in conversation with the author, 6 April 2021.

3 DISAPPEARING AND ENDANGERED ISLANDS

1 Plato's dialogues *Timeaus* and *Critias* (*c.* 430 BC) are the primary sources for the myth of Atlantis.

2 Extract included in David Christopher Lane, ed., *Plato's Sunken Island: The Historical-Myth of Atlantis* (Walnut, CA, 2020), pp. 7–8. See also Plato, *Timaeus* (London, 1965), p. 37.

3 Gavin Menzies, *The Lost Empire of Atlantis*: *History's Greatest Mystery Revealed* (New York, 2011).

4 The series ran for thirteen episodes in 1977–8. Mark Harris had webbed hands and feet, and possessed many superhuman traits, including being able to breathe underwater.

5 Reprinted in Smithson, 'Incidents of Mirror-Travel in the Yucatan', *Robert Smithson: The Collected Writings*, ed. Jack Flam (Berkley, CA, 1996), pp. 119–33.

6 Ibid., p. 131.

7 Ibid., p. 133.

8 Referenced in Joy Sleeman, 'The Possibility of an Island', in *Simon Faithfull: Does The World Exist When I'm Not There?* (Laconic, 2016), n.p.

9 Ron Graziani, *Robert Smithson and the American Landscape* (Cambridge, 2004), p. 36.

10 For his account and photographic record of the Yucatan 'Mirror Displacements' see Smithson, *The Collected Writings*, 'Incidents of Mirror-Travel in the Yucatan', pp. 119–33.

11 Smithson, *The Collected Writings*, p. 129.

12 The two artists shared an interest in archaeological sites and were in the UK when Smithson had work in the Institute of Contemporary Art show 'When Attitudes Become Form', which opened in September 1969. They visited the ruins at Old Sarum, Wiltshire, Pentre Ifan in Pembrokeshire, Dartmoor National Park and Oxted Quarry in Surrey (among other places) and documented their trip in photographs. Holt remembers the trip in an interview in *Tate Etc*, 25 (Summer 2012), www.tate.org.uk.

13 J. G. Ballard's novel *The Drowned World* (1962) is a prescient tale of the effects of a meteorological disaster, summarized in the back cover blurb (quoted above) of the 2014 edition (London, 1962). His 1965 novel *The Drought* (originally titled *The Burning World*) more clearly foresees the effects of manmade climate change, albeit caused here by solar instability. Polar ice caps have melted, and Europe is a network of giant lagoons.

14 Alastair Bonnett, *The Age of Islands: In Search of New and Disappearing Islands* (London, 2021), p. 157.

15 Ibid., p. 230.

16 Ibid., p. 157.

17 There are many international research institutes analysing the effects of the climate crisis on these SIDS. The United Nations office for Disaster Risk Reduction and research institutions such as the International Institute for Disaster Risk (IISD) have supported research and lobbying on behalf of small island communities and disastrous ecological developments. See, for example, from IISD: Leila Mead, 'Small Islands, Large Oceans: Voices on the Frontline of Climate Change', www.iisd.org, 29 March 2021.

18 T. J. Demos, *Decolonising Nature: Contemporary Art and the Politics of Ecology* (Berlin, 2016), p. 8.

19 Jaimey Hamilton Faris, 'Sisters of Ocean and Ice: On the Hydro-Feminism of Kathy Jetñil-Kijiner and Aka Niviâna's *Rise: From One Island to Another*', *Shima*, XIII/2 (2019), p. 76.

20 Ibid.

21 See, for example, Astrida Neimanis, *Bodies of Water: Posthuman Feminist Phenomenology* (London, 2017).

22 Predicted by the U.S. Geological Survey. See 'Marshall Islands Could Be Wiped Out by Climate Change – and Their Colonial History Limits Their Ability to Save Themselves', https://theconversation.com, accessed 1 November 2021.

23 German trading interests brought the islands under German colonial control, following their early settlement by French and Spanish 'explorers'. In 1914 they were taken over by the Japanese but captured by U.S. forces in 1944 during the Second World War Pacific Campaign. The U.S. took over administration in 1947, using the islands as a military site, and controversially as a nuclear test site. Between 1946 and 1958, 67 nuclear weapons were tested on inhabited Bikini and Enewetak Atolls, forcing the evacuation of exposed communities. In 1983 Marshall Islands became a sovereign self-governing nation, although the United States retained responsibility for defence and security.

24 Quoted in Cathie Koa Dunsford, 'Kaitiakitanga: Protecting Our Oceans, Islands and Skies by Inspiring a Climate Change', *Dreadlocks: Oceans, Islands and Skies*, Proceedings of the Oceanic Conference on Creativity and Climate Change, VI/VII (2010–11), p. 16.

25 Reproduced in the online exhibition catalogue *Inundation*: www.inundation.org, accessed 20 October 2020.

26 As described on Enomoto's website: 'Sounding', www.joyenomoto.com, accessed 20 October 2020.

27 Elizabeth DeLoughrey, 'Pacific Literature and the Environment: Nuclear Fallout as Climate Change', *Dreadlocks: Oceans, Islands and Skies*, Proceedings of the Oceanic Conference on Creativity and Climate Change, VI/VII (2010–11), pp. 127–42. For DeLoughrey's adaption of Virilio's ideas on the geopolitics of militarization, see DeLoughrey, 'Radiation Ecologies and the Wars of Light', *Modern Fiction Studies* (*MFS*), LV/3 (Fall 2009), pp. 468–98.

28 T. J. Demos has explored the intersection of contemporary art, environmental activism and 'political ecology' in his book *Decolonising Nature*. Demos argues for a definition of 'political ecology' that 'insist[s] on environmental matters of concern as inextricable from

social, political and economic forces' (p. 7). Some broader definitions of the relationship between art and ecology are explored in Andrew Brown, *Art and Ecology Now* (London, 2014).

29 In an article of 2008 the artist Dean Kenning looks at the ways in which contemporary artists (including Joseph Beuys and Mierle Laderman Ukeles) have engaged with ecological concerns in their work, arguing for an aesthetic practice that is 'dialectically grounded', and that raises disparate environmental concerns. 'Eco Art', *Art Monthly*, 313 (February 2008), pp. 1–4.

30 Greg Hilty, 'Imagining the Galápagos: The Artist in Nature's System', in *Galápagos*, ed. Bergit Arends and Siân Ede, exh. cat. Calouste Gulbenkian Foundation (London, 2012), p. 25.

31 Personal communication with the artist, 7 March 2023.

32 For details of conservation projects supported by 'Galápagos Conservancy' as posted on their blog in 2020: www.galapagos.org/newsroom/unravelling-the-silent-marine-invasion-in-galapagos, accessed 13 January 2023.

33 Dorothy Cross and Fiona Shaw (Ireland); Alison Turnbull, Marcus Coates, Tannia Kovats, Jeremy Deller, Kaffe Matthews, Semiconductor, Jyll Bradley and Alexis Deacon (UK); and Paulo Catrica and Filipa César (Portugal).

34 Arends and Ede, eds, *Galápagos*, p. 76.

35 Ibid.

36 'Making strange' is explained in a lecture given by Cross at MIT, 29 April 2009. See 'Guestbook Lecture: Dorothy Cross, April 29, 2009', www.youtube.com, accessed 20 March 2022.

37 Quoted in Fiona Shaw, 'The Isle Is Full of Noises', in *Galápagos*, ed. Arends and Ede, p. 117.

38 In another series, titled *Psyche; or, the Butterfly*, Turnbull researched the butterflies of the Pacific Rainforest in Chocó, Columbia. See *Psyche; or, the Butterfly: An Expanded Field Guide* (Más Arte Más Acción, London, 2018), which includes an essay by Marina Warner, 'The Mimic Net', pp. 52–62.

39 Personal communication with the artist, 19 June 2022.

40 Katrina Palmer, Portland Diary, 21 July 2014. I am grateful to Palmer for providing me with her (as-yet unpublished) diary, and for generously discussing her work with me.

41 See Gill Hackman, *Stone to Build London: Portland's Legacy* (Monkton Farleigh, 2014). Other well-known buildings include the Banqueting Hall in Whitehall and the National Gallery extension in London.

42 For details of the Artangel project, see 'End Matter', www.artangel.org.uk, accessed 21 May 2020.

43 'The peninsula carved by time out of a single stone': Thomas Hardy, *The Well-Beloved: A Sketch of a Temperament* (London, 2000), p. 3.

44 Katrina Palmer in conversation with the author, 25 January 2019.

45 Katrina Palmer, *End Matter* (Artangel, London, 2015), p. 22.

46 Katrina Palmer in conversation with the author, 2019.

47 See, for example, Trevor Barnes, *Dead Doubles: The Extraordinary Worldwide Hunt for One of the Cold War's Most Notorious Spy Rings* (London, 2020).

48 For a detailed history of Portland, see Stuart Morris, *Portland: An Illustrated History* (Wimborne, Dorset, 1985).

49 Palmer's notion of 'End Matter' is deliberately unsettled, echoing the contradictory notion of 'absent and present sculpture'. In an appendix to her book *End Matter*, she writes: 'What will the end matter refer to? If it refers to a second book, then the original book will not be complete. If the referred to text is absent, then the addendum, postscript, etc., will in fact not be end matter at all, but will be body matter, masquerading as end matter . . . The book will need both text and end matter in place, meaning the project is unresolved and unresolvable.' (*End Matter*, p. 74).

50 Ibid., p. 5.

51 Ibid.

52 Ibid.

53 Dan Barrow, 'Katrina Palmer: The Loss Adjusters', *The Wire*, 377 (July 2015), p. 71.

54 'Cobra Mist' was a long-range surveillance radar system operated by the United States. Planned to be sited in Turkey, to provide coverage of European Soviet airspace, it was moved to Orford Ness, from where it offered a view of most of Eastern Europe. Constructed during the 1960s and into 1970, the system was plagued by unresolved noise problems and was shut down in 1973. The buildings were subsequently occupied by a radio-transmitting service for the UK Foreign Office and the BBC World Service until 2011, and acquired by a private company, Cobra Mist Ltd, in 2015.

55 Sophia Davis, 'Military Landscape and Secret Science: The Case of Orford Ness', *Cultural Geographies in Practice*, xv/1 (2008), pp. 143–9.

56 In 2013 Trinity House decommissioned the lighthouse as a navigation aid.

57 Davis, 'Military Landscape and Secret Science', p. 149.

58 *Cobra Mist* was filmed in 16 mm anamorphic film and is 6 minutes, 45 seconds long.

59 Max Porter, cited on book jacket of Robert Macfarlane and Stanley Donwood, *Ness* (London, 2018).

60 Ilya Kaminsky, *I See a Silence* (Artangel, London, 2021).

61 Ibid., p. 5.

62 In the 1920s RAF Orford Ness was used for trials of navigational apparatus for military aircraft, although it was claimed publicly that this was for maritime navigation. From 1929, military aircraft were involved in trials. In 1934 the system was scrapped, and Black Beacon relegated to use as a store. With war looming, new homing systems were established in other UK fighter stations.

4 ISLAND DETENTIONS

1 Robben Island, in Cape Town's Cable Bay, was a penal colony largely for political prisoners, and is best known as the place where former South African president Nelson Mandela was imprisoned for eighteen years. It was made a UNESCO World Heritage Site in 1999.

2 Jude McCulloch, 'Christmas Island Detention Centre' (2007), cited in Alison Mountz and Linda Briskman, 'Introducing Island Detentions: The Placement of Asylum Seekers and Migrants on Islands', *Shima: The International Journal of Research into Island Cultures*, vi/2 (2012), pp. 21–6, p. 21.

3 Alison Mountz, 'Political Geography ii: Islands and Archipelagos', *Progress in Human Geography*, i–ii (2014), p. 2.

4 See John Scott and Zoe Staines, 'Charting the Place of Islands in Criminology: On Isolation, Integration and Insularity', *Theoretical Criminology*, xxv/4 (2020), www.journals.sagepub.com.

5 The Devil's Island penal system, with a death rate of up to 75 per cent, was strongly criticized in René Belbenoît's book *Dry Guillotine* (1938) before the prison was closed in 1953.

6 The film was not distributed in the UK or United States, following concerns about Polanski's sex offences.

7 An ex-prisoner and convicted murderer (he claimed innocence), Charrière's full story has since been disputed. For the original story, see 'Henri Charriere: Author of "Papillon"', *New York Times*, www.nytimes.com, 30 July 1973.

8 Many other novels and films have been inspired by Devil's Island, including Richard Oswald's German production *Dreyfus* (1930); and *Devil's Island* (1939, dir. William Clemens), starring Boris Karloff as Dr Charles Gaudet. A grim adventure film, *I Escaped from Devil's Island*, appeared in 1973 (dir. Jim Brown), and a remake of *Papillon* was also made in 2017 (dir. Michael Noer), starring Charlie Hunnam and Rami Malek.

9 Franz Kafka, *In the Penal Colony* [1914] (Kindle edition, 2014).

10 Michel Foucault, *Discipline and Punish: The Birth of the Prison* [1975] (London, 2020), p. 236.

11 T. J. Demos, *The Migrant Image: The Art and Politics of Documentary during Global Crisis* (Durham, NC, 2013), p. xiii.

12 Mountz and Briskman, 'Introducing Island Detentions', pp. 21–6.

13 Alessandra Von Burg, 'Citizenship Islands: The Ongoing Emergency in the Mediterranean Sea', *Media and Communication*, vii/2 (2019), pp. 218–29.

14 Cited by Niru Ratnam in 'Ai Weiwei's Aylan Kurdi Image Is Crude, Thoughtless and Egotistical', *The Spectator*, www.spectator.co.uk, 1 February 2016.

15 For example, the Indian sand artist Sudarsan Pattnaik's *Humanity Washed Ashore: Shame, Shame, Shame* (2015). See 'Syrian Toddler Aylan Kurdi Sand Sculpture By Sudarsan Pattnaik Goes Viral! #HumanityWashedAshore', www.india.com, accessed 21 December 2021.

16 'Alfredo Jaar on Europe's Failure to Welcome Refugees', *Art Newspaper*, www.theartnewspaper.com, 2 September 2016.

17 I am grateful to Alfredo Jaar for kindly providing information on the context of *The Gift*.

18 The camp was built to accommodate around 3,000 people, but by 2020 there were around 20,000 occupants.

19 Lauren Markham, 'A Disaster Waiting to Happen: Who Was Really Responsible for the Fire at the Moria Refugee Camp?', *The Guardian*, www.theguardian.com, 21 April 2022.

20 Anthony Downey, 'Scopic Reflections: Incoming and the Technology Exceptionalism', in *Richard Mosse* (London, 2017), p. 22.

21 'Richard Mosse in Conversation with Alona Pardo', ibid., p. 34.

22 Cited in online publication: *RA Collection: Art?*, 'The Leopard (WESTERN UNION: small boats)', www.royalacademy.org.uk, accessed 24 March 2022.

23 Various reviews are cited in Maya Ramsay, 'Re-Framing the Debate: The Art of Lampedusa', *Crossings: Journal of Migration and Culture*, VII/2 (October 2016), pp. 209–25.

24 'Mediterranean "a cemetery" – Maltese PM Muscat', www.bbc.co.uk, accessed 21 December 2021.

25 Nicholas Murray, 'The Lampedusa Cross', in *The Yellow Wheelbarrow* (Melos Press, 2019).

26 The United Nations Refugee Agency (UNHCR) and the International Organisation for Migration (IOM) confirmed the number of dead, including children. The boat's Tunisian captain was found guilty of manslaughter.

27 Matthew Collings, 'Venice Biennale 2019 Roundup', www.standard.co.uk, 13 May 2019.

28 Elizabeth DeLoughrey argues that the discourse of 'routes' encodes the vessels of a Pacific historiography: 'Whether rendered as a voyaging canoe, a naval ship, a drifting raft, or metaphorically as ethnic blood, the concept of the *vessel* is integral to territorial claims of indigenous sovereignty as well as (masculine) ethnic regionalism.' DeLoughrey, *Routes and Roots: Navigating Pacific and Caribbean Island Literatures* (Honolulu, HI, 2007), pp. 96–7. Although the Mediterranean migration 'routes' evoke a different regional imaginary, I suggest that migrant boats can carry some parallel symbolic meanings.

29 James Randall, *An Introduction to Island Studies* (Charlottetown, PEI, 2021). See his chapter 'Island Health and Epidemiology', pp. 149–64.

30 The island of Poveglia was featured on the American paranormal reality TV series *Scariest Places on Earth*, which aired from 2000 to 2006 on Fox Family and ABC Family channels.

31 See Tom Kington, '"Worlds Most Haunted Island" Up for Auction', www.telegraph.co.uk, 15 April 2014.

32 In Anthony Horowitz's *Alex Rider: Scorpia* (2005), Malagosto is several kilometres from Venice and owned by the criminal organization Scorpia.

33 Michel Foucault, *Discipline and Punish* [1975] (London, 2020), Section 3, Part 1: 'Docile Bodies', pp. 135–69.

34 See Mark William O'Hara, 'Foucault and Film: Theories and Representations of Mental Illness', PhD thesis, Miami University, 2014. The study examines six Hollywood films that explore mental illness, including Scorsese's *Shutter Island.* Lehane's book is also explored in Robab Beheshti and Mahdi Shafieyan, 'Foucauldian Docile Body in Dennis Lehane's *Shutter Island*', *Theory and Practice in Language Studies*, VI/10 (October 2016), pp. 2052–9.

35 Peter Bradshaw, 'Wes Anderson Unleashes a Cracking Canine Caper', *The Guardian*, 20 March 2018, *G2*: p. 12.

36 *Isle of Dogs* is a stop-motion animation film written and directed by Wes Anderson (2018). The screenplay is by Wes Anderson, with Roman Coppola, Jason Schwartzman and the Japanese writer and actor Kunichi Nomura, who also voices the dog-hating Mayor Kobayashi. A star-studded cast includes Bryan Cranston (Chief), Edward Norton (Rex), Bill Murray (Boss), Bob Balaban (King), Jeff Goldblum (King), Harvey Keitel (Gondo), Scarlett Johansson (Nutmeg), Tilda Swinton (Oracle) and Yoko Ono (scientist).

37 Justin Chang wrote in the *LA Times*: 'all these coy linguistic layers amount to their own form of marginalization, effectively reducing the hapless, unsuspecting people of Megasaki to foreigners in their own city.' This issue is not helped by the fact the leader of the pro-dog movement is an American foreign exchange student (Greta Gerwig). See Justin Chang, 'Wes Anderson's "Isle of Dogs" Is Often Captivating, But Cultural Sensitivity Gets Lost in Translation', www.latimes.com, 21 March 2018.

38 The play was immediately suppressed, and no known copy exists. I have no evidence that Anderson knew of it; rather, I am suggesting that the play offered a suitably mischievous – and prescient – legacy.

39 Although the leaders of the pack are indisputably male 'alpha' dogs, there are a few female protagonists with relatively important roles, including Nutmeg (Scarlett Johansson), a female ex-show dog who assists the canine resistance, Oracle (Tilda Swinton), Stacy (Greta Gerwig) and the scientist (Yoko Ono).

40 Bradshaw, 'Anderson Unleashes', p. 12.

5 ISLANDS OF 'WHITE GOLD'

1 For an accessible, well-researched history of Bunce Island, see 'Bunce Island History', Yale University Gilder Lehrman Center for the Study of Slavery, Resistance and Abolition, https://glc.yale.edu, accessed 1 March 2022.

2 Including Tim Carrier's *Family Across the Sea*, 1990.

3 See, for example, the work of Leon Wainwright, including his book *Timed Out: Art and the Transnational Caribbean* (Manchester, 2011).

4 Notions of 'decolonial island praxis' are explored in Macerena Gómez-Barris, 'Coloniality and Islands', *Shima*, XIII/2 (2019), pp. 1–10.

5 In 1802 Napoleon repealed the law in the French colonies, but slavery was only banned in France in 1848.

6 See Dale Tomich, 'Sugar Technology and Slave Labor in Martinique, 1830–1848', *West Indian Guide*, LXIII/1–2 (1989), pp. 118–34.

7 The debates around the economic and cultural effects of tourism on small islands are beyond the scope of this book. A useful introduction can be found in James Randall, *An Introduction to Island Studies* (Charlottetown, PEI, 2021), chapter 10: 'Island Tourism', pp. 183–206. See also Anthony Carrigan, *Postcolonial Tourism: Literature, Culture and Environment* (London, 2012).

8 See especially his *L'Intention Poetique* (The Poetic Intention), first published in 1969. Cited by Aragorn Eloff in 'Wandering the Shoreline with Edouard Glissant', *New Frame*, www.newframe.com, 7 May 2019.

9 In 'Cross Cultural Poetics', a lecture given in Madison (WI), Pittsburgh and Toronto in 1973. Published in English in Edouard Glissant, *Caribbean Discourse: Selected Essays* (Charlottesville, VA, 1989), pp. 98–157. For a discussion of 'creolization', see p. 140. The use of Glissant's ideas as a 'tool kit' to explore visual art and the geo-poetics of the Caribbean landscape have been usefully explored by Kate Keohane, 'Some Otherwhere: Édouard Glissant and the Caribbean Landscape in Contemporary Art', PhD thesis, University of St Andrews, 2020, https://research-repository.st-andrews.ac.uk.

10 Elizabeth Deloughrey, 'Island Writing, Creole Cultures', in *The Cambridge History of Postcolonial Literature* (Cambridge, 2012), pp. 802–3.

11 Ibid., p. 803. See Edward Kamau Brathwaite's *The Arrivants: A New World Trilogy* (Oxford, 1973), which includes his poems 'Rights of Passage', 'Islands' and 'Masks'.

12 Derek Walcott, *Selected Poems* (London, 2007), p. 123.

13 Ibid., pp. 123–4.

14 Leon Wainwright has developed related arguments in search of 'a more layered and contemporary account of aesthetics as a field of social practice'. He has mapped the complexities of 'diaspora aesthetics' to formulate his own multi-layered aesthetic philosophy of some diasporic art. See *Phenomenal Difference: A Philosophy of Black British Art* (Liverpool, 2017).

15 Hilary McD. Beckles, *The First Black Slave Society: Britain's Barbados, 1636–1876* (Kingston, Jamaica, 2016).

16 By 1660 Barbados generated more trade than all other English colonies combined. It was eventually surpassed by larger Caribbean islands such as Jamaica in 1713. In the nineteenth century sugar production dominated the economies of other islands including Martinique, Grenada, Saint Croix, Saint Dominique and Cuba.

17 Edward Kamau Brathwaite, 'Caribbean Man in Space and Time' [1975], *Small Axe*, XXV/3 (November 2021), pp. 90–104. See also Leigh Anne Duck, 'Plantation Cartographies and Chronologies', *American Literary History*, XXIV/4 (Winter 2012), pp. 842–52.

18 As described on the artist's site: 'In Defense of Beauty', https://annaleedavis.com, accessed 1 March 2022.

19 See the cross-disciplinary publication: Patricia Mohammed, ed., *Gendered Realities: An Anthology of Essays in Caribbean Feminist Thought* (Mona, Jamaica, 2002). See also Hilary McD. Beckles, *Centering Women: Gender Discourses in Caribbean Slave Society* (Princeton, NJ, 1999); and Barbara Bush, *Slave Women in Caribbean Society* (Kingston, Jamaica, 1990).

20 Artist's site (see endnote 18 above).

21 Brathwaite, 'Caribbean Man in Space and Time', p. 96.

22 See Annalee Davis, Jocelyn Gardner and Erica Moiah James, 'Introduction: Art as Caribbean Feminist Practice', *Small Axe*, 52 (March 2017), pp. 34–42.

23 Shown at Lewisham Arthouse, London, June–July 2017.

24 McLean recorded the sounds of everyday life on Jamaican-born Vanley Burke's allotment in Handsworth, Birmingham.

25 For a discussion of McLean's works on the theme of the chattel house see Gill Perry, *Playing at Home: The House in Contemporary Art* (London, 2013), pp. 208–14.

26 See Mark Watson and Robert Potter, *Low-Cost Housing in Barbados: Evolution or Social Revolution?* (Kingston, Jamaica, 1995), p. 56.

27 Personal communication with the artist, 5 July 2021.

28 In his analysis of modern Barbados, Hilary McD. Beckles explores the chattel house as a symbol of Black economic enfranchisement, building on research by Potter and Watson cited above. McD. Beckles, *Chattel House Blues: Making of a Democratic Society in Barbados* (Kingston, Jamaica, 2004), p. 140.

29 Potter and Watson, *Low-Cost Housing in Barbados*, p. 56.

30 Homi Bhabha, 'Of Mimicry and Man: The Ambivalence of Colonial Discourse', *October*, XXVIII: *Discipleship: A Special Issue on Psychoanalysis* (Spring 1984), pp. 125–33. Discussed in personal communication with the artist, 5 June 2021.

31 The Spanish called these free slaves 'maroons', derived from the word *cimaroon*, meaning 'fierce' or 'unruly'. The Jamaican Maroons occupied a mountainous region known as Cockpit Country, where they constructed crude fortresses and followed cultural traditions derived from Africa and Europe.

32 See Mavis Christine Campbell, *The Maroons of Jamaica, 1655–1796: A History of Resistance, Collaboration and Betrayal* (Trenton, NJ, 1990); and Lucille Mathurin Mair, *The Rebel Woman in the British West Indies during Slavery* (Kingston, Jamaica, 1995).

33 Trinidad became a British Crown Colony in 1802, and in 1889 Trinidad and Tobago were incorporated into a single Crown Colony.

34 See Miles Ogborn, 'Slavery, Freedom and the Jamaican Landscape', www.bl.uk, accessed 20 March 2021.

35 Apart from *The Precariat*, see her series of scaled-down chattel houses on stilts, *Primitive Matters* (2011/12), discussed in Perry, *Playing at Home*, pp. 209–14.

36 There is a growing literature on the culture of resistance among bondwomen in the American South and the Caribbean, including Stephanie M. H. Camp, *Closer to Freedom: Enslaved Women and Everyday Resistance in the Plantation South* (Chapel Hill, NC, 2004); Loucynda Jensen, 'Searching the Silence: Finding Black Women's Resistance to Slavery in Antebellum U.S. History', *PSU McNair Scholars Online Journal*, II/1 (2006); Hilary McD. Beckles, *Natural Rebels: A Social History of Enslaved Black Women in Barbados* (New Brunswick, NJ, 1989); and Barbara Bush, *Slave Women in Caribbean Society* (Kingston, Jamaica, 1990).

37 Entela Bilali, 'The Art of Quilting in Alice Walker's Fiction', Challenges Towards the Future, the 2nd International Conference on Research and Education, 30–31 May 2014, University of Shkodra, Albania.

38 'Bondwomen', a term that originated in the fourteenth century, is increasingly used by researchers as an alternative to 'female slaves' to describe women bound to labour without wages. I use both terms in this book.

39 Camp, *Closer to Freedom*, p. 67.

40 See Jennifer L. Morgan, *Laboring Women: Reproduction and Gender in New World Slavery* (Philadelphia, PA, 2004).

41 Walcott, *Selected Poems*, p. 123.

42 By the eighteenth century the cowrie had become the currency of choice along the trade routes of West Africa. It continued as a means of payment, also adopted by colonizers, until the early twentieth century. See M. Şaul, 'Money in Colonial Transition: Cowries and Francs in West Africa', *American Anthropologist*, CVI/1 (2004), pp. 71–84.

43 'Anansi stories' are Jamaican folktales that were brought to Jamaica by Ashanti slaves and handed down through generations. See Emily Zobel Marshall, *Anansi's Journey: A Story of Jamaican Cultural Resistance* (Kingston, Jamaica, 2012).

44 For an audience schooled in Western art history, they may also evoke the French-born artist Louise Bourgeois' series of huge metal spiders titled *Maman* (first cast in 1996), oversized symbols of maternal power and protection.

45 Personal communication with the artist, 1 June 2020.

46 Melanie Schwapp, 'Granny Dead', in *So Many Islands: Stories from the Mediterranean, Indian and Pacific Oceans*, ed. Nicholas Laughlin (London, 2018) pp. 63–70, p. 65.

47 Ibid., p. 65.

48 'She start calling me "Queenie" for "queen of the Maroons", and even though Mummy get vex and tell her my name is Pearl, she don't stop calling me "Queenie" till the name stick and everybody start calling me that. Even Mummy.' Ibid., p. 65.

49 'So Many Islands: Melanie Schwapp Speaks to Sabaya', www.youtube.com, accessed 1 March 2022.

50 Walcott, *Selected Poems*, p. 122.

51 Ibid., p. 115.

52 Alex Farquharson, 'Anew: To the Future, via the Past', in *Life between Islands: Caribbean-British Art, 1950s–Now*, ed. Alex Farquharson and David A. Bailey (London, 2021), p. 11.

53 The Tate Gallery was founded in 1889 (opened 1897) when Henry Tate donated his art collection and gallery funding to the nation. The origins of his wealth in sugar plantations and slavery are explored in a statement on the Tate site: 'History of Tate', www.tate.org.uk, accessed 20 March 2022.

54 The exhibition was timely, appearing in the wake of the global Black Lives Matter protests of 2020–21 and the British Windrush Scandal of 2018.

55 Farquharson, 'Anew: To the Future, via the Past', pp. 11–23.

56 Brathwaite, *The Arrivants: A New World Trilogy*.

57 For a useful review of various Caribbean artists' activities in Britain, see David A. Bailey, 'Caribbean Movements in Britain', in *Life between Islands*, ed. Farquharson and Bailey, pp. 25–35.

58 Although in South America on the Atlantic coast, Guyana is part of the Anglophone Caribbean, with close links to other islands.

59 Giulia Smith, 'Nature Erupts into Orchestras of Nemesis: The Ecological Imaginary', in *Life between Islands*, ed. Farquharson and Bailey, p. 45.

60 See Allison Thompson, 'Comin Rite Thru: Masquerade and Marches, Resistance and Revolution', in *Life between Islands*, ed. Farquharson and Bailey, p. 75.

61 This Super 8 film was among the original rushes for McQueen's film *Caribs' Leap* (2002), which focuses on the fate of Amerindians who first lived on Grenada, and the current state of the descendants of African slaves who form most of the island's modern population.

62 The terms 'cosmopolitan' and 'cosmopolitanism' have acquired a range of meanings across the social sciences, politics, cultural theory and visual culture. The contemporary relevance and usages of the terms are reviewed in Eleanor Byrne and Berthold Schoene, eds, 'Cosmopolitanism as Critical and Creative Practice', *Open Arts Journal*, 1, https://openartsjournal.org, accessed 20 June 2021. See also the work of Marsha Meskimmon, including her *Contemporary Art and the Cosmopolitan Imagination* (London, 2010). I have appropriated the term here to signal a set of hybrid cultural and aesthetic attitudes that are negotiated rather than romanticized.

63 Calvin Tomkins, 'Into the Unknown: Chris Ofili Returns to New York with a Major Retrospective', *New Yorker*, 29 September 2014, cited in Thompson, 'Comin Rite Thru', p. 75.

64 Matthew Ryder, *Chris Ofili*, exh. cat., New Museum, New York (2014), p. 133.

65 Nanette de Jong and Christian Mieves have suggested that the concept of flattening can be understood as an alternative way to analyse cultural meaning in Trinidadian Carnival. See N. De Jong and C. Mieves, 'The Trope of Flattening and the Complexities of Difference: Visual and Acoustic Accounts of Caribbean Carnival', *Anthurium: A Caribbean Studies Journal*, XIII/2 (2016), pp. 1–26.

66 Leon Wainwright, 'Solving Caribbean Mysteries: Art, Embodiment and an Eye for the Tropics', *Small Axe*, XII/1 (2008), p. 135. See also Wainwright. 'A Suitable Distance? Revisiting a Millennial Approach to Curating Art in the Caribbean', *Art Journal*, LXXXI/3 (2022), pp. 39–52.

67 Personal communication with the artist, 23 April 2022.

68 Candice Nembhard cites a U.S. Crime and Safety Report which describes 'an excess of violent crimes' . . . largely on account of the island being a 'major trans-shipment point for illicit drugs': 'Blue Power and Trinidad's Shifting Social History', in *Blue Power/Ar'n't I a Woman* (London, 2021), n.p.

6 IRISH ISLANDS: OF MYTHS AND MAPS

1 Skellig Michael was designated a UNESCO world heritage site in 1996. It is one of approximately eighty islands of significant size that make up the Irish archipelago. Only about twenty of these are inhabited, of which Achill Island in County Mayo is the largest. Hundreds of smaller islets are dotted around the Irish coast.

2 Skellig Michael features in Episode One of *Civilisation*, 'The Skin of Our Teeth', first broadcast in 1969. As a patrician scholar, Clark's approach to 'civilization' has subsequently been reappraised, including a rethinking of the term that underpins a BBC/Open University series of 2019, *Civilisations*.

3 First published by Seamus Heaney (1939–2013) in 1966 in his collection *Death of a Naturalist*.

4 As has been pointed out by Fionna Barber, to whom I am hugely indebted for her helpful feedback on an early draft of this chapter, and for her invaluable research on Irish art.

5 Edna O'Brien, *Mother Island* [1976] (New York, 1999), p. 2.

6 Ibid., p. 1.

7 See the work of Catherine Nash, including 'Gender and Landscape in Ireland' [1993], in *Sources in Irish Art: A Reader*, ed. Fintan Cullen (Cork, 2000), pp. 302–8.

8 'Dark Rosaleen' is a patriotic love poem by James Clarence Mangan, written in 1846, when acts of nationalism were outlawed. Ireland is disguised as Rosaleen.

9 One of the first films to be banned under the British Government's Broadcasting Ban (1988) on the voices of representatives from Sinn Féin and several Irish republican and loyalist groups on television and radio in the UK. The film was shown on Channel 4 in 1991: 'Mother Ireland. Aired on Channel Four 1991', www.youtube.com, accessed 4 October 2022.

10 The nature of Boland's revisionist critique is controversial. Some have claimed that her iconoclasm doesn't go far enough, revealing a tendency towards 'regressive essentialism'. However, Andrew J. Auge has argued that despite evidence of essentialism in individual poems, this is not in the overall trajectory of her work: 'There one finds an awareness that the underlying strata of the self – gender, nation, history – are neither seamless nor secure, but deeply fissured.' Andrew J. Auge, 'Fracture and Wound: Eavan Boland's Poetry of Nationality', *New Hibernia Review*, VIII/2 (Summer 2004), p. 122.

11 Eavan Boland, 'Mother Ireland', *Poetry Magazine: Contemporary Irish Poetry* (October/November 1995), p. 93.

12 The 1983 Eighth Amendment of the Irish Constitution inserted a subsection recognizing the equal right to life of the pregnant woman and the unborn. It ensured that legislation would be restricted to allowing abortion only in circumstances where the life of a pregnant woman was at risk. Despite the support of the Catholic hierarchy, it was finally repealed in 2018 by a vote of 66.4 per cent.

13 Fionna Barber, 'Elliptical Affinities: Art, Feminism and the Body', in *Elliptical Affinities: Irish Women Artists and the Politics of the Body, 1984 to the Present*, exh. cat., Highlanes Gallery (Drogheda, 2019). For an excellent account of the role of feminism and women artists within the broader field of Irish art, see Barber, *Art in Ireland Since 1910* (London, 2013).

14 Cited in Gill Perry, 'Witches, Housewives and Mothers: Crossing (Irish) Borders in the Body Politic', in *Elliptical Affinities*, ed. Barber, p. 19.

15 Temperance Lloyd, Mary Trembles and Susannah Edwards from Bideford, Devon, were tried as witches in 1682 at the Exeter Assises, although much of the evidence against them was hearsay. These three have been labelled as the last witches to be hanged in England, although there were subsequent cases.

16 *The Tower* was commissioned as part of the Magdalene Series at Rua Red, Dublin, discussed below, pp. 198ff.

17 Discussed in Nash, 'Gender and Landscape in Ireland', pp. 303–5.

18 See for example her *City Drawing* series (1997) or her *Black Map* series (2010).

19 Nash, 'Gender and Landscape in Ireland', p. 305.

20 John Millington Synge's controversial drama *The Playboy of the Western World*, first performed in 1907, raises these issues by giving his characters the dialect of the Mayo County Irish, influenced by the syntax and vocabulary of Gaelic, the ancient Celtic tongue of Ireland and Scotland.

21 Nash, 'Gender and Landscape', p. 306.

22 The different forms of 'primitivism' that Paul and Grace adopted and their subsequent separation are discussed in Barber, *Art in Ireland*, pp. 19–26.

23 Nash, 'Gender and Landscape in Ireland', p. 306.

24 The opening caption is reproduced in 'Man of Aran (1934)', www.screenonline.org.uk, accessed 29 December 2021.

25 Sheila O'Malley references the controversy in her *Film Comment* piece 'TCM Diary: Man of Aran', www.filmcomment.com, 6 March 2019. For a useful overview of Irish cinema in the twentieth century, see Kevin Rockett, Luke Gibbons and John Hill, *Cinema and Ireland* (London, 1988). See especially Part 2 of Chapter Seven: 'Romanticism, Realism and Irish Cinema', pp. 194ff.

26 Marina Warner, 'Passionate Cruces: The Art of Dorothy Cross', in *Dorothy Cross*, exh. cat., Irish Museum of Modern Art (Dublin, 2005), p. 28.

27 Declan Quirke, 'Folding Landscapes: The Maps of Tim Robinson', www.drawingmatter.org, 23 June 2021.

28 These myths and the origins of Aran patterns are discussed in Fionna Barber, 'The Entangled Map and Irish Art', in *Textiles, Community and Controversy: The Knitting Map*, ed. Jools Gibson and Nicola Moffat (London, 2015), pp. 30–31.

29 Warner uses the term 'bricoleur's ingenuity' in 'Passionate Cruces: The Art of Dorothy Cross', p. 28.

30 See, for example *Medusae*, a video made with Cross's zoologist brother, Professor Tim Cross, in 2000. See *Dorothy Cross*, 2005, pp. 88–9.
31 Ibid., p. 48.
32 Ibid.
33 Reproduced in Henry Wadsworth Longfellow, ed., *Poems of Places: An Anthology*, 31 vols (Dublin, 1876–9), vol. v.
34 Philip Marsden, *The Summer Isles: A Voyage of the Imagination* (London, 2019), p. 6.
35 For details of this legend and the 'reports' of Captain Nesbit, as told in 1675 by William Hamilton of Derry, see Donald S. Johnson, *Phantom Islands of the Atlantic: The Legends of Seven Lands that Never Were* (London, 1997), pp. 113ff. Various popular websites also recount the myths and legends, including: https://stairnaheireann.net, accessed 29 December 2021.
36 Johnson, *Phantom Islands of the Atlantic*, pp. 118–19.
37 Ibid., p. 119.
38 Barbara Freitag, *Hy Brasil: The Metamorphosis of an Island: From Cartographic Error to Celtic Elysium* (Brill, 2013).
39 Johnson, *Phantom Islands of the Atlantic*, p. 113.
40 Freitag (2013) has researched and traced Hy-Brasil's appeal for centuries of Irish writing, including Griffin's nineteenth-century poem.
41 At www.issu.com/tulcafestival/docs/final-t-prog, accessed 10 June 2021.
42 *Floating World* is a three-screen, sixteen-minute video installation with music by Johann Johannsson.
43 For an exploration of this history and its modern-day appropriations, see Lorna Siggins, 'The Caribbean Irish: The Other Emerald Isle', *Irish Times*, www.irishtimes.com, 16 April 2016.
44 'Joanne Laws Interview Clare Langan About the Themes and Influences in Her Films', *Magnetic Earth* (The Dock Arts, 2019), www.thedock.ie, accessed 20 April 2020.
45 Declan Long catalogue essay in *Clare Langan: The Floating World*, exh. cat., VISUAL Centre of Contemporary Art (Carlow, 2015), n.p.
46 *The Surrealist Map of the World* first appeared in a special issue of the Belgian periodical *Variétés* in 1929: 'Le Surréalisme en 1929'. An influential article by Jeremy W. Crampton explores maps as power, 'Maps as Social Constructions: Power, Communication and Visualization', *Progress in Human Geography*, XXV/2 (2001), p. 236.
47 See Meghan Kelly, 'Mapping Bodies, Designing Feminist Icons', *GeoHumanities*, VII/2 (2021) pp. 529–57.
48 Clarissa Farrell, 'Critique: Alice Maher and Rachel Fallon, "The Map"', *The VAN and mimiVAN*, https://visualartsireland.com, 26 January 2022.
49 I am indebted to the curator Maolíosa Boyle for supporting my study of *The Map*, and to Alice Maher and Rachel Fallon for answering my queries and providing invaluable information on the evolution and ideas behind their remarkable project. Other artists involved in the *Magdalene* series projects are the poet Sinéad Gleeson and the artist Jesse Jones.
50 As the writer Sue Hubbard has observed: 'If you were born in Heathen England, you may not be too familiar with Mary Magdalene . . . But if you've grown up in a Catholic country, particularly Ireland, her presence is ubiquitous.' Sue Hubbard, 'Alice Maher Rachel Fallon Explore The Magdalene', www.artlyst.com, 20 October 2021. For an excellent, poetic account by the writer Sue Rainsford, see 'The Map/We Are the Map, Rua Red, Dublin, 18 October 2021–29 January 2022', https://papervisualart.com, accessed 29 January 2022.
51 Maolíosa Boyle, curator's note in Alice Maher, Rachel Fallon, *The Map* (*The Magdalene Series*), exh. cat., Rua Red, (Dublin, 2021), n.p.
52 This interpretation is welcomed by the artists, who have encouraged multiple readings of their work (as explained in a seminar discussion of the work at Rua Red on 8 March 2022).
53 See Sharon Pace Macleod, *Celtic Myth and Religion: A Study of Traditional Belief* (London, 2011), especially pp. 199–200; Diana Leatham, *The Story of St Brigid of Ireland* (Leighton Buzzard, 1955).
54 For a brief discussion of strategies of metamorphosis, see Perry, 'Witches, Housewives and Mothers', pp. 20–22.
55 Maher described this 'eviscera' in a seminar discussion of the work at Rua Red on 8 March 2022.
56 These aspects are explored in Heather Hanna, *Women Framing Hair: Serial Strategies in Contemporary Art* (Cambridge, 2015). See especially 'Chapter Three: Flow, Tangle and Coil: Alice Maher's Feminine Tresses', pp. 55–92.
57 I am grateful to Sinéad Gleeson for permission to publish this extract from her poem.
58 Lynn Picknett, *Mary Magdalen* (New York, 2004), p. 2. For a recent research collection, see Claire McGettrick

et al., *Ireland and the Magdalene Laundries: A Campaign for Justice* (London, 2021).

59 Since the closure of Magdalene Laundries, research has revealed some disturbing statistics, including the illegal sale of these babies to American couples. See '2,000 Irish Children Were Illegally Adopted in US', www.irishcentral.com, 5 February 2013.

60 Picknett, *Mary Magdalen*, p. 5.

61 Discussed by Maher at a seminar at Rua Red, Dublin, 8 March 2022.

62 Barber, 'The Entangled Map and Irish Art', p. 26.

63 Rozsika Parker, *The Subversive Stitch: Embroidery and the Making of the Feminine* (London, 1984), p. 2.

7 FLOATING ISLANDS

1 See Stephanos Stephanides and Susan Bassnett, 'Islands, Literature and Cultural Translatability', in *Transtext(e)s Transcultures*, https://journals.openedition.org, accessed 23 September 2022.

2 Homer, *The Odyssey* (London, 2003), 10, 1–4.

3 Geographers, ethnographers and biologists from across the world have also been studying natural floating islands, which usually consist of floating aquatic plants, peat and mud, often found on marshlands and lakes, as in the famous La Rota in Posta Fibreno Lake, Italy. The Uru (or Uros) people of Peru and Bolivia live on more than forty floating islands made of reeds on Lake Titicaca, near Puno.

4 Richard Head, *The Floating Island* [1695] (Whitefish, MT, 2018).

5 Jules Verne, *The Floating Island; or, The Pearl of the Pacific* (New York, 1896).

6 W.J.T. Mitchell, ed., *Landscape and Power* (Chicago, IL, 1994), p. 1.

7 John Haber, 'Inside Out and Outside In', *Haber's Art Reviews*, www.haberarts.com, 24 September 2005.

8 Central Park was constructed on 314 hectares (778 ac) of land acquired by the city of New York and opened to the public in 1858.

9 Zittel explains the aims of this project in an interview first published in 2003, and republished in *Art 21* in November 2011: '"Pocket Property": Andrea Zittel', https://art21.org, accessed 16 March 2020.

10 In a series of works from the 1990s onwards, Zittel explored minimal, self-sufficient dwelling spaces in which everyday actions such as sleeping, eating, cooking and socializing are transformed into acts of art. For example, her 'A–Z West' is a group of small self-sufficient structures in the Californian desert, near Joshua Tree. See Richard Julin, *Andrea Zittel: Lay of My Land* (New York, 2011).

11 Richard McCoy, 'An Island in 100 Acres: An Interview with Andrea Zittel', www.magazine.art21.org, 21 January 2010.

12 This section includes a revised part-version of my essay published in *British Art Studies*: 'Landscaping Islands and Floating Histories in Contemporary British Art', *British Art Studies*, 10: 'Landscape Now', http://britishartstudies.ac.uk.

13 For a full illustrated account of the project see Alex Hartley et al., *Nowhereisland*, ed. Alex Hartley and Tania Kovats (London, 2015); and the website http://nowhereisland.org.

14 See discussion at pp. 216–17 of the *Nowhereisland* installation photographs at Liverpool in 2006. Much has now been written (across disciplines) on the nature and function of the archive and its theoretical underpinnings, including what has been described as 'the dialectic between storage and retrieval'. This is relevant to modern performance art and its photographic representations that (as some might argue) are perpetually reinstated as part of an ongoing work, although separate from the original event. In this sense, the archive becomes a part of the extended original work and is accorded value. In his book *Archive Fever: A Freudian Impression* (Chicago, IL, 1996), Jacques Derrida argues from Freudian psychoanalytic theory that the need to build and keep archives is a product of the repetition compulsion (also described as the 'death drive'). A key point made by Derrida that is relevant to this study is that the archivization produces as much as it records the event.

15 Claire Doherty, in 'Foreword' to Hartley, *Nowhereisland*, p. 11.

16 See, for example, Tim Burrows, 'Legacy, What Legacy? Five Years on the London Olympic Park Battle Still Rages', www.theguardian.com, 27 July 2017. Burrows argues that the promised 'affordable' housing commitment has not taken shape.

17 The ideological implications and ambitions of modernist architecture that 'reached for the skies' like a tower of Babel are discussed in Mark Crinson's fascinating

book *Rebuilding Babel: Modern Architecture and Internationalism* (London, 2017).

18 Lee Moran, 'Artist Gets £500,000 of Taxpayers' Money to Transport Vast Lump of Arctic Rock . . . and Take It on a Coastal Tour of Britain', www.dailymail.co.uk, 22 September 2011.

19 Claire Doherty, 'The Island as Social Form', in *Nowhereisland*, ed. Hartley and Kovats, p. 155.

20 Philip Hoare, *The Power of Islands*, quoted ibid., p. 113. Of course, 'utopia' is itself a much-debated notion, and Moore's *Utopia* an imaginary island society. Moreover, the term 'utopia' derives from the Greek terms *ou-topos* (meaning 'no place' or 'nowhere') and *eu-topos* (meaning 'good place'). Carl Gardner reflects on the problems of defining utopia and what the island should *not* be in his essay 'What Constitutes an Island State?', ibid., p. 108.

21 Ibid., pp. 156–7.

22 Debates rage among political theorists, sociologists and anthropologists as to what the concept of 'citizenship' means. A useful overview has been published by the Institute of Development Studies: Emma Jones and John Gaventa, eds, *Concepts of Citizenship: A Review*, IDS Bibliography 19 (Brighton, 2002).

23 Rana Dasgupta, *After Nations* (London, 2019).

24 The opening page of text of the 'Antarctica World Passport' (issued 2017) reads: 'The 1959 Antarctic Treaty counts 53 signatory nations who have declared Antarctica a common territory. The Madrid Protocol, ratified in 1991, has frozen mining until 2048 and banned industrial research or exploitation for 50 years. Military activity is similarly prohibited. Antarctica has become a land of peace, scientific research and international cooperation.'

25 Quoted ibid.

26 Tim Cresswell, *Place: An Introduction* (Oxford, 2015), p. 17.

27 Hartley, *Nowhereisland*, 'Moonrock', p. 175.

28 Doreen Massey, 'Landscape as a Provocation: Reflections on Moving Mountains', *Journal of Material Culture*, XI/1–2 (2006) p. 33. See also Massey's *For Space* (London, 2005).

29 See Alex Law's review of Jodie Matthews and Daniel Travers, *Islands and Britishness: A Global Perspective* (Newcastle upon Tyne, 2012) in *Island Studies Journal*, VII/1 (2012), p. 147.

30 Madeleine Bunting, 'Books about Our Island Mentality', *The Guardian*, 23 March 2019, p. 38.

31 Personal communication with the artist, 7 June 2021.

32 Elizabeth DeLoughrey, 'Island Writing, Creole Cultures', in *The Cambridge History of Postcolonial Literature* (Cambridge, 2012), pp. 802–3.

33 Edouard Glissant, *Caribbean Discourse* (Charlottesville, VA, 1989), p. 139.

8 GOING NORTH AND MELTING ICE

1 Roni Horn, 'Island Zombie', in *Island Zombie: Iceland Writings* (Princeton, NJ, 2020), p. 1.

2 The Icelandic mainland is a few degrees south of the Arctic Circle, which passes through Grimsey Island 40 kilometres (25 mi.) off the north coast.

3 Films include *Journey to the Centre of the Earth* (1959, dir. Henry Levin), starring James Mason and Pat Boone; *Journey to the Centre of the Earth* (2008, dir. Eric Brevig), starring Rick Schroder and Peter Fonda, was released as a DVD by The Asylum.

4 See Julie Reiss, 'Terra Incognita: Exhibiting Ice in the Anthropocene', in *Art, Theory and Practice in the Anthropocene*, ed. Reiss (Wilmington, DE, 2019), pp. 77–86.

5 Horn, 'Island Zombie', p. 1.

6 Roni Horn, *Island (Iceland): To Place*, vols 1–10 (New York and Cologne, 1990–2010); Roni Horn, *My Oz*, exh. cat., Reykjavik Art Museum (2007).

7 Horn, Keynote Speech, Reykjavik Art Museum, Reykjavik, 2006, reproduced in Horn, *My Oz*, p. 108.

8 Horn, interview with Jan Howard, in *Roni Horn* (London, 2000), p. 104.

9 Roni Horn, *Weather Reports You* (London and Gottingen, 2007), p. 194.

10 Horn, interview with Howard, p. 105.

11 Quoted in the Artangel booklet printed to accompany the project (2007), n.p.

12 Horn, *Weather Reports You*, pp. 9–10.

13 Ibid., p. 194.

14 Climate modellers are regularly updating predictions, as can be seen in the project and documentary *After Ice* (2021) from the University of Dundee in collaboration with the University of Iceland, which records the 'anthropogenically accelerated melt'. 'New Film Charts "Unprecedented" Decline of Iceland's Glaciers', www.dundee.ac.uk, accessed 21 February 2022.

15 Horn, *My Oz*, p. 103.
16 According to government figures, 73 per cent of electricity is provided by hydroelectric power and 26.8 per cent from geothermal energy: 'Iceland Is a Leader in Renewable Energy', www.visiticeland.com, accessed 23 June 2022.
17 'The Hidden Price of Iceland's Green Energy', www.savingiceland.org, accessed 23 June 2022.
18 This relates to my discussion in Chapter Three of the relevance of a range of artistic engagements with ecological concerns and 'eco-art'.
19 Horn, 'On the Obsolescence of Islands', *Island Zombie*, pp. 115–17.
20 Horn, *My Oz*, p. 10.
21 'Inner Geography: Interview with Jan Howard' [1994], quoted in *Roni Horn*, p. 102.
22 Briony Fer, 'On Site: Roni Horn', *ArtForum* (Summer 2007), pp. 173–6, www.artforum.com.
23 Horn has commented that the cold and dark provide 'the perfect climate for a game of chess, the ultimate indoor hobby . . . for a people beaten by the weather into being a people of few words (Artangel leaflet (2007), n.p.).
24 Horn, *Weather Reports You*, p. 10.
25 See Chapter Five for a discussion of the concept of 'cosmopolitanism'.
26 Claire Bishop, 'As if I Was Lost and Someone Suddenly Came to Give Me News about Myself', *Off Limits: 40 Artangel Projects* (London, 2002), p. 22.
27 Horn, *Weather Reports You*, p. 10.
28 Buckland organized a series of Cape Farewell expeditions to the Arctic, the Scottish Islands and the Andes (see 'Expeditions', www.capefarewell.com). Alex Hartley joined a Cape Farewell expedition to Svalbard in 2004. See Chapter Seven; and Andrew Brown, *Art and Ecology Now* (London, 2014), pp. 76–7.
29 Reiss, *Art, Theory and Practice in the Anthropocene*, p. 78.
30 First established in 1991 as a local art exhibition, from 1999 the festival was given an international profile and took on the name Lofoten International Art Festival.
31 See 'Lofoten International Art Festival LIAF', https://biennialfoundation.org, accessed 1 July 2022.
32 See www.lofotendeclaration.org, accessed 1 July 2022.
33 Oliver Basciano, 'Lofoten International Art Festival: Disappearing Acts', www.artreview.com, 25 November 2015.
34 Bruno Latour, 'Waiting for Gaia: Composing the Common World through Art and Politics', www.bruno-latour.fr, accessed 1 July 2022.
35 This island site is also the home of the contemporary art gallery, the Kaviar Factory, opened in 2013.
36 Orit Gat, 'Lofoten International Art Festival 2017, "I Taste the Future"', www.e-flux.com, accessed 2 July 2022.
37 Rachel Withers argues that *Artscape Nordland* 'offers an exemplary early model of good negotiating practice' for the commissioning of public art projects: 'How to Get Environmental Art Right', https://theconversation.com, accessed 2 July 2022.
38 Liv Helene Willumsen, *Witches of the North: Scotland and Finnmark* (Leiden, 2013).
39 For details of these trials, see ibid.

CONCLUSION: **ART ISLANDS, FUTURE ISLANDS AND END GAMES**

1 Laura Mansfield, 'The Island as a Model for the Interpretation and Development of Exhibitions of Contemporary Art beyond a Gallery Setting', PhD thesis, Manchester Metropolitan University (2015).
2 Mansfield's thesis included documentation of projects curated by the author that developed this island model. For example, her interactive game *Imaginary Islands – a Building Kit* invited individuals to construct imaginary island landscapes from illustrated cards. Ibid., p. 28ff.
3 Rosalind Krauss, 'The Cultural Logic of the Late Capitalist Museum', *October*, LIV (1990), pp. 3–7.
4 Frank Rose, 'The Swedish Museum that Babyborn Built', www.newyorktimes.com, 3 September 2015.
5 Kusama's *Yellow Pumpkin* has now been repaired and restored to its original position.
6 Cited by Lars Müller and Akiko Miki, *Insular Insight: Where Art and Architecture Conspire with Nature* (Baden, 2011), p. 18. Fukutake has explained his notion of 'public capitalism' arguing that his company objectives stand in opposition to 'financial capitalism'. He claims that money is not the sole objective of his economic activity; instead, 'Culture is my economics' (p. 28).
7 Ibid., p. 23.
8 See Phili Jodidio and Tadao Ando, *Tadao Ando at Naoshima: Art, Architecture, Nature* (Oakland, CA, 2006).
9 See 'Art House Project', https://benesse-artsite.jp, accessed 12 July 2022.

10 These issues and some problematic aspects of a 'globalized' art world are discussed in Gill Perry, 'Artists, Institutions and "Global" Art', in *Art after Empire: From Colonialism to Globalisation*, ed. Warren Carter (Manchester, 2018), pp. 98–131.
11 Cited in 'Hauser & Wirth's New Location on Isla del Rey Opens with Mark Bradford', www.artdaily.com, 27 July 2021.
12 Ibid.
13 Cited in Arden Sherman, 'Venice Biennale: Union of Comoros', *Dailyserving*, 24 June 2009.
14 Roni Horn, *Island Zombie: Iceland Writings* (Princeton, NJ, 2020), pp. 116–17.
15 Cited in Andrew Brown, *Art and Ecology Now* (London, 2014), p. 64.
16 Personal communication with the artist, 27 December 2022.
17 A prototype *Future Island* consisting of a large heated rock and wall graphics was shown at the 17th Venice Architecture Biennale in 2021. For the *Future Island* website and ongoing project, see 'Future Island: A Pioneer Landscape in Evolution on Albano University Campus', www.ooze.eu.com, accessed 23 January 2023.
18 Blum et al., 'Archipelagoes/Oceans/American Visuality', *Journal of Transnational American Visuality*, x/1 (2019), pp. 5ff.
19 In *Playing at Home: The House in Contemporary Art* (London, 2013), I explore some of the playful and subversive strategies adopted by women artists using the 'subversive potential of laughter' (pp. 19–20).
20 Issues explored in Gill Perry, ed., *Difference and Excess in Contemporary Art* (Oxford, 2004).
21 A useful exploration of the label 'feminist art' and its complicated relationship with art practices can be found in the Introduction to Hilary Robinson and Maria Elena Buszek, *A Companion to Feminist Art* (Oxford, 2019); for relevant explorations of gender and ecology see Alona Pardo, *RE/SISTERS: A Lens on Gender and Ecology*, exh.cat., Barbican Art Gallery (London, 2023), and Astrida Neimanis, *Bodies of Water: Posthuman Feminist Phenomenology* (London, 2017).
22 Andrea Schlieker, ed., *Cornelia Parker*, exh. cat., Tate Gallery (London, 2022), pp. 40–41.
23 Ibid.
24 Heidi Scott, 'Nature's Laboratories, Fiction's Fantasies: The Ecocritical Significance of Islands', *Academia Letters* (2021), p. 1, www.academia.edu.

BIBLIOGRAPHY

Arends, Bergit, and Siân Ede, eds, *Galápagos*, exh. cat., Calouste Gulbenkian Foundation, (London, 2012)

Armitage, David, and Alison Bashford, eds, *Pacific Histories: Ocean, Land, People* (Basingstoke, 2013)

Avery, Charles, *The Islanders: An Introduction* (London, 2008)

Baldacchino, Godfrey, 'The Coming of Age of Island Studies', *Tijdschrift voor Economische en Sociale Geografie*, cxv/3 (2004), pp. 272–83

—, 'Islands, Island Studies', *Island Studies Journal*, i/1 (2006), pp. 3–18

—, ed., *Bridging Islands: The Impact of Fixed Links* (New Brunswick, NJ, 2007)

—, 'Studying Islands: On Whose Terms? Some Epistemological and Methodological Challenges to the Pursuit of Island Studies', *Island Studies Journal*, iii/1 (2008), pp. 37–58

—, *The Routledge International Handbook of Island Studies* (London, 2018)

Ballard, J. G., *The Drowned World* (London, 1962)

—, *The Drought* (London, 1965)

—, *Concrete Island* (London, 1974)

Barber, Fionna, *Art in Ireland since 1910* (London, 2013)

—, 'The Entangled Map and Irish Art', in *Textiles, Community and Controversy: The Knitting Map*, ed. Jools Gibson, Nicola Moffat (London, 2015), pp. 30–31.

—, ed., 'Elliptical Affinities: Art, Feminism and the Body', in *Elliptical Affinities: Irish Women Artists and the Politics of the Body*, exh. cat., Highlanes Gallery (Drogheda, 2019)

Belting, Hans, Andrea Buddensieg and Peter Weibel, eds, *The Global Contemporary and the Rise of New Art Worlds* (Cambridge, MA, 2013)

Benitez-Rojo, Antonio, *The Repeating Island: The Caribbean and the Postmodern Perspective*, trans. James E. Maraniss (Durham, NC, 1996)

Billig, Volkmar, *Inseln: Geschichte einer Faszination* [Islands: The History of a Fascination] (Berlin, 2010)

Bishop, Claire, ed., *Participation, Documents of Contemporary Art* (London, 2006)

Blum, Hester, 'The Prospect of Oceanic Studies', *PMLA*, cxxv/3 (2010), p. 670

—, et al., 'Introduction to the Special Forum Archipelagoes/Oceans/American Visuality', *Journal of Transnational American Visuality*, x/1 (2019), pp. 1–21

Boettger, Suzaan, *Inside the Spiral: The Passions of Robert Smithson* (Minneapolis, MN, 2023)

Boland, Eavan, 'Mother Ireland', *Poetry Magazine: Contemporary Irish Poetry* (October/November 1995), p. 93

Bonnett, Alastair, *The Age of Islands: In Search of New and Disappearing Islands* (London, 2020)

Boyle, Charles [Jack Robinson], *Good Morning, Mr Crusoe* (London, 2019)

Brathwaite, Edward Kamau, *The Arrivants: A New World Trilogy* (Oxford, 1973)

—, *Middle Passages* (Newcastle upon Tyne, 1992)

—, 'Caribbean Man in Space and Time', *Small Axe*, xxv/3 (November 2021), pp. 90–104

Bregman, Rutger, *Humankind: A Hopeful History* (London, 2020)

Brown, Andrew, *Art and Ecology Now* (London, 2014)

Bush, Barbara, *Slave Women in Caribbean Society* (Kingston, Jamaica, 1990)

Camp, Stephanie M. H., *Closer to Freedom: Enslaved Women and Everyday Resistance in the Plantation South* (Chapel Hill, NC, 2004)

Campbell, Mavis Christine, *The Maroons of Jamaica, 1655–1796: A History of Resistance, Collaboration and Betrayal* (Trenton, NJ, 1990)

Cohen, Robin, *Island Societies* (Oxford, 2017)

Conkling, Philip, 'On Islanders and Islandness', *Geographical Review*, XCVII/2 (2007) pp. 191–201

Connell, John, 'Island Dreaming: The Contemplation of Polynesian Paradise', *Journal of Historical Geography*, XXIX/4 (2003), pp. 554–81

Cresswell, Tim, *Place: An Introduction* (Oxford, 2015)

Crofton, Ian, *Fringed with Mud and Pearls: An English Island Odyssey* (Edinburgh, 2021)

Cross, Dorothy, *Crossings* (London and Dublin, 2022)

Davis, Annalee, Jocelyn Gardner and Erica Moiah James, 'Introduction: Art as a Caribbean Feminist Practice', *Small Axe*, XXI/1, No 52 (March 2017), pp. 34–42

Davis, Sophia, 'Military Landscape and Secret Science: The Case of Orford Ness', *Cultural Geographies in Practice*, XV/1 (2008), pp. 143–9

De la Mare, Walter, *Desert Islands* (London, 1930)

Dean, Tacita, and Clarrie Wallis, *Tacita Dean* (London, 2001)

—, 'Tacita Dean: Selected Writings', in *Tacita Dean*, 6 vols (Paris, 2003), vol. I

—, *Tacita Dean: Teignmouth Electron* [1999] (Göttingen, Steidl, 2009)

Deleuze, Gilles, *Desert Islands and Other Texts, 1953–74* (Paris, 2004)

DeLoughrey, Elizabeth, *Routes and Roots: Navigating Pacific and Caribbean Island Literatures* (Honolulu, HI, 2007)

—, 'Radiation Ecologies and the Wars of Light', *Modern Fiction Studies* (*MFS*), LV/3 (Fall 2009), pp. 468–98

—, 'Pacific Literature and the Environment: Nuclear Fallout as Climate Change', *Dreadlocks: Oceans, Islands and Skies*, Proceedings of the Oceanic Conference on Creativity and Climate Change, VI/VII (2010–11), pp. 127–42

—, 'Island Writing, Creole Cultures', in *The Cambridge History of Postcolonial Literature*, (Cambridge, 2012), vol. II, pp. 802–3

—, *Allegories of the Anthropocene* (Durham, NC, 2019)

Demos, T. J., *The Migrant Image: The Art and Politics of Documentary during Global Crisis* (Durham, NC, 2013)

—, *Decolonising Nature: Contemporary Art and the Politics of Ecology* (Berlin, 2016)

—, *Visual Culture and Environment Today* (Berlin, 2017)

—, *Against the Anthropocene: Visual Culture and Environment Today* (Berlin, 2017)

—, Emily Scott and Subhankar Banerjee, *The Routledge Companion to Contemporary Art, Visual Culture and Climate Change* (London, 2021)

Enemoto, Joy Lehuanani, 'Reclaiming the 'Illi of Haukulu and 'Aihulama', in Hokulani K. Aikau and Vernadette Vicuña Gonzalez, *Detours: A Decolonial Guide to Hawai'i* (Durham, NC, 2019), pp. 173–81

Farquharson, Alex, and David A. Bailey, eds, *Life Between Islands: Caribbean-British Art 1950s–Now*, exh. cat., Tate Gallery (London, 2021)

Fer, Briony, *Louise Bourgeois: Imaginary Conversations*, exh. cat., National Museum of Norway, Oslo (2023)

Folley, Aideen, 'Understanding Islandness', *Annals of the American Association of Geographers*, 8 May 2023, pp. 1–18

Foucault, Michel, *Discipline and Punish: The Birth of the Prison* [1975] (London, 2020)

Fowkes, Maja and Reuben, *Art and Climate Change* (London, 2022)

Fowles, John, and Fay Godwin, *Islands* (London, 1978)

—, *The Magus* [1966] (London, 2004)

Franks, Jill, *Islands and the Modernists: The Allure of Isolation in Art, Literature and Science* (Jefferson, NC, and London, 2006)

Freitag, Barbara, *Hy Brasil: The Metamorphosis of an Island: From Cartographic Error to Celtic Elysium*, Textxet: Studies in Comparative Literature (Brill, 2013), vol. LXIX

Gaini, Firouz, and Helene Pristed Nielsen, eds, *Gender and Island Communities* (London, 2021)

Gerhardt, Christina, *Sea Change: An Atlas of Islands in a Rising Ocean* (Oakland, CA, 2023)

Giraudoux, Jean, *Suzanne and the Pacific*, trans. Ben Rya Redman (New York and London, 1923)

Glissant, Edouard, *Caribbean Discourse: Selected Essays* (Charlottesville, VA, 1989)

Godfrey, Mark, Susie Boyt and Bob Stanley, *Rodney Graham* (Oxford, 2017)

Gómez-Barris, Marcarena, and May Joseph, 'Coloniality and Islands', *Shima*, XIII/2 (2019), pp. 2–10

Graham, Rodney, et al., *Island Thought*, vol. I, Summer 1997, Canada, XLVII Biennale di Venezia (Ghent, 1997)

Grant, Catherine, and Dorothy Rowe, 'Decolonising Art History', *Art History*, LXIII/1 (2020), pp. 8–66

Graziani, Ron, *Robert Smithson and the American Landscape* (Cambridge, 2004)

Grydehøj, Adam, 'A Future of Island Studies', *Island Studies Journal*, XXII/1 (2017), pp. 3–16

—, and Yaso Nadarajah, 'Island Studies as a Decolonial Project', *Island Studies Journal*, XI/2 (2016)

Hall, Stuart, *Familiar Stranger: A Life between Two Islands* (Durham, NC, 2014)

Hamilton Faris, Jaimey, 'Sisters of Ocean and Ice: On the Hydro-Feminism of Kathy Jetñil-Kijiner and Aka Niviâna's *Rise: From One Island to Another*', *Shima*, XIII/2 (2019), pp. 76–99

Harris, Alexandra, Alan Hollinghust et al., *Landscape, Portrait, Still Life* (London, 2018)

Hartley, Alex, *Not Part of Your World*, exh. cat., Fruitmarket Gallery (Edinburgh, 2007)

—, *Nowhereisland*, with Tim Cresswell, Claire Doherty, Jeffrey Kastner and Tania Kovats (London, 2015)

Hau'ofa, Epeli, *We Are the Ocean: Selected Works* (Honolulu, HI, 2008)

Hay, Peter, 'A Phenomenology of Islands', *Island Studies Journal*, I/1 (2006), pp. 19–42

—, 'What the Sea Portends', *Island Studies Journal*, VIII/2 (2013), pp. 209–32

Hoare, Philip, *The Sea Inside* (London, 2014)

—, Doireann Ní Ghríofa and Declan Long, *Dorothy Cross: Crossing* (London and Dublin, 2022), pp. 161–6

Horn, Roni, *My Oz*, exh. cat., Reykjavik Art Museum (Reykjavík, 2007)

—, *Weather Reports You* (London and Göttingen, 2007
Island Studies Journal, https://islandstudiesjournal.org

—, *Island Zombie: Iceland Writings* (Princeton, NJ, and Oxford, 2020)

Jetñil-Kijiner, Kathy, *Iep Jaltok: Poems from a Marshallese Daughter* (Tucson, AZ, 2017)

Johnson, Donald S., *Phantom Islands of the Atlantic: The Legends of Seven Lands that Never Were* (London, 1997)

Julin, Richard, *Andrea Zittel: Lay of My Land* (New York, 2011)

Kafka, Franz, *In the Penal Colony* [1914] (Kindle edition, 2014)

Kaminsky, Ilya, *I See a Silence* (London, 2021)

Karides, Marina, 'Why Island Feminism?', *Shima*, XI/1 (2017), pp. 30–39

King, Natalie, 'Camping Paradise: I Am What I Am', in *Paradise Camp by Yuki Kihara*, ed. Natalie King, exh. cat., New Zealand Pavilion, Venice Biennale (Wellington and Melbourne, 2022)

Koa Dunsford, Cathie, 'Kaitiakitanga: Protecting our Oceans, Islands and Skies by Inspiring a Climate Change', *Dreadlocks: Oceans, Islands and Skies*, Proceedings of the Oceanic Conference on Creativity and Climate Change, VI/VII (2010–11)

Krauss, Rosalind, 'The Cultural Logic of the Late Capitalist Museum', *October*, LIV (1990), pp. 3–7

Lane, David Christopher, ed., *Plato's Sunken Island: The Historical-Myth of Atlantis* (Walnut, CA, 2020)

Laughlin, Nicholas, ed., *So Many Islands: Stories from the Caribbean, Mediterranean, Indian and Pacific Oceans* (London, 2018)

Lawrence, D. H., *The Man Who Loved Islands*, in *Love Among the Haystacks and Other Stories* (London, 1960)

Liang, Jack, *Rodney Graham: Vexation Island and Other Works: Another Day in Paradise*, exh. cat., Art Gallery of York University (Toronto, 1998)

Long, Declan, *Clare Langan: The Floating World* (Carlow, 2015)

McCall, Grant, 'Nissology: A Proposal for Consideration', *Journal of the Pacific Society*, XVII/2–3, 63–4 (1994), pp. 1–14

McCoy, Richard, 'An Island in 100 Acres: An Interview with Andrea Zittel', www.magazine.art21.org, 21 January 2010

McD. Beckles, Hilary, *Natural Rebels: A Social History of Enslaved Black Women in Barbados* (New Brunswick, NJ, 1989)

—, *Centering Woman: Gendered Discourse in Caribbean Slave Society* (Princeton, NJ, 1999)

—, *The First Black Slave Society: Britain's Barbados, 1636–1876* (Kingston, Jamaica, 2016)

McGettrick, Claire, et al., *Ireland and the Magdalene Laundries: A Campaign for Justice* (London, 2021)

Macmillan, Kate, *Empire of Islands: Contemporary Art and Unforgetting in Colonial Landscapes* (London, 2019

Mack, John, *The Sea: A Cultural History* (London, 2001)

Mansfield, Laura, 'The Island as a Model for the Interpretation and Development of Exhibitions of Contemporary Art beyond a Gallery Setting', PhD thesis, Manchester Metropolitan University (2015)

Mar, T. B., *Decolonisation and the Pacific* (Cambridge, 2016)

Marsden, Philip, *The Summer Isles: A Voyage of the Imagination* (London, 2019)

Massey, Doreen, *For Space* (London, 2005)

—, 'Landscape as a Provocation: Reflections on Moving Mountains', *Journal of Material Culture*, XI/1–2 (2006), pp. 33–48

Mathurin Mair, Lucille, *The Rebel Woman in the British West Indies during Slavery* (Kingston, Jamaica, 1995)

Matthews, Jodie, and Daniel Travers, *Islands and Britishness: A Global Perspective* (Newcastle upon Tyne, 2012)

Meskimmon, Marsha, *Contemporary Art and the Cosmopolitan Imagination* (London, 2010)

Mitchell, W.J.T., ed., *Landscape and Power* (Chicago, IL, 1994)

Mohammed, Patricia, ed., *Gendered Realities: An Anthology of Essays in Caribbean Feminist Thought* (Mona, Jamaica, 2002)

Morris, Stuart, *Portland: An Illustrated History* (Wimborne, Dorset, 1985)

Mountz, Alison, 'Political Geography II: Islands and Archipelagos', *Progress in Human Geography*, XXXIX/5 (2015), pp. 634–6

—, and Linda Briskman, 'Introducing Island Detentions: The Placement of Asylum Seekers and Migrants on Islands', *Shima*, VI/2 (2012), pp. 21–6

Müller, Lars, and Akiko Miki, *Insular Insight: Where Art and Architecture Conspire with Nature* (Baden, 2011)

Munroe, R. W., *Scottish Lighthouses* (Stornaway, 1979)

Nancollas, Tom, *Seashaken Houses: A Lighthouse History from Eddystone to Fastnet* (London, 2019)

Nash, Catherine, 'Gender and Landscape in Ireland' [1993], in *Sources in Irish Art: A Reader*, ed. Fintan Cullen (Cork, 2000), pp. 302–8

Neale, Tom, *An Island to Oneself* (London, 1966)

Neimanis, Astrida, *Bodies of Water: Posthuman Feminist Phenomenology* (London, 2017)

Nepomuceno, Nicole M., 'Yuki Kihara – Trouble in Paradise', *ArtAsiaPacific*, 129 (July/August 2009), www.artsasiapacific.com

Nicholson, Christopher, *Rock Lighthouses of Britain: The End of an Era?* (Caithness, Scotland, 1995)

Nunn, P. D., *Oceanic Islands* (Oxford, 1994)

Obeyesekere, Gananath, *The Apotheosis of Captain Cook: European Mythmaking in Pacific* (Princeton, NJ, 1997)

O'Brien, Edna, *Mother Ireland: A Memoir* [1976] (New York, 1999)

Olah, Nathalie, 'Cruel Voyeurism: Why Reality TV Shows Are Inherently Bad for Contestants' Mental Health', *New Statesman*, www.newstatesman.com, 5 June 2019

Owens, Craig, 'The Allegorical Impulse: Towards a Theory of Postmodernism', *October*, XII (Spring 1980), pp. 67–86

Palmer, Katrina, *End Matter* (Artangel, London, 2015)

Pardo, Alona, *RE/SISTERS: A Lens on Gender and Ecology*, exh.cat., Barbican Art Gallery (London, 2023)

Pearson, Nels, 'Recovering Islands: Scotland, Ocean and Archipelago in *To the Lighthouse*', *Twentieth-Century Literature*, LXIV/3 (2018), pp. 347–70

Perry, Gill, *Playing at Home: The House in Contemporary Art* (London, 2013)

—, 'Artists, Institutions and "Global" Art', in *Art after Empire: From Colonialism to Globalisation*, ed. Warren Carter (Manchester, 2018), pp. 98–131

—, 'Landscaping Islands and Floating Histories in Contemporary British Art', *British Art Studies*, 10 (2018): 'Landscape Now', https://britishartstudies.ac.uk/issues/issue-index/issue-10/landscaping-islands

—, 'Witches, Housewives and Mothers: Crossing (Irish) Borders in the Body Politic', in *Elliptical Affinities: Irish Women Artists and the Politics of the Body*, ed. Barber, exh. cat., Highlanes Gallery (Drogheda, 2019), pp. 19–27

—, ed., *Difference and Excess in Contemporary Art: The Visibility of Women's Practice* (Oxford, 2004)

Picknett, Lynn, *Mary Magdalen* (New York, 2004)

Pih, Darren, *Radical Landscapes: Art, Identity and Activism* (London, 2022)

Plato, *Timaeus* (London, 1965)

Pollock, Griselda, 'Feminism and Language', in *A Companion to Feminist Art*, ed. Hilary Robinson, Maria Elena Buszek (2019), pp. 261–81

Pugh, Jonathan, 'Island Movements: Thinking with the Archipelago', *Island Studies Journal*, VIII/1 (2013), pp. 9–34

—, 'The Relational Turn in Island Geographies: Bringing together Island, Sea and Ship Relations and the Case of the Landship', *Social and Cultural Geography*, XVII/8 (2016), pp. 1–20

—, 'Relationality and Island Studies in the Anthropocene', *Island Studies Journal*, XIII/2 (2018), pp. 93–110

—, 'The Power of Thinking with Islands', interview with L. DeAngelo and E. Angliker, *Mare Nostrum*, XXII/2 (2021) pp. 265–77

—, and David Chandler, *Anthropocene Islands: Entangled Worlds* (London, 2021)

—, and David Chandler, *The World as Abyss: The Caribbean and Critical Thought in the Anthropocene* (London, 2023)

Ramsay, Maya, 'Re-Framing the Debate: The Art of Lampedusa', *Crossings: Journal of Migration and Culture*, VII/2 (October 2016)

Randall, James E., *An Introduction to Island Studies* (Charlottetown, PEI, Canada, 2021)

Reiss, Julie, *Art, Theory and Practice in the Anthropocene* (Wilmington, DE, 2019)

Rhys, Jean, *Wide Sargasso Sea* [1966] (London, 1997)

Robinson, Hilary, and Maria Elena Buszek, eds, *A Companion to Feminist Art* (Oxford, 2019)

Ronström, Owe, 'Remoteness, Islands and Islandness', *Island Studies Journal*, XVI/2 (November 2021), pp. 207–97

Royle, Stephen M., *Islands: Nature and Culture* (London, 2014)

Rutazibwa, Olivia U., and Robbie Shilliam, *The Routledge Handbook of Postcolonial Politics* (London, 2018)

Said, Edward, *Orientalism: Western Concepts of the Orient* (New York, 1978)

Sampson, Barney, *Desert Islands and the Liquid Modern* (London, 2018)

Sant, Andrew, *The Lives and Times of the Islanders* (Nottingham, 2009)

Schlieker, Andrea, ed., *Cornelia Parker*, exh. cat., Tate Gallery (London, 2022)

Schwapp, Melanie, 'Granny Dead', in *So Many Islands*, ed. Nicholas Laughlin (London, 2018), pp. 63–70

Scott, Heidi, 'Havens and Horrors: The Island Landscape', *Interdisciplinary Studies in Literature and the Environment* (Oxford, 2014), pp. 1–22

—, 'Nature's Laboratories, Fiction's Fantasies: The Ecocritical Significance of Islands', *Academia Letters* (2021), pp. 1–4, www.academia.edu

Scott, John, and Zoe Staines, 'Charting the Place of Islands in Criminology: On Isolation, Integration and Insularity', *Theoretical Criminology*, XXV/4 (2020), www.journals.sagepub.com

Sharpley, Richard, 'Island Tourism or Tourism on Islands', *Tourism, Recreation, Research*, XXXVII/2 (2012), pp. 167–72

Shaxson, Nicholas, *Treasure Islands: Tax Havens and the Men Who Stole the World* (London, 2011)

Shell, Marc, *Islandology: Geography, Rhetoric, Politics* (Stanford, CA, 2014)

Shima: The International Journal of Research into Island Cultures, www.shimajournal.org

Sleeman, Joy, 'The Possibility of an Island', in *Simon Faithfull: Does the World Exist When I'm Not There?* (Laconic, 2016), n.p.

Smallman, Etan, 'Why I Made Captain Cook Lose His Breeches: Lisa Reihana on Her Colonial Epic Video', www.theguardian.com, 15 October 2018

Smithson, Robert, *Robert Smithson: The Collected Writings*, ed. Jack Flam (Berkeley, CA, 1966)

Spivak, Gayatri Chakravorty, 'Musings on the World-Island', *International Journal of Okinawan Studies*, III/1 (2012), p. 81

Stephanides, Stephanos, and Susan Bassnett, 'Islands, Literature and Cultural Translatability', *Transtext(e)s Transcultures: Journal of Cultural Studies*, I/3 (2008), pp. 5–21

Stratford, Elaine, ed., *Island Geographies: Essays and Conversations* (London, 2017)

—, 'Islands, the Anthropocene, and Decolonisation', *Antipode*, LV/4 (2023), pp. 1255–74

Syperek, Pandora, and Sarah Wade, eds, *Oceans: Documents of Contemporary Art* (London, 2023)

Thomas, Nicholas, *Discoveries: The Voyages of Captain Cook* (London, 2004)

—, *Islanders: The Pacific in the Age of Empire* (London, 2010)

—, *Oceanic Art* (London, 2019)

—, *Voyagers: The Settlement of the Pacific* (London, 2021)

—, *Possessions: Indigenous Art/Colonial Culture/ Decolonisation* (London, 2022)

—, *Gauguin and Polynesia* (London, 2024)

Uekötter, Frank, 'War, Peace and Guano', in *Dinh Q. Lê, the Colony*, ed. Jonathan Watkins and Jenine McGaughran (Manchester, 2016)

Verne, Jules, *The Floating Island; or, The Pearl of the Pacific* (New York, 1896)

Von Burg, Alessandra, 'Citizenship Islands: The Ongoing Emergency in the Mediterranean Sea', *Media and Communication*, VII/2 (2019), pp. 218–29

Wainwright, Jean, ed., *Ship to Shore: Art and the Lure of the Sea*, exh. cat., John Hansard Gallery (Southampton, 2018)

Wainwright, Leon, *Timed Out: Art and the Transnational Caribbean* (Manchester, 2011)

—, *Phenomenal Difference: A Philosophy of Black British Art* (Liverpool, 2017)

Warner, Marina, *Indigo; or, Mapping the Waters* (London, 1993)

—, 'Passionate Cruces: The Art of Dorothy Cross', in *Dorothy Cross*, exh. cat., Irish Museum of Modern Art (Dublin, 2005), p. 28

—, 'The Mimic Net', in *Alison Turnbull: Psyche; or, The Butterfly – An Expanded Field Work* (Más Arta Más Acción (London, 2018), pp. 52–62

Watson, Mark, and Robert Potter, *Low-Cost Housing in Barbados: Evolution or Social Revolution?* (Kingston, Jamaica, 1995)

Willumsen, Liv Helene, *Witches of the North: Scotland and Finnmark* (Leiden, 2013)

Wood, Paul, and Leon Wainwright, eds, *The West in the World* (Oxford, 2021)

Woolf, Virginia, *To the Lighthouse* [1927] (London, 2004)

Yarnall, Judith, *Transformations of Circe: The History of an Enchantress* (Urbana, IL, 1994)

Zobel Marshall, Emily, *Anansi's Journey: A Story of Jamaican Cultural Resistance* (Kingston, Jamaica, 2012)

ACKNOWLEDGEMENTS

Many artists, friends, colleagues, researchers and writers across disciplines have generously assisted my project. Their ideas and knowledge of island histories across the world have enriched my research. I have long admired the poetry of the Australian British poet Andrew Sant, known for his many publications on islands and islanders. His generic, often mischievous poems on island subjects relate to many of the themes of my book. He encouraged my project and kindly agreed to let me reproduce two thought-provoking, relevant poems to top and tail the text. Sant's anthology *The Lives and Times of the Islanders* (Shoestring Press, Nottingham, 2009) is the source for the two poems used. His most recent book is *Near the Border: New and Selected Poems* (Shoestring Press/Puncher and Wattmann, Nottingham, 2023). I am also grateful to his publishers, Shoestring Press, for supporting the inclusion of his work.

Several colleagues read all or parts of my text and gave me invaluable feedback and suggestions. I am hugely indebted to Michael Corris whose careful reading and detailed comments on an earlier draft helped to improve the final text. I have ranged across specialisms within and beyond art history and have benefited greatly from the comments on various chapters by Barney Samson, Fionna Barber, Leon Wainwright, Karen McLean, Davina Thackara and Barry Curtis. I am very grateful for early research support from Dilys Bidewell, and invaluable picture research by Eleanor Anderson. As I have nervously ventured into the multidisciplinary area of 'Island Studies' I must acknowledge the influence of the pioneering work of many scholars from other subject areas. They include Elizabeth DeLoughrey, Godfrey Baldacchino, Jonathan Pugh, David Chandler and Adam Grydehøj, among others. Jonathan Pugh was also kind enough to discuss ideas with me and helped to fertilize some of my art historical meanderings on the subject.

I am also hugely indebted to many of the artists discussed not only for their inspiring work, but also for queries answered and information and material provided, and the provision of high-resolution image files for reproduction. These include Rodney Graham, Karen McLean, Cornelia Parker, Alison Turnbull, Katrina Palmer, Kathy Jetñil-Kijiner, Joy Enomoto, Annalee Davies, Lisa Reihana, Gemma Anderson, Clare Langan, Antti Laitinen, Paolo Tamburella, Rachel Whiteread, Alfredo Jaar, Alex Hartley, Tania Kovats, Mike Perry, Kathy Prendergast, Alice Maher and Rachel Fallon, Jesse Jones, Dorothy Cross, Yuki Kihara, Ana Adahl, Marcus Coates and Ooze Architects. Many galleries and curators have also kindly supported the project and supplied images, including Nicholas Logsdail and Sharon Essor at the Lisson Gallery, London, Dale Mcfarland and Jane Hamlyn at Frith Street Gallery, London, Maoliosa Boyle at Rua Red Dublin, Rebecca Hossack at Rebecca Hossack Art Gallery, London, Aoife Ruane at Highlanes Gallery, Drogheda, Jaimey Hamilton Faris at the University of Hawai'i, Clive Coward at Tate Images, Hauser & Wirth London and Menorca, Victoria Miro Gallery, London, Alison Jacques Gallery, London, Block 336, Brixton, Walsall Art Gallery, Tate Gallery London, The British Library and Artangel Archives. Many innovative commissions on the island theme by the Arts Charity Artangel have inspired my research. Directors James Lingwood, Michael Morris and more recently Mariam Zulfiqar, have provided invaluable information on relevant projects. I am also grateful to Sinead Gleeson and Kathy Jetñil-Kijiner for kindly allowing me to reproduce extracts from their poems. Many friends and colleagues offered useful advice and discussed ideas, including Martin Harris, Jon Bird, Liz Rideal, Dilys Bidewell, Susan Siegfried, Alex Potts, Briony Fer, Anna Robins, Paul Wood, Emma Barker, Jonathan Watkins, Greg Hilty, Iwona Blazwick, Gilda Williams, Marcia Pointon, Lisa Tickner, Sandy Nairne, Steve Edwards, Ann Jones, Ray Forrest, Shannon Oksanen, Lucy Bland, Lynda Nead, Joanna Woodall, Jill Howitt, Liz Rivers and Tessa McWatt.

I am indebted to Michael Leaman and the staff at Reaktion Books, who enthusiastically took on a wide-ranging visual arts project with a daunting number of illustrations; Alex Ciobanu, Martha Jay and my copy-editor have done sterling work in helping to produce the book. Although it ranges across continents, my project has an emphasis on British and British ex-colonial works and the cost of reproductions was supported by a publications grant from the Paul Mellon Centre for Studies in British Art, for which I am deeply grateful. I owe so much to the support of my family and close friends, who have patiently listened to, encouraged and sometimes challenged my ideas on and about islands and art, over many years. I even dare to hope that my very young grandchildren Alfie and Lyra, who both have a passion for sea creatures and stories of ocean life, will one day read and enjoy the book. It is partly dedicated to them.

The book is primarily dedicated to the artist Rodney Graham (1949–2022). Before his death in 2022 he enthusiastically discussed my project with me. With his characteristic modesty and wry humour, he shared ideas, information and generously supplied images of his work. Based in Vancouver, he was a hugely talented artist, performer, photographer, filmmaker, painter and musician, whose diverse works used ironic quotation, reference and mimicry to question and enrich our relationship with the world. He was also a good friend of nearly thirty years. He is very much missed.

PHOTO ACKNOWLEDGEMENTS

The author and publishers wish to express their thanks to the sources listed below for illustrative material and/or permission to reproduce it. Every effort has been made to contact copyright holders; should there be any we have been unable to reach or to whom inaccurate acknowledgements have been made please contact the publishers, and full adjustments will be made to any subsequent printings. Some locations of artworks are also given below, in the interest of brevity:

© ADAGP, Paris and DACS, London 2024, photo Thierry Bal, courtesy Lucy + Jorge Orta: 109; © Anna Ådahl: 121, 122; Alamy Stock Photo: 12 (DreamWorks Pictures/TCD/Prod.DB), 17 (Photo 12), 27 (Ian Cowe), 28 (Peter Alvey), 33 (BFA/A24), 39 (dpa Picture Alliance Archive), 57 (Cindy Hopkins), 67 (Searchlight Pictures/Entertainment Pictures), 68 (Searchlight Pictures/Moviestore Collection Ltd), 69 (Tuul and Bruno Morandi/mauritius images GmbH), 90 (Masheter Movie Archive); © Gemma Anderson: 44; © Artangel, commissioned and produced by Artangel, 2007: 113, 115 (photo Stefan Altenburger), 116, 117; courtesy Artangel and Book Works, commissioned by Artangel in association with BBC Radio 4, presented on Portland by Artangel in association with b-side, with the support of the Henry Moore Foundation: 51; photo Thierry Bal, exhibition commissioned and produced by Artangel, presented in partnership with the National Trust: 53; © Black River Productions, Ltd/Mitch Epstein, courtesy of Galerie Thomas Zander, Cologne, used with permission (all rights reserved): 133; © Sonia Boyce, all rights reserved, DACS/Artimage 2024, photo William Cummins: 80; © Mark Bradford, photo Stefan Altenburger, courtesy the artist and Hauser & Wirth: 131; British Library, London: 70 (Maps K.Top.123.114), 77 (Maps K.Top.123.49); British Museum, London (2015,8039.1), © Francesco Tuccio, photo © The Trustees of the British Museum: 64; © David Buckland and Amy Balkin: 118; © 2023 CNES/Airbus (data SIO, NOAA, U.S. Navy, NGA, GEBCO): 1; courtesy Marcus Coates: 45, 46; © Dorothy Cross: 47, 91, 93; courtesy Annalee Davis: 71, 72; courtesy Tacita Dean, Frith Street Gallery, London and Marian Goodman Gallery, New York, Los Angeles and Paris: 29, 30; collection Dia Art Foundation, © Holt/Smithson Foundation/Licensed by ARS, New York and DACS, London: 36, 37 (gift of Nancy Holt); collection Dia Art Foundation, photo Gianfranco Gorgoni, 1970, © Holt/Smithson Foundation and Dia Art Foundation/Licensed by ARS, New York and DACS, London: 7; © The Easton Foundation/Licensed by VAGA at ARS, New York and DACS, London, photo Guri Dahl/LB Art: 126; © Estate of Donald Locke, photo © Tate (Oliver Cowling): 79; photo © Briony Fer, courtesy Peter Zumthor: 125; Getty Images: 3 (John Raymond Elliott/Fairfax Media), 18 (Robert Voets/CBS), 65 (Luca Zanon/Awakening), 108 (Andrea Baldo/LightRocket), 127 (Blom UK), 128 (Veronique Durruty/Gamma-Rapho); © Rodney Graham, courtesy Lisson Gallery, London: 14, 15, 34 (photo Ken Adlard); © Alex Hartley, courtesy the artist: 23, 25, 103, 104, 105, 106, 107; courtesy Hauser & Wirth: 130; © Holt/Smithson Foundation/Licensed by ARS, New York and DACS, London: 38, 101 (photo Andrew Cross); Irish Museum of Modern Art (IMMA), Dublin (Donation, Vincent & Noeleen Ferguson, 1996, IMMA.775), © Kathy Prendergast, photo courtesy the artist and IMMA: 88; Irish Museum of Modern Art (IMMA), Dublin (Purchase, 2000, IMMA.1351), © Pauline Cummins, photo courtesy the artist and IMMA: 92; courtesy Alfredo Jaar: 58, 59; courtesy Kathy Jetñil-Kijiner and Aka Niviâna: 40; courtesy Kathy Jetñil-Kijiner and Joy Lehuanani Enomoto: 41 (photo Kelly Ciurej), 42; © Joan Jonas/ARS, New York/DACS, London, courtesy the artist and Gladstone Gallery: 112; courtesy Jesse Jones: 87; © Isaac Julien, courtesy the artist and Victoria Miro: 62, 82; © Anish Kapoor, all rights reserved, DACS/Artimage 2024: 123; courtesy Yuki Kihara, photos Luke Walker: 20, 21; courtesy Tania Kovats: 110, 111; courtesy Antti Laitinen: 16; courtesy Clare Langan: 95; © The Late Estate of Broomberg & Chanarin, all rights reserved, DACS, London, courtesy the artists and Goodman Gallery, Johannesburg: 63; courtesy Dinh Q. Lê, commissioned by Artangel, Ikon, Birmingham, Han Nefkens H+F Collection and Proyecto Amil, Lima (with additional support from Catherine Petitgas, private collection, New York and Shoshana Wayne Gallery), and produced by Artangel and TANQ Studios: 26; Library of Congress, Prints and Photographs Division, Washington, DC: 9; © Richard Long, all rights reserved, DACS, London, photo Education Images/Universal Images Group via Getty Images: 129; courtesy Karen McLean: 73, 74, 75 (photo Mark Hinton), 76, 78, 85 (courtesy Block 336, London); © Emma McNally, commissioned for Artangel's Company of Angels, 2021: 55; © Steve McQueen, courtesy the artist, Thomas Dane Gallery, London and Marian Goodman Gallery, New York, Los Angeles and Paris: 83; © Alice Maher and Rachel Fallon, courtesy the artists: 97, 98, 99, 100; Middlesbrough Collection at MIMA, the Middlesbrough Institute of Modern Art (Purchased with Assistance from the Art Fund and Arts Council England/Victoria and Albert Museum Purchase Grant Fund), © Lubaina Himid, photo Jason Hynes, reproduced courtesy the artist, MIMA and Hollybush Gardens, London: 81; Museum of Fine Arts, Boston (Tompkins Collection – Arthur Gordon Tompkins Fund, 36.270): 4; National Gallery of Art, Prague (NG 480/2023), © courtesy Ai Weiwei Studio, photo © 2024 National Gallery Prague: 60; © Chris Ofili, courtesy the artist and Tate, London: 84; © OOZE 2021: 135; courtesy Cornelia Parker and Frith Street Gallery, London, photo © Tate (Matt Greenwood): 136; photos Gill Perry: 50, 52, 56; courtesy Mike Perry: 134; private collection, © Kathy Prendergast, photo courtesy the artist: 89; Queensland Art Gallery | Gallery of Modern Art, Brisbane (Purchased 2015 with funds from the Queensland Art Gallery | Gallery of Modern Art Foundation Appeal and Paul and Susan Taylor, 2015.045), © Lisa Reihana, photo courtesy QAGOMA: 19; photo Timothy Schenck, © Rachel Whiteread, courtesy the artist, the Trust for Governors Island and Luhring Augustine, New York: 24; Shutterstock: 2 (Two Arts/Cd/Kobal), 22 (Ingrid Abery); Shutterstock.com: 8 (Ppitooo), 43 (Peter Hermes Furian), 66 (Pandora Pictures), 86 (MNStudio), 114 (AventuraSur.photo), 120 (RuslanKphoto); Smithsonian American Art Museum, Washington, DC (Gift of William T. Evans, 1910.9.4): 6; © Tavares Strachan, courtesy the artist and Marian Goodman Gallery, New York, Los Angeles and Paris: 119; © Paolo W. Tamburella, courtesy the artist: 132; © Tatiana Trouvé, commissioned and produced by Artangel, presented by Artangel in partnership with the National Trust: 54; courtesy Alison Turnbull and Matt's Gallery, London: 48, 49; collection Vågan County, Norway, courtesy the Estate of Dan Graham and Lisson Gallery, London, photo TMAg/Shutterstock.com: 124; photo Wolfgang Volz/laif/Camera Press, © 1983 Christo and Jeanne-Claude Foundation: 5; collection Weatherspoon Art Museum at the University of North Carolina, Greensboro (Museum purchase with funds from the Dillard Paper Company for the Dillard Collection, 1969.1674), © Holt/Smithson Foundation/Licensed by ARS, New York and DACS, London: 35; © Catherine Yass, all rights reserved, DACS, London, photos courtesy the artist and Galerie Lelong, New York: 31, 32; Zentralbibliothek Zürich: 94; © Andrea Zittel, courtesy the artist, photo Thomas Stevenson: 102.

INDEX

Page numbers in *italics* refer to illustrations. Works of art can be found under artists' names. Exhibition titles are in inverted commas.

58th Venice Biennale 138–9
59th Venice Biennale 56

abbey of Kildare 200
Achill Island 188
Ådahl, Anna, *Impossible Image* 243–5, *244*
Admiralty Underwater Weapons Establishment 114
Aeana 27
Aegean islands 132
Aeolia 209
Africa 91, 128, 147, 164
Afterness (Artangel project) 119, 123–4
Age, The (newspaper) 9
Ai Weiwei 20, 129–32
  Law of the Journey 132
Akan folklore 164
Alcan 235–6
Alcatraz 125
Alcoa 235–6
Aldeburgh 116–17
Allan Poe, Edgar, *The Lighthouse* 70, 82
American Independence 63
Anansi 164, 282 n.43
Anderson, Gemma 32, 102
  Amblyrhynchus cristatus, Pahoehoe Lava, Blue Footed Booby Chimera 103
Anderson, Wes 20, 142, 143, 144, 280 n.36
  Isle of Dogs 142, 143
Anse Cafard 146
Anse Cafard Slave Memorial 146, *147*, 149
Anthropocene 18, 19, 196, 243, 272, n.29
Antigua 165
Aotearoa New Zealand 9, 12, 14, 20, 51–2, 56, 100
Aran Islands 187, 188–93
Archtor (steamer) 68
Arends, Bergit 105
Ariel 22, 26
Arken Museum of Modern Art, Denmark 252, *252*
Arsenale (Venice) 138–9
Art Basel 130
Art Newspaper 129–30
Artangel 66, 111, 115, 119, 235, 296–7
Artipelag 252–3
Arts Council 217, 220
Artscape Nordland (*Skulpturlandskap*) 246–7, *247*, 288 n.37
'Ata 9, 14, *10*
Athens 87
Atlantic Ocean 14, 73–4, 87, 94
Atomic Weapons Research Establishment (UK) 117–18, 121
Augusta (Sicily) 138
Australia 52, 97
Austvågøya 247–8

Bacon, Francis, *New Atlantis* 21, 87
Bahamas 241
Bailey, David A. 166
Baldacchino, Godfrey 16–17, 18, 271 n.17, 20
Ballantyne, R. M. 14
  Coral Island, The 14
Ballard, J. G. 22, 74, 93–4, 277 n.13
  Drowned World, The 93
  Drought, The 277 n.13
Baltic Sea 44
Bamburgh 73
Barbados 149–57, *150*, 165, 167, 281 n.16
Barber, Fionna 184, 207, 284 n.13, 28
Barbuda 165
Barca Nostra (Our Ship) project 137–8, 139
Barra (Scottish island) 22
Barton, Susan 15, 37
Basciano, Oliver 243
BBC (British Broadcasting Corporation) 111
BBC Radio 4 112–13
Beckles, Hilary McD. 149
Benesse House Museum (Naoshima) 254, *255*
Benjamin, Walter 245
Berlin 46
Bhabha, Homi K. 156
Big Harcar (rock) 73
Bilali, Entela 161–2
Birds, The (Hitchcock) 65
Biscayne Bay 23
Bishop, Claire 239
Black Beacon (Orford Ness) 123
Boccaccio, Giovanni, *Famous Women* 27

Bodega Bay 65
Bodrum 129
Boland, Eavan 182, 284 n.10
Mother Ireland 182
Bonnett, Alastair 93–4
Boston Harbor 85
Bourgeois, Louise 28, 208, 249–50, 264
Damned, the Possessed and the Beloved, The 249
Bowers Quarry (Portland) 116
Bowling, Frank 167
Boyce, Sonia 19, 167
Crop Over *169*
Boyle, Charles 35, 272 n.1,3, 273 n.1,2,3
Boyle, Maolíosa 199–200, 203–4, 285 n.49
Bradford, Mark, *Masses and Movements* 256–8, *257*
Branson, Richard 59
Bregman, Rutger 9, 12, 14
Humankind: A Hopeful History 9
Brexit 20, 214, 225, 226
Brice, Lisa 174
Briskman, Linda 128–9
Britain, Battle of 117
British Columbia 90
British Isles 167
British Museum 112, 137
British Virgin Islands 59
'Britishness' 225
Brook, Peter 10
Brooklyn Museum 241, *241*
Broomberg, Adam, and Oliver Chanarin, *The Bureaucracy of Angels* 134, *135*
Büchel, Christoph 138
Buckland, David, *Cape Farewell* project 240, 288 n.28
Ice Texts 240, *240*
Bunce Island 145, 149, 281 n.1
Bunting, Madeleine 225
Burman, Ben Lucien 37–8

Calabresi, Mario 130
Caliban 22, 26, 108
Calouste Gulbenkian Foundation 105, 107
Calypso 27
Camp, Stephanie 162
Canadian Pavilion (Venice) 42
Cape Farewell Arctic Expeditions 32, 240
Cape Town 125
Caribbean islands 19, 75, 139, 145–9, 166–72
Caribbean Sea 14, 94, 139, 146
Cast Away (film) 39–40
Cayman Brac 75–6
Cayman Islands 75
Chambers, Iain 123–4
Chanarin, Oliver (and Adam Broomberg) 134–5
Chang, Justin 143, 280 n.37
Channel Fleet 114
Channer, Alice, *Lethality and Vulnerability* *120*
Charles Darwin Foundation 104–5
Charles Darwin Research Station 107, 110
Charrière, Henri 126
Charvet, Jean-Gabriel 51, 274 n.40
Chesil Beach 93, 111
Chichu Museum 254
Chile 66
China 66–7
Chincha Islands 65, 66
Christian, Fletcher 43–4
Christo and Jeanne-Claude 23
Surrounded Islands *24*
Circe 27–8
Civilisation of 1969 (BBC series) 179, 283 n.2
Clark, Kenneth 179, 180
Coates, Marcus 32, 106–7
Galapagos Fashions *104*
Human Report (Blue Footed Booby) *105*
Cobra Mist (film) 118, 119, 278 n.54
'Cobra Mist' (radar station) 117
Coetzee, J. M., *Foe* 15, 37
Cohen, Robin 36
Coleridge, Samuel Taylor 82
Collings, Matthew 139
Columbus, Christopher 159
Comoros Islands 258–9
Djahazi 258–9, *258*
Connell, John 14, 50
Cook Islands 40
Cook, James (Captain) 14, 25, 50–54, 169
Copenhagen Climate Change Conference (2009) (COP15) 95
cosmopolitan 173, 240, 283 n.62
Country Life (magazine) 59–60
COVID-19 pandemic 20, 119
cowries 163–4
Cresswell, Tim 223
Cross, Dorothy 107–8, 189–90, 192–3
Stage *107*
Teacup *191*
Valentia Island *193*
Crowhurst, Donald 73, 74, 75, 77, 276 n.29
Cummins, Pauline, *Inis t'Oirr (Aran Dance)* *192*
Curry, Blue 77

d'Souza, Brian 124
Dafoe, Willem 82
Darwin, Charles 56, 102, 110
On the Origin of the Species 102
Dasgupta, Rana 221
After Nations 221
David Wyss, Johann, *Swiss Family Robinson* 14
Davis, Annalee 19, 150–54
Walker's Diary – An Effort at Disalienation *151*
In Defense of Beauty *153*
Davis, Sophia 118
D-Day 114
de la Mare, Walter 44
Desert Islands 44
De La Warr Pavilion, Bexhill 77
Dean, Tacita 71–4, 74–6
Disappearance at Sea II *72*
Teignmouth Electron, Cayman Brac *76*

Defoe, Daniel 14, 15, 34, 38, 41, 42
Robinson Crusoe 14, 15, 25, 35, 38, 41–4, *34*, 37
Delap, Maude 192
Deleuze, Gilles 21, 40, 49
DeLoughrey, Elizabeth 100, 148, 277 n.27
Demos, T. J. 94, 128, 277 n.28
Denmark 252
Devil's Island (Ile du Diable) 125–7
Devil's Island Prison 126–7
Diamond Beach (Martinique) 146
Dickinson, Emily 107
Dinh Q. Lê 66–7
Colony, The 66
Doherty, Clare 217, 220
Doig, Peter 174
Dolven, A. K. 246
Donne, John 16
Donwood, Stanley, and Robert Macfarlane 118–19
Ness (prose poem/play) 118–19
Dorset 93, 111, 114
Drake, Sir Francis 77
Dreyfus Affair 126–8
Dreyfus, Alfred 126, 127–8
Duffy, Carol Ann 27–8
Circe 28
Duffy, Patrick 88
Dujardin, Jean 126
Dutch 62
Dyrhólaey Lighthouse 232

'Earth' (Royal Academy exhibition) 44
Ecuador 101
Ede, Siân 105
Edge of the World, The (film) 64
Eggers, Robert 81, 82–3
Lighthouse, The 82
Eighth Amendment (Ireland 1983) 184, 205, 206, 284 n.12
Eilean Mòr 68–9, *69*
Elizabeth, St 161
'Elliptical Affinities: Irish Women Artists and the Politics of the Body' (exhibition) 184
England 71, 77, 93, 111, 114
'Englishness' 225
Enomoto, Joy Lehuanani 29, 97
Soundings 98, 99
Enright, Robert 42
Epstein, Mitch 260
Ocean Warwick Oil Platform, Dauphin Island, Alabama 261
European Union (EU) 125, 131

Fallon, Rachel 28, 198, 201, 205–6, 264
see also Map, The (with Alice Maher)
Farne Islands 71–3
Farquharson, Alex 166
feminist art 25, 29–30, 264–5, 289 n.21
Fer, Briony 237
Ferrer, José 126
Fiji 9, 165
Finnmark 249–50
First World War 64
Firth, Colin 77
Flaherty, Robert J. 188–9
Flannan Isles lighthouse 68–9, *69*
floating islands 209–28, 286 n.3
floating legacies and art making 210–13
nationhood and citizenship 217–24
Florida 23, 75, 88
Forfarshir (paddle steamer) 73
Fortey, Richard 33
Foucault, Michel, *Discipline and Punish* 128, 141–2
Fowles, John 15–16, 18, 60, 272 n.13
Islands 15
Magus, The 18
French Guiana 125
French Primitivism 188
Fukutake, Soichiro 254

Galápagos Islands 8, 19, 32–3, 101–11, *33, 102*
Gauguin, Paul 23, 54–6
Where Do We Come From? What Are We? Where Are We Going? 23
George III 52
Georgia Strait 90
Gerhardt, Christina, *HighWaterLine Honolulu* 100
Gibson, William 44
Giraudoux, Jean 15, 25, 37–8
Suzanne and the Pacific 15, 25
Gleeson, Sinéad, *We Are the Map* 203–4
Glissant, Édouard 146–8, 281, n.8
Golding, William 9–10, 15, 22
Lord of the Flies (novel) 9–10
Lord of the Flies (film) *11*
Goldsmiths College 158
Grace Darling 73, 75
Graham, Dan 246–8
Two-Way Mirror Triangle with One Curved Side/Nordscape Pavilion 247
Graham, Donald, *Keepers of the Light* 85–6
Graham, Rodney 15, 41–3, 46, 83–5, 85–6, 273, n.17–21, 297
Island Thought 43
Halcion Sleep 43
Lighthouse Keeper with Lighthouse Model, 1955 84
Vexation Island 41
Great Salt Lake 30
Greenland 96
Grenada 165, 172–3
Grenadines 165
Griffin, Gerald, *Hy-Brasail: The Isle of the Blest* (poem) 194, 196
Guano 66–8
Gulbenkian Galapagos Artists' Residency Programme 32–3, 105

Haiti 169–71
Hall, Stuart 166
Familiar Stranger: A Life between Two Islands 166
Hamilton Faris, Jaimey 96–7
Hamilton, Scott 12, 13
Hanks, Tom 39, 42
Hardy, Thomas 113–14

Harewood House 167
Harris, Robert 126
Hartley, Alex 60–61, 63–5, 213–17, 225, 228
Bird Attack (short film) *64*
Cape Farewell Arctic expedition 214, 216–17, 240, *217*
Gnomic Kilmuir 61
The Ship/Undiscovered Island 216
see also *Nowhereisland*
Hau'ofa, Epeli 13, 246
Hauser & Wirth 256
Hawai'i 47, 97
Hay, Peter 18, 272 n.26
Head, Richard, *The Floating Island* 210
Heaney, Seamus 193
Storm on the Island 179–80
Hebridean islands 64, 70, n.50, 51
Helios (god) 27
Henningsvaer, Lofoten Islands 242, 245–6, *242*
Henry, Paul 188
Hesperus (vessel) 68
Hilty, Greg 102, 105
Himid, Lubaina 19, 167, 169
Toussaint L'Ouverture 170
Hirta 63–4
HM Prison The Verne 115
HMS *Osprey* 114
Hoare, Philip 13–14, 220
Hoffman, Dustin 127
Höller, Carsten 219
Holt, Nancy 88, 93
Homer 21, 27, 171
Odyssey 209
Honolulu 100–101
Horn, Roni 28, 230–39, 260, 251
Island Zombie: Iceland Writings 230
My Oz 230
To Place 230, 232, 237
Vatnasafn/Library of Water 232, 234, 238
Water, Selected 236
Weather Reports You 232, 234
You Are the Weather 230, 238
Horowitz, Anthony, *Alex Rider* (series) 141
'Hotel Meridian' (exhibition) 46
Houses of Parliament 265, 266
How the Myth Was Made (documentary) 189–90
Hurricane Gilbert (1988) 75
Huxley, Aldous 22
Hy-Brasil 194–8, *195*

I Accuse! (1958) (drama film) 126
Iceland 17, 20, 28, 287 n.14,16
see also Northern and Arctic islands
Ihimaera, Witi, *The Whale Rider* (novel) 100
Ikon Gallery Birmingham 66
Indian Ocean 88, 94
Ingvarsdóttir, Fríða Björk 237
Inishmór island 187
Inujima 254
'Inundation' exhibition 100
Irish 'Atlantic Edge' 179, 187, 188
Isabela Island 102–3
Iseult, Irish princess (fictional character) 74
Isla del Rey 256–8, *256*
'island artists' 228, 264
Island of Blue Waters 92
Island Studies (academic journal) 16, 43
'island writers' 226–7
Isle of Bressay 59
Isle of Dogs (East London) 144
Isle of Dogs (film) 142–4
see also Anderson, Wes
Isle of Portland 93, 111–12, 116, 124
Isle of Skye 61, 70–71
Isolde 74, 75

Jaar, Alfredo 20, 129–31, 251
Gift, The 130, 131
Jab Molassies 173–4
Jakobsen, Björn 253
Jamaica 75, 158–60
Jamaican Cockpit Country 164
Jamaican Maroons 162
James, P. D., *The Lighthouse 70*
Japan 16, 142–4
Jean-Gabriel Charvet, *Les sauvages de la Mer Pacifique* 51–2
Jetñil-Kijiner, Kathy 29, 95–6, 97–9, *98*
Rise: From One Island to Another (2018) (video-poem) *95*
Sounding 98, 99
Johnson, Boris 219
Jonas, Joan, *Volcano Saga* 230, 231, *231*
Jones, Jesse 28, 183–4, 186
Tower, The 186
Tremble Tremble 184
Jonson, Ben, and Thomas Nashe, *The Isle of Dogs* 144
Julien, Isaac 20, 134–5, 167, 171
Paradise Omeros 171
Western Union 136
Jurassic Coast 93

Kafka, Franz, *In the Penal Colony* (novel) 67, 127–8
Kamakau, Samuel Mānaiakalani 52
Mo'oleo 52
Kamau Brathwaite, Edward 148
Kaminsky, Ilya, *I See a Silence* (poem) 119
Kapoor, Anish 219–20, 247
Eye in the Stone, The 246
Orbit 219
KGB spies 115
Kihara, Yuki 25–6, 56–7
Fonofono o le nuanua: Patches of the Rainbow 55
Paradise Camp 55
Kingdom of Tonga 97
Kings Cross Station 136
Klondike 85
Knitting Map, The (installation) 207
Kofe, Simon 95
Kosug, Daisuke, *Good Name* (*Bad Phrase*) 245

Kourbaj, Issam, *Dark Water, Burning World* (series) 137
Kovats, Tania 223–8, *225–6*
All the Islands of All the Seas 225–6, *226*
Only Blue (British Isles) 226, *227*
Krauss, Rosalind 251
Krohg, Christian 243
Kurdi, Alan 129–30, 279 n.14,15
Kusama, Yayoi 253–4
Yellow Pumpkin 253
Kyoto Protocol (2005) 235

Laitinen, Antti 44–5
It's My Island 44
Voyage 45
Lampedusa 129, 134, 136–7
Lampedusa Cross, The 137, *138*
'Land of Mu' 89
Langan, Clare 197–8
Floating World 196, 197
Latour, Bruno 243–4
laundresses 204–8, *207*
Lawrence, D. H. 22
Le Carré, John 115
Lehane, Dennis 141
Lehuanani Enomoto, Joy 97–8, *98*
Soundings 98,99
Lemuria 88, *89*
Lenape Native Americans 62
Lesbos 129–33
Lewis 68
Libya 136, 137
'Life between Islands' (Tate exhibition) 166, 169
Lighthouse, The (Eggers) (film) 81
Ligon, Richard 149
Lindenbrook, Oliver 237
Lloyd, Temperance 184
Located Labourer's Act 156
Locke, Donald 167
Plantation Series 167
Locke, Hew 167
Lofoten Declaration (2017) 243, 245
Lofoten International Art Festival (LIAF) 242–3, 245
Lofoten Islands 242–9, *242*
London 46, 51, 110, 136, 166, 174, 176
London Sinfonietta 136
Long Beach 90
Long John Silver (fictional character) 41
Longstone Lighthouse 71–4
Lord of the Flies (film) 10, 47, *11*
Lost (TV series) 47–8
Louis Stevenson, Robert, *Treasure Island* 14, 41–2
Love Island (TV series) 49, 55
Lund, Søren Robert 252

McCulloch, Jude 125
MacFarlane, Robert 118–19
Mack, John, 272, n.40
Mackenzie, Compton, *Whisky Galore* 22
McLean, Karen 19, 29, 154–64, 174, 176–7
Ar'n't I a Woman! 157, 159, 163
Blue Power 176
Precariat, The 154, 155
McMillan, Michael 167
McNally, Emma 122–3
A river that flows nowhere, to the sea 122
Untitled 122
McQueen, Steve 19, 167, 171, 172
Ashes 172
Magdalene Laundries 204, 205, 285 n.59
Maher and Fallon, *The Map* 28
Maher, Alice 28, 198, 201, 205–6, 264
see also *Map, The*
Malagosto (fictional island) 141
Maldives 94
Malta 77, 137, 165
Man from Atlantis, The (series) 88
Man of Aran (documentary) 188–9, *189*
Mana, Vika 12
Manhattan 63
Mansfield, Laura 251, 258, 288 n.1
Map of Broken Clear Glass (Atlantis) 90
Map, The (Alice Maher and Rachel Fallon) 198–208, 264, 285 n.49, 50, *97*
Detail of Architecture of Containment and Laundresses at Work 206
Detail of Island of Wild Oats 203
Detail of Slag Island 202
Maralinga 123
Marquesas islands 26, 56
Marsden, Philip,194
The Summer Isles 194
Marshall Islands 96–100
Marshall, H. E. 225
Our Island Story 225
Martinique 146, 147
Mary Magdalene 186, 199, 201–2, 204–5
Massachusetts 85
Massey, Doreen 224
Mauritius 165
Maxwell Davies, Peter 69
The Lighthouse 69–70
Mayan codex 89
Mediterranean islands 128–31, 165
Megasaki 142–3
Melilli 137
Melville, Hermann 82
Menzies, Gavin 87–8
Mercy, The (film) 77
Metamorphosis (Ovid) 27
Migrant Offshore Aid Station (MOAS) 130
'migration crisis' (2016) 129
Millbank 46
Minot, George 85
Minot's Ledge lighthouse 85
Misrata 136
Mitchell, W.J.T. 30
Landscape and Power 30
Mo'oleo 52
Montego Bay 75
Montserrat island 197
Monty Python's Flying Circus 46
Monuriki 39
Moore, Thomas
Utopia 21, 87, 220

Morholt, Irish knight (fictional character) 74
Mosher, Eve 100–101
HighWaterLine 100–101
Mosse, Richard 132–4
Incoming 133
Mother Ireland (film) 181–2
Mother Ireland 28, 180–87
Mountz, Alison 126, 128–9
Moutzouris, Kostas 132
Mozambique Canal 259, *258*
Murray, Nicholas 137

Nancollas, Tom 70
Naoshima 253–5
The Art House Project 254–6
Nash, Catherine 187, 188
Nashe, Thomas 144
Nasheed, Mohamed 94–5, *95*
National Gallery of the Cayman Islands 77
National Trust (1993) 118, 119
nationhood and citizenship 217–24
Natural History Museum (UK) 110
NBC 88
Neale, Tom 40–42
An Island to Oneself 40
Necker Island 59
Nepomuceno, Nicole M. 56
Nesbit, Captain John 194, 195
New Amsterdam 62
New Caledonia 126
New England coast 81
New Jersey 90
New York 62, 100
New Yorker (magazine) 44
New Zealand *see* Aotearoa New Zealand
Newsroom (journal) 12
Niviâna, Aka 96
North Africa 133, 136
North America 146
North Pacific Coast 85
North Sea 73
northern Africa 129
Northern and Arctic islands 229–50
ice melts and myths 236, 240–50
weather and Icelandic ice 230–39
northern Canada 70
Northern Ireland 181
Northumberland Coast 73
Norway
tourism 242
'Noten Eylandt' 62
Nowhereisland (Alex Hartley) 213–18, 251, *215*, *216*, *218*, 286 n.13, 14
nationhood and citizenship 217–18, 219, 220, 223–4
Nuku'alofa 9
'Nutten Island' 62
Nyholm, Kristoffer 69

O'Brien, Edna 181
Mother Ireland 181
Ofili, Chris 167, 174–6
Blue Devils 175
Okinawa 97
Olah, Nathalie 48
OOZE 262–3, 289 n.17
Future Island 263
Opera Theatre Company 192–3
Orford Ness 116–24
Orford Ness Lighthouse 118
Orgel, Stephen 22
Orta, Lucy and Jorge 221–3
Antarctica Project 222
Otolith Group 167
Outer Farne Islands 73
Outer Hebrides 61, 70
Ovid 27
Owens, Craig 31

Pacific Oceania 9, 10, 17, 19, 24, 29, 39, 50, 52, 94, 97, 98, 139
Palazzo Valguarnera-Gangi 134
Palmer, Katrina 111–16, 278 n.40, 49
End Matter 112–14, *113*, 115–16
Loss Adjusters, The 112
Quarryman's Daughters, The 113
Papillon (film) 126
Papua New Guinea 13
Paramin 174
Parker, Cornelia 17, 265–7
Island 267
Parker, Rozsika 208
Pattinson, Robert 82
Pearson, Nels 71
Perry, Mike 260–62
Island 262
Perse (Oceanid nymph) 27
Peru 65, 66
Philippines 97
Picknett, Lynn 205
Piper, Keith 167
'Plague Island' 20, 125, 272 n.33
Plato 87
Timaeus 87
Polanski, Roman, *An Officer and a Spy* (film), 126, 279 n.6
Pollard, Ingrid 167
Port of Molyvos 133
Porter, Max 119
Portland 111–13, 115, 116
Portland Bill Lighthouse 111
Portland Harbour 114
Portland Spy Ring 114–15
Porto Pozzallo 136
Poveglia 140
Powell, Michael 64
Prague 131–2
Prendergast, Kathy, *Body Maps* series 185–7, 198
To Alter a Landscape (Body Map Series) 185
Untitled 186
Prospero 21–2, 33
psychogeography 237
Puerta Ayora 107, 110
Pugh, Jonathan 17, 18–19, 271 n.21, 272 n.30

Queen Elizabeth Olympic Park 219, *219*
Queen Nanny 158, 165

Reihana, Lisa 14, 25–6, 50–54, 56, 57
in Pursuit of Venus [infected] 50, *51*

Reiss, Julie 241, 272 n.29
Rhys, Jean 26
Wide Sargasso Sea 26
Richardson, Emily 118, 119
Rio Tinto 235–6
RNLI Grace Darling Museum 73
Robben Island 125, 279 n.1
Robinson Crusoe (Defoe) 14, 15, 25, 35, 41–4, *34*
Crusoe's legacy 35–41, *37*, *38*, *40*
Robinson, Tim, *Arainn* 190, 191
Folding Landscapes 190–91
Royal Academy, London 44, 50–51
Royal Sovereign Lighthouse 77
Rozel Point 30
Ruane, Aoife 184
Ryan, Veronica 167

Saint Lucia 165
Sāmoa 56–7
Samson, Barney 16–17, 39, 47, 272 n.19, 273 n.13
Sanibel Island 88
Sant, Andrew 8, 268–70, 296
'Cargo' 8
'End Game' 268, 269
Santa Cruz 107
Santa Cruz Island 106
Santa Maria di Nazareth 140
Sappho 131
Schaffner, Franklin J. 127
Schwapp, Melanie 164–5
Granny Dead 165, *165*,
Scorsese, Martin 20, 141
Shutter Island 20, 141
Scott, Heidi 266
Scottish Hebridean islands 28
Seto Inland Sea 253, 254
sewing and embroidery 200–201, 207, 208
Shakespeare, William 14, 21, 26, 107
Shaw, Fiona 107, 108
Shaxson, Nicholas 59
Shetland Islands 59
Shima: The International Journal of Island Studies 16
Shrewsbury Museum and Art Gallery 107
Sicily 129, 134, 136
Sierra Leone 145
Simpson, Thomas 140–41
Blackened 140–41
Singapore 97
'Siting Vexation Island' 43
Skellig Michael 179, 180, 188, 197, 283 n.1,2
Small Island Developing States (SIDS) 94–7
Smalls, The (film) 82–3
Smith, Giulia 167
Smith, Marlene 167
Smithson, Robert 23, 30–32, 88–94, 210–11, 267, 277 n.11, 12
Floating Island to Travel Around Manhattan Island 211
Hypothetical Continent of Lemuria, The 89
Map of Broken Glass 90
Map of Clear Broken Glass 91
Mirror Displacement 92
Spiral Jetty 31
Snæfellsjökull volcano 229–30, *233*
So Many Islands (anthology) 165, 282 n.46
South Africa 125
South America 74
south Atlantic 74
South China Sea 66
South Pacific Oceania 52
Spain 66, 158–9
Speranza 28, 36–7
St Abb's 71–3
St Brigid's cloak 200–201
St Kilda 63–4
St Lucia 171–2
St Paul's Cathedral 112
St Vincent 165
Stabat Mater 192–3
Star Wars 179
Statue of Liberty 62
Steilneset Memorial 28, 249, 250, *248*
Stevenson, Robert Louis 82
Stonex, Emma, 69
Lamplighters, The 69
Stoney, George 189
Strachan, Tavares 240–41
The Distance between What We Have and What We Want (The Arctic Ice Project) 240
Stykkishólmur library 231–2, *232*
Suffolk coastline 123
Sulter, Maud 167
Sunday Times Golden Globe Race 73
Surrealist map of the World (1929) 198, *199*
Survivor (TV series) 48
Sycorax 22, 26
Syrian civil war 131

Tadao Ando 254
Tahiti 51, 52, 100
Taiwan 20
Tamburella, Paolo W. 258–9
Djahazi 258
Tasmania 9
Tate & Lyle 156
Tate, Henry 166
Tatum, Simon 77
Teignmouth Electron 73, 75, 77
see also Tacita Dean
Tempest, The (Shakespeare) 14, 21, 26, 107, 108
Terezin 132
Teshima 254
Thames, River 144
Third Republic 126
Thomas, Nicholas, 274 n.45, 274 n.37
Timaeus 87
Tobago 165, 173
Tonga 9, 10, 12, 14, 165
Tournier, Michel 15, 28, 36
Friday and the Other Island 15
Tower of London 112
Trelawny 161
Trinidad 159, 165, 173, 174
Trinidadian Blue Devil 173–4
Tristan da Cunha 74

Tristan, Cornish knight (fictional character) 74, 75
Trouvé, Tatiana 120–22
Residents, The 121
Tuccio, Francesco 137
TULCA Festival of Visual Arts 196–7
Turkey 129
Turnbull, Alison 32, 110–11, 278 n.38
Let's Progress from Me to Us 108
Specimens 110
Tuvalu 97

U.S. Guano Act (1856) 66
Uekötter, Frank 65
United Kingdom (UK) 20, 35, 63
United States (USA) 48, 66–7, 97, 125
Universal Declaration of Human Rights 221, 222
University of Hawai'i Manoa 97
University of London 158
University of Sheffield 129
Usumacinta River 92
Utah 30
Utopia 220, 287 n.20

Valentia Island 192–3, *193*
Valére, Laurent 146
Anse Cafard Memorial 147
Vanishing, The (film) 69
Vardø 249, 250
Vastria 132
Venice 42, 140–41, 259
Venice Art Biennale 41, 50, 258–9, 263, *258*
Verne, Jules 237
The Floating Island 210
Journey to the Centre of the Earth 229–30
Virgin Mary 192, 193
Virilio, Paul 100
Visconti, Luchino 134
Leopard, The (film) 134
Voyage de Guérison 74, 75

Wailing Woman Rock 179, 180
Wainwright, Leon, 176, 281 n.3, 14, 283 n.66
Wake, Thomas (fictional character) 82
Walcott, Derek 148–9, 164, 165–6, 171
Omeros 171–2
'The Schooner *Flight*' 165–6
Waldseemüller world map 257–8
Wales 82, 93
Wallis, Clarrie 75
Walsall Black Sisters 162–3
Warner, Marina 26, 272 n.44, 278 n.38, 284 n.26
Indigo; or, Mapping the Waters 26
Warner, Peter 9, 10, 12–13, *13*
Watson, Chris 118, 119, 123–4
Wells, H. G., *The Island of Doctor Moreau* 15
Werner's Nomenclature of Colours 110
West Africa 156
Western Australia 123
Weymouth 115
Whiteread, Rachel 62–3
Cabin 62
Williams, Aubrey 167
Willumsen, Liv Helene 249, 250
Wilson 39–40
Windward Maroons 158–60
witchcraft 249
wool sweaters 191–2
Woolf, Virginia 68, 70–71, 81
To the Lighthouse (Woolf) 70, 68, 81

Yarlow, Loretta 42–3
Yarnall, Judith 27
Yass, Catherine 71, 77–81
Lighthouse 79
Lighthouse (East) 80
Yucatan peninsula 88, 91

Zaya, Octavio 259
Zittel, Andrea 210, 211–13, 286 n.9, 10,11
A–Z Pocket Property 212
Island in 100 Acres 212–13
Zumthor, Peter 28, 249, 250
Steilneset Memorial 248